1967 MERCEDES BENZ
250 S
CHASSIS # 108012-12-048048
ENG # M-1081
     108.920-12-018064

Body & Paint
                    433·491 508

332G

108012 -12-7

2  02976  12336

# *Chilton's*

# Repair and Tune-up Guide

## for the

# MERCEDES-BENZ

*Illustrated*

PRODUCED BY THE AUTOMOTIVE BOOK DEPARTMENT

*Managing Editor:* JOHN MILTON

*Technical Editor and Writer:* JEFFREY W. HALLINGER

**CHILTON BOOK COMPANY**
PHILADELPHIA    NEW YORK    LONDON

Copyright © 1970 by Chilton Book Company
Published in Philadelphia by Chilton Book Company
and simultaneously in Ontario, Canada,
by Thomas Nelson & Sons, Ltd.
All rights reserved
Manufactured in the United States of America
by New City Printing Company

ISBN:   0-8019-5536-X
Library of Congress Catalog Card No. 70-131236

# ACKNOWLEDGMENTS

The Chilton Book Company expresses appreciation to the following firms for their generous assistance:

**A PIERBURG AUTO-U LUFTRAHRT-GERATEBAU KG**
Neuss/Rhein, Germany (Zenith carburetors)

**ARNOLT CORPORATION**
Warsaw, Indiana (Solex carburetors)

**CHAMPION SPARK PLUG COMPANY**
Toledo, Ohio

**DAIMLER-BENZ AG**
Stuttgart-Unterturkheim, Germany

**MERCEDES-BENZ OF NORTH AMERICA**
Fort Lee, New Jersey

**ROBERT BOSCH CORPORATION**
Long Island City, New York

**NOTE:** Although the information in this book is based on factory sources and is as complete as it was possible to make it at time of publication, the possibility exists that later changes were made which could not be included here. It must be recognized that such changes are the manufacturer's prerogative, and that the manufacturer cannot be held responsible for them, or the publisher's interpretation of factory information.

# *Contents*

# Chapter One

# Identification and Maintenance

## Introduction

The purpose of this book is to show the owner of a Mercedes-Benz how to perform the simple, routine maintenance and repairs that every car must have and, in some cases, to detail more complex work.

All repairs and maintenance are explained in light of the usual tools possessed by the home mechanic or average repair shop and, where special tools are necessary, alternate procedures are given. Jobs that are impossible, or very difficult, to perform without these tools are noted, but are referred to their rightful place—the authorized Mercedes-Benz dealer.

All models imported into the United States from about 1964 are covered, with the exception of the type 600. It is recognized that few if any 600 owners are interested in doing their own work and that the Mercedes-Benz dealer can provide the best service for this model. In general, however, the engine and transmission used in the 300 SEL/8 6.3 is identical to that used in the 600, with minor modifications for this application.

## Identification

When confronted with a parts ordering situation and a strange car, the first question usually asked is "What year is it?" Fortunately, Mercedes-Benz owners don't have this problem. It does not really matter what year your model was built, so long as the model series and the chassis numbers are known.

Since the Mercedes-Benz design is in continuous development and evolution, the newest developments are put into production as soon as they become available. Therefore, while it is true that arbitrary cut-off chassis numbers are chosen each year to designate the onset of the "new" model year, it does not necessarily mean that a 1968 car is radically different from a 1969 model. Especially, it does not mean that an "old" 1968 is now obsolete.

All this is great for the owner, but it presents a problem when ordering parts. The solution is found in the comprehensive Daimler-Benz identification plates, found in various places, but usually under the hood and on the door posts. Consulting

1

the illustration pertaining to your model (220, 230 S, etc.), find the locations of the chassis number plate, type plate and engine plate. With these numbers, plus the engine and other subsystem serial numbers, one is armed with all the information he needs to identify his car.

When ordering parts, it is necessary to give the complete chassis number, plus the numbers of the concerned area. For ex-

Type plate

Chassis number　　Body and paint　　Engine number

Identification plates.

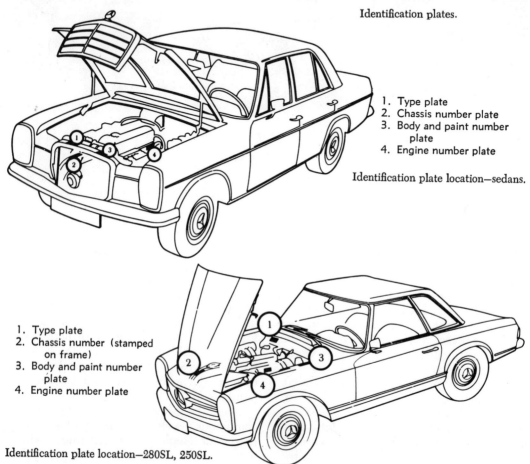

1. Type plate
2. Chassis number plate
3. Body and paint number plate
4. Engine number plate

Identification plate location—sedans.

1. Type plate
2. Chassis number (stamped on frame)
3. Body and paint number plate
4. Engine number plate

Identification plate location—280SL, 250SL.

1. Type plate
2. Chassis number
3. Body and paint number plate
4. Engine number plate

Identification plate location—230SL.

# Model/Engine Identification

| Model | Chassis | Engine Model | Engine Type |
|---|---|---|---|
| 190c | 110.010 | M121B.V. | 121.924 |
| 200 | 110.010 | M121B.XI | 121.940 |
| *190Dc | 110.110 | OM621.III | 621.912 |
| *200D | 110.110 | OM621.VIII | 621.918 |
| 230 | 110.011 | M180.VI | 180.945 |
| | | M180.X① | 180.949① |
| 220b | 111.010 | M180.IV | 180.940 |
| 220Sb | 111.012 | M180.V | 180.941 |
| 230S | 111.010 | M180.VIII | 180.947 |
| 250S | 108.012 | M108.I | 108.920 —1967 250S |
| 220SEb | 111.014 | M127.III | 127.982 |
| 250SE | 108.014 | M129.I | 129.980 |
| 230SL | 113.042 | M127.II | 127.981 |
| 250SL | 113.043 | M129.III | 129.982 |
| 220SEb/C | 111.021(coupe) | M127.V | 127.984 |
| 220SEb/C | 111.023(convt.) | M127.V | 127.984 |
| 250SE/C | 111.021(coupe) | M129.I | 129.980 |
| 250SE/C | 111.023(convt.) | M129.I | 129.980 |
| 300SE | 112.014(sedan) | M189.III(1st version) | 189.984(1st version) |
| 300SE | 112.015(long wb) | M189.V(2nd version) | 189.986(2nd version) |
| 300SE② | 112.021(coupe) | M189.IV(1st version) | 189.985(1st version) |
| 300SE② | 112.023(convt.) | M189.VI(2nd version) | 189.987(2nd version) |
| 300SEb | 108.015 | M189.VIII | 189.989 |
| 300SEL | 109.015 | M189.VII | 189.988 |
| 300SE③ | 112.021(coupe) | M189.VI | 189.987 |
| 300SE③ | 112.023(convt.) | M189.VI | 189.987 |
| *220D/8 | 115.110 | OM615 | 615.912 |
| 220/8 | 115.010 | M115 | 115.920 |
| 230/8⑤ | 114.015 | M180 | 180.954 |
| 250/8⑥ | 114.010 | M114 | 114.920 |
| 280S/8 | 108.016 | M130 | 130.920 —1970 |
| 280SE/8 | 108.018(sedan) | M130 | 130.980 |
| 280SE/8④ | 108.019(long wb) | M130 | 130.980 |
| 280SE/8 | 111.024(coupe) | M130 | 130.980 |
| 280SE/8 | 111.025(convt.) | M130 | 130.980 |
| 280SL/8 | 113.044 | M130 | 130.983 |
| 300SEL/8 2.8 | 109.016 | M130 | 130.981 |
| 300SEL/8 6.3 | 109.018 | M100 | 100.981 |

①   *INAT carburetors from chassis No. 017649.*
②   *To August, 1965.*
③   *From August, 1965.*
④   *Also known as 280SEL/8*
⑤   *Not imported after August, 1969.*
⑥   *Not imported after 1968.*
wb   *wheelbase*
convt.   *convertible*
\*   *diesel models (see Chapter 3)*

# Out of Production Models

| Model | Starting Serial No. | Ending Serial No. |
|---|---|---|
| 190c | 110.010—10—000001 | 110.010—10—130557 |
| 200 | 110.010—10—130558 | 110.010—10—200761 |
| 190Dc | 110.110—10—000001 | 110.110—10—225647 |
| 200D | 110.110—10—225648 | 110.110—10—387263 |
| 230 | 110.011—10—000001 | 110.011—10—040258 |
| 220b | 111.010—10—000001 | 111.010—10—069692 |
| 220Sb | 111.012—10—000001 | 111.012—10—161126 |
| 230S | 111.010—10—069693 | 111.010—10—110798 |
| 250S | 108.012—10—000001 | ④ |
| 220SEb | 111.014—10—000001 | 111.014—10—082687 |
| 250SE | 108.014—10—000001 | 108.014—10—055181 |
| 230SL | 113.042—10—000001 | 113.042—10—019832 |
| 250SL | 113.043—10—000001 | 113.043—10—005196 |
| 220SEb/C (coupe) | 111.021—10—000001 | 111.021—10—082990 |
| 220SEb/C (convt.) | 111.023—10—000001 | 111.023—10—082990 |
| 250SE/C (coupe) | 111.021—10—082991 | 111.021—10—089205 |
| 250SE/C (convt.) | 111.023—10—082991 | 111.023—10—089205 |
| 300SE (sedan) | 112.014—10—000001 | 112.014—10—005137 |
| 300SE (long wb) | 112.015—10—000001 | 112.015—10—005137 |
| 300SE (coupe)① | 112.021—10—000001 | 112.021—10—005137 |
| 300SE (convt.)① | 112.023—10—000001 | 112.023—10—005137 |
| 300SEb | 108.015—10—000001 | 108.015—10—002737 |
| 300SEL | 109.015—10—000001 | 109.015—10—002369 |
| 300SE (coupe)② | 112.021—10—005138 | 112.021—10—009875 |
| 300SE (convt.)② | 112.023—10—005138 | 112.023—10—009875 |

# Current Models

| Model | Starting Serial No. | Ending Serial No. |
|---|---|---|
| 220D/8 | 115.110—10—000001 | |
| 220/8 | 115.010—10—000001 | |
| 230/8 | 114.015—10—000001 | ⑤ |
| 250/8 | 114.010—10—000001 | |
| 280S/8 | 108.016—10—000001 | |
| 280SE/8 (sedan) | 108.018—10—000001 | |
| 280SE/8 (long wb)③ | 108.019—10—000001 | |
| 280SE/8 (coupe) | 111.024—10—000001 | |
| 280SE/8 (convt.) | 111.025—10—000001 | |
| 280SL/8 | 113.044—10—000001 | |
| 300SEL/8 | 109.016—10—000001 | |
| 300SEL/8 6.3 | 109.018—12—000001 | |

① To August, 1965.
② From August, 1965.
③ Also known as 280SEL/8.
④ Still in production, but not imported after 1968.
⑤ Not imported as of August, 1969.
wb    wheelbase
convt.    convertible

ample, when ordering pistons or a distributor cap you must give the engine number as well as chassis number. If you are ordering front suspension components, give the front axle number. Identification of the various subsystems is covered in their respective chapters, excepting engine identification.

The model/engine identification chart gives a picture of the model/engine/chassis combinations that have been imported to the United States since about 1964. Some models were in production much earlier and are included because of popularity.

All models that are now out of production, as well as current models, are shown in the next chart, along with their starting and ending chassis numbers. This is especially useful where the same designation has been carried over to a different vehicle.

An example of this is the 230. While the 230 is now out of production and the 230/8 has taken its place, the two have the same designation on the trunk lid. (The "/8" does not appear.) The chassis number immediately indicates whether you have a "new" 230, although the more modern styling should be a clue.

It should be noted that the center number (10 or 12) in the chassis number indicates the type transmission. A "10" indicates that the car is equipped with a manual transmission, while a "12" indicates an automatic. These numbers, of course, will vary with individual transmission options for individual cars.

On Mercedes-Benz models imported recently into the United States the certification plate has been relocated from the left windshield pillar to the center door pillar. This change was effected with the following chassis end numbers:

| Model | Chassis Type | Chassis End No. |
|---|---|---|
| 220 D/8 | 115 110 | 076 285 |
| 220/8 | 115 010 | 034 047 |
| 230/8 | 114 015 | 033 510 |
| 250/8 | 114 010 | 030 983 |
| 280 S/8 | 108 016 | 031 250 |
| 280 SE/8 | 108 018 | 031 833 |
| 280 SE/8 Cp./Conv. | 111 024/025 | 003 144 |
| 280 SEL/8 | 108 019 | 032 041 |
| 280 SL/8 | 113 044 | 010 704 |
| 300 SEL/8 | 109 016 | 002 047 |
| 300 SEL/8 6.3 | 109 018 | 002 390 |

# Periodic Maintenance

Periodic maintenance is, of course, best performed by a qualified Mercedes-Benz dealer, for he has both the experience and the tools necessary for a good job.

There are times, however, when it might be impossible for an owner to reach a dealer and he would have to do his own work. The following will help him and also those who like to do their own maintenance.

It must be remembered that any work not performed by the dealer *could* result in the invalidation of the warranty. If in doubt, check with the dealer.

Mercedes-Benz has established a series of periodic maintenance inspections to be performed at various mileages.

| Inspection | Interval |
|---|---|
| A | 180–600 miles (for new cars) |
| B | at 3,000 miles |
| C | every 6,000 miles (starting at 9,000 miles) |
| D | every 12,000 miles (starting at 6,000 miles) |
| E | every 12,000 miles |
| S/F | every spring and fall |

These inspections consist of two basic areas of concentration—lubrication, by grease gun or oil can, and bolt tightening. The maintenance charts and their accompanying captions illustrate the jobs to be done in these two areas for the latest models, but can be considered typical for earlier models as well.

## Recommended Oil Brands

Note: Based on latest information available at time of publication

Aerolene HD
*Amalie Motor Oil 1-2-3
Amalie XLO-HD S1
Atlantic Aviation Motor Oil
*Atlantic Imperial Motor Oil
Caltex Super RPM Delo Special
Castrol (HD)
*Castrol Super 10W-40
*Castrolite 10W-30
*Castrol XL 20W-50
Chevron Super (RPM) Delo Special
Chevron (RPM) Supreme Motor Oil
Dual HD Oil
Elk Pennsylvania Motor Oil xHD S1
*Esso Extra Motor Oil
Esso Motoroil
Essolube HD
Esso Uniflo

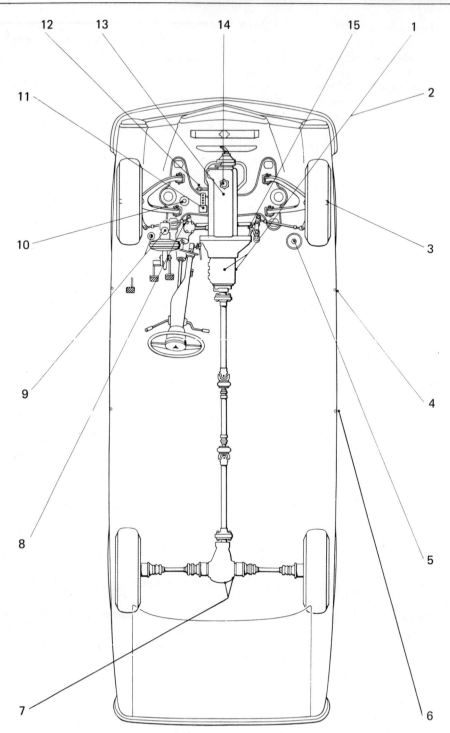

1. Automatic transmission drain plug
2. Manual transmission drain and fill plugs
3. Front wheel bearing
4. Front door hinges
5. Leveling device reservoir
6. Rear door hinges
7. Rear axle oil drain and fill plugs
8. Steering box oil fill plug
9. Brake and clutch reservoirs
10. Power steering reservoir
11. Fuel injection pump
12. Engine oil dipstick
13. Engine oil drain plug
14. Engine oil filler
15. Automatic transmission dipstick

Lubrication points—220D/8 engine and running gear.

Lubrication points—220D/8 engine and running gear.

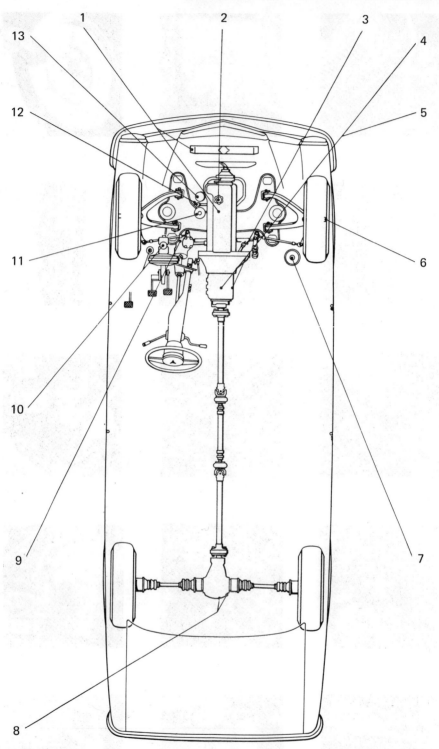

1. Crankcase drain plug (1)
   Oil cooler drain plug (2)
2. Oil fill cap
3. Automatic transmission dip-stick
4. Automatic transmission drain plugs
5. Manual transmission drain and fill plugs
6. Front wheel bearings
7. Leveling device reservoir
8. Rear axle drain and fill plugs
9. Steering box oil fill plug
10. Brake and clutch reservoirs
11. Power steering reservoir
12. Engine oil dipstick
13. Distributor cam felt

Lubrication points—230/8, 250/8 engine and running gear.

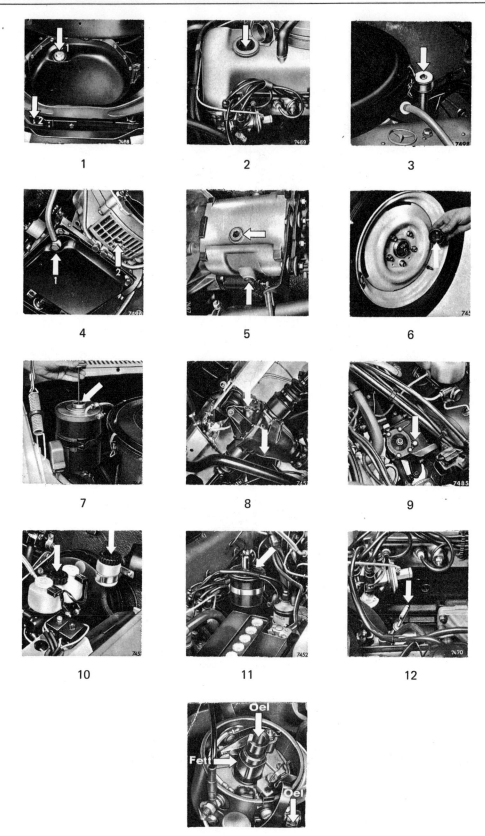

13

Lubrication points—230/8, 250/8 engine and running gear.

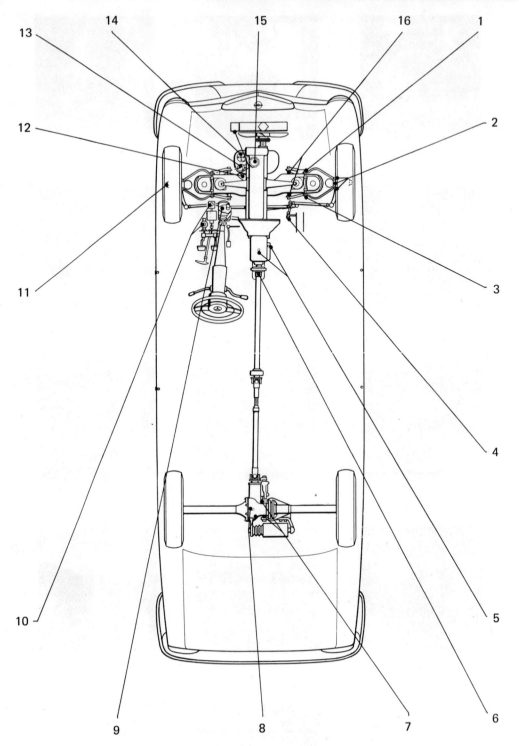

Lubrication points—280S/8, 280SE/8, 280SEC/8 engine and running gear.

1. Front, upper wishbone—right and left
2. Steering knuckle—right and left
3. Rear, upper wishbone—right and left
4. Intermediate steering rod bearing
5. Manual transmission oil drain and fill plugs
6. Front universal
7. Rear axle grease fittings
8. Rear axle oil drain and fill plugs
9. Steering box oil fill plug
10. Brake and clutch reservoirs
11. Front wheel bearings
12. Crankcase oil drain plug and oil cooler drain plug
13. Engine oil dipstick
14. Distributor cam felt
15. Oil filler cap
16. Front, lower wishbone—right and left

Lubrication points—280S/8, 280SE/8, 280SEC/8 engine and running gear.

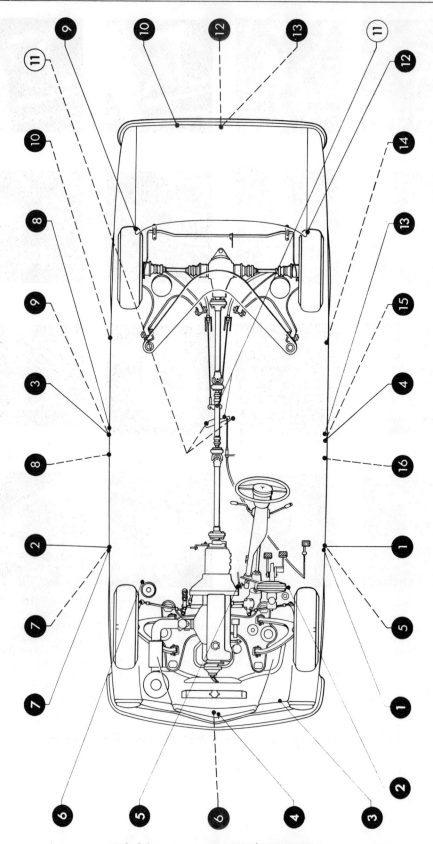

Body lubrication points—220/8, 230/8, 250/8.

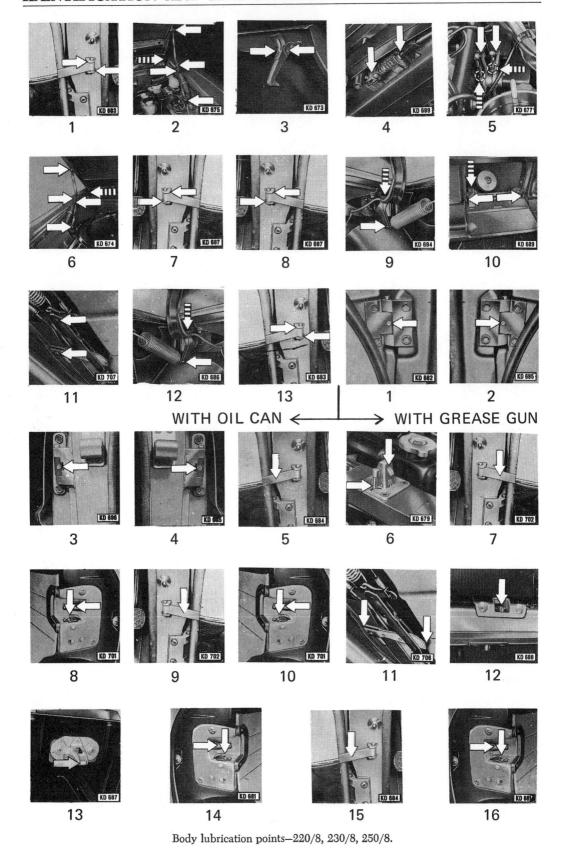

WITH OIL CAN ←⟶ WITH GREASE GUN

Body lubrication points—220/8, 230/8, 250/8.

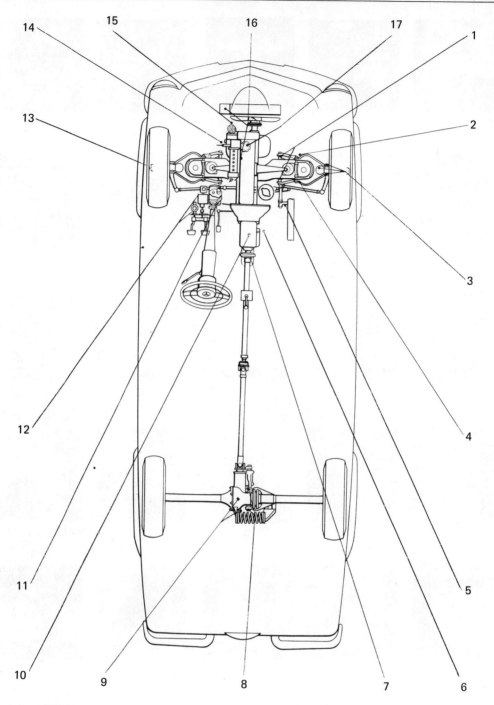

Lubrication points—280SL/8 engine and running gear.

1. Lower wishbone—right and left
2. Front upper wishbone—right and left
3. King pin—right and left
4. Rear, upper wishbone—right and left
5. Intermediate steering arm (unless sealed)
6. Manual transmission oil fill plug
7. Front universal
8. Rear axle grease fittings
9. Rear axle oil drain and fill plugs
10. Manual transmission oil drain plug
11. Steering box oil fill plug
12. Brake and clutch reservoirs
13. Front wheel bearings
14. Engine oil dipstick
15. Distributor felt
16. Crankcase drain plug and oil cooler drain plug
17. Engine oil fill cap

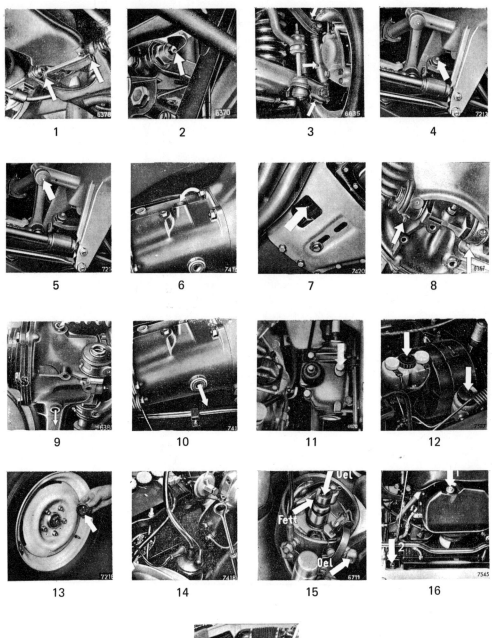

Lubrication points—280SL/8 engine and running gear.

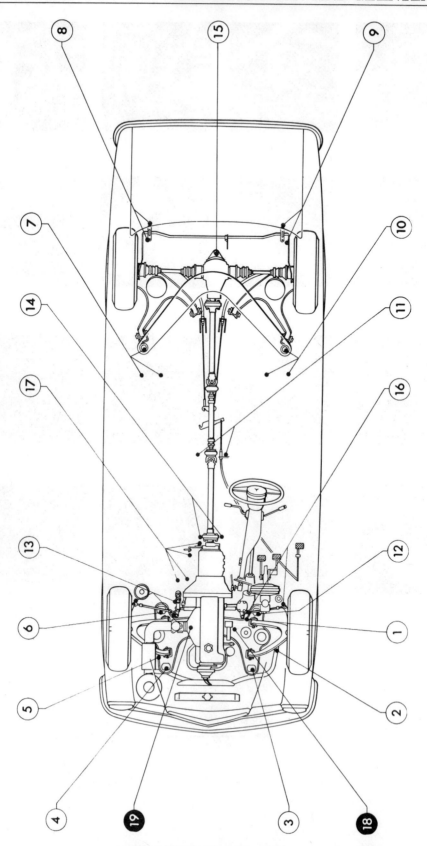

Bolt tightening locations—sedans.

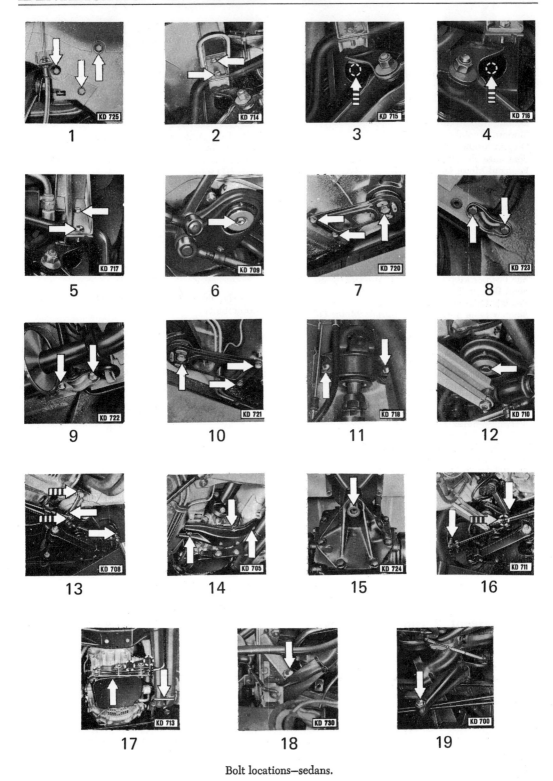

Bolt locations—sedans.

Gulflube Motor Oil HD
Gulfpride Motor Oil
*Gulfpride Single "G"
Inco HD S1
*Inco Multigrade Motor Oil 10W/30 S1
Innerlube HD
*Kendall ML6 Longlife Motor Oil
Kendall F-L Oil S-HD
*Kendall Superb Motor Oil
Modern Duolube HD Motor Oil
Oilzum Motor Oil HD S1
Pennstate Heavy Duty
Pennzoil Motor Oil with Z-7
Phillips 66 HDS Motor Oil (S-1)
Phillips Trop-Artic Motor Oil (S-1)
Quaker State HD Motor Oil
*Quaker State Super Blend Motor Oil
Royal Triton
Shell Rotella S
Shell X-100 Motor Oil
*Shell Super Motor Oil (20W/50)
*Shell Super Motor Oil 101 (10W/30)
#Shell Rotella T
Sinclair Dino Dinolene Motor Oil
*Sinclair Dino Supreme Multigrade Motor Oil
    10W-40
Sunoco HD Dynalube Motor Oil
Sunoco Ocnus HD (MIL) Oil
Super RPM Delo Special Lubricating Oil
Texaco S-1
*Texaco All Temperature Motor Oil 10W/30
Texaco Havoline Motor Oil
US Heavy Duty Motor Oil
Valvoline Super HPO HDM
*Valvoline All Climate
*Valvoline XLD Long Distance Oil
Veedol Motor Oil HD 900
*Veedol 10-30 Motor Oil HD
*Veedol Super 10-40 Motor Oil
Veedol Ashfree HD Plus Motor Oil
Veedol HDB
Wolf's Head Motor Oil
*Multigrade
#Not suitable for Diesel

## Lubricant Recommendations

| Unit | List No. | | | | | | | |
|---|---|---|---|---|---|---|---|---|
| | 1 | 2 | 3 | 4 | 5 | 6 | 7 | 8 |
| Rear axle | √ | (x) | | | | | | |
| Limited slip axle | | | √ | | | | | |
| Manual steering | √ | (x) | | | | | | |
| Water pump | √ | (x) | | | | | | |
| Manual transmission | | | | √ | (x) | (x) | | (x) |
| Power steering | | | | √ | (x) | (x) | | (x) |
| Auto. transmission | | | | √ | (x) | | | |
|   220/8—250/8 | | | | | | | √ | |
|   300 SEL/8  6.3 | | | | | | | √ | |

√   *Primary recommendation*

(x)  *Can be used if necessary*

## List 1
(SAE 90)

Amalie Multi-purpose Lube
Caltex Multipurpose Thuban EP 90
Castrol Hypoid B
Castrol Hypoid ELH
Chevron (RPM) Universal Gear Lubricant
Esso Gear Oil GX 90
Gulf Multi-purpose Gear Lubricant
Kendall Three Star Gear Lube
Pennzoil Gear Lubricant 4080 MP/4090 MP
Shell HD 90
Sinclair Extra Duty Gear Lube
Sunoco Multi-purpose Gear Lubricant (MPGL5)
Texaco Multigear Lube EP
Valvoline Gear Lubricant 18MD
Veedol Multigear HD

## List 2
(SAE 90)

Inco Hypoid Multipurpose Gear Oil
Mobilube GX
Quaker State Super Quadrolube
Shell Gear Oil (Hypoid)
Shell Spirax EP
Sunoco DB Hypgear BSA 708
Texaco Universal Gear Lubricant EP
Valvoline Hypoid X18

## List 3
(Limited slip)

Veedol Multigear Limited Slip Special

## List 4
(Automatic transmission fluid)
ATF

Amalie ATF Type A Suffix A
Caltex Texamatic Fluid AQ 1800A
Castrol TQ
Esso Automatic Transmission Fluid AQ—ATF
    2974A
Gulf ATF Type A Suffix A
HUB ATF
Inco ATF—AQ—ATF 2103A
Kendall Automatic Transmission Fluid
Mobil ATF 200 AQ—ATF—No. 752A
Mobilfluid 300
Pennzoil Hydra-Flo ATF Type A
Philube ATF
Quaker State Quadromatic ATF Type A
Sunoco Automatic Transmission Fluid AQ—
    ATF 737A
Texaco Texamatic Fluid AQ 1735A
Valvoline Valvomatic ATF Type A Suffix A
Veedol ATF Type A Suffix A 1407A
White Rose ATF Type A

## List 5
(Automatic transmission fluid)
ATF

Caltex Texamatic Fluid AQ 1800A
Castrol TQ—ATF—2418A

Chevron Automatic Transmission Fluid Type A-68
Esso Automatic Transmission Fluid AQ–ATF
   2974A
Mobil ATF 200 AQ–ATF–No. 752A
Shell Donax T6 AQ844A
Sunoco Automatic Transmission Fluid AQ– ATF
   737A
Texaco Texamatic Fluid AQ 1735A
Valvoline Transmission Fluid DB
Veedol ATF Type A Suffix A 1407A

## List 6
(Automatic transmission fluid)
ATF

Caltex Texamatic Fluid AQ 1800A
Texaco Texamatic Fluid AQ 1735A
Veedol ATF Type A Suffix A Special 735 MB600

## List 7
(Automatic transmission fluid)
Dexron

Castrol TQ (Dexron) B 10.658
Castrol TQ Dexron B 10.578
*Mobil ATF 220 Dexron B 10 104
Mobil ATF 220 Dexron B 10 467
Shell Automatic Transmission Fluid Dexron
   B 10 492
Shell Automatic Transmission Fluid Dexron
   B 10 378
Sunamatic 128 Dexron B 10 107
*Texamatic Fluid 6673 Dexron B 10 101
Veedol ATF Special B 101 Dexron
*Especially desirable

## List 8
(Transmission oils)

Castrol Gear Oil SDB
Chevron Gear Oil DB
Esso Gear Oil DB
Mobil Transmission Oil DB
Texaco Transmission Oil DB

## Diesel Engine Oil Recommendations

Oils that are particularly suitable for diesel engine use in 190Dc and 200D models, and which must be used in the 220D/8 for greatest engine life are as follows:

Castrol (HD)
Esso Engine Oil (HD)
Valvoline Super HPO HDM
Veedol High Detergency HD900

### Changing the Oil and Filter

The question is often asked, "When do I change the oil?" To understand the reasoning behind oil change intervals, perhaps it would be best to examine engine oil itself with relation to the job it has to perform.

Engine oil must have satisfactory dispersive power, the power to hold accumulated particles and chemical contaminants in suspension. This is why oil that appears "dirty" at oil change time is to be taken as a good sign—the contaminants are draining out of the engine and not forming sludge on internal parts. In conjunction with this is the necessity for detergent (washing) action. The detergent literally washes the inside of the engine and allows the oil to act as a cleaner as well as a lubricant. Other additives act to neutralize the acids which are a normal combustion byproduct of fuel burning and oil aging.

Oil must also perform functions relating to reduction of oxidation and corrosion and, perhaps most important, oil must have adequate lubricity, the ability to keep friction and wear to a minimum. Going hand in hand with this is the proper viscosity for the temperatures encountered.

The viscosity–temperature chart shows how ambient (surrounding) temperature should influence oil viscosity selection. For winter operation, a "W" is added after the SAE viscosity rating to indicate that oil's suitability for cold temperature. Oils classified 10W/30, for example, are suitable for both summer and winter operation.

| Ambient Temperature | SAE Rating |
| --- | --- |
| below —13° F. | SAE 5W |
| between —13° & +50° F. | SAE 10W (or corresponding multigrade) 10W/30 |
| above +32° F. | SAE 30W (or corresponding multigrade 10W/30 |
| above +86° F. | SAE 40 (or corresponding multigrade) 20W/40 |

Resistance to foaming and chemical breakdown under high temperatures is also a must, for oil also acts as an engine coolant. An engine very low on oil will almost always run hotter than one properly filled.

These requirements can be fulfilled only by the so-called HD oils (heavy-duty) with detergent action. Straight, uncompounded oils cannot meet the rigid requirements set by the factory for their close-

# Maintenance Intervals
(All Figures in Thousands of Miles)

| Model | Automatic Trans. Fluid | | Engine Oil | | Oil Filter | Oil Bath Air Filter | Inj. Pump Oil | Chassis | Heat Riser Valve |
|---|---|---|---|---|---|---|---|---|---|
| | Check & Refill | Change ⑨ | Check & Refill | Change | Change | Change | Check | Lube | Lube (Kerosene) |
| 190c | 3.0 | 12.0 | 3.0 | 6.0 | 6.0 | | | 3.0 ⑩ | 3.0 |
| 200 | 3.0 | 12.0 | 3.0 | 6.0 | 6.0 | | | 3.0 ⑩ | 3.0 |
| 190Dc | 1.9 | 11.4 | | 1.9 | 5.7 | 1.9 | 11.4 | 1.9 ⑪ | 5.7 |
| 200D | 3.0 | 12.0 | | 3.0 | 3.0 | 3.0 | 12.0 | 3.0 ⑩ | 6.0 |
| 230 | 3.0 | 12.0 | 3.0 | 6.0 | 6.0 | | | 3.0 ⑩ | 6.0 |
| 220b | 1.9 | 11.4 | 1.9 | 5.7 | 5.7 | | | 1.9 ⑪ | 5.7 |
| 220Sb | 1.9 | 11.4 | 1.9 | 5.7 | 5.7 | | | 1.9 ⑪ | 5.7 |
| 230S | 3.0 | 12.0 | 3.0 | 6.0 | 6.0 | | | 3.0 ⑩ | 6.0 |
| 250S | 3.0 | 12.0 | 3.0 | 6.0 | 6.0 | | | 3.0 ⑩ | 6.0 |
| 220SEb | 1.9 | 11.4 | 1.9 | 5.7 | 5.7 | | 5.7 | 1.9 ⑪ | |
| 250SE | 3.0 | 12.0 | 3.0 | 6.0 | 6.0 | | 12.0 | 3.0 ⑩ | |
| 230SL ⑭ | 1.9 | 11.4 | 1.9 | 5.7 | 5.7 | | 5.7 ⑮ | 1.9 ⑪ | |
| 250SL | 3.0 | 12.0 | 3.0 | 6.0 | 6.0 | | 12.0 | 3.0 ⑩ | |
| 220SEb/C① | 1.9 | 11.4 | 1.9 | 5.7 | 5.7 | | 5.7 | 1.9 ⑪ | |
| 250SE/C② | 3.0 | 12.0 | 3.0 | 6.0 | 6.0 | | 12.0 | 3.0 ⑩ | |
| 250SE/C③ | 3.0 | 12.0 | 3.0 | 6.0 | 6.0 | | 12.0 | 3.0 ⑩ | |
| 300SE④ | 1.9 | 11.4 | 1.9 | 5.7 | 5.7 | | 5.7 | 1.9 ⑪ | |
| 300SE⑤ | 1.9 | 11.4 | 1.9 | 5.7 | 5.7 | | 5.7 | 1.9 ⑪ | |
| 300SE⑥ | 1.9 | 11.4 | 1.9 | 5.7 | 5.7 | | 5.7 | 1.9 ⑪ | |
| 300SEb | 3.0 | 12.0 | 3.0 | 6.0 | 6.0 | | 12.0 | 3.0 ⑩ | |
| 300SEL | 3.0 | 12.0 | 3.0 | 6.0 | 6.0 | | 12.0 | 3.0 ⑩ | |
| 300SE⑦ | 3.0 | 12.0 | 3.0 | 6.0 | 6.0 | | 12.0 | 3.0 ⑩ | |
| 300SE⑧ | 3.0 | 12.0 | 3.0 | 6.0 | 6.0 | | 12.0 | 3.0 ⑩ | |
| 220D/8 | 3.0 | 12.0 | | 3.0 | 3.0 | 3.0 | 12.0 | 3.0 ⑩ | 6.0 |
| 220/8 | 3.0 | 30.0 | 3.0 | 6.0 | 6.0 | | | 3.0 ⑩ | 3.0 |
| 230/8 | 3.0 | 12.0 | 3.0 | 6.0 | 6.0 | | | 3.0 ⑩ | 3.0 |
| 250/8 | 3.0 | 12.0 | 3.0 | 6.0 | 6.0 | | | 3.0 ⑩ | 3.0 |
| 280S/8 | 3.0 | 12.0 | 3.0 | 6.0 | 6.0 | | | 3.0 ⑩ | 3.0 |
| 280SE/8 | 3.0 | 12.0 | 3.0 | 6.0 | 6.0 | | 12.0 | 3.0 ⑩ | |
| 280SEL/8 | 3.0 | 12.0 | 3.0 | 6.0 | 6.0 | | 12.0 | 3.0 ⑩ | |
| 280SE/8 ① | 3.0 | 12.0 | 3.0 | 6.0 | 6.0 | | 12.0 | 3.0 ⑩ | |
| 280SL/8 | 3.0 | 12.0 | 3.0 | 6.0 | 6.0 | | 12.0 | 3.0 ⑩ | |
| 300SEL/8 | 3.0 | 12.0 | 3.0 | 6.0 | 6.0 | | 12.0 | 3.0 ⑩ | |
| 300SEL/8 6.3 | 3.0 | 12.0 | 3.0 | 6.0 | 6.0 | | 12.0 | 3.0 ⑩ | |

①    *Coupe and convertible*
②    *Coupe*
③    *Convertible*
④    *Long wheelbase*
⑤    *Coupe to August, 1965*
⑥    *Convertible to August, 1965*
⑦    *Coupe from August, 1965*
⑧    *Convertible from August, 1965*
⑨    *Transmission oil filter every 30,000 miles*
⑩    *Every 1,500 miles or every month under adverse conditions, at least every two months regardless*

## Maintenance Intervals
(All Figures in Thousands of Miles)

| Model | Manual Trans. Oil Change | Power Steering Fluid Refill | Manual Steering Oil Refill | Rear Axle Oil Change | Level Control Fluid Refill | Brake Fluid Refill | Clutch Fluid Refill | Wheel Bearings Repack | Parking Brake Rails Lube | Door ⑫ Hinges ⑰ Lube |
|---|---|---|---|---|---|---|---|---|---|---|
| 190c | 12.0 | 3.0 | 12.0 | 12.0 | | 3.0 | 3.0 | 12.0 | 6.0 | 12.0 |
| 200 | 12.0 | 3.0 | 12.0 | 12.0 | | 3.0 | 3.0 | 12.0 | 6.0 | 12.0 |
| 190Dc | 11.4 | 1.9 | 11.4 | 11.4 | | 1.9 | 1.9 | 11.4 | 5.7 | 11.4 |
| 200D | 12.0 | 3.0 | 12.0 | 12.0 | | 3.0 | 3.0 | 12.0 | 6.0 | 12.0 |
| 230 | 12.0 | 3.0 | 12.0 | 12.0 | | 3.0 | 3.0 | 12.0 | 6.0 | 12.0 |
| 220b | 11.4 | 1.9 | 11.4 | 11.4 | | 1.9 | 1.9 | 11.4 | 5.7 | 11.4 |
| 220Sb | 11.4 | 1.9 | 11.4 | 11.4 | | 1.9 | 1.9 | 11.4 | 5.7 | 11.4 |
| 230S | 12.0 | 3.0 | 12.0 | 12.0 | | 3.0 | 3.0 | 12.0 | 6.0 | 12.0 |
| 250S | 12.0 | 3.0 | 12.0 | 12.0 | | 3.0 | 3.0 | 12.0 | 6.0 | 12.0 |
| 220SEb | 11.4 | 1.9 | 11.4 | 11.4 | | 1.9 | 1.9 | 11.4 | 5.7 | 11.4 |
| 250SE | 12.0 | 3.0 | 12.0 | 12.0 | | 3.0 | 3.0 | 12.0 | 6.0 | 12.0 |
| 230SL ⑭ | 11.4 | 1.9 | 11.4 | 11.4 | | 1.9 | 1.9 | 11.4 | 5.7 | 11.4 |
| 250SL | 12.0 | 3.0 | 12.0 | 12.0 | | 3.0 | 3.0 | 12.0 | 6.0 | 12.0 |
| 220SEb/C① | 11.4 | 1.9 | 11.4 | 11.4 | | 1.9 | 1.9 | 11.4 | 5.7 | 11.4 |
| 250SE/C② | 12.0 | 3.0 | 12.0 | 12.0 | | 3.0 | 3.0 | 12.0 | 6.0 | 12.0 |
| 250SE/C③ | 12.0 | 3.0 | 12.0 | 12.0 | | 3.0 | 3.0 | 12.0 | 6.0 | 12.0 |
| 300SE④ | 11.4 | 1.9 | | 11.4 | 1.9 ⑬ | 1.9 | 1.9 | 11.4 | 5.7 | 11.4 |
| 300SE⑤ | 11.4 | 1.9 | | 11.4 | 1.9 ⑬ | 1.9 | 1.9 | 11.4 | 5.7 | 11.4 |
| 300SE⑥ | 11.4 | 1.9 | | 11.4 | 1.9 ⑬ | 1.9 | 1.9 | 11.4 | 5.7 | 11.4 |
| 300SEb | 12.0 | 3.0 | | 12.0 | | 3.0 | | 12.0 | 6.0 | 12.0 |
| 300SEL | 12.0 | 3.0 | | 12.0 | 3.0 ⑬ | 3.0 | | 12.0 | 6.0 | 12.0 |
| 300SE⑦ | 12.0 | 3.0 | | 12.0 | 3.0 ⑬ | 3.0 | | 12.0 | 6.0 | 12.0 |
| 300SE⑧ | 12.0 | 3.0 | | 12.0 | 3.0 ⑬ | 3.0 | | 12.0 | 6.0 | 12.0 |
| 220D/8 | 12.0 | 3.0 | 12.0 | 12.0 | 3.0 | 3.0 | 3.0 | 12.0 | 6.0 | 12.0 |
| 220/8 | 12.0 | 3.0 | 12.0 | 12.0 | 3.0 | 3.0 | 3.0 | 12.0 | 6.0 | 12.0 |
| 230/8 | 12.0 | 3.0 | 12.0 | 12.0 | 3.0 | 3.0 | 3.0 | 12.0 | 6.0 | 12.0 |
| 250/8 | 12.0 | 3.0 | 12.0 | 12.0 | 3.0 | 3.0 | 3.0 | 12.0 | 6.0 | 12.0 |
| 280S/8 | 12.0 | 3.0 | 12.0 | 12.0 | 3.0 | 3.0 | 3.0 | 12.0 | 6.0 | 12.0 |
| 280SE/8 | 12.0 | 3.0 | 12.0 | 12.0 | 3.0 | 3.0 | 3.0 | 12.0 | 6.0 | 12.0 |
| 280SEL/8 | 12.0 | 3.0 | 12.0 | 12.0 | 3.0 | 3.0 | 3.0 | 12.0 | 6.0 | 12.0 |
| 280SE/8① | 12.0 | 3.0 | 12.0 | 12.0 | 3.0 | 3.0 | 3.0 | 12.0 | 6.0 | 12.0 |
| 280SL/8 | 12.0 | 3.0 | 12.0 | 12.0 | 3.0 | 3.0 | 3.0 | 12.0 | 6.0 | 12.0 |
| 300SEL/8 | 12.0 | 3.0 | | 12.0 | 3.0 | 3.0 | 3.0 | 12.0 | 6.0 | 12.0 |
| 300SEL/8 6.3 | | 3.0 | | 12.0 | 3.0 ⑬ | 3.0 | | 12.0 ⑯ | 6.0 | 12.0 |

⑪   *Every 1,000 miles under adverse conditions*
⑫   *At same mileage, oil miscellaneous hinges, joints, linkages, distributor felt*
⑬   *Antifreeze unit for air suspension below 41° F. Fill to top of corrugation with ethyl alcohol*
⑭   *To August, 1965. From August, 1965 same as 230S except injection pump interval*
⑮   *From August, 1965—12,000 miles*
⑯   *Also every spring and fall*
⑰   *At same mileage, grease water pump and wedge in contact breaker if applicable*

## Capacities

| Model | Fuel Tank (gals.) ** | Crankcase (qts.) Max. ** | Crankcase (qts.) Min. ** | Radiator (qts.) ** | Rear Axle (pts.) ** | Oil Filter (pts.) ** | Transmission (pts.) Man. ** | Transmission (pts.) Auto. ** | Power Steering (pts.) ** | Manual Steering (pts.) *** |
|---|---|---|---|---|---|---|---|---|---|---|
| 190c | 13 3/4 | 4 1/4 | 2 1/2 | 10 1/2 | 5 1/4 | 1 | 3 | 7 1/2 [1] | 3 | 5/8 |
| 200 | 17 1/4 | 4 1/4 | 2 1/2 | 10 1/2 | 5 1/4 | 1 | 3 | 7 1/2 [1] | 3 | 5/8 |
| 190Dc | 13 3/4 | 4 1/4 | 2 1/2 | 10 1/2 | 5 1/4 | 2 | 3 | 7 1/2 [1] | 3 | 5/8 |
| 200D | 17 1/4 | 4 1/4 | 2 1/2 | 10 1/2 | 5 1/4 | 2 | 3 | 7 1/2 [1] | 3 | 5/8 |
| 230 | 17 1/4 | 5 3/4 | 3 3/4 | 14 3/4 | 5 1/4 | 1 | 3 | 7 1/2 [1] | 3 | 5/8 |
| 220b | 17 1/4 | 5 3/4 | 3 3/4 | 12 | 5 1/4 | 1 | 3 | 8 [3] | 3 | 5/8 |
| 220Sb | 17 1/4 | 5 3/4 | 3 3/4 | 12 | 5 1/4 | 1 | 3 | 8 [3] | 3 | 5/8 |
| 230S | 17 1/4 | 5 3/4 | 3 3/4 | 12 | 5 1/4 | 1 | 3 | 8 [3] | 3 | 5/8 |
| 250S | 21 1/2 | 5 3/4 [4] | 3 3/4 | 11 | 5 1/4 | 1 | 3 | 8 [3] | 3 | 5/8 |
| 220SEb | 17 1/4 | 5 3/4 | 3 3/4 | 12 | 5 1/4 | 1 | 3 | 8 [3] | 3 | 5/8 |
| 250SE | 21 1/2 | 5 3/4 [4] | 3 3/4 | 11 | 5 1/4 | 1 | 3 | 8 [3] | 3 | 5/8 |
| 230SL | 17 1/4 | 5 3/4 | 3 3/4 | 11 1/2 | 5 1/4 | 1 | 3 | 8 [3] | 3 | 5/8 |
| 250SL | 21 1/2 | 5 3/4 [4] | 3 3/4 | 13 1/2 | 5 1/4 | 1 | 3 | 8 [3] | 3 | 5/8 |
| 220SEb/C | 17 1/4 | 5 3/4 | 3 3/4 | 12 | 5 1/4 | 1 | 3 | 8 [3] | 3 | 5/8 |
| 250SE/C | 21 1/2 | 5 3/4 [4] | 3 3/4 | 11 | 5 1/4 | 1 | 3 | 8 [3] | 3 | 5/8 |
| 300SE | 21 1/2 | 6 1/4 | 4 1/4 | 17 3/4 | 5 1/4 | 1 | 3 | 10 [6] | 3 1/4 | |
| 300SE* | 21 1/2 | 6 1/4 | 4 1/4 | 17 3/4 | 5 1/4 | 1 | 3 | 10 [6] | 3 1/4 | |
| 300SEb | 21 1/2 | 6 1/4 | 4 1/4 | 17 3/4 | 5 1/4 | 1 | 3 | 10 [6] | 3 1/4 | |
| 300SEL | 21 1/2 | 6 1/4 | 4 1/4 | 17 3/4 | 5 1/4 | 1 | 3 | 10 [6] | 3 1/4 | |
| 220D/8 | 17 1/4 | 4 1/4 [8] | 2 1/2 | 11 1/4 | 2 1/2 | 2 | 3 | 9 3/4 [5] | 3 | 5/8 |
| 220/8 | 17 1/4 | 4 1/4 | 2 1/2 | 11 | 2 1/2 | 1 | 3 1/2 | 8 3/4 [2] | 3 | 5/8 |
| 230/8 | 17 1/4 | 5 3/4 [4] | 3 3/4 | 11 | 2 1/2 | 1 | 3 1/2 | 9 3/4 [5] | 3 | 5/8 |
| 250/8 | 17 1/4 | 5 3/4 [4] | 3 3/4 | 10 1/2 | 2 1/2 | 1 | 3 1/2 | 9 3/4 [5] | 3 | 5/8 |
| 280S/8 | 21 1/2 | 5 3/4 [4] | 3 3/4 | 11 | 5 1/4 | 1 | 3 | 8 [3] | 3 | 5/8 |
| 280SE/8 | 21 1/2 | 5 3/4 [4] | 3 3/4 | 11 1/4 | 5 1/4 | 1 | 3 | 8 [3] | 3 | 5/8 |
| 280SL/8 | 21 1/2 | 5 3/4 [4] | 3 3/4 | 13 1/4 | 5 1/4 | 1 | 3 | 8 [3] | 3 | 5/8 |
| 300SEL/8 | 21 1/2 | 5 3/4 [4] | 3 3/4 | 11 | 5 1/4 | 1 | 3 | 8 [3] | 3 | 5/8 |
| 300SEL/8 6.3 | 27 3/4 | 6 3/4 | 5 1/4 | 19 | 5 1/4 | 2 | | 16 1/2 [7] | 3 1/4 | |

* Coupe and convertible, first and second versions.
** All figures rounded off to nearest quarter.
*** Rounded off to the nearest eighth.
[1] Initial filling — 9 1/2 pts.
[2] Initial filling — 11 3/4 pts.
[3] Initial filling — 10 pts.
[4] With oil cooler — 6 1/4 qts.
[5] Initial filling — 11 1/2 pts.
[6] Initial filling — 12 pts.
[7] Initial filling — 18 1/2 pts.
[8] Oil cooler added after chassis No. 052 894; add 1 pt. extra.

tolerance engines; therefore, it must be emphasized that non-detergent oil should never be used except in an emergency. If such oil is used for any length of time, the reuse of a detergent oil may result in sludge deposits being lifted from the internal parts and circulated through the engine, resulting in increased engine wear. In cases like this, the engine should be flushed out by the dealer before reinstalling detergent oil.

Brands of oil approved for use in Mercedes-Benz automobiles can be found in the listing in this chapter. If the oil is topped up or changed, it is not strictly necessary to stay with the same *brand* of oil, so long as detergent qualities and viscosity remain essentially the same. *Frequent* switching of oil brands is, however, not recommended, since the resulting mixture may lose some of its effectiveness.

If the proper grade (viscosity) oil is used, of an approved type, it is not necessary, or desirable, to add special "patent" oil additives. While these may not do any harm, they certainly don't do anything to help a properly maintained engine in good condition.

Oil change intervals are set by the factory, but it must be remembered that individual car usage should determine the interval. Any change or deterioration of the engine oil will depend on a multitude of factors, some of which are:
1. Design of the engine.
2. Operating conditions (high speed vs. city driving, dust conditions, heat).
3. Quality of fuel used (especially with diesel engines).
4. Oil dilution by fuel (as when car is cranked excessively during starting).
5. Contamination of the oil by water (as with a blown head gasket).
6. Efficiency of the oil filter.
7. Oil capacity of the engine.
8. Oil consumption (how much oil was added between changes).
9. Oil additive concentration (depends on brand).

The oil change intervals given in the table are, then, only average, safe values for normal operating conditions. Miles traveled are certainly the most obvious method of determining oil change interval, but probably the most inaccurate. A better way would be to consider the operating

time of the engine in hours, as the large fleet owners do with good results.

If the car is not used often, the oil must be changed at least once every six months, regardless of miles traveled, since the normal deterioration of the oil through chemical changes will take place regardless.

Diesel engines are subject to greater lower end loads than gasoline engines, therefore it is vital that oil recommendations be followed for long bearing life.

For all engines, it is possible in a pinch to use brands of oil other than those recommended, but in no circumstances should "re-manufactured" oils be used. If in doubt about a brand of oil, go to the highest viscosity rating possible for increased protection and change to a recommended brand as soon as possible.

There are almost as many "expert" opinions about break-in oils for rebuilt engines

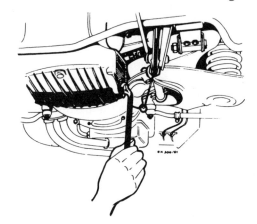

Engine oil drain plug.

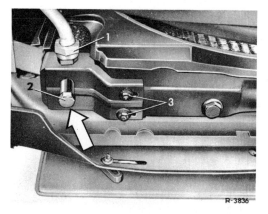

1. Pipe joint
2. Oil drain plug
3. Hold-down nuts

Oil cooler.

as there are "experts". Mercedes-Benz engines are filled at the factory with a high-grade, blended NON-DETERGENT oil. This oil is loaded with various anti-corrosion additives, however. If the factory break-in oil cannot be obtained from the dealer, use a 50–50 mixture of an unblended, heavy-duty, non-detergent oil and a recommended brand S-1 HD oil for the first 300–600 miles.

It is generally thought that a good SAE 5 or 10 "straight" oil is best for break-in purposes. To use such an oil in 90° F. temperatures would obviously do the engine little good under normal circumstances, and to use it to break in a newly rebuilt engine would be foolhardy. The viscosity should be chosen according to the prevailing temperatures.

The engine oil is changed by removing the drain plug in the oil pan (see illustration). It is best to drain the oil while hot, because particles and contaminants will then be in suspension and drained out with the oil.

If the car has an oil cooler, the oil must be drained by removing the drain plug at the bottom of the cooler (see illustration). It is recommended that the oil filter be removed before draining the oil cooler in order to provide a pressure release in the oil system, ensuring complete draining. The copper and copper-asbestos gaskets on the oil pan and oil cooler plugs may be re-used if they are not scored badly, but it is advisable to renew them after a few oil changes to prevent seepage.

Tightening torque for the oil pan drain plug is approximately 36 ft.lbs., for the oil cooler drain plug 14 ft.lbs. and for the lower oil filter bolt 29 ft.lbs.

The oil filter is located on the lower left-hand side of the engine on most models. It is either a full-flow or a combined full and partial-flow type, depending on application.

To remove the filter element, loosen the bolt (2) and carefully remove the housing (1) and filter element, being careful not to spill the oil. Clean the inside of the housing with a kerosene-soaked, lint-free rag to remove any sediment, then insert a new filter element. Make sure that the pressure spring (7) is properly installed before inserting the element—its absence will result in no filtering action. As can be seen in this illustration, the bolt that holds the housing is, in this case, on top. An oil drain plug is provided on the side of the filter housing to allow pre-draining the housing before removal.

Another type of oil filter construction used is shown here. The nylon filter screen (3) should be cleaned every 3,000 miles in kerosene. The two openings (a) should be stoppered with washers and a bolt and the filter blown out with *low pressure* air.

On all filter types, inspect the housing gasket carefully for scars or breakage. Make sure the gasket is properly seated in its bore to prevent leakage.

All new Mercedes-Benz automobiles are equipped with a special fine-pore filter element for break-in purposes. This should be replaced at the first service inspection (A—180–600 miles). If the engine is rebuilt, it is necessary to use this type filter again, but under no circumstances should it be used for other than break-in.

**Manual Transmission**

To drain the transmission oil, remove the lower drain plug and drain oil into a pan.

Oil filter.

Seal filter element at "a" and blow through with compressed air.

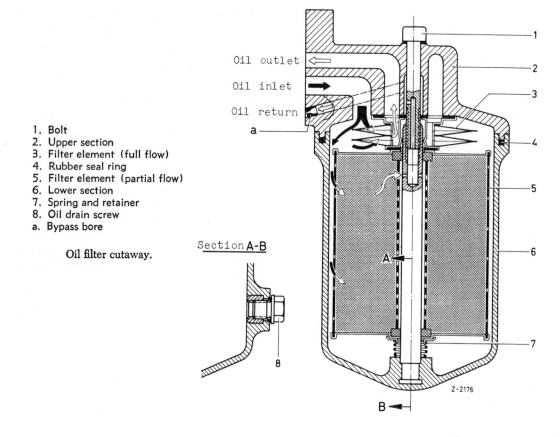

Oil outlet
Oil inlet
Oil return

1. Bolt
2. Upper section
3. Filter element (full flow)
4. Rubber seal ring
5. Filter element (partial flow)
6. Lower section
7. Spring and retainer
8. Oil drain screw
a. Bypass bore

Oil filter cutaway.

Section A-B

Z-2176

## Chart Showing Automatic Transmissions
## with Model Application and Type of Fluid To Be Used

| Automatic Transmission Part No. | Model Application | Type A Suffix A | Type B Dexron |
|---|---|---|---|
| 108 270 07 01 | 280SL/8, 280S/8, 280SEL/8, 300SEL/8 (109.016) | X | |
| 109 270 09 01 | 300SEL/8 6.3 | | X |
| 110 270 01 01 | 190c up to chassis No. 110010-12-086351 | X | |
| 110 270 05 01 | 190Dc — 200D | X | |
| 110 270 14 01 | 190c — 200 | X | |
| 110 270 20 01 | 230 | X | |
| 111 270 01 01 | 220b, 220Sb, 220SEb, 230S | X | |
| 111 270 13 01 | 220b, 220Sb, 220SEb, 230S | X | |
| 112 270 01 01 | 300SE, 300SEb, 300SE, (112.015) | X | |
| 112 270 09 01 | 300SE, 300SE Cp/Cv., 300SEb, 300SEL (109.015) | X | |
| 112 270 16 01 | 300SE, 300SE Cp/Cv., 300SEb, 300SEL (109.015) | X | |
| 113 270 01 01 | 230SL, 250S, 250SL, 250SE, 250SE Cp/Cv. | X | |
| 114 270 01 01 | 230/8, 250/8 | | X |
| 115 270 02 01 | 220/8 | | X |
| 115 270 04 01 | 220D/8 | | X |

The upper fill plug can be loosened at this time to provide a pressure release.

It is advisable that the transmission oil be hot when draining so that most of the metal particles that are a result of normal wear are in suspension. Before inserting the drain plug, blow off any metal chips with compressed air.

### Automatic Transmission

To further enlarge on the previous table listing applicable fluids, the following chart shows individual models and the general type of fluid required for transmission oil changes. Any transmission requiring Type A Suffix A fluid may be topped up with Dexron B fluid between oil changes, but the Type A fluid must be used at other times. The reverse, however, is not true. Transmissions requiring Dexron B type fluids must be topped up with only this type fluid.

To check the transmission oil level, have the engine running and at normal operating temperature with the selector in Park. The car should be on level ground.

Pull out the dipstick, wipe with a lint-free cloth, and reinsert. Pull the dipstick again and check the oil level; it should be between the upper and lower marks.

The most important thing to remember is that the engine be warm, for the dipstick will read below the lower mark, even if full, when the engine and transmission are cold.

Normally, when fluid is low, an audible sucking sound can be heard from the oil pump, and the fluid will be foamy.

If fluid must be added, carefully pour

Draining automatic transmission.

through a strainer-type funnel into the dipstick opening.

To recheck after filling, shift the transmission through all its ranges with engine running to ensure that all the servos are filled up.

Excess transmission oil always should be siphoned off if overfilled, because prolonged use will result in transmission damage.

The difference between the upper and lower marks on the dipstick is 0.5 liter for older models and 0.3 liter for the "/8" series.

To drain transmission on models having a drain plug in the transmission oil pan,

Refilling automatic transmission.

Converter drain plug (1).

Automatic transmission—220/8–250/8.

simply remove the plug and drain the fluid into a container. The transmission should be at operating temperature and the car on level ground for this (see illustration). Then, remove the screen cover to expose the torque converter drain plug (1) (see illustration). Unscrew this plug and drain oil, then reinstall both plugs and the cover.

On the 220/8–250/8 series transmissions, a transmission oil filter has been incorporated. Refilling procedures remain the same, but to change the oil the drain plug (1) at the bottom of the dipstick tube must be removed, then the plug (2) on the torque converter. As in older versions, the converter may have to be rotated to bring the plug into view. Always use a new drain plug gasket.

To change the filter, remove the four attaching bolts (3) that hold the oil pan to the transmission. Be careful when removing these bolts that you don't drop the

protective plates (4). *CAUTION: The oil pan will still have oil in it. Remove the filter (6) by removing the two screws (5). The filter cannot be cleaned, replace it.* It is extremely important that the gaskets on both filter and oil pan are not kinked during installation. Refill and check as previously outlined.

*CAUTION: On 220 D/8, 220/8, 230/8 and 250/8 models, some owner's manuals INCORRECTLY list ATF Type A, Suffix A fluid for these automatic transmissions. Dexron B fluid, of an approved type (see list), is the only fluid to be used.*

The transmission used on the 280 SL/8, 280SE/8 and 300 SEL/8 is drained by unscrewing the drain plug (1) (see illustration) and draining the fluid into a container. The torque converter is drained by removing the ventilated clutch housing cover (2) and rotating the drain plug into view, then loosening the plug.

To change the filter, remove the oil pan

Automatic transmission—280/8–300SEL/8.

Transmission oil filter—220/8–250/8.

Transmission oil filter—280/8–300SEL/8.

bolts and the two oil lines (5 and 6). The filter (7) (see illustration) is removed by loosening the box socket screw (8). Reinstall by reversing removal procedure, being careful not to pinch gaskets. Always use new gaskets on both drain plugs. Refill and check as previously outlined.

**Rear Axle**

To drain the rear axle, first jack up the car from the rear and support the axle tubes on jack stands. The reason for this is, if the axle tubes are allowed to hang free, oil runs down into them and complete draining is impossible. If the axle is then filled up to the specified level and the car lowered, the oil level is too high and foaming and leakage through the breather results.

After jacking up the rear, remove the bottom drain plug and loosen the top plug for pressure release. After the fluid has drained, replace the bottom plug and refill from the top. It is important that the proper lubricant be used (see list), especially in limited slip differentials.

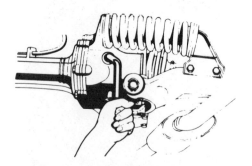

Rear axle oil fill plug.

The limited slip differential can be filled *only* with Veedol Multigen Limited Slip Special lubricant. Identification of this type differential is by a plate attached to the rear axle housing, reading "Achtung Spezial—Öl Sperrdifferential." (Caution! Special oil—limited slip differential.)

Two oil changes are necessary before regular maintenance begins. The first of these is at the "A" inspection (180–600 miles), the second at the "B" inspection (3,000 miles). Thereafter, the oil must be *checked* every 12,000 miles and replenished only if necessary. No further oil *changes* are necessary, unless the differential is rebuilt.

**Power Steering**

The hydraulic fluid reservoir is connected to the steering box by hydraulic hoses. The pump allows the car to be steered with greater ease, but fluid loss would not result in steering loss because the power steering unit provides an assist only. If steering effort suddenly became greater, the fluid reservoir should be the first thing to check.

Remove the wingnut and cover and observe the fluid level. At normal operating temperature, the fluid should reach the mark on the side of the reservoir, with the engine idling. If the fluid is checked cold, it is normal for the level to be slightly less than ½″ below the mark.

Never overfill the reservoir as foaming may result. If the fluid looks "milky" or cloudy, it may indicate an air leak somewhere in the system. In any event, all gaskets should be inspected for kinks and

Limited slip differential identification plate.

Typical power steering fluid reservoir.

all hoses for leaks each time the level is checked.

Every 30,000 miles the filter element in the reservoir should be changed. To do this, remove the wingnut and cover, then remove the pressure spring and plate. The filter element can then be removed and another installed. Always check that gaskets are not kinked or broken during cover installation.

## Manual Steering

To check level in manual steering box, remove filler plug as illustrated on lubrication charts. Top up with SAE 90 gear lube of recommended type. It is not necessary to change the oil in this unit. Recommended lubricants can be found in the lists in this chapter.

## Chassis Lubrication

The grease nipples on the upper and lower A-frames, king pins, driveshaft, rear axle pivot, steering intermediate lever, and door hinges should be greased regularly as outlined in the *Maintenance Interval* chart.

Good general procedure is to wipe all dirt and old grease from the fittings before applying the grease gun—grit can be injected into the fitting along with the new grease. The best way to protect the fittings is to use small plastic caps made especially for the purpose on all fittings exposed to dirt, or wrap the nipples with a small piece of aluminum foil after each grease job. All excess grease should be wiped from around fittings after greasing to keep dirt build-up to a minimum.

Recommended chassis greases are:
    Caltex Marfak 1
    Esso
    Mobilgrease No. 4
    Texaco Marfak 1
    Valvoline
    Veedol VC

## Wheel Bearings

Wheel bearings should be repacked at intervals recommended in the *Maintenance Interval* chart.

To remove the wheel bearings, first remove the brake drum or, in the case of disc brakes, remove the brake caliper. (See Chapter 7 for this job, because it differs for various makes of disc brake systems.)

| | |
|---|---|
| 1. Clamp nut | 2. Washer |
| 1a. Index screw | 3. Outer wheel bearing |

Wheel bearing removal.

| | |
|---|---|
| 1. Seal | 4. Outer race |
| 2. Ring | 5. Outer race |
| 3. Inner race | 6. Inner race |

Wheel bearings disassembled.

Then, pull the grease retainer from the front wheel hub, using a large pair of channel lock pliers or equivalent. Loosen the Allen screw (1a) of the clamping nut (1), as shown in the illustration, then remove the clamping nut and washer.

To remove the front hub, it may be necessary to use a puller of some type, although gentle tapping with a hammer should loosen it enough to allow pulling by hand. On cars with disc brakes, the brake disc will come off with the hub. The wheel bearings are found inside the hub, in the sequence illustrated.

Using the correct amount of grease, liberally coat both bearings (3 and 6), making sure no grease gets on the brake drum

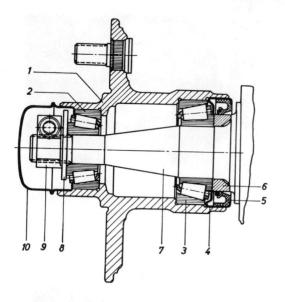

1. Front wheel hub
2. Outer annular taper
   roller bearing
3. Inner annular
   taper roller
   bearing
4. Puller ring
5. Seal
6. Spacer ring
7. Wheel spindle
8. Washer
9. Clamp nut
10. Hubcap

First version wheel bearings.

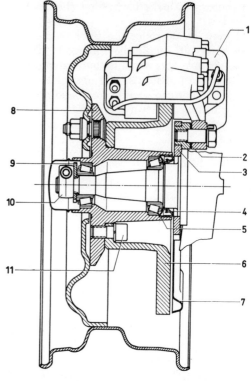

1. Brake caliper
2. Shim
3. Bracket for brake
   caliper
4. Seal
5. Puller ring
6. Brake disc
7. Cover plate
8. Front wheel hub
9. Washer
10. Clamp nut
11. Hexagon socket
    screw
    with lockwasher

Second version wheel bearings.

or disc in the process. The correct amount of grease is approximately 65–85 grams (2–3 oz.).

It is very important that the wheel bearings have the proper preload to prevent failure. Tighten the clamping nut until the hub can just be turned by hand. Then, loosen the clamping nut and tap the wheel spindle sharply with a hammer.

Ideally, end-play of the hub should be set using a dial indicator. If one is not available, the hub can be checked by hand by pulling in and out on the flange. End-play should not exceed 0.080″.

**Automatic Level Control**

The automatic leveling unit maintains the rear of the car in a level condition regardless of the load. The system consists of a leveling valve, an oil pump and a reservoir, plus a leveling unit at each rear wheel in place of shock absorbers.

The system is fully automatic and the only maintenance required at periodic intervals is a check of the oil level in the reservoir, as illustrated in the *Lubrication* charts. The oil in the system is a special type, available in Europe but usually found only at authorized Mercedes-Benz dealers in the United States. It must be emphasized that only the special oil should be used in this system.

**Air Cleaner**

Air cleaners are of two general types— dry filter element and oil bath.

In general, dry elements should be cleaned every 4,800 miles (16,000 miles for phase II series with dry air filters) and replaced every 80,000 miles. Of course, if conditions are dusty, the filter should be cleaned and/or replaced more frequently, since a dirty filter can result in decreased performance and poor fuel economy. Dry filters should never be moistened with oil or cleaned with solvent of any kind.

Dry elements can be removed for clean-

1. Air suction tube
2. Lower part of air intake silencer
3. Air filter element
4. Upper part of air intake silencer
5. Hexagon nut
6. Rubber tube
7. Retaining plate
8. Engine air-vent line

Air cleaner—190c.

2. Upper part of air intake silencer
3. Rubber band
4. Carburetor intake scoop
5. Air suction tube

Air cleaner—220b, 220Sb.

Air cleaner—220SEb, 300SE.

ing as follows: on 190c models, remove the upper section of the air cleaner (4) by removing the clamp which holds it to the carburetor. On 220b and 220Sb models, the rubber band (3) serves the same purpose, and on 220SEb and 300SE, the air hose (6).

On the 190c, remove the nut (5) (on others, unsnap the catches), remove the screws (1) and push the air intake manifold (2) toward the rear until the screws are clear of the manifold slots, then swing aside. Unsnap the catches and remove

Filter screen location—phase II models.

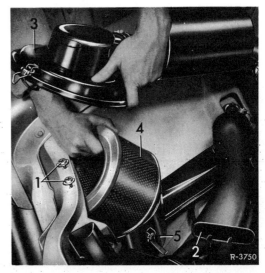

1. Fixing screws
2. Air intake
3. Top half
4. Air cleaner element
5. Housing

Air cleaner—220/8.

1. Fixing screws   2. Top half   3. Element

Air cleaner—230/8, 250/8.

Cleaning dry element.

upper section of the air cleaner and the element.

On Models 230/8 and 250/8, remove the engine vent hose, then remove the screws (1) and unsnap the catches.

To clean dry elements, simply tap on a solid surface to loosen dirt, then blow through with compressed air at no more than 70 psi. Before installing element, clean the inside of the air cleaner body with a kerosene-soaked, lint-free rag.

Oil bath air cleaners are so designed that air flows through the intake opening between the element and housing to the oil bath chamber, where heavy dirt particles are precipitated. The remaining dust is deposited on the oil-wet filter element.

The nature of this type filter requires that the oil be changed regularly and the element cleaned in kerosene, the interval depending on prevailing dust conditions. Under normal circumstances, the element should be cleaned and the oil changed every 5,000–8,000 miles. Under severe dust conditions, however, Mercedes-Benz recommends doing this every week, or every day if conditions are really severe.

When servicing the air cleaner, remove the old oil from the lower housing and wash out housing with kerosene. The oil level should never be too high or too low. If the level is too low, the filter will not work efficiently; if it is too high, some oil may be sucked into the carburetor.

When checking the oil level, it is best to allow the oil to drain completely from the filter element; this usually takes about 15 minutes.

Airflow in oil bath air cleaner.

Oil level in oil bath air cleaner.

On the 220D/8, the oil level can be checked after about five minutes of draining. Normal oil level is between the two punched arrows. *NOTE: During periods of extreme cold (below 5° F.), the motor oil normally used can be replaced with shock absorber fluid or a 70/30 mixture of motor oil and kerosene.*

1. Air suction tube
2. Top half
3. Bottom half
4. Clamp springs
5. Fixing plate

Air cleaner—220D8.

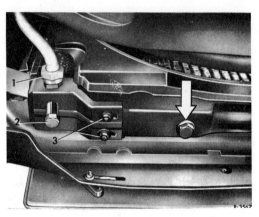

Radiator drain plug—cars with oil cooler.

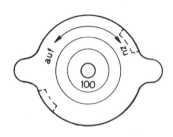

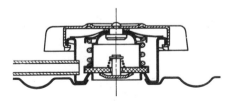

Radiator cap.

Radiator drain plug—cars without oil cooler.

## Cooling System

The cooling system consists of the radiator, water pump, thermostat and associated hoses and lines.

Perhaps the most important of these, from a maintenance point of view, is the radiator and the coolant used. As of this writing, the radiator is filled at the factory with a permanent antifreeze solution that is suitable for year-round use, except under extreme temperature range and load conditions (e.g., pulling a trailer in the mountains with the air conditioning on). Antifreeze should be changed at least once every year and replaced with one of the approved brands.

To check the coolant level, carefully turn the radiator cap counterclockwise ("auf"= open, "zu"=closed) to the first notch and allow pressure to escape. After pressure is relieved, the cap can be removed. If the coolant is hot, the correct level is about ½" above the plate that is visible in the filler neck. If cold, the level should be right at the plate.

The proper cap is marked with a "100", indicating that the overpressure valve opens at 1 atmosphere (14.7 psi) and the vacuum valve at 0.1 atmosphere (1.47 psi).

The factory recommends that certain anti-rust and anti-scale additives be added to the coolant each time the system is drained and flushed. Such approved treating agents are made by Castrol, Gulf, Mobil, Shell, Valvoline and Veedol, and are readily available in the United States.

To drain the cooling system, turn the heater lever to the "warm" position, carefully open the radiator cap to the first

Drain plug on side of block.

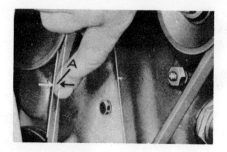

Checking fanbelt tension, A=½".

notch to relieve pressure, then remove the cap. Open the radiator drain plug and the plug on the engine block. Be careful not to open the oil cooler drain plug—see illustrations. Remove the heater hose where it enters the cylinder head and bend the hose downwards to drain the heater core.

To refill, reinstall plugs and heater hose, set heater levers to "warm" position and slowly fill radiator to visible full mark (plate). Start the engine and allow it to

idle for about one minute with radiator cap off. Check the coolant level and top up if necessary.

Before installing plugs, clean the threads and coat with graphite grease or Molykote; tightening torque is 4–6 ft.lbs. Some approved Molykote lubricants are Molykote G Paste, Molykote M Dispersion, Molykote BR2-S grease and Dow Corning 3450 Paste.

If the coolant temperature goes too high, first check the coolant level and top up if necessary. *CAUTION: Never pour cold water into a hot radiator. Use hot water only, as cylinder head could crack.* Check all hose connections for breaks, as well as

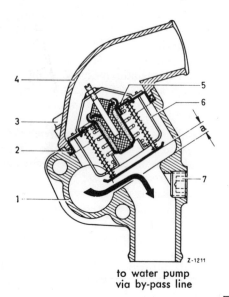

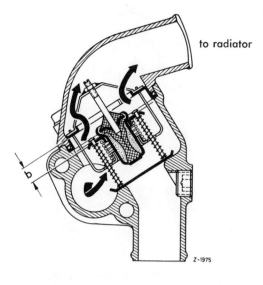

to radiator

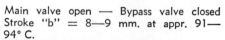

to water pump
via by-pass line

Thermostat action.

Main valve closed — Bypass valve fully open
Stroke "a" = 6—6.5 mm. from 0 to appr. 74—78°C.
    1. Cooling water thermostat
    2. Sealing ring
    3. Hexagon socket screw
    4. Cover

Main valve open — Bypass valve closed
Stroke "b" = 8—9 mm. at appr. 91—94° C.
    5. Corrugation
    6. Cooling water thermostat element
    7. Plug

the engine block. Check the fanbelt tension (½″ deflection when pushed with thumb) and the engine oil. If there are traces of water in the oil, chances are that a head gasket has blown.

Ignition timing advanced too far will also cause overheating, see Chapter 2.

Check the fan operation by allowing the car to idle until hot. The fan should cut in before the temperature gauge reaches the red line. If it does not, the coupling is defective and must be replaced.

Thermostats are of various types, some for winter use and some for summer. In general, summer thermostats open at a lower temperature than winter types to aid in cooling. The thermostat is an integral part of the cooling system and should never be removed completely, because to do so would *not* aid in cooling.

If the radiator is rusted or filled with sludge, a cleaning agent is available at Mercedes-Benz dealers for flushing the system. The cleaner should remain in the system for at least 24 hours, under normal operating conditions, for best results.

Scale can be removed by using a different cleaning agent, also available at the dealer. This agent also should be kept in the system for 24 hours. *CAUTION: Each agent must be used separately.*

After drawing out the cleaner, always flush the cooling system with clean water from a garden hose, with all drain cocks open, then blow out the radiator core ribs with compressed air to remove bugs and dirt. Cracked hoses should be replaced.

Radiator mount and thermostat location.

If the cleaning agents don't work, as with a badly rusted radiator, the radiator must be removed and sent to an authorized radiator shop for cleaning.

To remove the radiator, drain the coolant and the oil cooler (if so equipped). Then, remove the fan shroud and loosen the upper and lower hose clamps. Remove the hoses at the radiator, being careful not to crush the outlets. If the hoses are deteriorated it is best to cut them away with a sharp knife.

Unscrew the connections of the engine oil cooler and transmission oil cooler (automatic). Detach the hold-down bolts and

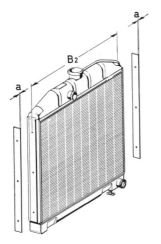
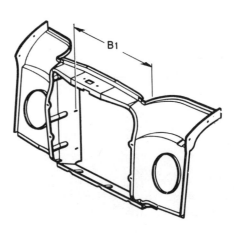

Measurements needed to determine spacer thickness.

the rubber pads on each side of the radiator and pull the radiator upward.

On the 230 SL, the bleeder hose from the radiator top tank must be removed, as well as the battery and hood.

When reinstalling, always measure the distance B1 and B2 (as illustrated). If the distances "a" (thickness of rubber pads) added to B2 do not equal B1, shims must be added, otherwise the radiator will be overstressed and the solder joints will tend to crack. ("Horseshoe" shims are available at most auto parts jobbers.)

Always make sure that the fan clears the shrouding all around *before* starting the engine, and that there is sufficient clearance between all hoses and the fanbelts.

To prevent further corrosion, install any of the approved anti-rust additives.

### APPROVED ANTIFREEZE BRANDS*

Caltex Antifreeze
Castrol Antifreeze
Chevron Antifreeze
Esso Antifreeze
Gulf Antifreeze and Summer Coolant
Mobil Permazone
Prestone Antifreeze
Shell Antifreeze
Sinclair Antifreeze
Valvoline Antifreeze
Veedol Frostfree

*Based on information January, 1969; antifreeze available in the United States. *NOTE: Due to the various compositions of different brands of antifreeze, refer to the capacities chart in this chapter and apply information to particular brand recommendations to obtain adequate protection.*

Fuel filter, showing hold-down bolt (1).

### Fuel Injection Pump

The oil level in the fuel injection pump should be checked at the indicated interval (see chart) and, if necessary, topped up with engine oil.

To check oil level, back out the screw (5) several turns. Any excess oil will seep out of this opening. To fill, unscrew the filter (6) and squirt oil into the opening until it flows out around the bleed screw (5).

### Fuel Filters

Trouble-free operation of the fuel injection pump is largely dependent on the purity of the fuel used. For this reason, the fuel filter should be replaced regularly (every 25,000–30,000 miles). In the case of diesel engines, two filters are used.

To remove the main filter element on gasoline-engined cars, loosen bolt (1) and remove housing downward. Remove the old element, clean the housing and install

Fuel injection pump, showing bleed screw (5) and hand pump (4).

| 1. Pre-filter | 3. Bleed screw |
|---|---|
| 2. Main filter | 4. Hand pump |

Diesel fuel filters.

new element. If fuel filter seems exceptionally dirty due to impure fuel, it may be wise to change it every 10,000 miles or so.

On diesel models, the small pre-filter (1) is transparent, thus making it easy to see accumulated dirt. It should be cleaned every 30,000 miles by removing the two connecting hoses and rinsing in kerosene. Low pressure compressed aid applied to the "out" side will facilitate dirt removal.

The main filter (2) can be checked for contamination by opening the air bleed screw (3) on the filter cover and pumping the hand pump (4) on the injection pump. If the filter is clear, fuel will pour out of the bleeder hole in a steady stream. If the filter is blocked, you can expect only a dribble.

## Windshield Wipers

Windshield wiper rubbers should be replaced at least once a year, as they are subject to deterioration from wear and atmospheric pollution. In any case, check wipers each spring and fall as part of normal maintenance procedure. If the wiper rubbers are worn it is not necessary to replace the entire assembly, as the rubbers are available separately.

## Storage Tips

If the car is to be stored for any period of time (over six weeks), special methods of preservation will ensure proper operation. The main thing to remember is that clean parts will last longer than dirt-covered ones. With this in mind, it is a good idea to clean the engine and under-carriage thoroughly at a spray-type car wash. The detergent and high pressure water remove corrosion-producing deposits hard to reach normally, especially when a good commercial degreasing agent is used. It is a good idea to cover the distributor cap with a plastic bag while doing this.

After the car has dried thoroughly, remove any visible rust deposits with a scraper or sandpaper, then drain the engine oil and fill with new break-in oil (anti-corrosive) or fresh HD oil, using a new oil filter. Add a mixture of 95% fuel and 5% 10W break-in oil to the fuel tank. Replace the injection pump oil with a 20W/20 break-in oil and remove the pump cover and spray the spring section with 30W break-in oil. After reinstalling the pump

cover, spray the outside of the pump with engine oil.

Run the engine up to operating temperature. Add a good anti-corrosive agent to the radiator before this run. Disconnect the fuel line of carbureted engines at the fuel pump and allow the carburetors to run dry. (Do not do this with injected engines, gasoline or diesel.)

Remove the spark plugs or glow plugs and crank the engine several times to remove combustion gases. To prevent fuel from entering the cylinders of injected engines, move the adjusting lever of the pump control rod to "stop". If the pump has pneumatic governors, the control cable at the adjusting lever must be disconnected as well.

Squirt about 10 cc. of 30W engine oil into each cylinder. After the engine is cool, crank it over and squirt about 150 cc. of the same oil down the carburetor or throttle valve, then reinsert spark or glow plugs.

Remove the camshaft cover/s and spray the valve train with 30W engine oil, then reinstall. Empty the fuel tank and seal off all openings with tape.

Close off all openings of the engine and exhaust system with oiled paper or cardboard and tape; coat with paint or tar. Remove all V-belts and spray the entire engine with SAE 30 engine oil, as well as the front and rear suspension.

## Bolt Tightening

When vehicles or component parts are designed, certain types of bolts are chosen on the basis of the material and shape of the parts to be connected, the expected load, and the available space.

In order to ensure that these bolts are properly fastened, specifications are given for torque values to be applied. These specifications are usually given in ft.-lbs. To determine these factory specified values accurately, a torque wrench, reading in ft.-lbs., is necessary.

Frequently the cylinder head bolts are not tightened sufficiently after disassembly because the breakaway torque is higher than the actual tightening torque. As a result, the apparently correct torque reading can represent an insufficiently tight condition in which the prescribed torque value actually is not achieved.

For the "/8" (1968 onward phase II) passenger cars, some bolts must be tightened by angle of rotation. These bolts are pretightened with a small tightening torque and finally turned a prescribed number of degrees of angle. An example of this is the flywheel bolts.

The bolt thread should be lightly lubricated with engine oil before insertion.

Other lubricants, such as graphite or molybdenum disulphide greases, should not be used, as they reduce the coefficient of friction and cause inaccurate torque readings. With "blind hole" bolts, special care must be exercised. The tapped hole must be free of oil or dirt, otherwise the bolt will not fit closely at the head, even if correctly tightened.

# Gasoline Engine
# Troubleshooting and Tune-up

## Part I
## Troubleshooting a
## Non-Starting Engine

There are four basic areas to examine when an engine will not start—cranking system, ignition system, fuel system and engine compression.

### Cranking—Starter Does Not Turn Engine

Turn on the headlights (high beam) and try cranking the engine. If the engine does not turn over, and the lights stay bright, there could be an open circuit at the starter switch or motor, or the starter brush contacts might not be contacting the armature. See Chapter 5 for further starter motor tests.

If the lights dim very slightly, the starter drive might not be engaging the engine, or there might be resistance at the starter switch or in the cable connections. Check the connections for looseness or corrosion first.

If the lights become very dim, or go out altogether, it could be that the battery is simply too low to turn the engine over, or again, the cables at the battery might be loose or the connections corroded. Also, the starter motor itself might be jammed or shorted internally, or the engine seized up. In the case of the latter, check the oil level. If no oil shows on the dipstick, or if the oil is contaminated by water, further checking may require partial engine disassembly. *CAUTION: If the car is towed or pushstarted in this condition, a broken crankshaft or bent connecting rod could result. Water leakage into the cylinders through a blown head gasket causes a condition of hydrostatic lock. Water will not compress, and if the engine is forced to turn over against this trapped water, something will usually break. Remove the spark plugs to check for water before ever attempting to pushstart.*

### Starter Turns Engine

If the starter cranks the engine at normal speed, and the lights still dim considerably, the problem could be a weak battery, corroded or loose terminals, or a defective cable. After visually inspecting the connections and cables, test the battery in the

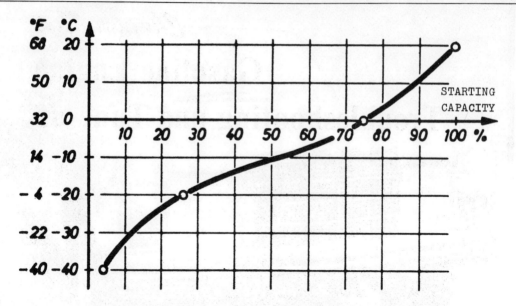

How starting capacity decreases with decreasing temperature.

## Battery Specifications

| Model | Battery Capacity (Ah @ 20 hrs.) | Model | Battery Capacity (Ah @ 20 hrs.) | Model | Battery Capacity (Ah @ 20 hrs.) |
|---|---|---|---|---|---|
| 190c | 52⑤ | 250SE | 55 | 220D/8 | 88 |
| 200 | 44 | 230SL | 55⑦ | 220/8 | 44 |
| 190Dc | 66 | 250SL | 55 | 230/8 | 44 |
| 200D | 66 | 220SEb/C① | 55⑦ | 250/8 | 44 |
| 230 | 44 | 250SE/C① | 55 | 280S/8 | 55 |
| 220b | 52⑤⑥ | 300SE③ | 66 | 280SE/8③① | 55 |
| 220Sb | 52⑤⑥ | 300SE①② | 66 | 280SL/8 | 55 |
| 230S | 44 | 300SEb | 66 | 300SEL/8 | 66 |
| 250S | 44 | 300SEL | 66 | 300SEL/8 6.3 | 66 |
| 220SEb | 55⑦ | 300SE①④ | 66 | | |

① Coupe and convertible.
② To August, 1965.
③ Long wheelbase.
④ From August, 1965.
⑤ Second version; first version—56.
⑥ From March, 1965—44.
⑦ Second version; first version—60.

Acid level—5mm. above separator or level mark.

| Specific gravity— | Full charge | 1.280 (1.230 tropics) |
|---|---|---|
| | Half charge | 1.210 (1.160 tropics) |
| | Discharged | 1.140 (1.090 tropics) |

| Charging current— | Initial | 5% |
|---|---|---|
| | Standard | 10% |
| | Quick | 75% |

Maximum acid temperature during charging—40°C. (104°F.)

| Freezing temperature— | Full charge | —68°C. (—40 tropics) |
|---|---|---|
| | Half charge | —40°C. (—13 tropics) |
| | Discharged | —12°C. (—13 tropics or —6 for phase II models) |

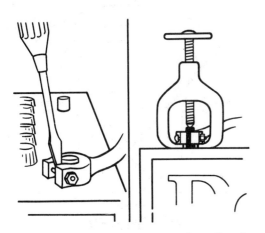

Left, checking cable connection; right, pulling battery terminal clamp using a puller.

Checking battery cell voltage.

| SPECIFIC GRAVITY READING | CHARGED CONDITION |
|---|---|
| 1.260-1.280 | Fully Charged |
| 1.230-1.250 | Three Quarter Charged |
| 1.200-1.220 | One Half Charged |
| 1.170-1.190 | One Quarter Charged |
| 1.140-1.160 | Just About Flat |
| 1.110-1.130 | All The Way Down |

following manner: with a screwdriver blade inserted between battery post and cable connection, twist gently to insure a good metal to metal contact, then try cranking the engine. If starter speed picks up, it can be assumed that the connection was bad. The battery terminals cannot be hammered on or otherwise subjected to severe shock, because internal battery damage can result. If the connection will not come off the terminal easily, use a puller as illustrated.

To accurately test the electrical condition of the battery, a load suited to the battery size, and adjustable with a rheostat, is used. Since this test gear is not readily available, however, general practice is to use a commercial cell tester containing a fixed resistance, which indicates the voltage drop of each cell under a fixed load. If the battery is fully charged, the drop should not exceed 1.8 volts over 10 seconds (see illustration).

The specific gravity test is the most common way of determining battery condition. This is accomplished using a hydrometer. The illustration and battery table give

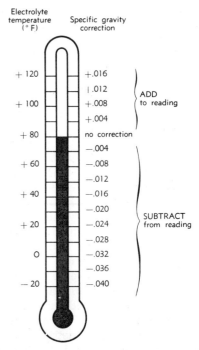

The effect of temperature on specific gravity readings.

average readings for normal and discharged batteries; the effect of temperature on hydrometer readings is also illustrated.

If the battery is discharged, the water level must be brought up to cover the plates using distilled water only, never acid. The charger is then hooked up, observing correct polarity, and the battery is charged at one-tenth its rated capacity. Acid temperature must be kept below the figures listed in the table and, if temperature gets higher, the charging rate must be decreased and the time of charging increased. If the battery is in poor condition, having sulphated (white) plates, charge at only 1% of its rated capacity. Charging is completed when cell voltage or specific gravity no longer increase appreciably over a one hour period. Fully charged, each cell should read 2.6–2.7 volts with the charger connected and on. The cell voltage will normally drop to about 2.2 volts within two hours after charging. After charging is completed, top up battery with distilled water, using no special additives, and grease terminals with a good grease (Bosch Ft1V40 is recommended).

If the engine still will not start, the ignition system then must be checked.

**Ignition System**

Remove a spark plug wire and, holding it with gloves or insulated pliers, position it about ¼″ away from the engine block. Now, crank the engine with the starter motor, observing the spark.

### Weak Spark/No Spark

There are many factors that could cause this condition—points dirty or pitted, poor electrical connections in the primary ignition circuit (from battery through switch to coil), defective high tension (center) wire, defective coil, defective condenser, reversed coil polarity, defective rotor, cap or simply a wet ignition system.

The first step is to visually inspect the entire ignition system for bad connections, broken wires or moisture. Remove the distributor cap and inspect the breaker points. They should be unpitted and clean (not oily). You may find that the points are gray-colored. This is normal, and should be considered detrimental only when accompanied by pitting. Do not file

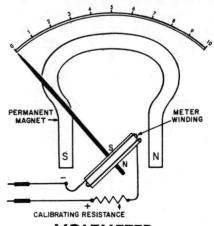

**VOLTMETER**

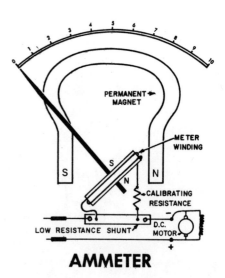

**AMMETER**

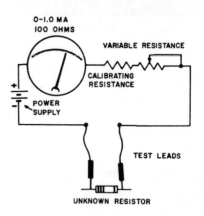

**OHMMETER**

the points—this removes their protective coating and shortens their life.

At this time, it might be opportune to discuss a few useful electrical testing instruments.

A voltmeter measures voltage, or the electrical "pressure" pushing current through a unit or circuit. The meter is connected across the terminals of the unit being tested, and the reading will be the difference in pressure (voltage drop) between the two terminals.

An ammeter is used to measure the current, or amount of electricty, flowing through a unit or circuit. Ammeters are always connected in series, (in the line) with the unit or circuit being tested.

An ohmmeter is used to measure electrical resistance in a unit or circuit. An ohmmeter has a self-contained power supply and is always connected across (in parallel with) the terminals of the unit or circuit being tested.

While not *absolutely* necessary for on-the-spot diagnosis, these three instruments should be in the toolbox of every serious amateur mechanic, and their small cost is more than justified by the great increase in diagnostic capability achieved.

For example. the spark plug wires can be checked for continuity using the ohmmeter. Placing the instrument on its lowest scale or, in the case of radio suppression wires, the middle scale, read across both ends of each wire. Standard copper/steel wire should read very low, depending upon length, whereas radio wires should read not more than about 30,000 ohms.

If the car has no ammeter, one should be temporarily hooked up following the basic schematic below. Wire No. 1 goes from the voltage regulator to the lights and accessories. Wire No. 2 (dotted line) is temporarily disconnected and the ammeter connected between the starter solenoid and the voltage regulator terminals.

Individual cars may have slightly different wiring, therefore it is best to consult the wiring diagrams in Chapter 5 for specific cases.

With the ammeter hooked up, crank the engine. The ammeter will indicate no reading, discharge, or a normal (centered) but unsteady reading.

No reading indicates that the points are not closing or are burned, the ignition switch defective, coil winding open, or the primary winding grounded.

A discharge indicates the points are not opening (set too close), the condenser is shorted, the contact arm grounded (points), coil primary shorted to ground or primary wire grounded.

A normal, but unsteady, reading indicates that the high tension wire is open or grounded, coil is defective, distributor cap and/or rotor is cracked, or that there is moisture on the spark plug wires or distributor cap.

The coil can be checked for continuity, both primary and secondary windings, in the following manner:

To check the coil primary, switch the ohmmeter to its lowest scale, connect test

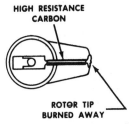

Rotor defects to look for.

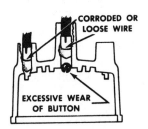

Distributor cap defects to look for.

Ammeter hook up points (see text).

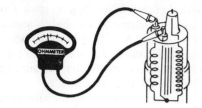

Checking coil primary resistance.

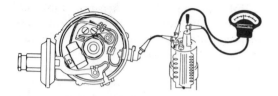

Checking coil secondary windings.

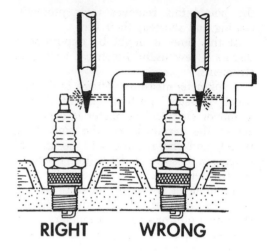

**RIGHT**     **WRONG**

Coil polarity test.

leads across primary terminals of coil (after disconnecting leads to these terminals) and take a reading. Coils should check out at between 1 and 2 ohms, depending on model. In any case, if a coil shows no resistance, or exceedingly high resistance, it should be replaced.

The secondary windings are checked by switching the ohmmeter to its highest scale, connecting one test lead to the high tension (center) wire at the distributor cap and the other lead to the coil distributor terminal (one which is normally connected to the distributor contact points). A good coil should read between 4,000 and 8,000 ohms, although some high performance units can read as high as 13,000 ohms. If the reading is much below 4,000 ohms, the coil may have shorted secondary turns; if the reading is greater than 40,000 ohms, the secondary windings are open, the high tension lead has too high resistance, or the connections are poor.

Reversed coil polarity can result in hard starting or poor performance. Switching the primary coil leads is easy to do and, while the engine will still run, a 14–20% decrease in efficiency can be expected. As other components age (e.g., spark plugs, points), this lack of coil efficiency becomes more apparent.

To check coil polarity, hold an ordinary pencil (with gloves) between a disconnected spark plug wire (engine running) and ground. If polarity is correct, the

The effects of incorrect coil polarity on a spark plug electrode.

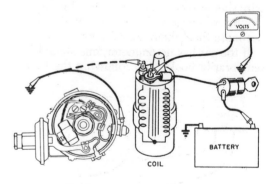

Checking ignition primary circuit.

spark will jump from wire-to-pencil-to-ground. The condition of the spark plug electrode will indicate reversed polarity as well as (see illustration).

The next step is to check the primary ignition circuit. The engine should be

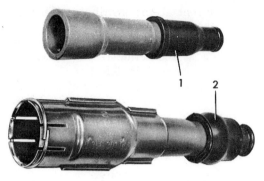

1. Far-range unit (1,000 ohms)
2. Short-range unit (5,000 ohms)

Radio interference suppressors.

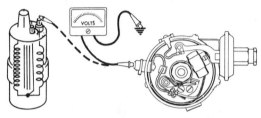

Checking ignition primary circuit—distributor side.

warm for this test, if possible. Ground the coil terminal connected to the contact points, using a jumper wire. Connect the voltmeter between the other coil primary terminal and ground. Jiggle the ignition switch, while on, and watch the meter. If the needle wavers over a large range, the ignition switch is probably defective.

With the switch on, engine not running, the voltmeter should read 5.5–7 volts. Crank the engine and check the reading—it should be at least 9 volts.

Check the spark plug wire suppressors for excessive resistance, using an ohmmeter. The far range interference suppressor (000 159 2185) should read 1,000 ohms, the close range suppressors (000 156 30 10 and 000 156 32 10) should read 5,000 ohms. If these values are extremely high, in the 20,000 ohm range for example, the suppressors should be replaced.

The series resistor (ballast) can be by-passed by a relay to increase the starting voltage, and, as an additional measure,

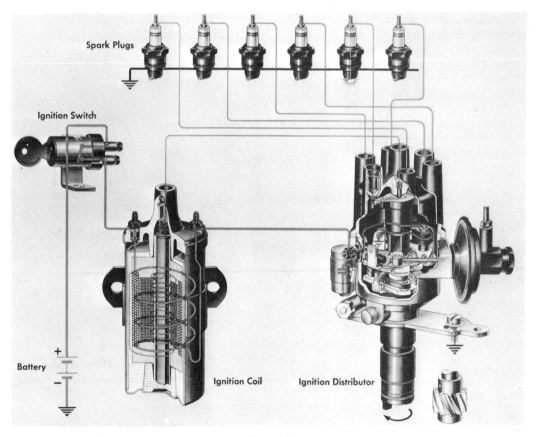

Typical ignition system.

both the ignition coil and the ballast resistor of the six-cylinder engine can be installed on four-cylinder models. In this case, the series resistor must be bypassed either by using the relay or by connecting it to starter terminal No. 16 of the new type starter motor.

On six-cylinder engines, the ballast resistor can be replaced by the Beru WZ03 (color white) for increased starting efficiency.

To check the distributor side of the primary circuit, switch the voltmeter to a full-scale range of at least 20 volts. Then connect one voltmeter lead to ground, the other to the coil terminal having the wire going to the contact points. Remove the high tension wire from the distributor cap and ground it, then close the ignition switch and slowly bump the engine over to open and close the contact points. As the points open and close, the voltmeter should read one-third to one-half battery voltage. Normally, with the engine stopped and points open, the voltage should be the same as battery voltage; with the points closed, it should be close to zero.

If, while cranking, the voltage remains near zero, check for . . .

1. No current at the distributor. Disconnect the primary wire that goes to contact points at coil terminal and read voltage at the terminal. If voltage is present, the wire is defective.
2. Points not opening because of close adjustment or worn distributor cam lobes. Dual point systems may have one set not opening, the other operating normally.
3. Points grounded where lead goes through distributor body.
4. Dead shorted condenser. To check condenser, connect one lead of ohmmeter to body of condenser, the other to its lead. If the meter shows even a small reading, the condenser is shorted and must be replaced.

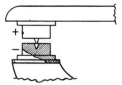 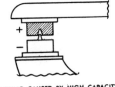

PITTING CAUSED BY LOW CAPACITY | PITTING CAUSED BY HIGH CAPACITY

Point pitting caused by incorrect condenser.

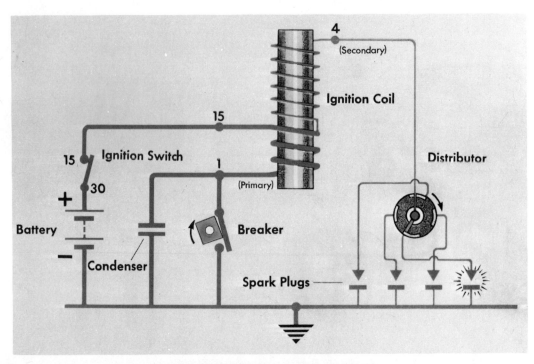

Typical ignition system in schematic form.

Visual inspection of the contact points indicates the condition of the condenser as well. A shorted (no capacity) condenser will cause metal to be transferred from the negative to the positive contact. A condenser with too great a capacity will cause metal to be transferred from positive to negative contact (see illustration).

In any case, the result is rapid pitting of the points, and condensers always should be replaced when replacing contact points as a good general preventive maintenance procedure.

Another area not to be overlooked is the ballast resistor. This often-neglected unit plays an important role in limiting the primary current through the coil and contact points. It helps to prolong point life at low engine speeds when the points remain closed for a longer length of time and it also protects against excessive build-up of primary current when the ignition switch is turned on with the engine stopped and the points closed.

GOOD SPARK

If the spark is normal looking (e.g., "powerful"), the problem is probably in the fuel system, although very wet, wide-gapped spark plugs or ignition timing mal-adjusted can cause a no-start condition.

**Fuel System**

If the entire ignition system checks out, and the no-start condition still exists, the fuel system is the next logical area to check. Assuming there IS gasoline in the tank (check the tank, the gauge could be defective), there should be gasoline at the carburetors or fuel injection unit. Loosen the connection from the fuel pump, remove the line and hold it over a can. Crank the engine with the starter. If fuel spurts out of the line, either the carburetors are flooded, the choke is not operating properly, dirt or water is blocking the carburetors, or, more seriously, water is leaking into the cylinders.

## Fuel Pump Specifications

| Model | Pump Type | Delivery Pressure psi @ Starter Speed | psi @ Idle Speed | Measuring Point | psi @ 3,000 rpm | Discharge Pressure psi @ Idle Speed | psi @ 3,000 rpm | Vacuum ① mm. Hg. Idle Speed | mm. Hg. Starter Speed |
|---|---|---|---|---|---|---|---|---|---|
| 190c 200, 230 220b 220Sb 230S 250S | DVG diaphragm ⑦ | 1.77-2.35 | 2.21-2.94 | Behind pump outlet | | | | | 230-320 |
| 220/8 230/8 250/8 | APG diaphragm | 1.77-2.35 | 2.21-2.94 | Behind pump outlet | | | | | 230-320 |
| 190Dc 200D 220D/8 | Bosch FP/K22M2/8 | | 1.20-2.20 | Between inj. pump & main filter | 32.0 | 29.0 | 37.0 | 2.9-5.9 | |
| 220SEb 300SE ② | Bosch FP/ESB5RC25/ 12AI | 8.8-13.2 ③ | | Behind find filter | | 17.6 ③④ | | | |
| 230SL 250SE 250SL 300SE 300SEb 300SEL ⑤ | Bosch FP/ESB5RC25/ 12AI | 13.2-16.1 ③ | | Behind fine filter | | 19.1 ③⑥ | | | |

① Measured in front of pump inlet.
② With two-cylinder injection pump.
③ With engine not running and a minimum of 11 volts at terminals.
④ Measured behind damper unit in fuel return line.
⑤ With six-cylinder injection pump.
⑥ Behind fuel overflow valve on injection pump.
⑦ Pump tappet clearance — .016-.020".

*CAUTION: Remove the center high tension wire from the coil and distributor cap to reduce the possibility of a spark-induced fire.*

If gasoline is not present at the fuel line, there could be a clogged fuel filter, blocked vent opening in gas tank cap, an air leak in the fuel supply line, a clogged fuel line, or a broken fuel pump.

To clear a clogged fuel line, remove the line from the tank to fuel pump at the pump and blow through the line with compressed air. You should hear bubbling at the tank filler if the line is clear. *CAUTION: Do not use high-pressure compressed air.*

To check fuel pump pressure, disconnect the feed line from the pump to the carburetors and insert a T-fitting, with appropriate fittings or short sections of neoprene hose, into the line. Attach a 0–10 psi pressure gauge to the T and crank the engine. To check fuel volume, disconnect the T-fitting and hold the open end of the fuel discharge line to the mouth of a graduated container.

Delivery pressure of the Bosch electric

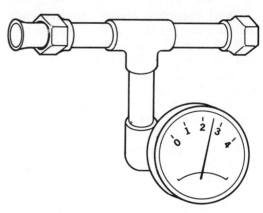

Fuel pressure test gauge.

| 1. Threaded union with check valve (delivery side) | 4. Terminal 31 |
| 2. Screw plug | 5. Threaded union (suction side) |
| 3. Terminal 30 | 6. Pump cover |

Bosch electric fuel pump.

fuel pump used on fuel injected models is measured between the fuel filter and damper unit; it should not be less than 5.9 psi with a minimum terminal voltage of 10 volts @ 3.1–3.5 Amperes. As with mechanical pumps, check the filter for stoppage before assuming the pump is faulty. *NOTE: It is not necessary, or desirable, for the engine to be running; turn on the ignition and pump should work.*

Measure delivery volume at a point behind the return line damper nut. *NOTE: Use new fuel filter element. Volume should be 3.5 qts. per minute with 10 volts @ 3.1–3.5 Amperes at pump terminals.*

Check the pump-to-motor seal for leakage by disconnecting the bypass pipe (4). With pump warm (after shutting off engine) there should be no rapid dripping.

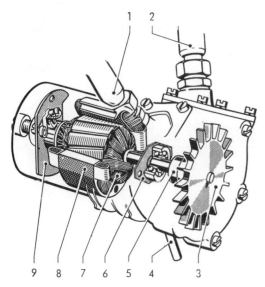

| 1. Connection, delivery side, with check valve | 4. Leak-off pipe |
| | 5. Slide ring seal |
| | 6. Mounting plate |
| 2. Connection, suction side | 7. Armature |
| | 8. Laminated pole |
| 3. Vane | 9. Brush holder plate |

Bosch electric fuel pump internal parts.

The pump itself can be cleaned of dirt by removing the pump cover (6), after match-marking the cover and case. *NOTE: Maximum impeller play on key is ±18°.*

Although greatly reduced as a direct result of improved fuel technology and fuel induction system design, vapor lock still exists under certain temperature conditions and acceleration attitudes. Because of pressure drop in the fuel line, on the suction side of the pump, there is a tendency for fuel to boil at a lower temperature than is normal. Also, the volume of fuel in its vapor state is over 1,000 times greater than its volume as a liquid, thus aggravating this condition by reducing the weight of the fuel being delivered. When occupied by vapor instead of liquid fuel, the pump is in a state of vapor lock, and is thus prevented from delivering a continuous flow of fuel to the carburetors or injectors. This results in "missing" and, in extreme cases, engine stoppage or non-starting. One easy way to get rid of vapor lock is to let the car cool down, thus allowing the vapor to condense as a liquid. This, however, is only a temporary measure and, if conditions remain the same, the problem can recur. For a more permanent solution, the line can be wrapped with asbestos tape covered with shiny aluminum foil.

Checking engine compression with a recording-type instrument.

## Engine Compression

Compression is measured for each individual engine and, as there are often production variations, compression specifications are now given only as a range for Mercedes-Benz automobiles. To check compression, run the engine until normal operating temperature has been reached. (In cases where the engine will not start, a compression test can be used for diagnostic purposes, but readings should be considered only in light of other individual cylinder readings for the same engine, and a percentage of difference between cylinders should be calculated.)

Remove the spark plug wires, blow all foreign matter from the vicinity of the spark plug wells, then loosen plugs one turn. Replace plug wires, start engine and "blip" the throttle once or twice to clear the cylinders of dislodged carbon particles. Stop the engine and remove the plug wires and spark plugs, then remove the air cleaner and block the throttle butterflies

open. Either hook up a remote starting switch, or have an assistant crank the engine through about four revolutions, holding the compression gauge firmly against the spark plug opening. Record the reading and proceed to the other cylinders.

Comparing the compression readings of each cylinder should help to determine any problems that might exist. For example, if the compression readings of two adjoining cylinders are low and approximately equal, while the other cylinders are more or less normal, a blown head gasket between those two cylinders is indicated. If all the readings are high but one, it indicates that either the head gasket is blown to the atmosphere in that cylinder, or perhaps that a valve is burned or warped, a valve seat cracked, a piston broken, a head cracked, or that there are cracked piston rings.

If all the readings are more or less uniformly low, it could indicate worn or broken piston rings, or valve clearances set too close. If the valves are set too close, they are prevented from fully closing, thus venting compression pressure into the exhaust or intake manifolds.

To further narrow down the possibilities, squirt some 30W oil into each cylinder and recheck the compression. If the compression remains the same, it indicates trouble of some type in the cylinder head area, either gasket or valves. If the compression noticeably increases, it could be piston rings or pistons. It must be noted, however, that these tests are not the ultimate in good engine diagnosis, and that other factors should be considered before removing the cylinder head. Pay particular attention to the valve adjustment, making sure it is correct before beginning a major repair job.

# Part II
# Troubleshooting a Poorly-Running Engine/Tune-up

If the engine starts and runs, but poorly, the poor running condition normally falls into two categories—lack of power and rough running (misfiring).

### Engine Lacks Power

This is by far the most common cause for complaint among all car owners, and all automobiles, no matter how well made, require a certain amount of engine maintenance to keep them running smoothly. Usually a general "feel" that the car "just doesn't have it any more" is enough to justify checking the fourteen items listed following:

1. Poor compression (see Part I).
2. Ignition timing.
3. Ignition points dirty or pitted (see Part I).
4. Spark plugs dirty or improperly gapped.
5. Vacuum advance unit.
6. Carburetors/fuel injection (see Chapter 6).
7. Valve timing.
8. Fuel pressure/vapor lock (see Part I).
9. Clogged or restricted exhaust system (muffler, dented tailpipe).
10. Clogged air cleaner.
11. Overheating engine.
12. Excessive internal friction.
13. Slipping clutch or automatic transmission (see Chapter 8).
14. Drag in chassis which retards free running of car (see Chapters 9 and 10).

### Engine Runs Rough or Misfires

In the case of a rough running, misfiring engine, the first step is to determine which cylinder is causing the trouble. The fastest way to do this, lacking sophisticated test equipment, is to short one spark plug at a time, while the engine is running.

Using a pair of insulated pliers, pull each plug wire off in turn. The cylinder/s affected can then be located, since removing a plug wire from a misfiring cylinder will have no effect on the rough running condition, while removing a wire from a "good" cylinder still operating properly will cause a definite increase in the roughness. Of course, if the roughness exists only at higher engine speeds, the problem must be isolated by trial and error—especially if the problem exists only under load.

Assuming a weak cylinder is located, remove a spark plug from a normal cylinder and switch with the spark plug of the affected cylinder. (Or, if all cylinders seem bad, replace all the plugs.) If the roughness moves along with the spark plug, the plug is bad and needs cleaning/regapping or replacement. It is recommended that all the plugs be cleaned and regapped at the same time, and that this operation be done only once. After a plug has been regapped once, it has been burned away to such an extent that it no longer has the proper heat range.

The spark plug illustrations show some some typical spark plugs and the damage they are subject to. It should be noted that spark plug condition is closely related to engine performance, and, as a result, can be a useful diagnostic tool.

Some Mercedes-Benz automobiles are equipped with Platinum spark plugs. These spark plugs must be regapped more carefully than "normal" types, and, while their lifespan may be longer, they are also subject to the "once only" regapping rule.

To regap a Platinum plug, the body electrode is slightly bent forward by light strokes applied at the arrowed portion of its outer casing (see illustration).

Heat range is a term used to describe the cooling characteristics of spark plugs. Plugs with longer-nosed insulators take a longer time to dissipate heat effectively, and are termed "hot" plugs. The reverse is also true, shorter-nosed

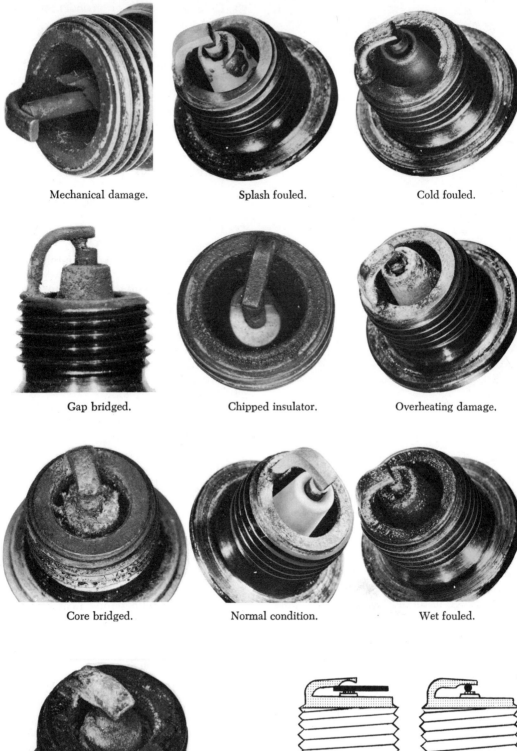

Mechanical damage.

Splash fouled.

Cold fouled.

Gap bridged.

Chipped insulator.

Overheating damage.

Core bridged.

Normal condition.

Wet fouled.

Scavenger deposits (lead).

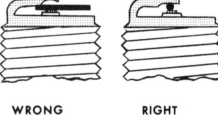

**WRONG**

**RIGHT**

How to gap spark plugs.

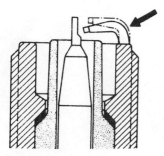

Platinum spark plug.

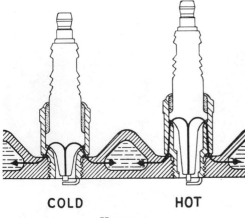

COLD       HOT

Heat range.

plugs dissipate heat rapidly, and are thus called "cold" plugs. It is generally advisable to use the factory-specified spark plugs. However, in conditions of extreme hard usage (e.g., driving cross country in August), going to the next cooler heat range is all right. The same is true if most driving is done in the city or over short distances, go to the next hotter range spark plug to eliminate spark plug fouling.

If there is no apparent change in the roughness of the engine after switching spark plugs, check the plug lead going to that cylinder, the distributor cap tower of the affected cylinder and the compression of the cylinder (see Part I).

If there is no particular cylinder that is a problem, or if the miss exists only at higher engine speeds, the following are some areas to check:

### IDLE-SPEED MISS

1. Plug gaps too wide.
2. Defective spark plugs.

3. Defective coil or condenser (see Part I).
4. Defective breaker points (see Part I).
5. Sticking point breaker arm.
6. Incorrect breaker point gap.
7. Timing too far advanced or retarded.
8. Loose connection in primary ignition circuit (see Part I).
9. Defective ignition switch (see Part I).
10. Worn distributor shaft bushings.
11. Defective distributor rotor.
12. Defective spark plug wires (see Part I).
13. Incorrect carburetor adjustment (see Chapter 6).
14. Dirt or water in fuel.
15. Vapor lock (see Part I).
16. Air leak where intake manifold meets head.
17. Air leak at manifold/carburetor seat.
18. Worn intake valve guides.
19. Valves sticking open.
20. Valves warped or burned (see Part I).
21. Broken valve spring.
22. Incorrect valve clearance.
23. Cracked valve seat.
24. Worn camshaft lobe/s.
25. Sticking piston rings (see Part I).
26. Broken piston rings (see Part I).
27. Scored cylinder walls.
28. Broken piston (see Part I).
29. Blown head gasket (see Part I).
30. Warped cylinder head or block (see Part I).

### HIGH-SPEED MISS

1. Weak point breaker arm spring.
2. Weak fuel pump, delivering diminishing pressure as speed increases.
3. Points set too wide.
4. Spark plugs with wrong heat range installed.
5. Excessive carbon build-up in cylinders and on pistons.
6. Loose timing chain.

After the trouble has been isolated and corrected, it is advisable that all factors affecting engine performance be checked. In other words, a complete tune-up would not be out of order for, if one component has failed, the others may be on the brink of doing so.

Tune-up procedures normally include cleaning and regapping the spark plugs (covered previously), setting or replacing

# Tune-up Specifications

| Model | Engine Type | Spark Plugs ▲ | Plug Gap (in.) | Point Gap (in.) | Point Dwell (deg.) | Valve Clearance (in.) Intake | Valve Clearance (in.) Exhaust | Valve Timing (deg.) Intake Opens * | Ignition Timing (deg.) ** | Idle Speed Manual Transmission N | Idle Speed Automatic Transmission N | Idle Speed Automatic Transmission D | Cranking Compression Pressure (psi) Normal Range | Minimum |
|---|---|---|---|---|---|---|---|---|---|---|---|---|---|---|
| 190c | 121.924 | L87Y | .020 | .016-.020 | 48-52 | .003 | .006 | 10 B | 48 | 800-850 | 850-950 | 600 ⑨ | 139-154 | 117 |
| 200 | 121.940 | N6Y | .023 | .016-.020 | 48-52 | .003 | .007 | 11 B | 43 | 800-850 | 850-950 | 600 ⑨ | 147-162 | 125 |
| 230 | 180.945 / 180.949 ① | N6Y | .023 | .016-.020 | 37-41 | .003 | .007 | 11 B | 37 | 750-800 | 800-850 | 550 ⑨ | 147-162 | 125 |
| 220b | 180.940 | N6Y | .023 | .012-.016 | 37-41 | .003 | .006 | 10 B | 35 | 750-800 | 800-850 | 550 ⑨ | 147-162 | 125 |
| 220Sb | 180.941 | N6Y | .023 | .012-.016 | 37-41 | .003 | .006 | 10 B | 35 | 750-800 | 800-850 | 550 ⑨ | 147-162 | 125 |
| 230S | 180.947 | N6Y | .023 | .012-.016 | 37-41 | .003 | .007 | 11 B | 37 | 750-800 | 800-850 | 550 ⑨ | 147-162 | 125 |
| 250S | 108.920 | N6Y | .023 | .012-.016 | 37-41 | .003 | .007 | 11 B | 37 | 750-800 | 800-850 | 550 ⑨ | 147-162 | 125 |
| 220SEb | 127.982 | N6Y | .023 | .012-.016 | 37-41 | .003 | .006 | 10 B | 28 | 750-800 | 750-800 | 600 ⑨ | 147-162 | 125 |
| 250SEb | 129.980 | N6Y | .020 | .012-.016 | 37-41 | .003 | .007 | 11 B | 30 | 750-800 | 750-800 | 750 ⑨ | 162-177 | 132 |
| 250SE/c ② | 129.980 | N6Y | .020 | .012-.016 | 37-41 | .003 | .007 | 11 B | 30 | 750-800 | 750-800 | 750 ⑨ | 162-177 | 132 |
| 230SL | 127.981 | N6Y | .020 | .012-.016 | 37-41 | .003 | .007 | 10 B | 30 | 750-800 | 750-800 | 600 ⑨ | 162-177 | 132 |
| 250SL | 129.982 | N6Y | .020 | .012-.016 | 37-41 | .003 | .007 | 11 B | 30 | 750-800 | 750-800 | 750 ⑨ | 162-177 | 132 |
| 220SEb/c ② | 127.984 | N6Y | .023 | .012-.016 | 37-41 | .003 | .006 | 10 B | 28 | 750-800 | 750-800 | 600 ⑨ | 147-162 | 125 |
| 300SE ④ | 189.984 | N6Y | .020 | .014-.018 | 47-51 | .004 | .010 | 7 B | 28 | 650-700 | 680-720 | 600 ⑨ | 147-162 | 125 |
| 300SE ⑤ | 189.986 ⑤ | N6Y | .020 | .014-.018 | 47-51 | .004 | .008 | 18 B | 28 | 650-700 | 680-720 | 600 ⑨ | 147-162 | 125 |
| 300SE ④ | 189.986 ④ | N6Y | .020 | .014-.018 | 47-51 | .004 | .008 | 18 B | 28 | 650-700 | 680-720 | 600 ⑨ | 147-162 | 125 |
| 300SE ⑥ ⑦ | 189.987 ⑥ | N6Y | .020 | .014-.018 | 47-51 | .004 | .008 | 18 B | 28 | 650-700 | 680-720 | 600 ⑨ | 147-162 | 125 |
| 300SEb | 189.989 | N6Y | .020 | .014-.018 | 47-51 | .004 | .010 | 18 B | 28 | 650-700 | 680-720 | 600 ⑨ | 147-162 | 125 |
| 300SEL | 189.988 | N6Y | .020 | .014-.018 | 47-51 | .004 | .010 | 18 B | 28 | 650-700 | 680-720 | 600 ⑨ | 147-162 | 125 |
| 220/8 | 115.920 | N6Y | .023 | .016-.020 | 48-52 | .003 | .008 | 11 B | 43 | 850-950 | 850-950 | 600 ⑨ | 147-162 | 125 |
| 230/8 | 180.954 | N6Y | .023 | .012-.016 | 37-41 | .003 | .007 | 11 B | 37 | 800-900 | 800-900 | 650-700 | 147-162 | 125 |
| 250/8 | 114.920 | N6Y | .023 | .012-.016 | 37-41 | .003 | .007 | 11 B | 37 | 800-900 | 800-900 | 650-700 | 147-162 | 125 |
| 280S/8 | 130.920 | N6Y | .023 | .012-.016 | 37-41 | .003 | .007 | 11 B | 37 | 800-900 | 800-900 | 650-700 | 147-162 | 125 |
| 280SE/8 ⑧ | 130.980 | N6Y | .020 | .012-.016 | 37-41 | .003 | .007 | 11 B | 30 | 700-800 | 700 | 700 | 162-177 | 132 |
| 280SL/8 | 130.983 | N6Y | .020 | .012-.016 | 37-41 | .003 | .007 | 11 B | 30 | 700-800 | 700 | 700 | 162-177 | 132 |
| 300SEL/8 | 130.981 | N6Y | .020 | .012-.016 | 37-41 | .003 | .007 | 11 B | 30 | 700-800 | 700 | 700 | 162-177 | 132 |
| 300SEL/8 6.3 | 100.981 | UN12Y | .020 | .012-.016 | 34-38 | .004 | .010 | 4B-2A | 26 ⑪ | 550 | 550 | 600 | 147-162 | 125 |

① INAT carburetors.
② Coupe and convertible.
③ First version.
④ Long wheelbase.
⑤ Second version.
⑥ Convt. to Aug., 1965.
⑦ From Aug., 1965; same engine as previous second version 300 SE convt.
⑧ Sedan, coupe, convertible and long wheelbase 230 SEL/8.

NOTE: For carburetor settings, see Chapter 6.

⑨ In gear with power steering in lock position.
⑩ Coupe to Aug., 1965.
⑪ At 3,000 rpm.
▲ For normal driving. See Appendix for other applications and plug types.
* Preload test value of .016". See Chapter 2 for procedure and additional timing values.
** At 4,500 rpm, vacuum line disconnected and plugged. See Distributor Advance Values Chart.

A After top dead center.
B Before top dead center.
NOTE: On dual-point distributors, check each set separately by inserting insulator between each contact set in turn. Dwell values given are total both sets.
NOTE: To counteract wearing of fiber contact block, adjust dwell to lower end of range (wider gap).

contact points, checking distributor cap and rotor, setting the ignition timing, setting the valve clearance and checking and adjusting the carburetors or fuel injection system (covered in Chapter 6). Valve timing, although not a normal tune-up procedure. is included here because of the great effect it has on overall engine performance.

## Ignition Contact Points, Rotor and Distributor Cap

When setting ignition contact points, it is advisable to observe the following general rules:

1. If the points are used, they should not be adjusted using a feeler gauge. The gauge will not give an accurate reading on a pitted surface.
2. Never file the points—this removes their protective coating and results in rapid pitting.
3. When using a feeler gauge to set new points, be certain that the points are fully open. The fiber rubbing block must rest on the highest point of the cam lobe.
4. Always make sure a feeler gauge is free of oil or grease before setting points.
5. Make sure the points are properly aligned and that the feeler gauge is not tilted. If points are misaligned, bend the fixed contact support only, never the movable breaker arm.

A dwellmeter virtually eliminates errors in point gap caused by distributor cam lobes being unequally worn, or human error. In any case, point dwell should be checked as soon as possible after setting with a feeler gauge, because it is a far more accurate check of point operation

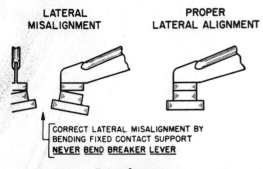

LATERAL MISALIGNMENT          PROPER LATERAL ALIGNMENT

CORRECT LATERAL MISALIGNMENT BY BENDING FIXED CONTACT SUPPORT NEVER BEND BREAKER LEVER

Point alignment.

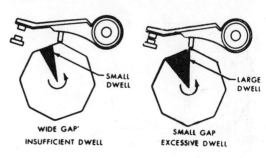

WIDE GAP'
INSUFFICIENT DWELL          SMALL GAP
EXCESSIVE DWELL

Dwell as a function of point gap.

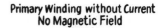

Primary Winding without Current
No Magnetic Field

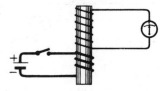

Cutting-in Process
Development of Magnetic Field

DC Current in Primary Winding
Constant Magnetic Field

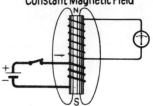

Interrupting Process
Collapse of Magnetic Field

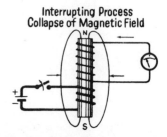

Ignition coil theory of operation.

under normal operating conditions. The dwellmeter is also capable of detecting high point resistance (oxidation) or poor connections within the distributor.

The dwellmeter, actually a modified voltmeter, depends on the nature of contact point operation for its usefulness. In this electro-mechanical system, a fiber block slides, under tension, over a cam (see illustrations). The angle (in black) that the block traverses on the cam, during which time current is made available to the coil primary winding, is an inverse function of point gap. In other words, the wider the gap, the smaller the "dwell" (expressed in degrees); the closer the gap, the greater the "dwell".

Because the fiber block wears down gradually in service, it is good practice to set the dwell on the low side of any dwell range (smaller number of degrees) given in specifications. As the block wears, the dwell becomes greater (toward the center of the range) and point life is increased between adjustments.

To connect the dwellmeter, disconnect and plug the distributor vacuum line, switch the meter to the six-, four- or eight-cylinder range, as the case may be, and connect one lead to ground. The other lead should be connected to the coil distributor terminal (the one having the wire going to contact points). Zero the meter, start the engine and gradually allow it to assume normal idle speed (see *Tune-up Specifications*). The meter should agree with the specifications. Any excessive variation in dwell indicates a worn distributor shaft or bushings, or perhaps a worn distributor cam or breaker plate.

It is obvious from the above procedure that some means of measuring engine rpm must also be employed when checking dwell. If the car is equipped with a tachometer, as in SL models and 300 SEL 6.3, the process is simplified. If not, an external tachometer must be employed. Hook up is the same as for the dwellmeter, and both can be used in conjunction. Most commercial dwellmeters have a tachometer scale built in, and switching between them is possible.

To replace the contact points, remove the distributor cap, rotor and plate. Remove the distributor contact holder (3) by removing screw (4) and prying the cable

A. Contact breaker pair (contact closed)
1. Connecting terminal from low-voltage cable 1 to ignition coil and to cable from breaker arm
2. Bosses on contact breaker plate
3. Contact holder with adjusting slot
4. Fixing screw for contact holder
5. Vacuum box with diaphragm
6. Notch on distributor housing rim of distributor for cylinder 1
7. Pull rod for vacuum control

Distributor components—single contact set.

from the connecting terminal (1), or by removing the connecting terminal screw (depending on design). To reinstall, reverse removal procedure, remembering to check that the distributor cam is properly lubricated with a tiny amount of grease.

To adjust points initially, set block at the highest spot on the cam and set gap to approximate center of range by inserting a screwdriver into the adjusting slot of the contact holder (3) between the two bosses (2). In some cases, the points are adjusted by turning an eccentric cam with a small screwdriver. While it is possible to set the gap using a feeler gauge, it is much more accurate to use the dwellmeter.

The 300 SEL 6.3 engine has a dual-point distributor, similar to models used on previous 300 series engines. To check dwell with this distributor, each point set must be blocked off, in turn, using a fiber plate or other insulator. Dwell angle, in this case, is checked at starter cranking speed, ignition switch on and center coil wire removed.

To check total dwell, replace the distributor cap, start the engine and run at 4,000 rpm. The dwell angle may drop not more than 3° from previous check, and must be over 32° in any case. If angle is less than 32°, replace the points.

To replace the points, remove the distributor plate and rotor, then remove contact sets A and B (see illustration). This can be accomplished by removing the cotter pins from the bearing posts and removing screws (10 and 13). Remove the screw from the cable terminal, then remove the points.

To install, reverse the above procedure, making sure that the points are parallel to each other when closed. The lubrication felt should be moistened with a drop of oil at this time.

To adjust the point gap, loosen screw (13) for set A and screw (10) for set B. Then, turn eccentric screws (11 and 14) to obtain an approximate .012–.016″ gap. Tighten screws (10 and 13) and check dwell. If it is out of specification, adjust each set identically, in small increments, until proper value for both sets is obtained.

Due to the general increase in the use of rock salt on winter roads, the ignition system is more subject to corrosion and cross-firing of spark plug wires and to surface discharge across the distributor cap. In addition to standard commercial ignition sprays, it is advisable when conducting a tune-up to change the ignition system components to update and protect the system.

Since October, 1967 all cars have been equipped with a new-type distributor cap, which is made of polyester and pre-sprayed on the inside for moisture protection. When the new cap is employed, it is also possible to use a new-type rotor, also made of polyester with polycarbonate radio suppression built-in.

The new caps have the same parts numbers as the old-type caps, but they can be easily recognized by their shiny inner coating. The following parts numbers are applicable:

190c, 200 _____000 158 18 02
220b, 250 SE _____000 158 16 02
300 SE, 300 SEL _____000 158 17 02

The new-type rotor, part No. 000 158 20 31 (for 200–250 SE models), is to be used with all four- and six-cylinder models having a CAST-IRON distributor housing, a conical rotor seat and a 0.513″ diameter rotor driveshaft.

Rotor 000 158 21 31 is to be used ONLY

A. Contact breaker point set
   (points open)
P. Contact breaker point set
   (points closed)
1. Distributor shaft with 4 cams
2, 3. Slide for movable breaker arm
4. Base plate with contact
   breaker point set A
5. Pull rod for vacuum advance
6. Mark for cylinder 1
7. Adjusting cam-head bolt (for
   correcting ignition interval
   between both contact breaker
   point sets)
8. Intermediate plate (adjustable on base
   plate) with contact breaker point
   set B
9, 12. Fastening screw of intermediate plate
   (with contact breaker point set B)
10, 13. Fastening screw of contact breaker point
   set
11, 14. Adjusting cam-head screw for contact
   breaker point gap and/or dwell angle
   adjustment
15. Vacuum box with diaphragm

Distributor components—double contact sets.

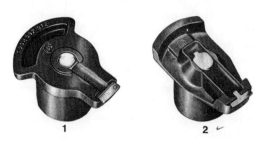

1. Old type (part No. 000 158 15 31)
2. New type (part No. 000 158 20 31)

Distributor rotors.

with a new-type distributor having an ALUMINUM housing, cylindrical rotor seat and a 0.562″ diameter rotor driveshaft.

By using force, the rotor, 000 158 20 31, can be pushed onto the rotor driveshaft of the aluminum distributor, but the rotor will not make good contact with the carbon center button of the cap. The other rotor, 000 158 21 31, can be slipped onto the older cast-iron distributor, but it will wobble and damage the cap. Do not interchange these rotors.

In addition to these parts, a protective cover for the distributor, part No. 000 158 06 85, has been made available for all four- and six-cylinder distributors. If the cover is not presently installed, a longer high-tension wire (25.19″) is needed. This can be ordered, along with the cover, under part No. 130 150 09 18.

Rubber distributor cover protects against moisture, salt and dirt.

When installing this cover on fuel-injected engines, make sure that the spark plug wires go underneath the fuel injection tubes.

Also, on the 300 SEL/8, a modification of the hose between the air suspension pump and the antifreeze container is necessary. The end connected to the rear fitting of the antifreeze container must be removed and connected to the front fitting. The plug removed from the front fitting can be used to block the fitting just vacated, and the hose shortened to 9⅝″ for clearance.

## Ignition Timing

Setting the ignition timing varies somewhat for different models, but in general, there are two ways of doing it. One is by use of a "timing" light or stroboscope; the other is more simple and involves using a small 12-volt light bulb with two leads soldered to its terminals. It must be noted that the latter method is not to be considered a substitute for a strobe light, and is generally only useful for finding approximate timing values after the distributor has been removed.

To set the timing using a strobe light,

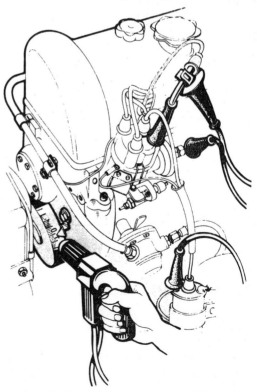

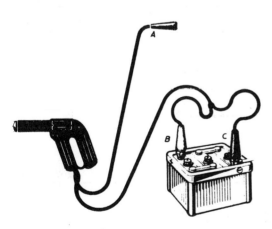

A. To No. 1 cylinder
B. To battery positive terminal
C. To battery negative terminal

Timing light hook up.

Checking timing using a strobe light.

first make sure that the contact gap (or dwell) is correct—timing is influenced by this value. Then, connect the timing light leads to the battery posts, observing correct polarity, and the third lead into No. 1 spark plug wire at some point. A good way to do this is to slip a small nail into the appropriate distributor cap tower, then connect the lead to the nail.

Run the engine at the speed specified in the *Tune-up Specifications* while shining the light on the timing index area. Timing is normally checked at 4,500 rpm (3,000 rpm for 6.3) with the vacuum line disconnected and plugged. *CAUTION: Make sure cables are out of the fan.*

Timing is adjusted by loosening the distributor clamp bolt and rotating the distributor. To advance timing, rotate the distributor opposite the normal direction of rotation; to retard timing, rotate in the normal direction.

The *Distributor Advance Values* table gives timing values for various engine

## Distributor Advance Values

| Model | Bosch Distributor Number | Basic Timing Test Light ±1° | Basic Timing Strobe Light (starter speed)* | Dynamic Timing (No Load) 800 rpm w/o & w vacuum | 1,500 rpm w/o vacuum | 3,000 rpm w/o vacuum | 4,500 rpm w/o vacuum | Range of Vacuum Advance | Start of Vacuum Advance at No-Load rpm |
|---|---|---|---|---|---|---|---|---|---|
| 190c | VJUR4BR27T | 2°B | 3°B | 8-13°B | 22-27° | 28-32° | 37-41° | 11 ±3° | 1,000-1,200 |
| 200 | IFUR4 0231 115 052 ⑧ / 0231 115 060 ⑦ | 5°A | 6°B | 9-15°B / TDC ±2° | 23-29° / 24-31° | 29-35° / 31-37° | 43° / 43° | 11 ±3° | 1,000-1,200 |
| 230, 230S, 250S | IFUR6 0231 116 038 | 1°B | 3°B | 5-15°B | 20-27° | 25-31° | 37° | 10 ±3° | 1,400-1,600 |
|  | ✢ IFUR6 0231 116 048 | 1°B | 3°B | 5-15°B | 20-27° | 25-31° | 37° | 10 ±3° | 1,800-2,000 |
|  | IFUR6 0231 116 052 ⑦ |  |  | TDC ② | 19-28° | 29-35° | 37° |  |  |
| 220b, 220Sb | VJUR6BR47T 0231 116 038 | 2°A | TDC | 4-11° | 18-23° | 23-27° | 33° | 11 ±2° | 1,400-1,600 / 1,800-2,000 ① |
| 220SEb, 220SEb/C | VJUR6BR45T | 2°A | TDC | TDC | 11-15° | 26° | 26° | 14 ±3° | 800-1,000 |
|  | VJUR6BR49T | 2°A | TDC | 0-3°B | 11-15° | 26° | 26° | 14 ±3° | 800-1,000 |
|  | VJUR6BR61T | 4°B | 6°B | 4-7°B | 15-19° | 26° | 26° | 14 ±3° | 800-1,000 |
| 250SE, 250SL, 250SE/C | IFUR6 0231 11 6047 | 3°B | 5°B ② |  | 13-20° | 30° | 30° |  |  |
|  | IFUR6 0231 11 6051 ⑦ | 6°B | 8°B ② | 2°A ±2° | 12-19° | 30° | 30° |  |  |
| 230SL | VJUR6BR49 | 2°B | 4°B | 4-7°B | 15-19° | 30° | 30° | 14 ±3° | 800-1,000 |
|  |  |  |  | 8°B | 10-12° | 30° | 30° | 14 ±3° | 800-1,000 |
| 300SE | ZV/PBUR6RI | 1°B | 3°B | 8-15°B | 21-26° | 26° | 26° | 11 ±2° | 800-1,000 |
| 300SE ③ ④ | ZV/PBUR6RIT 0231 141 001 | 3°B | 4°B | 8-15°B | 21-26° | 26° | 26° | 11 ±3° | 800-1,000 |
| 300SE ⑤ | PFUR6 0231 141 002 | 3°B | 4°B | 8-18°B | 21-28° | 28° | 28° | 11 ±3° | 800-1,000 |
| 300SEb, 300SEL | PFUR6 0231 141 004 ⑥ | TDC | 1°B | 2°B | 14-24° | 28° | 28° | 8 ±3° | 800-1,000 |
| 220/8 | JFUR4 0231 115 065 |  |  | 2°A +3/2° ⑨ |  |  | 43° |  |  |
|  | JFUR4 0231 115 060 ⑦ | 5°B |  | TDC ±2° | 25-32° | 31-37° | 43° |  |  |
| 230/8 250/8 | JFUR6 0231 116 052 ⑦ | TDC |  | TDC | 19-28° | 29-35° | 37° | 10 ±3° | 1,800-2,000 |
| 280S/8 | JFUR6 0231 116 052 ⑦ | TDC |  | TDC | 19-28° | 29-35° | 37° | 10 ±3° | 1,800-2,000 |
| 280SE/8, 280SL/8 | JFUR6 0231 116 051 ⑦ |  |  | 2°A ±2° ⑨ | 12-19° | 30° | 30° | 10 ±3° |  |
| 300SEL/8 | JFUR6 0231 116 051 ⑦ |  |  | 2°A ±2° ⑨ | 12-19° | 30° | 30° | 10 ±3° |  |
| 300SEL/8 6.3 | TFUR8 0231 119 004 ⑦ |  |  | 2°A ±2° | 13-21° | 26° | 26° | 10 ±3° | 600-620 |

\* With spark plugs installed.
① 250S, 230S, 230 with 180.949 engine.
② Without vacuum advance.
③ Long wheelbase.
④ Coupe to August, 1965.
⑤ Coupe and convertible from August, 1965.
⑥ Manual transmission only.
⑦ Exhaust emission control only.
⑧ Without exhaust emission control.
⑨ With vacuum advance only.

NOTE: *See advance curve graphs in Appendix.*
NOTE: *The timing light check at cranking speed is only for finding approximate ignition timing values. To help eliminate errors, check cylinders No. 1 and No. 4 on four-cylinder engines, No. 1 and No. 6 on six-cylinder engines; the values should vary not more than 1.5°.*

speeds, with and without the vacuum line connected. This enables one to measure the full range of the automatic advance unit. Hook up the timing light and a tachometer and run the engine at various speeds (with vacuum connected) and plot the values against rpm. The total advance curves can be found in graphic form in the Appendix. To adjust the advance curve, adjust the stop nut on the pull rod which connects the vacuum advance diaphragm to the breaker plate. Screwing the nut in advances the spark and decreases the range and vice-versa.

On the 220/8, however, the vacuum unit cannot be adjusted properly and, therefore, must be replaced if the advance curve is incorrect. (Distributor No. 0231115064.)

To set the basic timing after the distributor has been removed, connect a small 12-volt test lamp between ground and the coil distributor terminal. Remove No. 1 spark plug and the coil high-tension lead. Slowly bump the engine over, holding a finger loosely in the spark plug hole. When the rotor of the distributor comes around to the mark on the housing, and the finger is

forced out of the spark plug hole by compression pressure, the proper conditions for setting timing are established.

With the key on and a wrench on the crankshaft sprocket (never use the camshaft sprocket) nut, turn the engine over slowly in the direction of normal rotation until the light bulb just lights. Note the position of the timing marks with relation to the pointer. The values should correspond with those for static timing given in the *Distributor Advance Values* chart. If an adjustment is to be made, always rotate the engine through a complete engine cycle to come up on No. 1 again, in order to take up slack in the distributor drive.

The values obtained in this check are usually 1–2° later than those obtained by using a strobe light at starter speed. "Later" means that the light bulb might light at perhaps 2° BTDC, whereas the strobe would indicate 3½° BTDC for the same setting.

Checking the timing at starter speed, using the strobe light, is identical to that check made at 4,500 rpm, excepting that all spark plug wires except No. 1 are

1. Ball pin base
2. Annular spring
3. Ball pin head
4. Rocker arm
5. Spring clamp
6. Camshaft
7. Pressure piece
8. Valve cone half
9. Valve spring retainer and sealing ring retainer
10. Outer valve spring
11. Inner valve spring
12. Pressure piece
13. Snap-ring
14. Valve guide
15. Valve
16. Sealing ring

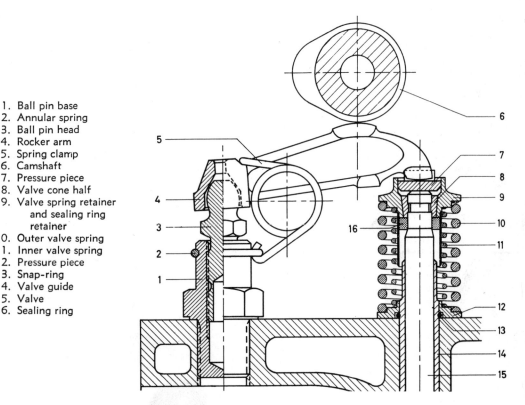

Valve arrangement—gasoline engines except 300SE.

grounded to prevent accidental starting.

To set the ignition timing on the 300 SEL/8 6.3 V8 engine, disconnect the vacuum line from the distributor and plug it. With the strobe light connected to No. 1 spark plug wire, run the engine at 3,000 rpm and observe timing mark (26° BTDC). If necessary, loosen distributor clamp and rotate distributor to obtain correct value. To advance timing, turn against direction of rotation; to retard timing, turn in same direction as rotation.

It is necessary then, because of the dual-point design, to check the timing at No. 5 cylinder. The values obtained should be the same for both cylinders No. 1 and No. 5. If not, reset intermediate plate (8) and/or contact sets A and B (see illustration) with respect to each other by loosening screws (9 and 12), then turning bolt (7)

to reset intermediate plate (8). The dwell angle might have to be reset at this time as well.

This distributor is best set up on an ignition test stand at the dealer, as the points have to be perfectly synchronized for perfect operation.

### Valve Clearance

Valve (tappet) clearance should be checked with the engine cold. On the 190c, 220b, 220 Sb and 220 Seb, clearance is measured between the sliding surface of the rocker arm and the cam base circle of the camshaft. The newer 220/8, 230/8 and 250/8 series engines also have clearance measured in this manner.

On the 300 SE series, however, clearance is measured between the valve stem end and the adjusting screw or ball socket.

1. Adjusting screw and ball cup for exhaust valve
2. Rocker arm (exhaust)
3. Valve spring retainer and sealing ring retainer for exhaust valve
4. Sealing ring (exhaust)
5. Cylinder head
6. Valve guide (exhaust)
7. Exhaust valve
8. Valve seat ring (exhaust)
9. Valve seat ring (intake)
10. Intake valve
11. Valve guide (intake)
12. Washer
13. Sealing ring retainer (intake)
14. Sealing ring (intake)
15. Inner valve spring
16. Outer valve spring
17. Valve spring retainer (intake)
18. Valve cone halves
19. Rocker arm (intake)
20. Adjusting screw (intake)
a = Distance between jointing surface cylinder head and intake valve spring retainer
b = Distance between joining surface cylinder head and exhaust valve spring retainer

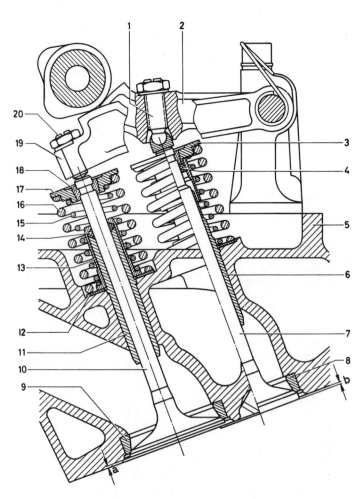

Valve arrangement—300SE.

To measure clearance, remove spark plug wires and high-tension wire. Detach the air vent line at the valve cover and remove the cover screws and cover. Some models have a plastic vacuum line routed close to the cover. This line cannot be kinked or bent, therefore it is best to remove it entirely by disconnecting each end and lifting it out of the way. Also, on some models, such as the 220 Seb and 300 SE, the air control shaft running over the valve cover must be removed, as well as the air cleaner.

Check the cylinder head bolts for correct torque and, if necessary, tighten to specifications (see Chapter 4).

Rotate the camshaft by turning the crankshaft pulley bolt with a 22 mm. wrench until the lobe of the cam is not pressed against the rocker arm, but is on the opposite side of, and at right angles to, the sliding surface of the rocker arm (see illustration). Some models, such as the 300 SE, have holes in the vibration damper plate to assist in crankshaft rotation. In this case, a screwdriver may be used, carefully, to turn the pulley.

Insert the proper feeler gauge between the sliding surface of the rocker arm and the cam base circle, or, in the case of the 300 SE, between the valve stem and the adjusting screw. Adjust until the feeler can just be pulled through with a little tension.

Adjustment is accomplished by turning

Torque wrench adapter for adjusting ball pin.

the ball pin (3) at the hex collar. To increase clearance, screw the ball pin head inward; to decrease, screw outward. This adjustment ideally should be performed using a special adapter and a torque wrench. The illustration shows what this adapter looks like and how it is used. The shape of the tool is dictated by the need for accurate torque readings since, using it, the wrench can be directly lined up with the ball pin head.

In any case, the torque of the ball pin head in its base should be 10–11 ft.-lbs. (14.4–25 ft.-lbs for phase II models). If the torque is too little, the ball pin head will tend to vibrate and clearance will not remain as set.

If the tappet clearance is too small and the ball pin head cannot be screwed in far enough to remedy it, a thinner pressure piece can be installed in the spring retainer (9). Standard thickness is 0.177" (4.5 mm.), but pieces are available in 0.137" (3.5 mm.) and 0.0985" (2.5 mm.) thicknesses as well.

To replace the pressure piece, the rocker arm must be removed; see Chapter 4 for the job. On the 300 SE, the clearance is adjusted by unscrewing the locknut on the rocker arm and turning the adjusting screw in or out.

Adjusting valve clearance.

During extremely cold weather (—13° F.), the intake valve clearance may be opened up to aid cold starting. When the weather warms up, however, the clearance must be reset to normal values.

| Model | Winter | Summer |
|---|---|---|
| 300 SEL/8  6.3 | .006″ | .004″ |
| 220/8 | .005″ | .003″ |
| 230/8 | .005″ | .003″ |
| 250/8 | .005″ | .003″ |
| 250 S | .005″ | .003″ |
| 280 S/8 | .005″ | .003″ |
| 280 SE/8 | .005″ | .003″ |
| 280 SL/8 | .005″ | .003″ |
| 300 SEL/8 | .005″ | .003″ |

## Valve Timing

Checking valve timing is too inaccurate at the standard tappet clearance, therefore timing values are given for an assumed tappet clearance of 0.4 mm. (0.016″).

To check timing, remove the rocker cover and spark plugs. Cut the degree wheel from the back endpaper of this book and glue it to a piece of stiff cardboard, bakelite or aluminum. A pointer must be made out of a bent section of $\frac{3}{16}$″ brazing rod or coathanger wire, and attached to the engine as illustrated. *NOTE: If the degree wheel is attached to the camshaft as shown, values read from it must be doubled.*

With a 22 mm. wrench on the crankshaft pulley, turn the engine, in the direction of rotation, until the TDC mark on the vibration damper registers with the pointer (see inset) and the distributor rotor points to the No. 1 cylinder mark on the housing. Turn the loosened degree wheel until the pointer lines up with the 0° (OT) mark, then tighten it in this position. Continue turning the crankshaft in the direction of rotation until the camshaft lobe of the associated valve is vertical (e.g., points away from the rocker arm surface). To take up tappet clearance, insert a feeler gauge thick enough to raise the valve slightly from its seat between the rocker arm cone and the pressure piece (see illustration).

The next step involves the use of a dial indicator. Attach the indicator to the cylinder head so that the feeler (3) rests against the valve spring retainer of No. 1 cylinder intake valve. Preload the indicator at least 0.008″, then set to zero, making

## Valve Timing Figures

| Model | camshaft code number① | Intake valve | | Exhaust valve | | Mini. dist. betw. intake valve and piston with crankshaft adjusted to 5° after intersection TDC |
|---|---|---|---|---|---|---|
| | | opens BTDC | closes ATDC | opens BTDC | closes ATDC | |
| 190c | 42 ③ 46 ④ 49 ⑤ | 10° | 46° | 44° | 12° | .0351″ |
| 190Dc 200D | 02 ③ 12 ④ 13 ⑤ 17 ⑥ | 12.5° | 41.5° | 45° | 9° | .0394″ ⑦ |
| 200 | 50 ⑥ | 11° | 53° | 47° | 21° | |
| 220b 220Sb 220SEb | 61 ② 70 ③ 79 ④ 82 ⑤ | 10° | 46° | 44° | 12° | |
| 230 230S | 86 | 11° | 53° | 47° | 21° | |
| 230SL | 76 ④ 84 ⑤ | 10° | 58° | 51° | 23° | .0351″ |
| 250S 250SE 250SL | 86 | 11° | 53° | 47° | 21° | |
| 300SE ⑧ | 39 ② 42 ③ | 7° | 47° | 49.5° | 11.5° | |
| 300SE ⑨ 300SEb 300SEL | 46 | 18° | 58° | 53° | 15° | |
| 220/8 | 61 | 11° | 47°* | 48°** | 16° | .0351″ |
| 220D/8 | 18 | 12.5° | 41.5°* | 45°** | 9° | .0507″ ⑦ |
| 230/8 250/8 | 0835 | 11° | 47°* | 48°** | 16° | .0351″ |
| 280S/8 280SE/8 280SE/C/8 | 0835 | 11° | 47°* | 48°** | 16° | .0351″ |
| 280SE/8 300SEL/8 | 0935 | 12° | 56°* | 53°** | 21° | .0351″ |
| 300SEL/8 6.3 # | left-16 right-17 same | L-5° R-7° 2.5° | L-50°* R-48°* 52.5°* | L-40°** R-42°** 37.5°** | L-15.5° R-13.5° 18° | .0351″ |

① The code number on individual camshafts is stamped on the end face.
② Hollow shaft.
③ Solid shaft for external lubrication with grooved bearings.
④ Solid shaft for external lubrication without grooved bearings (except No. 1).
⑤ Solid shaft for external lubrication without grooved bearings.
⑥ Cams
⑦ On models 200D and 220D/8, the minimum distance (.058″) between
   the exhaust valve and piston head at 5° before TDC must also be measured.
⑧ With engine types 189.984 and 189.985.
⑨ With engine types 189.986 and 189.987.
* ABDC
** BBDC
# Top line—with new chain; bottom line—after 12,000 miles, both sides.

sure the feeler (3) is exactly perpendicular on the valve spring retainer. It may be necessary to bleed down the chain tensioner at this time to facilitate readings.

Turn the crankshaft in the normal direction of rotation, again using a wrench on the crankshaft pulley, until the indicator reads 0.016″ less than zero reading.

Note the reading of the degree wheel at this time, remembering to double reading if wheel is mounted to camshaft sprocket. Again turn the crankshaft until the valve

1. Pointer for graduation on crankshaft
2. TDC mark or graduation on degree wheel of crankshaft
3. Degree wheel from end-paper
4. Pointer on camshaft
5. Dial micrometer with feeler and holder
6. Bracket for camshaft cover
7. Distributor rotor arm
8. Mark on distributor housing for 1st cylinder

Adjusting valve timing.

1. Feeler gauge
2. Valve spring retainer
3. Dial indicator prod
4. Dial indicator holder
5. Dial indicator

Adjusting valve timing.

is closing and the indicator again reads 0.016″ less than zero reading. Make sure, at this time, that preload has remained constant, then note the reading of the degree wheel. The difference between the two degree wheel readings is the timing angle (number of degrees the valve is open) for that valve.

The other valves may be checked in the same manner. comparing them against other and the opening values given in the *Tune-up Specifications*. It must be remembered that turning the crankshaft contrary to the normal direction of rotation results in inaccurate readings. If valve timing is not to specification, the easiest way of bringing it in line is to install an offset Woodruff key in the camshaft sprocket. This is far simpler than replacing the entire timing chain, and it is the factory-recommended way of changing valve timing provided the timing chain is not stretched too far or worn out. Offset keys are available in the following sizes:

| *Offset* | *Part No.* | *For a correction at crankshaft of* |
|---|---|---|
| 2° (.7 mm.) | 621 991 04 67 | 4° |
| 3°20′ (.9 mm.) | 621 991 02 67 | 6½° |
| 4° (1.1 mm.) | 621 991 01 67 | 8° |
| 5° (1.3 mm.) | 621 991 00 67 | 10° |

The Woodruff key must be installed with the offset toward the "right", in the normal direction of rotation, to effect advanced valve opening; toward the "left" to retard.

Advancing the intake valve opening too much can result in piston and/or valve damage. (The valve will hit the piston.) To check the clearance between the valve head and the piston, the crankshaft must be positioned at 5° ATDC (on intake stroke). The procedure is essentially the same as for measuring valve timing.

As before, the dial indicator is set to zero after being preloaded, then the valve is depressed until it touches the top of the piston. As the normal valve head-to-piston clearance is approximately .035", you can see that the dial indicator must be preloaded at least .042" so there will be enough movement for the feeler.

If the clearance is much less than .035", the cylinder head must be removed and checked for carbon deposits. If none exist, the valve seat must be cut deeper into the head. Always set the ignition timing after installing an offset key.

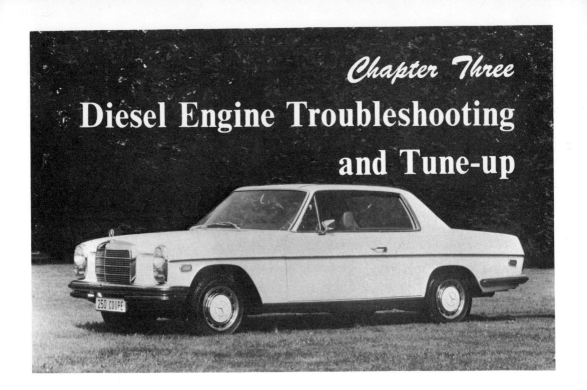

# Chapter Three

# Diesel Engine Troubleshooting and Tune-up

The diesel and gasoline engines used by Mercedes-Benz differ essentially in only one way—how the fuel is ignited. Both types are four-stroke cycle engines, that is, their operating cycles consist of (1) an intake stroke, whereby air (or air-fuel mixture) is pulled into the combustion chamber, (2) a compression stroke, during which the air (or air-fuel mixture) is compressed and heated, (3) a power stroke, caused by the burning (ignition) of the injected fuel and air mixture, and (4) an exhaust stroke, which literally pushes the burnt and unburnt gases out of the engine.

A diesel engine does not have an ignition system as such, although there are glow plugs for starting. To ignite its fuel-air mixture, the diesel depends on the heating effect of compression pressure. If the pressure is high enough, through high compres-

## FOUR STROKE DIESEL CYCLE

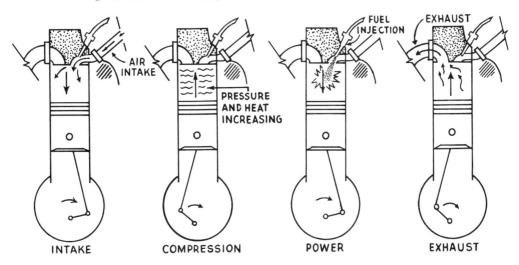

INTAKE          COMPRESSION          POWER          EXHAUST

## General Diesel Engine Specifications

| Model | Engine Model | Engine Type | Bore & Stroke (mm.) | Displace. (cc.) | Compress. Ratio | Firing Order | No. of Cyl. | H.P. @ rpm (SAE) | Torque & rpm (ft. lbs.) | Number Main Bear. |
|---|---|---|---|---|---|---|---|---|---|---|
| 190Dc | OM621.III | 621.912 | 87 x 83.6 | 1,988 | 21:1 | 1-3-4-2 | 4 | 60 @ 4,200 | 87 @ 2,400 | 3 |
| 200D | OM621.VIII | 621.918 | 87 x 83.6 | 1,988 | 21:1 | 1-3-4-2 | 4 | 60 @ 4,200 | 87 @ 2,400 | 5 |
| 220D/8 | OM615 | 615.912 | 87 x 92.4 | 2,197 | 21:1 | 1-3-4-2 | 4 | 65 @ 4,200 | 96 @ 2,400 | 5 |

sion ratios and combustion chamber design, the fuel-air mixture will ignite of its own accord.

The diesel, having no ignition system, is simplified to an extent, although the timed fuel injection required may offset this to a degree. Advantages lie in increased fuel economy using lower grades of fuel, along with long life due to rugged construction.

## Part I
## Troubleshooting a Non-Starting Engine

Any discussion of diesel engine troubleshooting must involve fuel injection, since

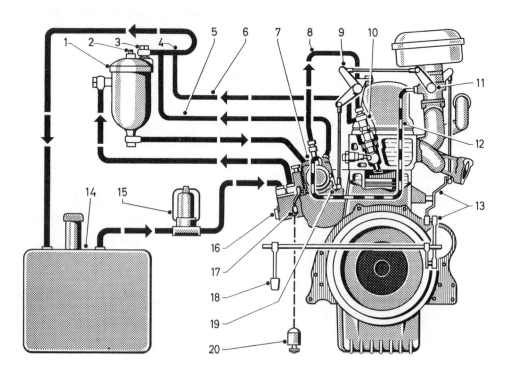

1. Main fuel filter
2. Vent screw
3. Hollow screw with throttle screw
4. Fuel return line
5. Overflow line
6. Injection nozzle leakage line
7. Injection pump
8. Pressure line from injection pump to injection nozzle
9. Angular lever for auxiliary mechanical control
10. Injection nozzle
11. Venturi control unit
12. Vacuum line with throttle screw
13. Linkage and lever for accelerator pedal control
14. Fuel tank
15. Fuel prefilter
16. Fuel feed pump with hand pump
17. Adjusting lever
18. Accelerator pedal
19. Lever for auxiliary mechanical control
20. Heater plug starting switch with starting and stopping cable

Diesel operation in schematic form.

most poor running conditions stem from a malfunction in this system. The illustration shows a typical engine and its fuel injection system in schematic form.

The fuel feed jump, driven by the injection pump, acts the same as the fuel pump of any gasoline engine, pumping fuel from the tank to the engine. The fuel passes through two fuel filters, the transparent prefilter and the larger main filter. From there it goes into the suction chamber of the injection pump, in which a constant fuel pressure is maintained by the overflow valve. At a *minimum* pressure of 11.8 psi surplus fuel flows back into the fuel tank via this valve. The fuel pump has a pumping capacity much greater than is necessary in order to keep the chamber always full of bubble-free fuel.

The injection pump plungers force the fuel from the suction chamber through the pump pressure valves into the injection lines—thence to the injection nozzles, at a spray pressure of 1564–1706 psi. The spray

must pass through the prechamber before reaching the main combustion chamber. Surplus fuel at the injectors is passed through leakage lines into the fuel tank.

The fuel volume is influenced by the accelerator pedal position, engine load and speed, and controlled by the pneumatic governor on the rear of the injection pump.

If the engine will not start, as usually happens in cold weather with a poorly maintained car, try turning the idle speed adjuster knob all the way counterclockwise, pre-glow for a full minute, push the clutch all the way in and the accelerator pedal halfway down. Then, try to start the engine. If the engine does not start after 10–15 seconds, pre-glow again and repeat the procedure. If the engine fires a few times but just won't catch, hold the starter on for a longer period.

This assumes, of course, that the starter motor turns the engine over at all. The most common cause of the starter not working, or working sluggishly, is a low battery, sometimes in combination with "summer" oil. The diesel, having such a high com-

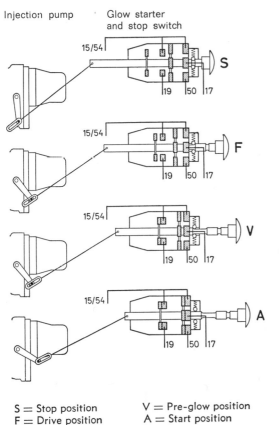

S = Stop position     V = Pre-glow position
F = Drive position     A = Start position

Starting cable positions.

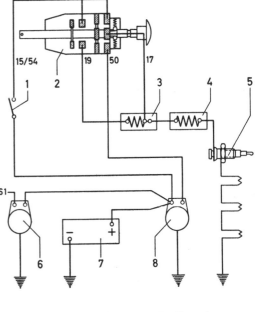

1. Main switch
2. Push pull switch
3. Glow plug control
4. Resistor
5. Glow plug
6. Generator
7. Battery
8. Starter

Diesel starting system.

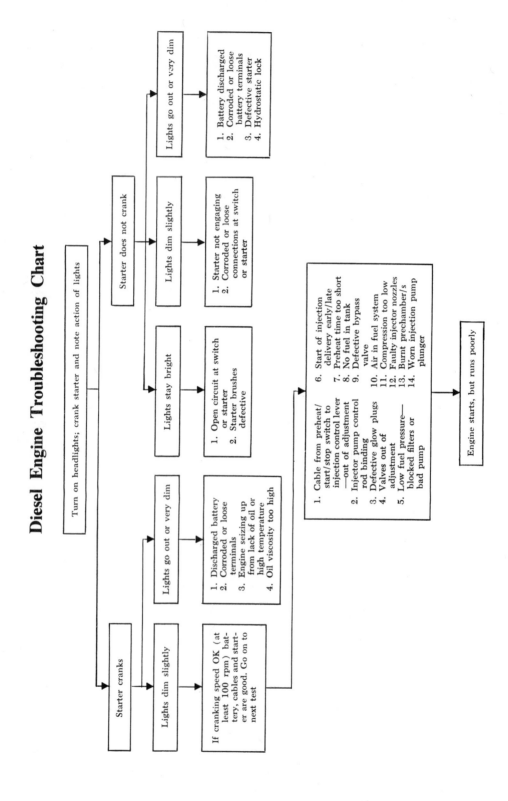

## Diesel Engine Troubleshooting Chart

Turn on headlights; crank starter and note action of lights

**Starter cranks**

Lights dim slightly → If cranking speed OK (at least 100 rpm) battery, cables and starter are good. Go on to next test

Lights go out or very dim →
1. Discharged battery
2. Corroded or loose terminals
3. Engine seizing up from lack of oil or high temperature
4. Oil viscosity too high

**Starter does not crank**

Lights stay bright →
1. Open circuit at switch or starter
2. Starter brushes defective

Lights dim slightly →
1. Starter not engaging
2. Corroded or loose connections at switch or starter

Lights go out or very dim →
1. Battery discharged
2. Corroded or loose battery terminals
3. Defective starter
4. Hydrostatic lock

1. Cable from preheat/start/stop switch to injection control lever—out of adjustment
2. Injector pump control rod binding
3. Defective glow plugs
4. Valves out of adjustment
5. Low fuel pressure—blocked filters or bad pump
6. Start of injection delivery early/late
7. Preheat time too short
8. No fuel in tank
9. Defective bypass valve
10. Air in fuel system
11. Compression too low
12. Faulty injector nozzles
13. Burnt prechamber/s
14. Worn injection pump plunger

Engine starts, but runs poorly

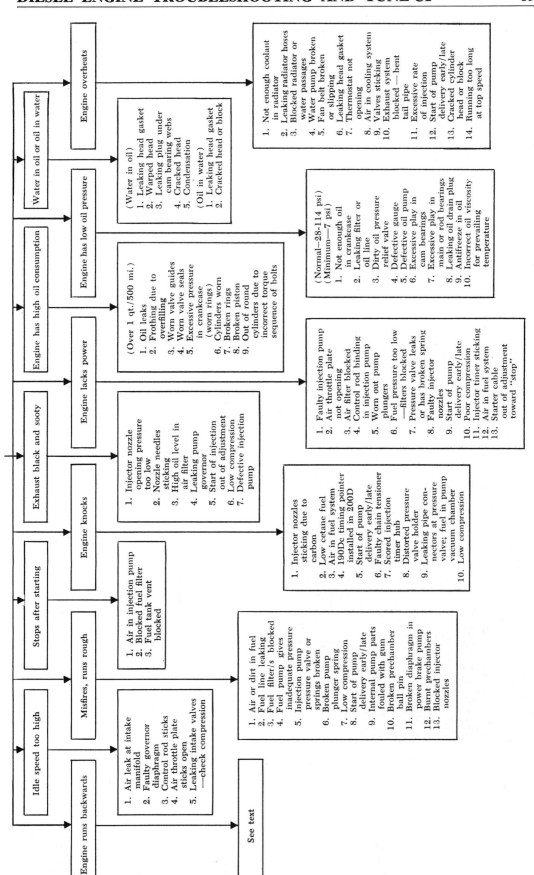

pression ratio (21:1) is difficult to turn over with high viscosity oil working against it. Battery and starter tests can be found in Chapter 2.

If, after checking the battery, starter, cables, and oil, the engine still will not start, a check of one, or all, of the following areas is in order:

1. Cable from pre-glow/start-stop switch to injection control lever.
2. Injection pump control rod.
3. Compression pressure (including valve adjustment).
4. Glow plugs.
5. Fuel pressure.
6. Start of injection pump delivery.

## Cable

To adjust the cable, first disconnect the ground cable from the negative battery post. Push the control knob all the way in to the "stop" position. In this position, the adjusting lever on the injection pump will be pushed completely forward. Next, pull the knob to the "start" position. In this position, the pin of the adjusting lever should rest against the end of the eye (2).

Now, release the knob. The adjusting lever should return to the "driving" position. In both this and the pre-glow position, the adjusting lever pin must clear the eye end by at least .080″. If not, adjust the cable by loosening the bolt and moving the coil spring outer housing (4) with relation to the angle bracket (3). Also, make sure the adjusting lever (1) is firmly attached to the pump shaft by tightening the clamp screw. Check the cable and adjusting lever for free movement and check that the lever is pulled all the way back when the knob is pulled to the starting position. Reconnect the battery cable and try to start the engine. *NOTE: If both the start and stop positions cannot be adjusted properly, it is best to sacrifice a little starting delivery to gain a full stop position on the lever.*

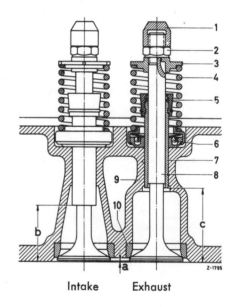

Intake     Exhaust

1. Adjusting lever (starting and stopping cable lever)
2. Eye with rubber molding of starting and stopping cable
3. Angle bracket
4. Coil spring

1. Cap nut
2. Hexagon nut
3. Valve spring disk
4. Valve spring
5. Valve seal
6. Valve rotator
7. Valve guide— exhaust
8. Exhaust valve
9. Cylinder head
10. Valve seat— exhaust

a = Distance from separating line of cylinder head to valve disk
b = Distance from separating line of cylinder head to front face of intake valve guide
c = Distance from separating line of cylinder head to front face of exhaust valve guide

Starting cable adjustment.

Diesel valve set-up, showing rotator.

## Diesel Tune-up Specifications

| Model | Valve clearance ①② | | Intake valve opens (deg.) ⑤ | Injection pump setting (deg.) | Injection nozzle pressure (psi) | | Idle speed (rpm) ③ | Cranking compression pressure (psi) |
| | Intake (in.) | Exhaust (in.) | | | New | Used | | |
|---|---|---|---|---|---|---|---|---|
| 190Dc | .004④ | .016 | 12.5B | 26B | 1564—1706 | 1422—1706 | 700—800 | 284—327 |
| 200D | .004④ | .016 | 12.5B | 26B | 1564—1706 | 1422—1706 | 700—800 | 284—327 |
| 220D/8 | .004④ | .016 | 12.5B | 24B | 1564—1706 | 1422—1706 | 700—800 | 284—327 |

B = *Before Top Dead Center*
① *With cold engine.*
② *With warm engine — intake .008, exhaust .018*
③ *Manual transmission in neutral, automatic transmission in drive range.*
④ *In cold weather (below 5°F.), increase to .006 cold.*
⑤ *See Chapter 2 for more complete specifications.*

### Control Rod

The control rod runs through the center of the injection pump, one end sticking out of the end housing, covered with a protective cap. If this rod is sticking in the stop position, no fuel is delivered to the injectors and the engine will not start. Remove the end cap and check the rod for binding.

### Compression

The section on compression testing found in Chapter 2 applies to diesel engines as well. The only difference in testing is that the glow plugs instead of the spark plugs are removed for the test. Individual cylinder pressures should not vary more than 45 psi.

Don't forget, valve clearances set too close will result in poor compression readings for the diesel, too. See Part II of this chapter for adjustment procedures.

Some engines have a valve rotator (6) installed. If this rotator fails, compression will be low. Usually, the replacement of the rotator will bring compression back up to par.

### Glow Plugs

The glow plugs provide a means for ignition during starting and perform the same *function* as normal spark plugs, although they do so in a different manner.

The light on the dashboard indicating when the glow plugs are hot enough to fire can also serve as a troubleshooting aid. If the light does not glow, it usually indicates a faulty plug.

Testing glow plugs.

Test the plugs by having an assistant hold the starting knob in the preheat position while shorting the plugs to ground, in turn, with a screwdriver. Each plug should produce a spark if working properly. While bridging the connections, the light should light. If, after disconnecting the ground lead (10) of the preheating system, the light still stays lit, a short circuit in the system is indicated. This is usually caused by a carboned up plug electrode or by a lead touching the cylinder head. Check the leads first. If they seem O.K., pull the knob to the preheat position and disconnect one plug power lead at a time, starting from the ground end, until the light goes out, indicating the faulty plug.

Glow plugs can be cleaned, but it is better to replace them if they are badly carboned. To remove the plugs, loosen the cable (10), if this has not been done al-

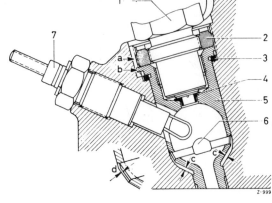

1. Union nut for mounting the injection line
2. Hex. nut for mounting the fitting
3. Fitting
4. Connection head of leak oil line
5. Hollow screw
6. Nozzle holder
7. Glow plug
8. Bus bar
9. Connection insulator
10. Connection cable or ground cable resp. (on both outer glow plugs)
11. Knurled nut

Diesel starting and injection components.

a. Groove in cylinder head
b. Lug securing prechamber
c. Distance between prechamber (5) and cylinder head
d. Max. permissible measure of a retracted ball pin with respect to the outer dia. of the prechamber (.020")
1. Nozzle holder
2. Threaded ring
3. Seal ring between prechamber and cylinder head
4. Seal ring between prechamber and nozzle holder (nozzle plate)
5. Prechamber (ball pin version)
6. Ball pin in the prechamber
7. Glow plug

Glow plug and prechamber.

ready, by removing the knurled nut (11). Unscrew the other nuts and remove the insulators (9) and the bus bars (8). Using a 21 mm. socket, unscrew and remove the glow plugs.

Before installing new plugs, clean the ducts and prechamber bores with a stiff bristle brush or a small scraper. The ball pin in the prechamber is easy to break, so don't go much deeper than 2″ into the plug hole. Crank the engine a few times to blow out any carbon particles loosened by the scraping, then insert the plugs. Do not exceed 35 ft.-lbs. torque.

It might be a good idea to recheck these new plugs to ensure that all connections are tight and not grounded and that the plugs are not faulty.

**Fuel Pressure**

The fuel pump is mounted on the side of the fuel injection pump, and can be easily identified by the hand priming pump. Its job, like that of the gasoline engine fuel pump, is to deliver a constant fuel volume, at adequate pressure, to the injection pump. With the diesel engine it is extremely important that the fuel is air-free, without bubbles. A fuel bypass valve is located in the injection pump to maintain constant fuel pressure for the engine load. This valve opens at a pressure of 14.7–22 psi, sending excess fuel back into the supply system.

As with most things mechanical, accurate testing is possible only with the proper instruments. A general check of fuel pressure can be made, however, if one assumes that the bypass valve is functioning properly. Disconnect the return line at the fitting and hold the line over an open coffee can. Start the engine and watch the line. If fuel comes out, it can be assumed that the fuel pressure is sufficient, as a pressure of at least 14.7 psi is required to open a good bypass valve.

It is also good practice to check the dis-

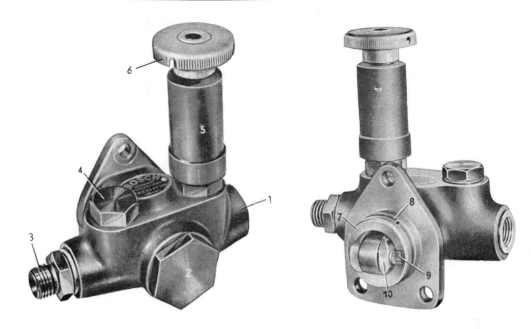

1. Connector at suction end
2. Screw plug to plunger
3. Connector at discharge end
4. Screw plug to pressure valve
5. Hand pump and cap lug to suction valve
6. Handle of hand feed pump
7. Roller tappet guide
8. Guard ring
9. Guide pin and/or guide plate on roller tappet
10. Roller tappet

Diesel fuel pump.

charge line from the fuel filter, as a blocked filter will deliver no fuel. Check the tank before assuming the worst about a fuel pump—gauges have been known to be wrong. It may be a good idea to disconnect the input line from the fuel tank and blow back through it with low-pressure compressed air. A line free of debris will allow the air to bubble in the tank. *CAUTION: High pressure air will blow out the fuel tank filter.*

Defective fuel pumps should be replaced, as it is not really feasible to rebuild them without the proper tools. To check the pump, unscrew the hand pump and remove the suction valve. Unscrew the plug (4) covering the pressure valve and remove the valve. Worn valve seats can be reground sometimes, but it is better to replace them. To check the plunger, remove the plug (2) and pull the plunger and spring. If it is badly scored or worn the pump must be replaced. If the pump is only clogged with gum, it is possible to clean it with lacquer thinner or carbon tet, but a new rubber O-ring should be used on the hand pump during reassembly.

## Start of Injection Pump Delivery

As the piston comes up on compression stroke, there is a delay, caused by the fuel having to come from the pump to the injector nozzle, which must be compensated for. For example, if injection takes place too early, temperatures may not yet be high enough for ignition (piston has not come up far enough to compress the air). To compensate for this lag, the injection pump begins to deliver fuel to the nozzle 26° before top dead center is reached for 190 Dc and 200 D and 24° BTDC for 220 D/8.

To check the start of delivery, remove the negative battery cable and set the piston of No. 1 cylinder at top dead center by lining up the TDC mark on the crankshaft pulley with the pointer. If TDC is achieved, both intake and exhaust valves of No. 1 cylinder will be closed (springs not compressed).

This can be checked by removing the camshaft cover and observing the relationship of the rockers to the valve stems. Now, using a wrench on the crankshaft

1. Pipe union
2. Rubber sealing ring
3. Coil spring
4. Sealing ring
5. Pressure valve plate with pressure valve

Pressure valve components.

1. Adjustment lever of injection pump
2. Hand-operated fuel pump
3. Jaws for locking two pipe unions
4. Tachometer drive
5. Overflow pipe
6. Bleed screw
7. Fuel container
8. Fuel return lines

Measuring start of pump delivery.

pulley nut (never use the camshaft pulley nut, as the timing chain rails will be damaged), turn the engine over 1¾ turns, in the normal direction of rotation.

Unscrew the injection line at the pipe union of the first pump cylinder (see illustration). Remove pipe union (1), rubber O-ring (2), spring (3) and the pressure valve. Replace the union and screw on an overflow pipe (5) (see illustration).

Detach the starting cable from the lever at the injection pump and make sure that the lever is in the full delivery position. If this is not done the test may be inaccurate.

Either connect an auxiliary fuel container to the injection pump or fill the main fuel filter by operating the hand pump (2) and cracking the bleed screw (6) to ensure that the fuel is air-free.

With the wrench on the crankshaft pulley, turn the engine over slowly in the normal direction of rotation until the fuel stream from the overflow pipe stops dripping. *NOTE: Another drop may follow 10–15 seconds later, but this is normal.*

At this point, the pump piston covers the intake core in the pump cylinder and the start of delivery point has been reached. The crankshaft pointer should read 26° BTDC or 24° BTDC, depending on model.

Repeat the test by continuing to turn the crankshaft in the direction of rotation—two turns. At the end of the second revolution the fuel should cease dripping again at the proper point.

A. Solid fuel stream
B. Fuel begins to drip
C. One drop follows 10-15 seconds later

Overflow pipe during test.

To adjust the start of delivery, loosen the bolts of the front flange and rotate the pump toward the engine to begin delivery earlier, or away from the engine to delay delivery. It may be necessary to disconnect the injector tubes so that the pump will be free enough to rotate.

Remove all test equipment and reassemble, using a new seal (4) in the pressure valve assembly. The pressure valve assembly pipe union must be tightened to exactly 25 ft.-lbs. with the threads coated with Vaseline. Bleed the fuel system by opening bleed screw (6) and pumping the hand pump to evacuate any air. Reattach the starting cable and adjust as mentioned previously.

---

## Part II
## Troubleshooting a Poorly Running Engine/Tune-up

---

A careful study of the troubleshooting chart will reveal most of the symptoms of poor running associated with diesel engines of this type, along with their probable causes. You will also note that many items are found in more than one column, because the breakdown or malfunctioning of one component part could cause any number of problems, depending on whether other components are involved in this breakdown. For instance, a blocked fuel filter could cause the engine to stop immediately after starting, cause it to misfire or run badly, or even not start at all. In such cases of multiple listings, test or repair procedures given for one will be valid for all, unless specifically stated otherwise.

Many of the problems listed have been covered in Chapter 2; therefore, that chapter should be referred to in such cases. Compression testing, for example, is fully explained, as are the causes of poor compression. Many of the other items have obvious corrective measures.

In order to eliminate repetition, then, the most common testing and repair procedures follow in no particular order or sequence. Simply consult the troubleshooting chart and find the associated test.

### Engine Runs Backward

Under the right conditions the diesel engine can run backward (although poorly)

accompanied by smoke issuing from the air cleaner. This is not a common condition, but one that can be damaging to the engine.

For example, if reverse gear is accidentally engaged while coasting forward, or if the engine stalls under load and restarts itself, the engine can run backward. To stop it, engage a gear and let out the clutch suddenly, or block the exhaust pipe with a rag. This can also happen if an attempt is made to start the engine without preheating. If the switch is moved from the start to the preheat position, the beginning of preheat may coincide with engine revolutions, causing extremely early ignition. If this happens, the air filter will quickly catch fire and the engine can seize up due to lack of oil, so quick action is necessary.

Since 1962, diesel engines have had a check throttle valve installed to prevent

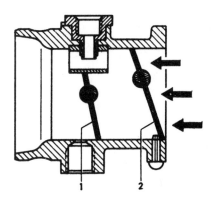

1. Throttle valve
2. Check throttle valve

Air check valve to prevent engine from running backwards. Arrows show the valve closed, as it would be if engine attempted to run backwards.

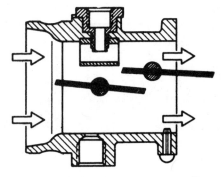

Air check valve as it operates normally.

this situation, so a check of that valve will usually isolate the problem. Lubricate the valve every 5,000 miles with engine oil to prevent recurrence.

## Engine Stops After Starting

Can be caused by blocked fuel tank, fuel filter, or an air-locked injection pump. Remove tank filler cap and try starting the engine. Remove fuel line to injection pump and crank engine. Check fuel volume. Bleed fuel system.

## Idle Speed Too High

Air leaks at the intake manifold can be located by squirting some soapy water at any suspected joints with the engine running. Solution will be sucked in or bubble if a leak exists.

The injection pump governor diaphragm cannot be checked accurately unless the pump is placed on a test stand. It is possible, however, to determine roughly whether or not the governor is operating. First, with the engine idling, squirt a soapy water solution over the intake manifold, vacuum line, governor housing and air venturi housing joints to check for leakage.

Remove the starting cable from the control lever of the injection pump and remove the sleeve (3) over the control rod. Unscrew vacuum line at (1) and actuate the control lever (2), making sure the control rod goes to its full stop position, while holding thumb over fitting (1).

Release control lever and observe control rod. If diaphragm of the pump gover-

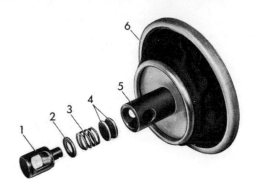

1. Compensator pin
2. Shim for compensator spring
3. Compensator spring
4. Shims for compensator spring
5. Sleeve
6. Diaphragm

Vacuum diaphragm components.

1. Prod of dial indicator
2. Sleeve of diaphragm
3. Piece of tubing
4. Pin, 6 mm. in diameter
5. Compensator pin

Assembling and checking diaphragm assembly.

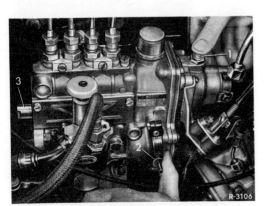

1. Vacuum union
2. Control lever
3. Protector sleeve over control rod

Checking vacuum chamber.

nor is functioning, the control rod will move slightly, but will be restrained by vacuum produced in the housing. Removing the thumb should allow the control rod to move. If this test indicates the diaphragm to be faulty, remove the four bolts and take out the diaphragm for inspection.

It is possible, although not the best procedure, to replace the diaphragm with the injection pump in place, but care must be taken in assembly. For example, it is easy to lose the compensator mechanism components (1, 4 and 5 in illustration). It is also necessary to use a dial indicator to measure the maximum compensator travel (see illustrations).

To measure this travel, obtain a pin 6 mm. in diameter (approximately 0.235″) and insert it through the sleeve (2) of the old diaphragm and compensator pin (5). Placing the assembly on a large socket (3) is necessary for stability. Set up the gauge as illustrated, with the prod tip on the end of the compensator pin, slightly preloaded. Press down on the prod and measure existing travel (maximum travel is .043″–.105″).

Disassemble the old diaphragm and insert the shims into the new one. Now measure maximum travel of the diaphragm. The difference in readings should not exceed .0024″. Shims are available to make corrections.

### Uneven Running, Metallic Noise, Blue Smoke

The usual cause of this condition is a broken ball pin in the prechamber, a jammed injection nozzle or a leaky vacuum pump system.

With the car stationary, rev the engine a few times and note the exhaust. If intermittent clouds of black smoke are emitted, it indicates one or more of the injection nozzles is faulty. To determine which nozzle is malfunctioning, allow the engine to idle. Loosen the cap nuts (7) of each injection tube, one at a time, about ½ turn,

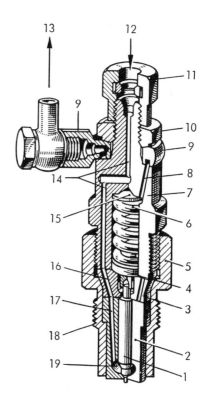

1. Jet needle
2. Nozzle assembly
3. Nozzle element
4. Thrust pin
5. Cap nut for fixing injection nozzle
6. Compression spring
7. Nozzle holder
8. Drain hole in the nozzle holder
9. Through-way jointing piece with annular canal for leak-off oil union
10. Hexagon nut for fixing the through-way jointing piece
11. Cap nut for fixing the injection pipe
12. Fuel feed
13. Leak-off oil drain back to fuel tank
14. Pressure canal in the nozzle holder
15. Special washers belonging to compression spring (machined steel disks)
16. Annular groove and feed bores in nozzle element
17. Annular groove and pressure canal in nozzle assembly
18. Mounting thread
19. Pressure chamber in nozzle assembly

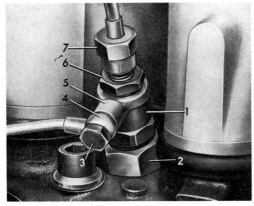

1. Nozzle holder
2. Cap nut of nozzle holder assembly
3. Hollow bolt
4. Union head of leak-off oil pipe
5. Through-way jointing piece
6. Hexagon nut anchoring the through-way jointing piece
7. Cap nut anchoring the injection pipe

Injection nozzle.

Nozzle holder/injection assembly.

then retighten. If there is no change in the rough idle, it indicates a faulty nozzle. A good nozzle will be indicated by a further roughening of the idle when the cap nut is unscrewed.

To remove the nozzle, take off the cap nut (7) and unscrew the nut (6) that holds the banjo fitting (5 and 3). Remove bolt (3) and the overflow line. Then, unscrew the nozzle assembly and seal (6).

Examine the prechamber for carbon deposits and clean it if necessary. To disassemble the nozzle holder, remove the cap nut (5) (see illustration) with a 27 mm. box wrench, then pull out the nozzle assembly (2) and jet needle (1). Remove the nozzle element (3), thrust pin (4) and spring (6) from the nozzle holder. It is very easy to crush or distort the nozzle holder, therefore do *not* clamp it in a vise to disassemble. Individual nozzle components are run-in together and never should be interchanged.

Nozzle testing requires special equipment capable of producing accurately measured pressure while allowing observation of the spray pattern. Since this equipment is not readily available, and jury-rigged setups do not produce good results, it is recommended that the dealer do any nozzle testing.

In any case, malfunctioning nozzles are usually only carboned up and, if care is exercised, they can be hand-cleaned.

Brush any carbon away using a brass-bristle brush or a piece of kerosene-soaked wood. Never use a steel scraper, because any burrs will ruin the injector. Using a sharpened brass rod, scrape any deposits from the grooves and orifices, then soak in solvent and blow out with compressed air. Examine for burrs or scratches and out-of-round injection holes, then check that the jet needle moves freely in the nozzle. Immerse the assembly in diesel fuel and pull the jet needle about one-third out of the nozzle, then release it. The jet should fall of its own weight.

In emergency situations, burrs keeping the jet from sliding may be removed by lapping with fine valve grinding compound. Damaged seating surfaces, however, usually will not be restored by lapping; therefore, it is best to replace such damaged units.

Assemble the unit carefully, checking the illustrations for correct parts assembly.

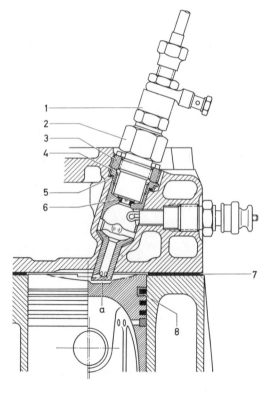

| | |
|---|---|
| 1. Nozzle holder | 5. Sealing ring |
| 2. Cap nut of nozzle holder | 6. Seal |
| 3. Threaded ring | 7. Cylinder head gasket |
| 4. Prechamber | 8. Piston ring liner |
| | a. Piston base recess |

Nozzle holder installed.

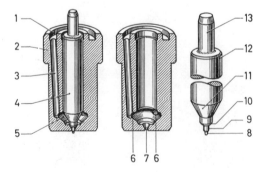

| | |
|---|---|
| 1. Annular groove | 7. Mouth of nozzle |
| 2. Nozzle assembly | 8. Injection pin |
| 3. Intake bore | 9. Throttle pin |
| 4. Jet needle | 10. Needle seating surface |
| 5. Pressure chamber | 11. Thrust shoulder |
| 6. Mouth of intake bore in pressure chamber | 12. Needle shaft |
| | 13. Thrust shank |

Injector nozzle.

Any dirt will prevent free operation of the jet. When tightening the cap nut, do not exceed 50 ft.-lbs.—excessive torque may distort the nozzle and cause the jet needle to bind. *CAUTION: Always use new seals when reassembling and installing injectors, and never try to stop leaks by overtightening connections.*

### Uneven Running, Droning Noise, Very Heavy Blue Smoke

This condition is usually caused by a cracked diaphragm in the power brake vacuum pump. Engine oil is sucked through the crack into the vacuum hose, then into the intake manifold. The result can be burned prechambers if not corrected in time, as well as general carbon build-up in the combustion chamber. Remove the hose from the vacuum pump to the intake manifold. If it is filled with oil, the prechambers must be examined for damage. If the prechamber is scorched badly or burnt away, it must be replaced. Unfortunately, special tools are required for this job. In light of the difficulty sometimes encountered in removal even *with* the special tools, it is almost certain that any substitute will not work, and may even damage the cylinder head. Leave this job to the dealer and confine activity to general scraping and cleaning of the chamber. This usually will be sufficient if the condition was caught in time. To alleviate the cause of the problem, the vacuum pump diaphragm must be replaced.

To check the diaphragm, detach the vacuum hose between the pump and the power brake and, using a T-fitting connector similar to the one illustrated, hook a vacuum gauge into the line. With the engine running at 2,000 rpm, the gauge should show a little over 21 in. Hg. (vacuum) after about 10 seconds.

### Engine Knocks

"Knocking" of the engine falls into four general categories:

1. Knocking during idling.
2. Knocking under partial load at low speed.
3. Knocking under partial load at high speed.
4. Hard knocking, engine shaking on mounts.

Unless the noise has some mechanical cause, bad connecting rod bearings for instance, diesel knock can be considered harmless to everything but the driver's ears.

#### KNOCKING DURING IDLING

This is a normal condition with diesel engines and nothing really can be done about it. Injection nozzle replacement, although often done, is not a guarantee that the noise will stop. In fact, the new clean nozzles will often make the noise more pronounced.

#### KNOCKING AT PARTIAL LOAD AT LOW SPEED

This usually occurs with a cold engine, and becomes less as the engine heats up. The most common cause of this is use of diesel fuel with too low a cetane rating (equivalent to "octane" for gasoline). Try mixing about a quart of engine oil with each tank of fuel or change fuel brands. A list of suppliers of diesel fuels appears in the Appendix, each of whom will send a service station directory of their diesel stations on request.

Oftimes air in the fuel system will cause this problem as well. Check all fuel lines and hoses, from the tank all the way up. The fuel filter and hand pump can also develop leaks. Bleed the fuel system, as described previously in this chapter, and check the fuel pump vacuum (idle speed= 6–12 in. Hg.) and pressure (open pressure of relief valve at idle=11–21 psi).

Although highly unlikely at this late date, some 200 D engines may have had timing pointers installed from the 190 Dc engine. This will retard the ignition by 3°

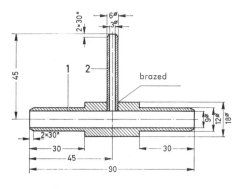

T-fitting for vacuum test.

or so. Check the pointer with the illustration and table.

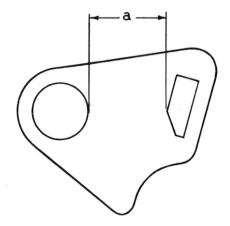

*Pointer*

| Type | Part Number | Measurement |
|------|-------------|-------------|
| 190 Dc | 121 032 01 15 | a = 1″ (25.0 mm.) |
| 200 D | 121 032 02 15 | a = 1¹⁄₁₆″ (27.0 mm.) |

Check the start of fuel delivery, as previously outlined, and check the fuel filters as outlined in Chapter 1.

Injection lines of a different diameter may be exchanged for older types to eliminate knocking. The new lines are ¹⁄₁₆″ (1.5 mm.) in diameter (inside).

### KNOCKING AT PARTIAL LOAD AT HIGHER SPEEDS

This type of knocking usually happens in third gear traveling at 30–45 mph. It can be distinguished by the fact that it gets louder as the engine heats up.

This is often caused by a faulty timing chain tensioner. When the chain loses tension it vibrates, causing a rattle. In addition, the injection timer hub can be scored to such a degree that injection timing is retarded.

To accurately check the chain tensioner requires special test equipment. However, if the tensioner is bad enough to cause chain rattle, it will suffice to remove it, clamp it down, fill it with oil and bleed it, then push down slowly. If the tensioner is good, it will require quite high pressure to compress, and will compress only very slowly.

To remove the tensioner, first take off the camshaft cover and drain the radiator to a level below the thermostat housing. Remove the housing and the idler pulley bracket. The tensioner now can be easily removed. Check the tensioner and, if necessary, replace it. Parts are available separately, but the pressure pin (9) and housing (4) *must* be replaced together for proper operation.

To bleed the tensioner after installation, fill the oil case in the cylinder head with engine oil and, using a screwdriver, push the tension sprocket bearing as far as it will go (see illustration). Slowly release the tensioner, making sure the oil case is filled with oil at all times. Repeat the procedure until no air bubbles issue and

Timing pointer.

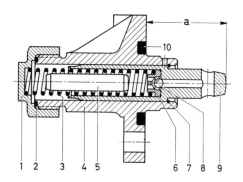

| | |
|---|---|
| 1. Cap nut | 6. Ball retainer |
| 2. Sealing ring | 7. Snap-ring |
| 3. Pressure spring | 8. Ball |
| 4. Housing | 9. Pressure pin |
| 5. Pin | 10. O-ring |

Chain tensioner.

Bleeding chain tensioner.

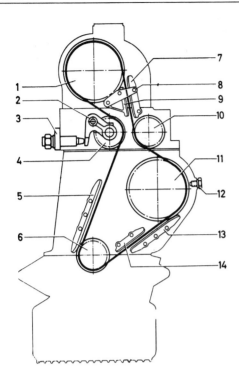

1. Camshaft sprocket
2. Idler sprocket support with idler sprocket
3. Chain tightener
4. Idler sprocket
5. Guide rail, outer
6. Crankshaft sprocket
7. Guide rail, outer
8. Holder for guide rail, inner
9. Guide rail, inner
10. Guide sprocket
11. Intermediate sprocket
12. Locking screw
13. Guide rail, outer
14. Guide rail, inner

Timing chain configuration—190Dc, 200D.

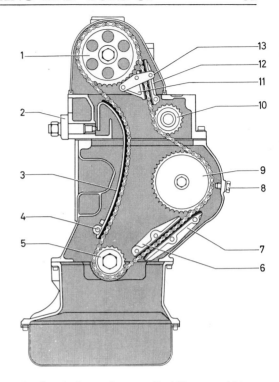

1. Camshaft sprocket
2. Chain tensioner
3. Tensioning rail
4. Pivot pin for tensioning rail
5. Crankshaft sprocket
6. Inner chain guide
7. Outer chain guide
8. Safety screw
9. Idling gear (drive for injection timer, injection pump and oil pump)
10. Diverter sprocket
11. Inner sliding rail
12. Outer sliding rail
13. Inner sliding rail retainer

Timing chain configuration—220D/8.

there is no free-play on the tensioner.

The injection timer can be removed and checked in the following manner:

1. Remove radiator (on 220 D/8).
2. Detach vacuum and pressure hoses from vacuum pump. Remove vacuum pump.
3. Remove cover screws and cover. Remove hex nut and washer from shaft.
4. Remove camshaft cover.
5. Remove hex screw and holder along with inner guide rail (on 190 Dc and 200 D.)
6. Remove the camshaft sprocket bolt.
7. Turn the crankshaft, using a wrench on the pulley nut, in the direction of rotation until the TDC mark for 222 D/8 models and the 45° BTDC mark on 190 Dc and 200 D models coincides with pointer.

8. Matchmark the position of the chain with the injection timer. (Use paint dots.)
9. Matchmark position of chain on camshaft sprocket.
10. Remove chain tensioner.
11. On 220 D/8, remove screw (13) and the inner and outer sliding rails (11 and 12).
12. Pull the camshaft sprocket, making sure the thrust washers are not lost.
13. Unscrew locking screw and pull the upper guide rail pivot pin.
14. Using a strip of sheet metal or cardboard between the chain and the gear teeth, remove chain from the intermediate sprocket.
15. Pry off the injection timer, being careful not to turn over the engine or camshaft.

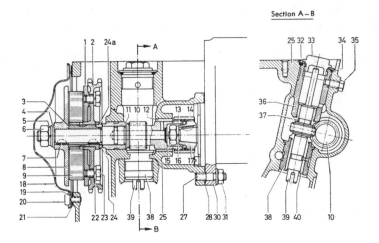

Section A – B

1. Segment plate of the injection timing device
2. Intermediate sprocket
3. Bushing
4. Washer
5. Lockwasher
6. Hex nut
7. Woodruff key
8. Segment flange of inj. timing device
9. Centrifugal weight roller of the inj. timing device
10. Intermediate gear shaft (driveshaft for injection pump and for helical gear 39 or for oil pump)
11. Bearing bushing, front
12. Bearing bushing, rear
13. Coupling sleeve
14. Snap-ring
15. Hex nut
16. Lockwasher
17. Follower
18. Cover
19. Lockwasher
20. Fill. hd. screw
21. Gasket
22. Lockwasher
23. Hex hd. screw
24. Butting ring (steel washer)
24a. Grooved pin
25. Cylinder crankcase
27. Stud bolt
28. Gasket
30. Injection pump
31. Hex nut with washer
32. Washer
33. Screw plug
34. Rubber ring
35. Hex hd. screw
36. Pressure piece
37. Bearing bushing
38. Bearing body
39. Helical gear (drive for oil pump and revolution counter)
40. Bearing bushing

Injection timer and tachometer drive.

Inspect the timer. If scored badly or broken internally, replace it, remembering to transfer matchmarks from old timer. When reassembling, follow removal procedure in reverse, being careful to line up the matchmarks. A bent piece of brazing rod will hold the guide rail in place while inserting the pivot pin. Don't forget to bleed the chain tensioner.

### HARD KNOCKING AND SHAKING OF ENGINE

The main cause of this is a sticking injector nozzle. These can be tested as described earlier in this chapter, as well as the pressure valve holders, another cause of the problem.

Leaks between the pipe connectors and pressure valve holders can cause fuel to leak into the governor vacuum chamber. Replacement of the seals will stop the problem, but the fuel must be drained from the vacuum chamber. Unscrew the oil level plug (see Chapter 1) and loosen the governor housing bolts. Drain the fuel by pulling the housing away.

### Injection Pump

In many cases of poor running, the injection pump itself is at fault. Fuel that is extremely gritty will cause wear of the pump plungers, and plunger springs can break in service. Accurate testing of the pump must be carried out on a test stand. Aside from testing the governor vacuum and control rod, little else other than visual inspection for broken or worn parts can be accomplished without this apparatus.

To remove the pump for service, unscrew all injection lines, the vacuum line and fuel lines. Plug the lines, then detach the connecting rod for the auxiliary mechanical control and the starting cable at the adjusting lever. Turn the crankshaft,

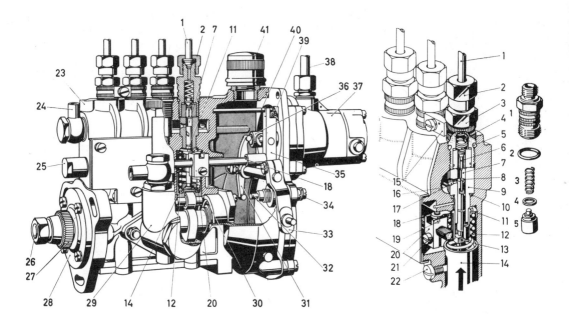

1. Pressure pipe (injection pipe)
2. Cap nut
3. Pipe union
4. Valve spring
5. Seal between pipe union and injection pump housing
6. Pressure valve with pressure valve holder
7. Pressure chamber
8. Plunger $\Big\} =$ forming pump element
9. Cylinder
10. Seal
11. Governor sleeve with steering arm
12. Tappet spring
13. Plunger vane
14. Roller tappet
15. Clamping jaws (to grip the pipe unions)
16. Suction chamber
17. Control bore (feed and return bore)
18. Control rod
19. Pin on control sleeve rotating lever
20. Adjustable clamping piece with guide groove
21. Clamp screw
22. Tappet guide screw
23. Injection pump housing
24. Fuel feed union
25. Control rod guide bearing and start-metering stop
26. Camshaft (drive side)
27. Link stud
28. Bearing base-plate with gasket and centering
29. Fuel feed pump
30. Journal bearing
31. Rocker arm
32. Stop pin for full load stop
33. Setting lever
34. Setting lever stop, also adjustment screw with full load stop
35. Guide lever
36. Diaphragm pin with pressure pin and compensator spring
37. Diaphragm assembly
38. Vacuum line
39. Diaphragm
40. Guide pin
41. Air cleaner and oil filler bore

Diesel fuel injection pump.

in the normal direction of rotation, to line up the 45° BTDC mark with the pointer (No. 1 piston on compression stroke). Matchmark the pump and flange. Unscrew the nut at the bell-shaped support, then the front flange hold-down nuts. Pull the pump from the crankcase, then remove the coupling sleeve from the pump drive collar or driveshaft. New pumps do not come with the splined drive collar, therefore the old one must be removed if the pump is to be exchanged. Using a puller similar to the one illustrated, carefully remove the collar and Woodruff key.

To install the pump, note that the crankshaft has not moved from the 45° BTDC position, then insert the Woodruff key into its groove in the driveshaft, making sure the shaft is dirt free. Install the drive collar and hex nut, using a tape-wrapped pair of pliers to hold the collar while tightening the nut. It is extremely important that the splines are not damaged in any way during this operation. Try sliding the coupling sleeve onto the drive collar. If it slides on easily, it can be pressed onto the driveshaft (see illustration). Remove the oil overflow pipe plug at the rear of the injec-

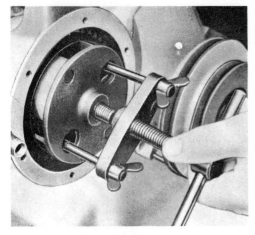
Removing injection timer.

Matchmarks on drive collar.

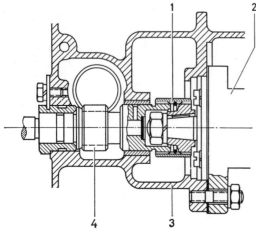

1. Coupling sleeve
2. Injection pump
3. Crankcase

4. Idling gear shaft
(driveshaft for
injection pump
and oil pump)

Injection pump drive.

tion pump and adjust start of delivery position by aligning marks as illustrated. Apply light finger pressure to the follower in a direction opposite normal direction of rotation (left). This pressure should cause the drive collar to jump two teeth. Grease the paper gaskets with Vaseline and install them to side of crankcase, then install pump, finger-tightening the bolts in the slotted holes. Turn the crankshaft in direction of rotation to 26° BTDC (or 24° BTDC for 220 D/8) and check the start of delivery, as outlined previously.

## Diesel Engine Tune-up

Some of the tune-up procedures have been covered in the troubleshooting section. For those who are not having any problems and wish to tune their engines as part of normal maintenance procedure, these tune-up jobs are listed below. (Starred items have been covered previously.)

1. Adjust idle speed.
*2. Check pneumatic governor for leakage.
3. Adjust idle control cable.
4. Adjust additional mechanical control (Stupser).
5. Adjust no-load maximum speed (governor).
6. Adjust full-load maximum speed (governor).
7. Adjust for minimum exhaust smoke.
8. Adjust valves.
*9. Check start of delivery.
*10. Check glow plugs and prechamber.
*11. Check and adjust start/stop cable.

While not a regular tune-up procedure, checking and adjustment of valve timing should be done, as it can affect performance to a considerable degree. It is also good practice to check this if the chain tensioner has been removed or replaced to rectify a noise condition (see Chapter 2 for general procedure).

**Idle Speed Adjustment**

To adjust idle speed, start the engine and allow it to come to normal operating temperature. Turn the idle control knob on the dashboard to the extreme right to get enough slack in the cable (4). It may

1. Vent line of crankcase ventilation system
2. Connecting rod (approximate length 310 mm.)
   to control valve lever
   (Venturi control unit)
3. Angle relay lever
4. Idle adjustment cable
5. Vacuum line between injection pump governor
   and Venturi control unit
6. Connecting rod (approximate length 205 mm.)
   to additional mechanical control lever
   (butt bolt)
7. Lever of additional mechanical control
   (butt bolt)

Diesel control linkage.

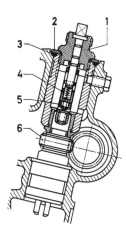

| | |
|---|---|
| 1. Revolution counter drive or adapter | 5. Cylindrical screw with hexagon socket |
| 2. Cover plate | |
| 3. Rubber ring | 6. Helical gear (driving oil pump and revolution counter) |
| 4. Follower or connecting piece between adapter and helical gear | |

Tachometer drive and oil pump drive.

be necessary to readjust the cable bracket to get the required free-play.

Since there is no electric ignition system, a mechanical tachometer take-off drive is provided, as shown in the illustration. (If such a tachometer is not available, adjust the idle speed by ear to about 700–800 rpm, manual transmission in neutral and automatic in drive, with the parking brake on fully and the wheels chocked. The ammeter light will go out when sufficient speed is reached.

To adjust the idle speed, turn the idle screw on the air intake in or out. If the vacuum line(5) is leaking, the idle speed will not drop when the screw is turned, so make sure both the line connections and the pneumatic governor are good before proceeding. Drain any fuel that might have leaked into the governor housing by unscrewing the oil level plug and loosening the governor housing bolts.

## Idle Control Cable

Turn the idle control knob on the dashboard to the extreme right and adjust the

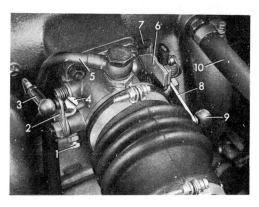

1. Full-load stop screw
2. Front control valve
3. Connecting rod from front control valve lever
   to angle lever for injection pump butt
   bolt operation
4. Idle stop screw
5. Vacuum line to injection pump
6. Check valve lever with stop for automatic
   opening and rubber damping (in this
   position the check valve is open)
7. Follower on rear control valve lever for
   automatic opening of check valve
8. Rear control valve lever
9. Connecting rod (approx. 250 mm. long) to
   reversing lever, pushrod, control shaft,
   pedal lever, foot-plate
10. Power brake line to vacuum pump

Air venturi and associated linkage.

cable to provide .004″–.008″ clearance between the adjusting ring and the relay lever. The cable must be checked for binding as well, and lubricated if necessary.

## Additional Mechanical Control

This control mechanism helps to eliminate idle speed variations, i.e., "hunting".

With the idle speed properly adjusted, detach the connecting rods [(2) (6) and (9) in illustration] and measure their length, center to center between ball sockets.

Connecting rod No. 2–310 mm. (12.1″)
Connecting rod No. 6–205 mm. (8.1″)
Connecting rod No. 9–250 mm. (9.8″)

With the rods adjusted, detach connecting rod No. 6 from the relay lever (3) and push it down until it rests against the idle stop. In this position, clearance between the ball socket and head should be .04″. If it requires more than .04″ lift to reattach the connecting rod, unscrew the ball socket.

## Maximum Speed Adjustment, No-Load Conditions

This adjustment must be made using a tachometer. The purpose of this adjustment is to limit the maximum engine revolutions so that the engine will never exceed its design speed in service. First, warm up the engine and press the accelerator to the floor. The full-load stop at the air venturi should be contacted by the linkage and the engine speed should not exceed 5,000 rpm. The speed can be adjusted by turning the full-load stop screw (1). If the throttle plate is already all the way open and the speed is not up to par, the injection pump control spring tension may be increased by shimming (see illustration). A .004″ shim will usually increase the engine speed by about 120–150 rpm, depending on the original tension of the spring.

*CAUTION: At first glance this appears to be an easy way to increase the engine speed range, thus the power output. Unfortunately, the power output decreases sharply above 5,000 rpm, and the reliability of the engine suffers as well, to the point of almost certain bearing failure or crankshaft destruction.*

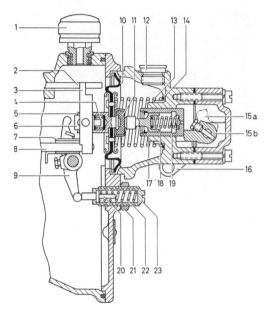

1. Air cleaner
2. Guide rod
3. Guide lever
4. Compensator spring
5. Diaphragm sleeve
6. Compensator pin
7. Start-metering stop
8. Control rod
9. Double-link rocker
10. Diaphragm
11. Rubber buffer
12. Vacuum union to vacuum chamber
13. Control spring
14. Backing ring
15a. Switch cam, full-load position
15b. Switch cam, idle position
16. Lever for automatic auxiliary governor system
17. Stop stud (butt bolt)
18. Auxiliary spring
19. Butt bolt housing or spring housing, sliding
20. Stop stud for full-load stop
21. Setting nut
22. Spring
23. Full-load stop screw

Vacuum system in idle position.

## Maximum Speed at Full-Load

If all aspects of engine and chassis performance have been checked and/or adjusted to produce optimum power and the car will not reach its maximum speed, the full-load stop screw can be adjusted further, or the injection pump control spring tension can be increased slightly. However, under no circumstances should the engine speed under no-load conditions be allowed to go over 5,000 rpm. If no-load engine speed is O.K., check the speedometer for accuracy, using a stopwatch and a turnpike measured mile.

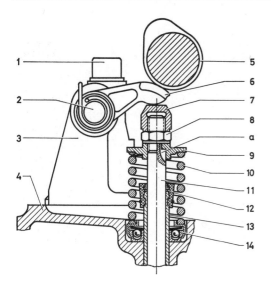

a. Groove in valve
   shaft
1. Extending screw
2. Rocker arm shaft
3. Rocker arm block
4. Cylinder head
5. Camshaft
6. Rocker arm
7. Cap nut
8. Hexagon nut
9. Valve spring re-
   tainer and seal-
   ing ring retainer
10. Valve spring
11. Valve shaft
12. Valve sealing ring
13. Valve guide
14. Valve rotator

Valve arrangement on diesel engines (220D/8 shown).

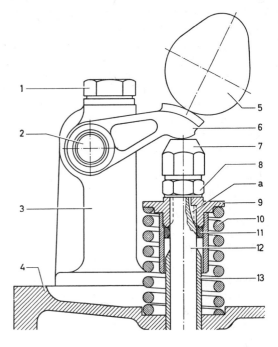

a. Groove in valve
   stem
1. Necked-down bolt
2. Rocker arm shaft
3. Rocker arm
   bracket
4. Cylinder head
5. Camshaft
6. Rocker arm
7. Cap nut
8. Hex nut
9. Valve spring re-
   tainer with seal
   ring holder
10. Valve spring
11. Rubber seal ring
12. Valve stem
13. Valve guide

On 190Dc and 200D, align camshaft with rocker arm as shown for valve adjustment.

| Model | Max. speed in second gear (mph) | Max. speed in third gear (mph) | Top speed (mph*) |
|---|---|---|---|
| 190 Dc | 34 | 54 | 77 |
| 200 D | 34 | 54 | 80 |
| 220 D/8 | 35 | 57 | 83 |

*Depends on transmission power drain.
*NOTE: The best full-load engine speed is 4,350 rpm.*

## Exhaust Smoke Emission

If the emission of black exhaust smoke seems excessive, test in the following manner: make all engine checks and adjustments and, with the engine fully tuned, road test the car on a slight grade. Accelerate in third gear from about 15 mph to the third-gear shift point mark on the speedometer. Have a passenger watch the exhaust smoke while doing this. If the smoke remains black and can be seen extending three or four feet behind, the maximum fuel delivery rate is too high. Adjust by screwing in the full-load stop screw on the *injection pump governor* about ¼ turn (see illustration). Repeat the road test and adjust in small increments until the smoke disappears. *CAUTION: Do not exceed ½ turn total.*

If the smoke level is still objectionable, the full-load stop screw on the *air venturi* can be adjusted to reduce maximum speed slightly, or the injection pump start of delivery can be retarded 2°.

## Valve Adjustment

Valve adjustment for diesel engines is basically the same as that given for gasoline engines in Chapter 2. On the diesel, however, the feeler gauge must be inserted between the rocker arm (6) and the cap nut (7), as in the illustration.

Remove the camshaft cover and turn the engine, using a wrench on the crankshaft pulley nut (22 mm.), until the TDC mark and the pointer line up.

This job can be accomplished easily if someone helps. First, a wrench must be placed on the valve spring retainer hex nut as illustrated (17). The hex nut (8) then must be loosened with another open end wrench, (bent to fit) (14), while the cap nut (7) is held with another wrench (16). The illustration shows this set up clearly.

Turn the cap nut (7) to adjust, then tighten the locknut (8) and recheck. Go on to the other cylinders as described in Chapter 2, turning the crankshaft to TDC position for each adjustment.

### Valve Timing

Follow the procedure in Chapter 2 for this job (glow plugs are removed instead of spark plugs). After valve timing is checked, measure the distance between the exhaust valve and the piston at 5° BTDC as well as the intake valve to piston clearance at 5° ATDC. (All measurements taken at top of exhaust stroke.) The clearance must be at least .050", intake and exhaust.

6. Rocker arm
7. Cap nut
8. Hexagon nut
9. Valve spring retainer with sealing ring retainer
14. Special wrench (621 589 01 01 00)
15. Feeler gauge
16. Special wrench (621 589 01 01 00)
17. Special wrench (621 589 00 03 00)

Adjusting valves on diesel engine.

Engine service procedures are basically the same as those for American-built engines. The only differences are in the valve gear service.

The illustration shows how to depress the valve spring using a special Mercedes-Benz tool. Automotive jobbers usually

---

## Valve and Cylinder Head Service

### Valve Seal Installation— Head Installed

In cases of excessive oil consumption traced to faulty valve stem seals, the seals can be replaced with the head installed.

Remove the camshaft cover and any obstructing linkage, then turn the engine over by hand to bring the pistons of the affected cylinders up to TDC.

Break the center out of an old spark plug and braze an air fitting onto it. Screw the fitting into the spark plug hole of the affected cylinder and maintain at least 180 psi pressure in the cylinder. This will hold the valve closed. It is important that the piston be exactly at top dead center, otherwise the air pressure will turn the engine over.

1. Valve retainer      2. Magnet

Removing valve spring with cylinder head installed.

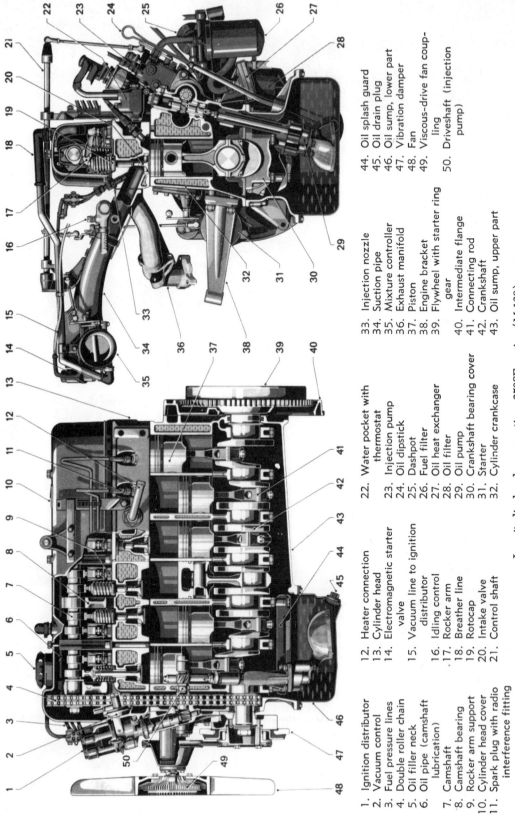

Longitudinal and cross-section—250SE engine (M 129).

1. Ignition distributor
2. Vacuum control
3. Fuel pressure lines
4. Double roller chain
5. Oil filler neck
6. Oil pipe (camshaft lubrication)
7. Camshaft
8. Camshaft bearing
9. Rocker arm support
10. Cylinder head cover
11. Spark plug with radio interference fitting
12. Heater connection
13. Cylinder head
14. Electromagnetic starter valve
15. Vacuum line to ignition distributor
16. Idling control
17. Rocker arm
18. Breather line
19. Rotocap
20. Intake valve
21. Control shaft
22. Water pocket with thermostat
23. Injection pump
24. Oil dipstick
25. Dashpot
26. Fuel filter
27. Oil heat exchanger
28. Oil filter
29. Oil pump
30. Crankshaft bearing cover
31. Starter
32. Cylinder crankcase
33. Injection nozzle
34. Suction pipe
35. Mixture controller
36. Exhaust manifold
37. Piston
38. Engine bracket
39. Flywheel with starter ring gear
40. Intermediate flange
41. Connecting rod
42. Crankshaft
43. Oil sump, upper part
44. Oil splash guard
45. Oil drain plug
46. Oil sump, lower part
47. Vibration damper
48. Fan
49. Viscous-drive fan coupling
50. Driveshaft (injection pump)

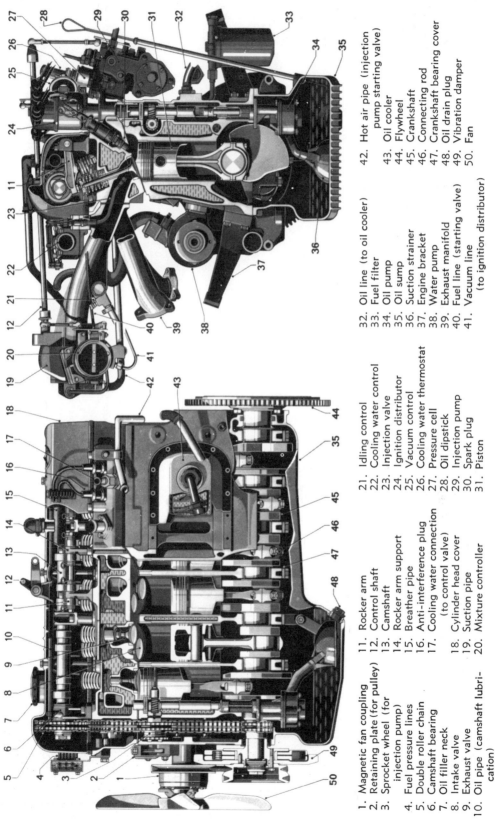

1. Magnetic fan coupling
2. Retaining plate (for pulley)
3. Sprocket wheel (for injection pump)
4. Fuel pressure lines
5. Double roller chain
6. Camshaft bearing
7. Oil filler neck
8. Intake valve
9. Exhaust valve
10. Oil pipe (camshaft lubrication)
11. Rocker arm
12. Control shaft
13. Camshaft
14. Rocker arm support
15. Breather pipe
16. Anti-interference plug
17. Cooling water connection (to control valve)
18. Cylinder head cover
19. Suction pipe
20. Mixture controller
21. Idling control
22. Cooling water control
23. Injection valve
24. Ignition distributor
25. Vacuum control
26. Cooling water thermostat
27. Pressure cell
28. Oil dipstick
29. Injection pump
30. Spark plug
31. Piston
32. Oil line (to oil cooler)
33. Fuel filter
34. Oil pump
35. Oil sump
36. Suction strainer
37. Engine bracket
38. Water pump
39. Exhaust manifold
40. Fuel line (starting valve)
41. Vacuum line (to ignition distributor)
42. Hot air pipe (injection pump starting valve)
43. Oil cooler
44. Flywheel
45. Crankshaft
46. Connecting rod
47. Crankshaft bearing cover
48. Oil drain plug
49. Vibration damper
50. Fan

Longitudinal and cross-section—300SE engine (M 189).

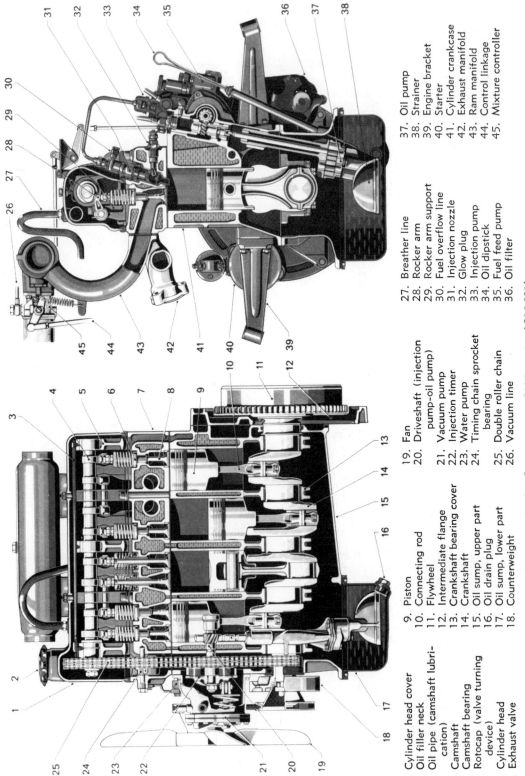

Longitudinal and cross-section—200D engine (OM 621).

1. Cylinder head cover
2. Oil filler neck
3. Oil pipe (camshaft lubrication)
4. Camshaft
5. Camshaft bearing
6. Rotocap (valve turning device)
7. Cylinder head
8. Exhaust valve
9. Piston
10. Connecting rod
11. Flywheel
12. Intermediate flange
13. Crankshaft bearing cover
14. Crankshaft
15. Oil sump, upper part
16. Oil drain plug
17. Oil sump, lower part
18. Counterweight
19. Fan
20. Driveshaft (injection pump–oil pump)
21. Vacuum pump
22. Injection timer
23. Water pump
24. Timing chain sprocket bearing
25. Double roller chain
26. Vacuum line
27. Breather line
28. Rocker arm
29. Rocker arm support
30. Fuel overflow line
31. Injection nozzle
32. Glow plug
33. Injection pump
34. Oil dipstick
35. Fuel feed pump
36. Oil filter
37. Oil pump
38. Strainer
39. Engine bracket
40. Starter
41. Cylinder crankcase
42. Exhaust manifold
43. Ram manifold
44. Control linkage
45. Mixture controller

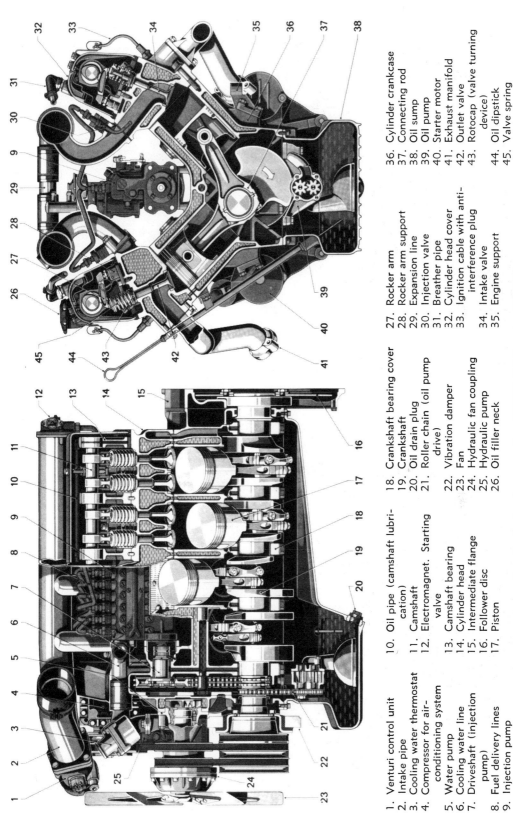

1. Venturi control unit
2. Intake pipe
3. Cooling water thermostat
4. Compressor for air-conditioning system
5. Water pump
6. Cooling water line
7. Driveshaft (injection pump)
8. Fuel delivery lines
9. Injection pump
10. Oil pipe (camshaft lubrication)
11. Camshaft
12. Electromagnet. Starting valve
13. Camshaft bearing
14. Cylinder head
15. Intermediate flange
16. Follower disc
17. Piston
18. Crankshaft bearing cover
19. Crankshaft
20. Oil drain plug
21. Roller chain (oil pump drive)
22. Vibration damper
23. Fan
24. Hydraulic fan coupling
25. Hydraulic pump
26. Oil filler neck
27. Rocker arm
28. Rocker arm support
29. Expansion line
30. Injection valve
31. Breather pipe
32. Cylinder head cover
33. Ignition cable with anti-interference plug
34. Intake valve
35. Engine support
36. Cylinder crankcase
37. Connecting rod
38. Oil sump
39. Oil pump
40. Starter motor
41. Exhaust manifold
42. Outlet valve
43. Rotocap (valve turning device)
44. Oil dipstick
45. Valve spring

Longitudinal and cross-section—300SEL/8 6.3 engine (M 100).

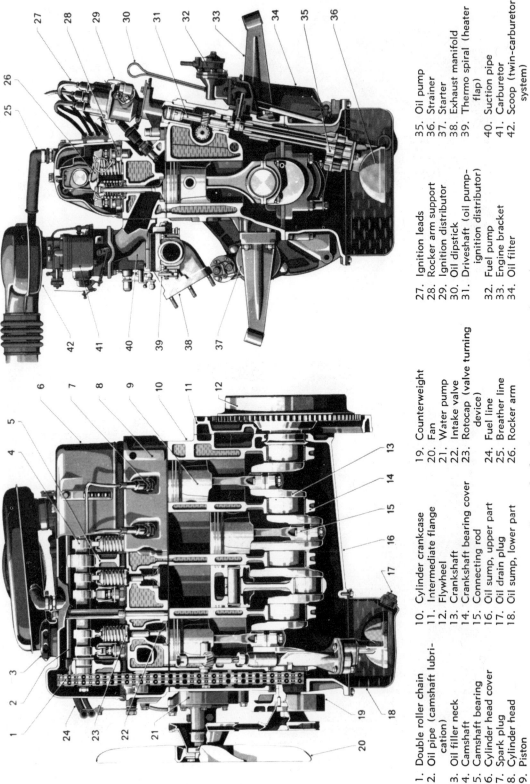

1. Double roller chain
2. Oil pipe (camshaft lubrication)
3. Oil filler neck
4. Camshaft
5. Camshaft bearing
6. Cylinder head cover
7. Spark plug
8. Cylinder head
9. Piston
10. Cylinder crankcase
11. Intermediate flange
12. Flywheel
13. Crankshaft
14. Crankshaft bearing cover
15. Connecting rod
16. Oil sump, upper part
17. Oil drain plug
18. Oil sump, lower part
19. Counterweight
20. Fan
21. Water pump
22. Intake valve
23. Rotocap (valve turning
    device)
24. Fuel line
25. Breather line
26. Rocker arm
27. Ignition leads
28. Rocker arm support
29. Ignition distributor
30. Oil dipstick
31. Driveshaft (oil pump–
    ignition distributor)
32. Fuel pump
33. Engine bracket
34. Oil filter
35. Oil pump
36. Strainer
37. Starter
38. Exhaust manifold
39. Thermo spiral (heater
    flap)
40. Suction pipe
41. Carburetor
42. Scoop (twin-carburetor
    system)

Longitudinal and cross-section—200 engine (M 121).

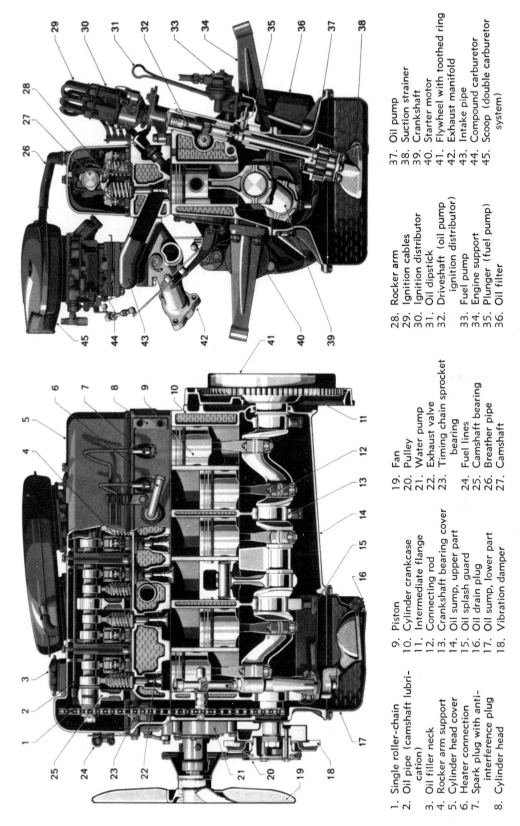

1. Single roller-chain
2. Oil pipe (camshaft lubrication)
3. Oil filler neck
4. Rocker arm support
5. Cylinder head cover
6. Heater connection
7. Spark plug with anti-interference plug
8. Cylinder head
9. Piston
10. Cylinder crankcase
11. Intermediate flange
12. Connecting rod
13. Crankshaft bearing cover
14. Oil sump, upper part
15. Oil splash guard
16. Oil drain plug
17. Oil sump, lower part
18. Vibration damper
19. Fan
20. Pulley
21. Water pump
22. Exhaust valve
23. Timing chain sprocket bearing
24. Fuel lines
25. Camshaft bearing
26. Breather pipe
27. Camshaft
28. Rocker arm
29. Ignition cables
30. Ignition distributor
31. Oil dipstick
32. Driveshaft (oil pump ignition distributor)
33. Fuel pump
34. Engine support
35. Plunger (fuel pump)
36. Oil filter
37. Oil pump
38. Suction strainer
39. Crankshaft
40. Starter motor
41. Flywheel with toothed ring
42. Exhaust manifold
43. Intake pipe
44. Compound carburetor
45. Scoop (double carburetor system)

Longitudinal and cross-section—230S engine (M 180).

## General Engine Specifications

| Model | Engine Model | Engine Type | Bore and Stroke (mm.) | Displace. (cc.) | Compress. Ratio | Firing Order | Number Cylinders | Horsepower @ rpm (SAE) | Torque @ rpm (ft. lbs.) | Max. rpm | Number Main Bearings |
|---|---|---|---|---|---|---|---|---|---|---|---|
| 190c | M121B.V | 121.924 | 85.00x83.60 | 1,897 | 8.7:1 | 1-3-4-2 | 4 | 90 @ 5,200 | 113 @ 2,700 | 6,000 | 3 |
| 200 | M121B.XI | 121.940 | 87.00x83.60 | 1,988 | 9.0:1 | 1-3-4-2 | 4 | 105 @ 5,200 | 113 @ 3,600 | 6,000 | 5 |
| 230 | M180.VI | 180.945 | 82.00x72.80 | 2,306 | 9.0:1 | 1-5-3-6-2-4 | 6 | 118 @ 5,400 | 137 @ 3,800 | 6,000 | 4 |
|  | M180.X [1] | 180.949 | 82.00x72.80 | 2,306 | 9.0:1 | 1-5-3-6-2-4 | 6 | 135 @ 5,600 | 145 @ 4,200 | 6,000 | 4 |
| 220b | M180.IV | 180.940 | 80.00x72.80 | 2,195 | 8.7:1 | 1-5-3-6-2-4 | 6 | 105 @ 5,000 | 133 @ 3,300 | 6,000 | 4 |
| 220Sb | M180.V | 180.941 | 80.00x72.80 | 2,195 | 9.0:1 | 1-5-3-6-2-4 | 6 | 124 @ 5,200 | 139 @ 3,700 | 6,000 | 4 |
| 230S | M180.VIII | 180.947 | 82.00x72.80 | 2,306 | 9.0:1 | 1-5-3-6-2-4 | 6 | 135 @ 5,600 | 145 @ 4,200 | 6,000 | 4 |
| 250S | M108.I | 108.920 | 82.00x78.80 | 2,496 | 9.0:1 | 1-5-3-6-2-4 | 6 | 146 @ 5,600 | 157 @ 4,200 | 6,300 | 7 |
| 220SEb | M127.III | 127.982 | 80.00x72.80 | 2,195 | 8.7:1 | 1-5-3-6-2-4 | 6 | 134 @ 5,000 | 152 @ 4,100 | 6,000 | 4 |
| 250SE | M129.I | 129.980 | 82.00x78.80 | 2,496 | 9.5:1 | 1-5-3-6-2-4 | 6 | 170 @ 5,600 | 174 @ 4,500 | 6,300 | 7 |
| 250SE/C [2] | M129.I | 129.980 | 82.00x78.80 | 2,496 | 9.5:1 | 1-5-3-6-2-4 | 6 | 170 @ 5,600 | 174 @ 4,500 | 6,300 | 7 |
| 230SL | M127.II | 127.981 | 82.00x72.80 | 2,306 | 9.5:1 | 1-5-3-6-2-4 | 6 | 170 @ 5,600 | 159 @ 4,500 | 6,500 | 4 |
| 250SL | M129.III | 129.982 | 82.00x78.80 | 2,496 | 9.5:1 | 1-5-3-6-2-4 | 6 | 170 @ 5,600 | 174 @ 4,500 | 6,500 | 7 |
| 220SEb/C [2] | M127.V | 127.984 | 80.00x72.80 | 2,195 | 8.7:1 | 1-5-3-6-2-4 | 6 | 134 @ 5,000 | 152 @ 4,100 | 6,000 | 4 |
| 300SE | M189.III [3] | 189.984 | 85.00x88.00 | 2,996 | 8.7:1 | 1-5-3-6-2-4 | 6 | 185 @ 5,200 | 204 @ 4,000 | 6,000 | 7 |
| 300SE [4] | M189.V [3] | 189.986 | 85.00x88.00 | 2,996 | 8.8:1 | 1-5-3-6-2-4 | 6 | 195 @ 5,500 | 203 @ 4,100 | 6,000 | 7 |
| 300SE [6] | M189.IV [3] | 189.985 | 85.00x88.00 | 2,996 | 8.7:1 | 1-5-3-6-2-4 | 6 | 185 @ 5,200 | 204 @ 4,000 | 6,000 | 7 |
| 300SE [2] [8] | M189.VI [5] | 189.987 | 85.00x88.00 | 2,996 | 8.8:1 | 1-5-3-6-2-4 | 6 | 195 @ 5,500 | 203 @ 4,100 | 6,000 | 7 |
| 300SEb | M189.VIII | 189.989 | 85.00x88.00 | 2,996 | 8.8:1 | 1-5-3-6-2-4 | 6 | 195 @ 5,500 | 203 @ 4,100 | 6,000 | 7 |
| 300SEL | M189.VII | 189.988 | 85.00x88.00 | 2,996 | 8.8:1 | 1-5-3-6-2-4 | 6 | 195 @ 5,500 | 203 @ 4,100 | 6,000 | 7 |
| 220/8 | M115 | 115.920 | 87.00x92.40 | 2,197 | 9.0:1 | 1-3-4-2 | 4 | 116 @ 5,200 | 142 @ 3,000 | 6,000 | 5 |
| 230/8 [9] | M180 | 180.954 | 81.75x72.80 | 2,292 | 9.0:1 | 1-5-3-6-2-4 | 6 | 135 @ 5,600 | 145 @ 3,800 | 6,300 | 4 |
| 250/8 | M114 | 114.920 | 82.00x78.80 | 2,496 | 9.0:1 | 1-5-3-6-2-4 | 6 | 146 @ 5,600 | 161 @ 3,800 | 6,300 | 7 |
| 280S/8 | M130 | 130.920 | 86.50x78.80 | 2,778 | 9.0:1 | 1-5-3-6-2-4 | 6 | 157 @ 5,400 | 181 @ 3,800 | 6,500 | 7 |
| 280SE/8 [10] | M130 | 130.980 | 86.50x78.80 | 2,778 | 9.5:1 | 1-5-3-6-2-4 | 6 | 180 @ 5,750 | 193 @ 4,500 | 6,500 | 7 |
| 280SL/8 | M130 | 130.983 | 86.50x78.80 | 2,778 | 9.5:1 | 1-5-3-6-2-4 | 6 | 180 @ 5,750 | 193 @ 4,500 | 6,500 | 7 |
| 300SEL/8 | M130 | 130.981 | 86.50x78.80 | 2,778 | 9.5:1 | 1-5-3-6-2-4 | 6 | 180 @ 5,750 | 193 @ 4,500 | 6,500 | 7 |
| 300SEL/8 6.3 | M100 | 100.981 | 103.00x95.00 | 6,332 | 9.0:1 | 1-5-4-8-6-3-7-2 | 8 | 300 @ 4,100 | 434 @ 3,000 | 5,250 | 5 |

[1] INAT carburetors from chassis No. 110,011-10-317649.
[2] Coupe and convertible.
[3] First version.
[4] Long wheelbase.
[5] Second version.
[6] Coupe to August, 1965.
[7] Convertible to August, 1965.
[8] From August, 1965. (Same engine as previous second version 300SE convertible)
[9] Not imported as of August, 1969.
[10] Sedan, coupe, convertible and long wheelbase (280SEL/8).

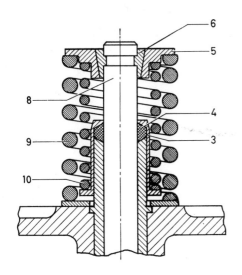

1. Snap-ring
2. Valve spring washer
3. Sealing ring retainer
4. Silicone valve seal
5. Valve spring retainer
6. Valve retainer
7. Pressure piece
8. Intake valve
9. Outer valve spring
10. Inner valve spring

Intake valve—300SE.

stock similar inexpensive tools, and one of these can be adapted, or one can be manufactured out of ¼″ flat stock, suitably bent and hardened, and some heavy washers.

Striking the valve stem sharply with a hammer sometimes loosens stubborn retainers, but this should not be done unless absolutely necessary. The diagrams show some typical valve seal configurations; but it is best to examine the seals you are working on and compare with new ones, because different versions were used in production.

## Cylinder Head Removal

In order to perform a valve job or to inspect cylinder bores for wear, the head must be removed. While this may seem fairly straightforward, some precautions must be observed to ensure that valve timing is not disturbed.

Drain the radiator and remove all hoses and wires. Remove the camshaft cover and associated throttle linkage, then press out the spring clamp (2) from the notch in the rocker arm (3). Push the clamp outward over the ball cap of the rocker, then depress the valve, using a tool similar to the

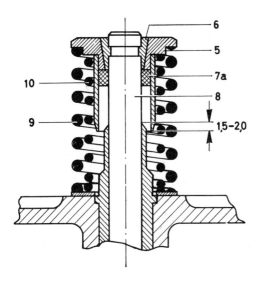

1. Snap-ring
2. Thrust collar
3. Sealing ring retainer
4. Valve seal
5. Valve spring retainer
6. Valve keeper
7. Pressure piece
8. Exhaust valve
9. Outer valve spring
10. Inner valve spring

Exhaust valve—300SE.

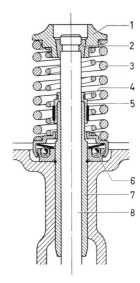

1. Valve spring retainer
2. Valve keeper
3. Outer valve spring
4. Inner valve spring
5. Teflon valve seal
6. Rotocap
7. Valve guide
8. Valve

Intake and exhaust valve—230SL.

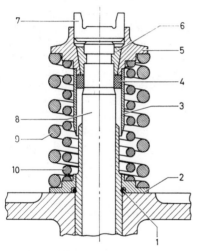

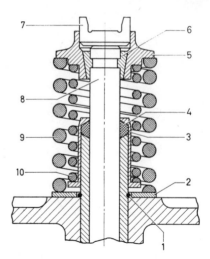

Exhaust valve—220b, 220Sb, 220SEb. Intake and exhaust valve—190c.

Intake valve—220b, 220Sb, 220SEb.

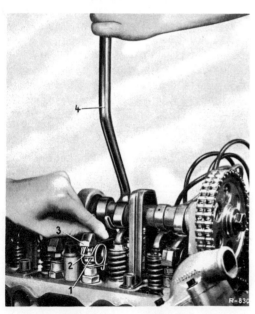

1. Ball pin head          4. Tool for removal
2. Spring clamp              (112 589 08 -
3. Rocker arm                61 00)

Removing valve train.

one described above, or a large screwdriver, and lift the rocker arm out of the ball pin head (1).

Remove the rocker arm supports and the camshaft sprocket nut. On diesels, the rockers and their supports must be removed together. Using a suitable puller, remove the camshaft sprocket, after having first marked the chain, sprocket and cam

for ease in assembly. Remove the sprocket and chain and wire it out of the way. *CAUTION: Make sure the chain is securely wired so that it will not slide down into the engine.*

Unbolt the manifolds and exhaust header pipe and push them out of the way, then loosen the cylinder head hold-down bolts in the reverse order of that shown in torque diagrams for each model. It is good practice to loosen each bolt a little at a time, working around the head, until all are free. This prevents unequal stresses in the metal.

Reach into the engine compartment and gradually work the head loose from each end by rocking it. Never, under any circumstances, use a screwdriver between the head and block to pry, as the head will be scarred badly and may be ruined.

**Timing Chain Replacement**

This operation can be done with everything in place. Remove only the camshaft cover, spark plugs, chain tensioner (see Chapter 3) and the rocker arm blocks.

With a high-speed grinder, grind off two chain rivets and remove one link. Connect the end of the new chain to one end of the old using a removable link (similar to ones used on motorcycle chains). Now, simply pull the old chain out from the other end while feeding in the new chain. *NOTE: Go in normal direction of rotation.* Make sure the new chain turns the camshaft as it goes around. Unhook the old chain and

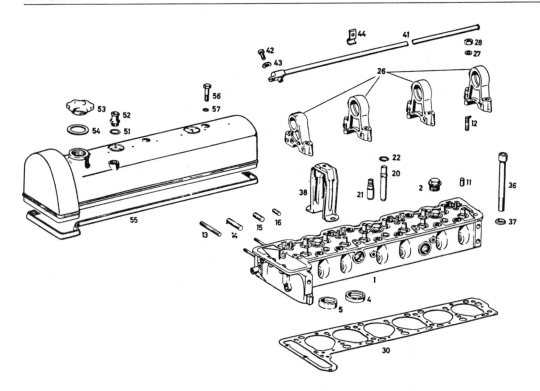

Six-cylinder head and associated parts—250SL, 280SL illustrated.

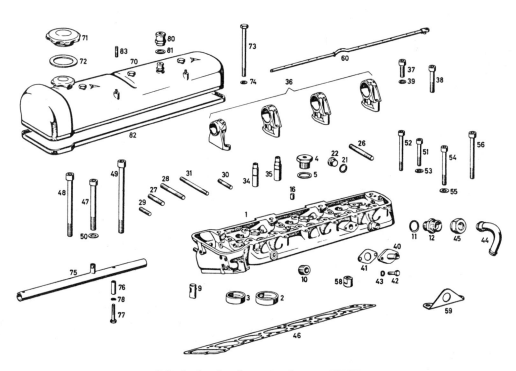

Cylinder head and associated parts—300SE.

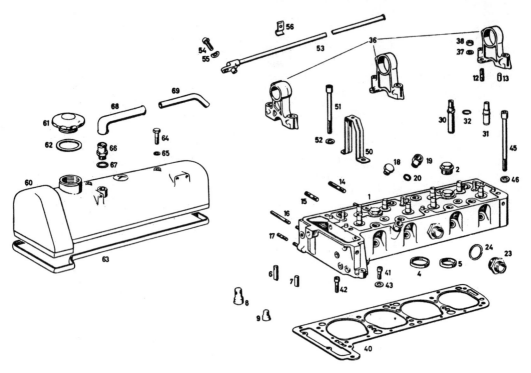

Four-cylinder head and associated parts.

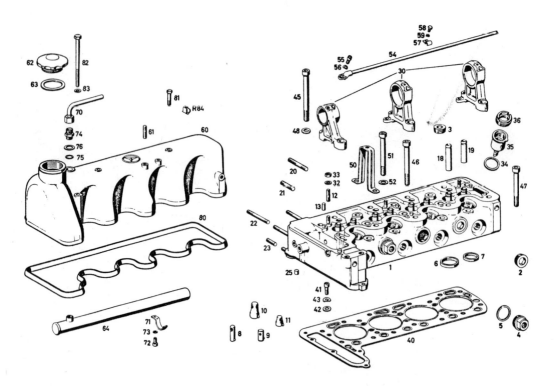

Diesel cylinder head and associated parts.

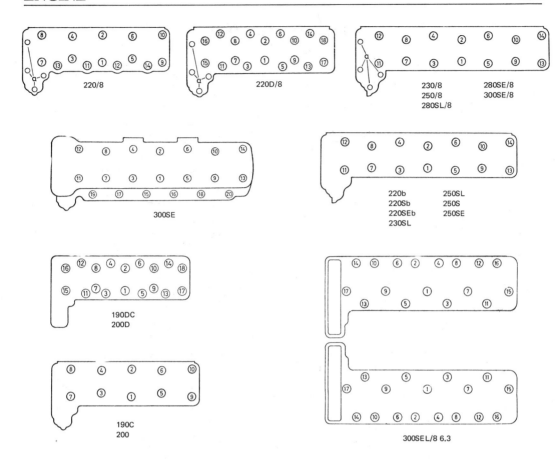

Cylinder head torque sequence.

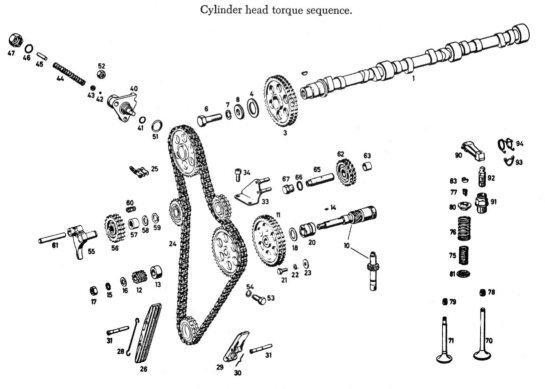

Six-cylinder valve train—250SL, 280SL illustrated.

# Torque Specifications
(Ft.lbs.)

| Model | Cylinder head bolts | | Rocker arm mounting bolts | Rocker block bolts | Connecting rod cap bolts | Main Bearing cap bolts | Flywheel bolts | | Oil pan bolts | Spark or glow plugs |
|---|---|---|---|---|---|---|---|---|---|---|
| | Cold ① | Hot ② | | | | | Man. | Auto. | | |
| 190c | 58 | 65 | 72 | | 27 | 65 | 40+3.5 | 33+3.5 | 5.8 | 21—26 |
| 200 | 58 | 65 | 72 | | 27 | 65 | 40+3.5 | 33+3.5 | 5.8 | 21—26 |
| 190Dc | 65 | 65 | | 27 | 27 | 65 | 40+3.5 | 33+3.5 | 5.8 | 36 |
| 200D | 65 | 65 | | 27 | 27 | 65 | 40+3.5 | 33+3.5 | 5.8 | 36 |
| 230 | 58 | 65 | 72 | | 44 | 58 | 47+3.5 | 47+3.5 | 5.8 | 21—26 |
| 220b | 58 | 65 | 72 | | 27 | 65 | 40+3.5 | 33+3.5 | 5.8 | 21—26 |
| 220Sb | 58 | 65 | 72 | | 27 | 65 | 40+3.5 | 33+3.5 | 5.8 | 21—26 |
| 230S | 58 | 65 | 72 | | 44 | 58 | 47+3.5 | 47+3.5 | 5.8 | 21—26 |
| 250S | 58 | 65 | 72 | | 43 | 58 | 69+3.5 | 69+3.5 | 5.8 | 21—26 |
| 220SEb | 58 | 65 | 72 | | 27 | 58 | 47+3.5 | 47+3.5 | 5.8 | 21—26 |
| 250SE | 58 | 65 | 72 | | 43 | 58 | 69+3.5 | 69+3.5 | 5.8 | 21—26 |
| 230SL | 58 | 65 | 72 | | 27 | 58 | 69+3.5 | 47+3.5 | 5.8 | 21—26 |
| 250SL | 58 | 65 | 72 | | 43 | 58 | 69+3.5 | 69+3.5 | 5.8 | 21—26 |
| 220SEb/C | 58 | 65 | 72 | | 27 | 58 | 47+3.5 | 47+3.5 | 5.8 | 21—26 |
| 250SE/C | 58 | 65 | 72 | | 43 | 58 | 69+3.5 | 69+3.5 | 5.8 | 21—26 |
| 300SE | 72 | 80 | | 27 | 27 | 36±1.4 | 32+1.4 | 32+1.4 | 5.8 | 21—26 |
| 300SEb | 72 | 80 | | 27 | 27 | 36±1.4 | 32+1.4 | 32+1.4 | 5.8 | 21—26 |
| 300SEL | 72 | 80 | | 27 | 27 | 36±1.4 | 32+1.4 | 32+1.4 | 5.8 | 21—26 |
| 220D/8 | 65 | 65 | | 27 | 40 | 65 | 21+7③ | 21+7③ | 8 | 36 |
| 220/8 | 58 | 65 | 58 | | 40 | 65 | 21+7③ | 21+7③ | 8 | 22 |
| 230/8 | 58 | 65 | 58 | | 45-2.1 | 58 | 21+7③ | 21+7③ | 8 | 22 |
| 250/8 | 58 | 65 | 58 | | 45-2.1 | 58 | 21+7③ | 21+7③ | 8 | 22 |
| 280S/8 | 72 | 80 | | | 45 | 65 | 21+7③ | 21+7③ | 8 | 22 |
| 280SE/8 | 72 | 80 | | | 45 | 65 | 21+7③ | 21+7③ | 8 | 22 |
| 280SL/8 | 72 | 80 | | | 45 | 65 | 21+7③ | 21+7③ | 8 | 22 |
| 300SEL/8 | 72 | 80 | | | 45 | 65 | 21+7③ | 21+7③ | 8 | 22 |

*NOTE: Lubricate all bolts with engine oil before insertion; do not use Molykote.*

① *36 ft.lbs. for M 10 bolts.*
② *43 ft.lbs. for M 10 bolts.*
③ *Plus tightening angle — 220/8, 220D/8: 60° + 10°*
*230/8, 250/8,*
*280S/8, 280SE/8,*
*280SL/8, 300SEL/8: 90° + 10°.*

## Crankshaft Specifications

| Model | Stand. Main Bearing Journal Diam. (mm.) | Stand. Connect. Rod Bearing Journal Diam. (mm.) | Journal out-of-round Tolerance (mm.) | Maximum Journal Taper (mm./in.) | Journal Fillet Radii (mm./in.) | Flywheel Flange Runout (mm./in.) | Maximum Unbalance (cm. g.) | Main Bearing Oil Clearance (mm./in.) | Crankshaft End-Play (mm./in.) |
|---|---|---|---|---|---|---|---|---|---|
| 190c | 69.955–69.965 | 51.955–51.965 | .005–.01 | .01/.0004 | 2.5–3.0/.097–.117 | .010/.0004 | 15 | .045–.060/.0017–.0023 | .100–.175/.004–.007 |
| 200 | 69.955–69.965 | 51.955–51.965 | .005–.01 | .01/.0004 | 2.5–3.0/.097–.117 | .010/.0004 | 15 | .045–.060/.0017–.0023 | .100–.175/.004–.007 |
| 190Dc | 69.955–69.965 | 51.955–51.965 | .005–.01 | .01/.0004 | 2.5–3.0/.097–.117 | .010/.0004 | 15 | .045–.060/.0017–.0023 | .100–.175/.004–.007 |
| 200D | 69.955–69.965 | 51.955–51.965 | .005–.01 | .01/.0004 | 2.5–3.0/.097–.117 | .010/.0004 | 15 | .045–.065/.0017–.0025 | .100–.175/.004–.007 |
| 230 | 59.955–59.965 | 47.955–47.965 | .005–.01 | .01/.0004 | 2.5–3.0/.097–.117 | .012/.0005 | 15 | .045–.060/.0017–.0023 | .100–.175/.004–.007 |
| 220b | 59.955–59.965 | 47.955–47.965 | .005–.01 | .01/.0004 | 2.5–3.0/.097–.117 | .012/.0005 | 15 | .045–.060/.0017–.0023 | .100–.175/.004–.007 |
| 220Sb | 59.955–59.965 | 47.955–47.965 | .005–.01 | .01/.0004 | 2.5–3.0/.097–.117 | .012/.0005 | 15 | .045–.060/.0017–.0023 | .100–.175/.004–.007 |
| 230S | 59.955–59.965 | 47.955–47.965 | .005–.01 | .01/.0004 | 2.5–3.0/.097–.117 | .012/.0005 | 15 | .045–.060/.0017–.0023 | .100–.175/.004–.007 |
| 250S | 59.955–59.965 | 47.955–47.965 | .005–.01 | .01/.0004 | 2.5–3.0/.097–.117 | .012/.0005 | 15 | .045–.060/.0017–.0023 | .100–.175/.004–.007 |
| 220SEb | 59.955–59.965 | 47.055–47.965 | .005–.01 | .01/.0004 | 2.5–3.0/.097–.117 | .012/.0005 | 15 | .045–.060/.0017–.0023 | .100–.175/.004–.007 |
| 250SE | 59.955–59.965 | 47.055–47.965 | .005–.01 | .01/.0004 | 2.5–3.0/.097–.117 | .012/.0005 | 15 | .045–.060/.0017–.0023 | .100–.175/.004–.007 |
| 230SL | 59.955–59.965 | 47.055–47.965 | .005–.01 | .01/.0004 | 2.5–3.0/.097–.117 | .012/.0005 | 15 | .045–.060/.0017–.0023 | .100–.175/.004–.007 |
| 250SL | 59.955–59.965 | 47.055–47.065 | .005–.01 | .01/.0004 | 2.5–3.0/.097–.117 | .012/.0005 | 15 | .045–.060/.0017–.0023 | .100–.175/.004–.007 |
| 250SE/C | 59.955–59.965 | 47.055–47.065 | .005–.01 | .01/.0004 | 2.5–3.0/.097–.117 | .012/.0005 | 15 | .045–.060/.0017–.0023 | .100–.175/.004–.007 |
| 300SE | 59.950–59.970 | 51.950–51.970 | .005–.01 | .01/.0004 | 2.5–3.0/.097–.117 | .015/.0006 | 20 | .030–.055/.0012–.0023 | .100–.240/.004–.010 |
| 300SEb | 59.950–59.970 | 51.950–51.970 | .005–.01 | .01/.0004 | 2.5–3.0/.097–.117 | .015/.0006 | 20 | .030–.055/.0012–.0023 | .100–.240/.004–.010 |
| 300SEL | 59.950–59.970 | 51.050–51.970 | .005–.01 | .01/.0004 | 2.5–3.0/.097–.117 | .015/.0006 | 20 | .030–.055/.0012–.0023 | .100–.240/.004–.010 |
| 300SE/C | 59.950–59.970 | 51.050–51.970 | .005–.01 | .01/.0004 | 2.5–3.0/.097–.117 | .015/.0006 | 20 | .030–.055/.0012–.0023 | .100–.240/.004–.010 |
| 220D/8 | 69.955–60.965 | 51.955–51.965 | .005–.01 | .01/.0004 | 2.5–3.0/.097–.117 | .010/.0004 | 15 | .045–.065/.0017–.0025 | .100–.240/.004–.010 |
| 220/8 | 69.955–69.965 | 51.955–51.965 | .005–.01 | .01/.0004 | 2.5–3.0/.097–.117 | .010/.0004 | 15 | .045–.065/.0017–.0025 | .100–.175/.004–.007 |
| 230/8 | 59.955–59.965 | 47.955–47.965 | .005–.01 | .01/.0004 | 2.5–3.0/.097–.117 | .012/.0005 | 15 | .045–.065/.0017–.0025 | .100–.175/.004–.007 |
| 250/8 | 59.955–59.965 | 47.955–47.965 | .005–.01 | .01/.0004 | 2.5–3.0/.097–.117 | .012/.0005 | 15 | .045–.065/.0017–.0025 | .100–.175/.004–.007 |
| 280S/8 | 59.955–59.965 | 47.955–47.965 | .005–.01 | .01/.0004 | 2.5–3.0/.097–.117 | .012/.0005 | 15 | .045–.065/.0017–.0025 | .100–.175/.004–.007 |
| 280SE/8 | 59.955–59.965 | 47.955–47.965 | .005–.01 | .01/.0004 | 2.5–3.0/.097–.117 | .012/.0005 | 15 | .045–.065/.0017–.0025 | .100–.175/.004–.007 |
| 280SEL/8 | 59.955–59.965 | 47.955–47.965 | .005–.01 | .01/.0004 | 2.5–3.0/.097–.117 | .012/.0005 | 15 | .045–.065/.0017–.0025 | .100–.175/.004–.007 |
| 280SL/8 | 59.955–59.965 | 47.955–47.965 | .005–.01 | .01/.0004 | 2.5–3.0/.097–.117 | .012/.0005 | 15 | .045–.065/.0017–.0025 | .100–.175/.004–.007 |
| 300SEL/8 2.8 | 59.955–59.965 | 47.955–47.965 | .005–.01 | .01/.0004 | 2.5–3.0/.097–.117 | .012/.0005 | 15 | .045–.065/.0017–.0025 | .100–.175/.004–.007 |
| 300SEL/8 6.3 | 69.955–69.965 | 54.940–54.960 | .005–.01 | .01/.0004 | 2.5–3.0/.097–.117 | .015/.0006 | 40 | .045–.065/.0017–.0025 | .100–.240/.004–.010 |

# Cylinder Head Specifications

| Model | Height of New Head (mm.) | Maximum Material Removal (mm./in.) | Maximum Longitudinal Eccentricity (mm./in.) | Maximum Lateral Eccentricity (mm./in.) | Total Compress. Space with Head Installed (cc.) | Compress. Ratio (:1) | Combust. Chamber Volume with Valves and Plugs (cc.) |
|---|---|---|---|---|---|---|---|
| 190c | 84.8—85.0 | 1.0/.039 | 0.1/.0039 | 0/0 | 60.8—64.1 | 8.7 | 51.1—52.1 |
| 200 | 84.8—85.0 | 1.0/.039 | 0.1/.0039 | 0 | 61.4—64.6 | 9.0 | 49.5—50.5 |
| 190Dc | 84.8—85.0 | 0.8/.031 | 0.1/.0039 | 0 | 23.5—25.5③② | 21.0 | |
| 200D | 84.8—85.0 | 0.8/.031 | 0.1/.0039 | 0 | 23.5—25.5③② | 21.0 | |
| 230 | 84.8—85.0 | 0.8/.031 | 0.1/.0039 | 0 | ④ | ④ | ④ |
| 220b | 84.8—85.0 | 0.8/.031 | 0.1/.0039 | 0 | ① | ① | ① |
| 220Sb | 84.8—85.0 | 0.8/.031 | 0.1/.0039 | 0 | ① | ① | ① |
| 230S | 84.8—85.0 | 0.8/.031 | 0.1/.0039 | 0 | ④ | ④ | ④ |
| 250S | 84.8—85.0 | 0.8/.031 | 0.1/.0039 | 0 | ④ | ④ | ④ |
| 220SEb | 84.8—85.0 | 0.8/.031 | 0.1/.0039 | 0 | ① | ① | ① |
| 250SE | 84.8—85.0 | 0.8/.031 | 0.1/.0039 | 0 | 48.0—50.7 | 9.5 | 40.7—41.7 |
| 230SL | 84.8—85.0 | 0.8/.031 | 0.1/.0039 | 0 | 45.3—48.0 | 9.5 | 37.5—38.5 |
| 250SL | 84.8—85.0 | 0.8/.031 | 0.1/.0039 | 0 | not available | 9.5 | not available |
| 250SE/C | 84.8—85.0 | 0.8/.031 | 0.1/.0039 | 0 | 48.0—50.7 | 9.5 | 40.7—41.7 |
| 300SE | See illus. A & B | 0.8/.031 | 0.08/.0031 | 0 | 62.0—65.0 ② | 8.8 | |
| 300SEb | See illus. A & B | 0.8/.031 | 0.08/.0031 | 0 | 62.0—65.0 | 8.8 | |
| 300SEL | See illus. A & B | 0.8/.031 | 0.08/.0031 | 0 | 62.0—65.0 | 8.8 | |
| 300SE/C | See illus. A & B | 0.8/.031 | 0.08/.0031 | 0 | 62.0—65.0 | 8.8 | |
| 220D/8 | 84.8—85.0 | 0.8/.031 | 0.1/.0039 | 0 | 27.0—28.0③② | 21.0 | |
| 220/8 | 84.8—85.0 | 1.0/.039 | 0.1/.0039 | 0 | 67.8—71.1 | 9.0 | 57.6—58.6 |
| 230/8 | 84.8—85.0 | 0.8/.031 | 0.1/.0039 | 0 | 47.0—49.7 | 9.0 | 37.6—38.6 |
| 250/8 | 84.8—85.0 | 0.8/.031 | 0.1/.0039 | 0 | 51.0—53.7 | 9.0 | 42.4—43.4 |
| 280S/8 | 84.8—85.0 | 0.8/.031 | 0.1/.0039 | 0 | not available | 9.0 | not available |
| 280SE/8 | 84.8—85.0 | 0.8/.031 | 0.1/.0039 | 0 | not available | 9.5 | not available |
| 280SEL/8 | 84.8—85.0 | 0.8/.031 | 0.1/.0039 | 0 | not available | 9.5 | not available |
| 280SL/8 | 84.8—85.0 | 0.8/.031 | 0.1/.0039 | 0 | not available | 9.5 | not available |
| 300SEL/8 2.8 | 84.8—85.0 | 0.8/.031 | 0.1/.0039 | 0 | not available | 9.5 | not available |
| 300SEL/8 6.3 | See illus. D | 0.5/.020 | 0.08/.0031 | 0 | 98.0—102.0 | 9.0 | 86.7—88.7 |

① *As of engine numbers:*

| | |
|---|---|
| 180 940—10—044 200 | 127 982—10—031 774 |
| 180 940—12—000 517 | 127 982—12—004 498 |
| 180 941—10—091 448 | 127 984—10—006 556 |
| 180 941—12—003 491 | 127 984—12—001 611 |

| Combustion Chamber | Compress. Ratio (:1) | Total Compress. Space (cc.) | Compress. Space in Head (cc.) |
|---|---|---|---|
| No. 1 cylinder | 8.7 | 49.5-53.1 | 39.0-40.0 |
| No. 2 cylinder | 8.5 | 48.2-50.8 | 37.7-38.7 |
| No. 3-6 cylinders | 8.3 | 46.9-49.5 | 36.4-37.4 |

② *Total compression space with cylinder head installed is determined by piston shape.*

③ *Prechamber end to cylinder head surface distance 'c' must be readjusted to 0.2145—0.2301" if head is milled by installing a thicker gasket at (13) (illustration C).*

④

| Model | | 230, 230S, 250S | | 230, 230S | 250S | 230, 230S | 250S |
|---|---|---|---|---|---|---|---|
| Combustion Chamber | Compress. Ratio (:1) | Total Compress. Space (cc.) | | | | Compress. Space in Head (cc.) | |
| No. 1 cylinder | 8.6 | 49.3-52.6 | | 53.4-57.0 | 40.1-41.1 | 44.3-45.3 | |
| No. 2 cylinder | 8.8 | 48.0-51.2 | | 52.0-55.5 | 38.8-39.8 | 42.9-43.9 | |
| No. 3-6 cylinders | 9.0 | 47.0-49.2 | | 51.0-53.7 | 37.6-38.6 | 41.6-42.6 | |

# Valve Specifications

| Model | Minimum Valve Head Edge Thickness (mm./in.) | | Valve Seat Width (mm.) | | Valve Seat Angle (deg.) | Valve Stem Diameter (mm.) | |
|---|---|---|---|---|---|---|---|
| | intake | exhaust | intake | exhaust | | intake | exhaust |
| 190c | 1.0/.039 | 1.5/.058 | 1.25—2.00 | 1.25—2.00 | 45+15' | 8.970 | 9.950 |
| 200 | 1.0/.039 | 1.5/.058 | 1.25—2.00 | 1.25—2.00 | 45+15' | 8.970 | 9.950 |
| 190Dc | 1.0/.039 | 1.5/.058 | 1.25—2.00 | 1.25—2.00 | 45+15' | 8.920 | 9.920 |
| 200D | 1.0/.039 | 1.5/.058 | 1.25—2.00 | 1.25—2.00 | 45+15' | 8.920 | 9.920 |
| 230 | 1.0/.039 | 1.5/.058 | 1.25—2.00 | 1.25—2.00 | 45+15' | 8.970 | 9.950 |
| 220b | 1.0/.039 | 1.5/.058 | 1.25—2.00 | 1.25—2.00 | 45+15' | 8.970 | 9.950 |
| 220Sb | 1.0/.039 | 1.5/.058 | 1.25—2.00 | 1.25—2.00 | 45+15' | 8.970 | 9.950 |
| 230S | 1.0/.039 | 1.5/.058 | 1.25—2.00 | 1.25—2.00 | 45+15' | 8.970 | 10.950 |
| 250S | 1.0/.039 | 1.5/.058 | 1.25—2.00 | 1.25—2.00 | 45+15' | 8.970 | 10.950 |
| 220SEb | 1.0/.039 | 1.5/.058 | 1.25—2.00 | 1.25—2.00 | 45+15' | 8.970 | 9.950 |
| 250SE | 1.0/.039 | 1.5/.058 | 1.25—2.00 | 1.25—2.00 | 45+15' | 8.970 | 10.950 |
| 230SL | 1.0/.039 | 1.5/.058 | 1.25—2.00 | 1.25—2.00 | 45+15' | 8.970 | 9.950 |
| 250SL | 1.0/.039 | 1.5/.058 | 1.25—2.00 | 1.25—2.00 | 45+15' | 8.970 | 10.950 |
| 250SE/C | 1.0/.039 | 1.5/.058 | 1.25—2.00 | 1.25—2.00 | 45+15' | 8.970 | 10.950 |
| 300SE | 1.0/.039 | 1.8/.070 | 1.50—2.00 | 1.50—2.00 | 45+15' | 8.970 | 11.950 |
| 300SEb | 1.0/.039 | 1.8/.070 | 1.50—2.00 | 1.50—2.00 | 45+15' | 8.970 | 11.950 |
| 300SEL | 1.0/.039 | 1.8/.070 | 1.50—2.00 | 1.50—2.00 | 45+15' | 8.970 | 11.950 |
| 300SE/C | 1.0/.039 | 1.8/.070 | 1.50—2.00 | 1.50—2.00 | 45+15' | 8.970 | 11.950 |
| 220D/8 | 1.5/.058 | 1.5/.058 | 1.30—1.60 | 2.60—2.90 | 30+15' | 9.920 | 9.940 |
| 220/8 | 1.0/.039 | 1.5/.058 | 1.25—2.00 | 1.25—2.00 | 45+15' | 8.970 | 10.940 |
| 230/8 | 1.0/.039 | 1.5/.058 | 1.25—2.00 | 1.25—2.00 | 45+15' | 8.970 | 10.940 |
| 250/8 | 1.0/.039 | 1.5/.058 | 1.25—2.00 | 1.25—2.00 | 45+15' | 8.970 | 10.940 |
| 280S/8 | 1.0/.039 | 1.5/.058 | 1.25—2.00 | 1.25—2.00 | 45+15' | 8.970 | 10.940 |
| 280SE/8 | 1.0/.039 | 1.5/.058 | 1.25—2.00 | 1.25—2.00 | 45+15' | 8.970 | 10.940 |
| 280SEL/8 | 1.0/.039 | 1.5/.058 | 1.25—2.00 | 1.25—2.00 | 45+15' | 8.970 | 10.940 |
| 280SL/8 | 1.0/.039 | 1.5/.058 | 1.25—2.00 | 1.25—2.00 | 45+15' | 8.970 | 10.940 |
| 300SEL/8 2.8 | 1.0/.039 | 1.5/.058 | 1.25—2.00 | 1.25—2.00 | 45+15' | 8.970 | 10.940 |
| 300SEL/8 6.3 | 1.0/.039 | 1.5/.058 | 1.25—2.00 | 1.25—2.00 | 45+15' | 8.970 | 11.940 |

*Illustrations for page 104*

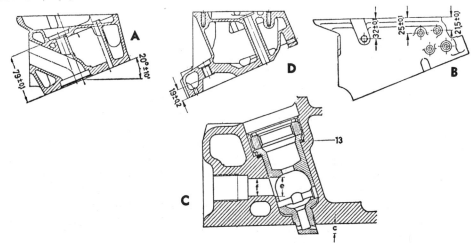

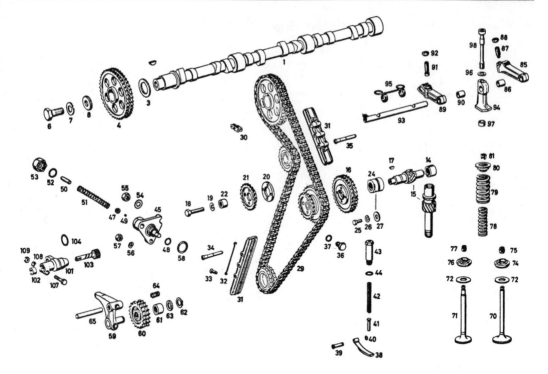

Valve train—300SE.

connect the new one together with the removable link, inserting the link from front
to rear with the closed end facing direction
of rotation (see illustration).

Install and bleed the chain tensioner,
then install rocker arm blocks and adjust
valve clearance. Check the valve timing,
as described in Chapter 2, and correct, if
necessary, using an offset Woodruff key, or
by removing the camshaft sprocket and
resetting the chain the necessary number
of teeth. Reinstall spark plugs and camshaft cover.

## Valve Grinding

Although a satisfactory job can be done
using a small hand valve lapper and compound, it is advisable to have the valves
and seats machine finished, then hand-
lapped. This is especially true if the valves
have been running hot—valve head warpage and bent stems are seen more easily
on a machine.

First, remove the valves using a C-type
spring compressor. Arrange all valves and
springs, in order, for ease in asembly. (A
board with ⅜″ holes and pegs makes a
handy valve and spring holder.)

With a medium wire brush, preferably

1. Spring clip               2. Link

Timing chain link.

in an electric drill, clean all ports and combustion chambers and blow out with compressed air. *CAUTION: Coarse brushes
will score aluminum.*

Wash head with gasoline and blow dry,
then inspect carefully for cracks or burned
valve seats. Place a straightedge diagonally
across the head surface, after cleaning all
pieces of gasket from it. Try to insert
feeler gauge between the head and

straightedge at several points. If a .002″ gauge (or thicker) goes through, the head should be milled. *CAUTION: Respect machining tolerances in the tables—too much material removal can result in valve or piston damage. Diesel heads require a gasket under the prechamber if the head is milled—see table and diagram.*

Now, wire brush the valves to remove all lead and carbon deposits. All warped or burnt valves, or valves with bent stems, must be discarded. After grinding, examine the edge of the valve head. If a "knife-edge" exists, the valve must be discarded, since the thin metal will burn away rapidly.

Measure the stem wear with a micrometer. Any valves with stems worn over specification must also be discarded. No valve seal can work properly with worn stems to contend with, and oil burning will result.

While not strictly necessary, it is a good idea to replace all the valves if three or four seem bad. Check that all springs are straight, not broken and all of the same height, then assemble the valves, using wheel bearing grease to hold the retainers during assembly.

After assembly, measure the assembled height of springs. All should be the same height, within .015″ or so. If not, remove the "longer" springs and place shims (available at automotive jobbers) under these springs to bring them to specification. This is necessary to maintain equal valve closing pressure.

Place a straightedge across the valve stems and check that they are all the same, again within .015″ or so. If they are not, either the stems can be machined or the valve seats "sunk". This is not absolutely necessary, but rocker arm geometry will be upset, with attendant wear, if the stems are all of a different height.

When installing the cylinder head, make sure all gasket surfaces are clean and that the gasket doesn't move. (Pilot studs are a big help here.) Always use a new head gasket and torque the head bolts evenly, a little at a time and in the proper sequence, until all are tight. Adjust valves and run the engine for about 15 minutes, then retorque the bolts. They often loosen after the head gasket seats. The bolts should be tightened again after about 500 miles of

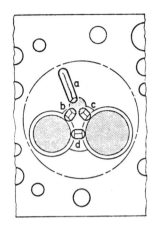

a. Crack from the bore of the prechamber to the center of the cylinder head
b. Crack extending to exhaust valve seat
c. Crack extending to intake valve seat
d. Crack across intake and exhaust valve seats

Typical cracks found in cylinder head—diesel engine illustrated. Cracks at "a" are not dangerous if less than 0.60″ long. Any cracks at "b", "c" and "d" necessitate head replacement.

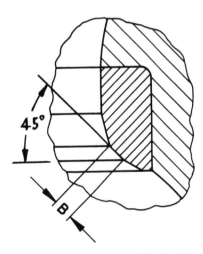

Valve seat angle and width ("B").

normal operation, and the valves readjusted.

## Engine Service

### Checking Condition of Cylinders

With the cylinder head off, examine the bores after wiping them with a clean rag.

# Piston Specifications

| Model | Standard Bore Diameter (mm.) | Piston Sidewall Clearance (mm./in.) | Piston Pin Diameter (mm.) | Piston Pin Running Fit (mm.) | Max. Weight Deviation in Engine Pistons (g.) | Rods (g.) | Piston Ring End Gap (mm.) ⑤ | Piston Ring Groove Clear. (mm.) |
|---|---|---|---|---|---|---|---|---|
| 190c | 85.000–85.022 | .03–.04/.0012–.0015 | 25.994–26.000 | .012–.023 | 4.0 | 5.0 | ① | .055–.077③ |
| 200 | 87.000–87.022 | .03–.04/.0012–.0015 | 26.000–25.995 | .012–.023 | 4.0 | 5.0 | ② | .060–.092③ |
| 190Dc | 87.000–87.022 | .07/.0027 | 26.000–25.995 | .012–.023 | 4.0 | 5.0 | ① | .080–.112③ |
| 200D | 87.000–87.022 | .07/.0027 | 26.000–25.995 | .012–.023 | 4.0 | 5.0 | ① | .080–.112③ |
| 230 | 82.000–82.022 | .03–.04/.0012–.0015 | 25.000–24.995 | .012–.023 | 4.0 | 5.0 | ② | .060–.092③ |
| 220b | 80.000–80.019 | .03–.04/.0012–.0015 | 23.994–24.000 | not avail. | 4.0 | 5.0 | ① | .080–.112 |
| 220Sb | 80.000–80.019 | .03–.04/.0012–.0015 | 23.994–24.000 | not avail. | 4.0 | 5.0 | ① | .080–.112 |
| 230S | 82.000–82.022 | .03–.04/.0012–.0015 | 23.994–24.000 | not avail. | 4.0 | 5.0 | ② | .060–.092 |
| 250S | 82.000–82.022 | .03–.04/.0012–.0015 | 25.000–24.995 | not avail. | 4.0 | 5.0 | ② | .060–.092 |
| 220SEb | 80.000–80.019 | .03–.04/.0012–.0015 | 23.994–24.000 | not avail. | 4.0 | 5.0 | ① | .080–.112 |
| 250SE | 82.000–82.022 | .03–.04/.0012–.0015 | 25.000–24.995 | not avail. | 4.0 | 5.0 | ② | .060–.092 |
| 230SL | 82.000–82.022 | .03–.04/.0012–.0015 | 23.994–24.000 | not avail. | 4.0 | 5.0 | ① | .060–.092 |
| 250SL | 82.000–82.022 | .03–.04/.0012–.0015 | 25.000–24.995 | not avail. | 4.0 | 5.0 | not avail. | not avail. |
| 250SE/C | 82.000–82.022 | .03–.04/.0012–.0015 | 25.000–24.995 | not avail. | 4.0 | 5.0 | ② | .060–.092 |
| 300SE | 85.000–85.022 | .03–.04/.0012–.0015 | 25.994–26.000 | .007–.018 | 4.0 | 5.0 | ① | .060–.092 |
| 300SEb | 85.000–85.022 | .03–.04/.0012–.0015 | 26.000–25.995 | .007–.018 | 4.0 | 5.0 | ① | .060–.092 |
| 300SEL | 85.000–85.022 | .03–.04/.0012–.0015 | 26.000–25.995 | .007–.018 | 4.0 | 5.0 | ① | .060–.092 |
| 300SE/C | 85.000–85.022 | .03–.04/.0012–.0015 | 26.000–25.995 | .007–.018 | 4.0 | 5.0 | ① | .060–.092 |
| 220D/8 | 87.000–87.022 | .02–.03/.0008–.0012 | 26.000–25.995 | .012–.023 | 4.0 | 5.0 | not avail. | not avail. |
| 220/8 | 87.000–87.022 | .02–.03/.0008–.0012 | 25.000–24.995 | .012–.023 | 4.0 | 5.0 | not avail. | not avail. |
| 230/8 | ④ | .02–.03/.0008–.0012 | 25.000–24.995 | .012–.023 | 4.0 | 5.0 | not avail. | not avail. |
| 250/8 | 82.000–82.022 | .02–.03/.0008–.0012 | 25.000–24.995 | .012–.023 | 4.0 | 5.0 | not avail. | not avail. |
| 280S/8 | 86.500–86.522 | .02–.03/.0008–.0012 | 25.000–24.995 | .012–.023 | 4.0 | 5.0 | not avail. | not avail. |
| 280SE/8 | 86.500–86.522 | .02–.03/.0008–.0012 | 25.000–24.995 | .012–.023 | 4.0 | 5.0 | not avail. | not avail. |
| 280SEL/8 | 86.500–86.522 | .02–.03/.0008–.0012 | 25.000–24.995 | .012–.023 | 4.0 | 5.0 | not avail. | not avail. |
| 280SL/8 | 86.500–86.522 | .02–.03/.0008–.0012 | 25.000–24.995 | .012–.023 | 4.0 | 5.0 | not avail. | not avail. |
| 300SEL/8 2.8 | 86.500–86.522 | .02–.03/.0008–.0012 | 25.000–24.995 | .012–.023 | 4.0 | 5.0 | not avail. | not avail. |
| 300SEL/8 6.3 | 103.000–103.022 | .02–.03/.0008–.0012 | 26.000–25.995 | .007–.018 | 4.0 | 8.0 | ① | .06–.092 |

①   Top  – .55–.70/.022–.028  
    II   – .45–.60/.018–.023  
    III  – .30–.45/.012–.016  
    IV  – .30–.45/.012–.016  

②   3 Ring Pistons (No Ring No. IV)  

③   I  See Space  
    II & III & IV .040 – .072  
    IV Type 300 SEL/8 6.3 – .05–.082  

④   Engine No. 180.945  
                180.949   82.000–82.022  
                180.954   81.750–81.772  

⑤   If Rings are fitted with Molybdenum, the end gap is 0.15–0.2 mm. less than the indicated figures.

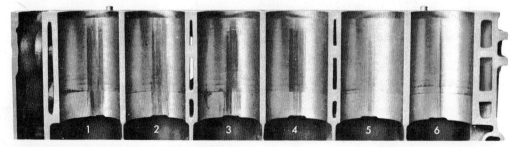

1, 2, 3 Piston skirt seizure resulted in this pattern. Engine must be rebored

4. Piston skirt and oil ring seizure caused this damage. Engine must be rebored

5, 6 Score marks caused by a split piston skirt. Damage is not serious enough to warrant reboring

Cylinder wall damage.

# Connecting Rod Specifications

| Model | Connecting Rod Big End Internal Diam. (mm.) | Connecting Rod Small End Internal Diam. (mm.) | Connecting Rod Bore Out-of-Round Max. (mm./in.) | Connecting Rod Length (mm.) | Connecting Rod Bearing Clearance (mm./in.) | Connecting Rod Side-Play (mm./in.) |
|---|---|---|---|---|---|---|
| 190c | 55.600—55.619 | 29.000—29.021 | .01/.0004 | 148.95—149.05 | .045—.060/.0018—.0023 | .110—.260/.004—.010 |
| 200 | 55.600—55.619 | 29.000—29.021 | .01/.0004 | 148.95—149.05 | .045—.060/.0018—.0023 | .110—.260/.004—.010 |
| 190Dc | 55.600—55.619 | 29.000—29.021 | .01/.0004 | 148.95—149.05 | .045—.060/.0018—.0023 | .110—.260/.004—.010 |
| 200D | 55.600—55.619 | 29.000—29.021 | .01/.0004 | 148.95—149.05 | .045—.060/.0018—.0023 | .110—.260/.004—.010 |
| 230 | 51.600—51.619 | 28.000—28.021 | .01/.0004 | 124.95—125.05 | .045—.060/.0018—.0023 | .110—.260/.004—.010 |
| 220b | 54.000—54.019 | 27.000—27.021 | .01/.0004 | 134.95—135.05 | .045—.060/.0018—.0023 | .110—.260/.004—.010 |
| 220Sb | 54.000—54.019 | 27.000—27.021 | .01/.0004 | 134.95—135.05 | .045—.060/.0018—.0023 | .110—.260/.004—.010 |
| 230S | 51.600—51.619 | 28.000—28.021 | .01/.0004 | 124.95—125.05 | .045—.060/.0018—.0023 | .110—.260/.004—.010 |
| 250S | 51.600—51.619 | 28.000—28.021 | .01/.0004 | 124.95—125.05 | .045—.060/.0018—.0023 | .110—.260/.004—.010 |
| 220SEb | 54.000—54.019 | 27.000—27.021 | .01/.0004 | 134.95—135.05 | .045—.060/.0018—.0023 | .110—.260/.004—.010 |
| 250SE | 51.600—51.619 | 28.000—28.021 | .01/.0004 | 124.95—125.05 | .045—.060/.0018—.0023 | .110—.260/.004—.010 |
| 230SL | 51.600—51.619 | 27.000—27.019 | .01/.0004 | 124.95—125.05 | .045—.060/.0018—.0023 | .110—.260/.004—.010 |
| 250SL | 51.600—51.619 | 28.000—28.021 | .01/.0004 | 124.95—125.05 | not avail. | not avail. |
| 250SE/C | 51.600—51.619 | 28.000—28.021 | .01/.0004 | 124.95—125.05 | not avail. | not avail. |
| 300SE | 55.600—55.619 | 29.000—29.021 | .01/.0004 | 163.95—164.05 | not avail. | not avail. |
| 300SEb | 55.600—55.619 | 29.000—29.021 | .01/.0004 | 163.95—164.05 | .050—.070/.0020—.0028 | .110—.260/.004—.010 |
| 300SEL | 55.600—55.619 | 29.000—29.021 | .01/.0004 | 163.95—164.05 | .050—.070/.0020—.0028 | .110—.260/.004—.010 |
| 300SE/C | 55.600—55.619 | 29.000—29.021 | .01/.0004 | 163.95—164.05 | .050—.070/.0020—.0028 | .110—.260/.004—.010 |
| 220D/8 | 55.600—55.619 | 29.000—29.021 | .01/.0004 | 148.95—149.05 | not avail. | not avail. |
| 220/8 | 55.600—55.619 | 29.000—29.021 | .01/.0004 | 148.95—149.05 | not avail. | not avail. |
| 230/8 | 51.600—51.619 | 28.000—28.021 | .01/.0004 | 124.95—125.05 | not avail. | not avail. |
| 250/8 | 51.600—51.619 | 28.000—28.021 | .01/.0004 | 124.95—125.05 | not avail. | not avail. |
| 280S/8 | 51.600—51.619 | 28.000—28.021 | .01/.0004 | 124.95—125.05 | not avail. | not avail. |
| 280SE/8 | 51.600—51.619 | 28.000—28.021 | .01/.0004 | 124.95—125.05 | not avail. | not avail. |
| 280SEL/8 | 51.600—51.619 | 28.000—28.021 | .01/.0004 | 124.95—125.05 | not avail. | not avail. |
| 280SL/8 | 51.600—51.619 | 28.000—28.021 | .01/.0004 | 124.95—125.05 | not avail. | not avail. |
| 300SEL/8 2.8 | 51.600—51.619 | 28.000—28.021 | .01/.0004 | 124.95—125.05 | not avail. | not avail. |
| 300SEL/8 6.3 | 58.050—58.150 | 29.000—29.021 | .01/.0004 | 165.95—166.05 | .045—.065/.0018—.0026 | .22—.35/.0088—.0140 |

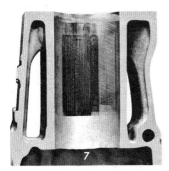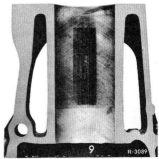

7. Ring seized longitudinally, causing a score mark 1 3/16" wide, on the land side of the piston groove. The honing pattern is destroyed and the cylinder must be rebored

8. Result of oil ring seizure. Engine must be rebored
9. Oil ring seizure here was not serious enough to warrant reboring. The honing marks are still visible

Cylinder wall damage.

Honing marks should be visible through any scuff marks and there should be no deep scores. If the walls are scored, the cylinder must be honed. Cylinders of the 300 SE worn beyond specification may *not* be overbored, because the thin liners will not stand up under heat after being further thinned. New liners must be installed, or the entire block replaced.

There may be a slight ridge at the top of the cylinder at the point where the piston reverses its travel. Even if the cylinders are good, this ridge must be removed before the pistons are replaced. Otherwise, it may damage the piston rings or lands.

The best check of cylinder condition is done with an inside micrometer. With the pistons at bottom dead center, measure the bore at positions (1), (2) and (3) on the diagram. Measure both along the "A" axis and the "B" axis to get a true picture of wear.

Generally, a cylinder greater than .0016" out of round must be rebored. A difference of .0012" between points (3) or (4) and point (6), (with engine disassembled), or any general wear in excess of .0050" also requires cylinder reboring. In general, .0004" wear between points (1) and (6) per 6,000 miles is "normal" wear.

Inspect the piston tops for cracks, after scraping carbon deposits, and check the top block surface for cracks. Use a straightedge to check for warpage in the same manner as the cylinder head was checked.

If it is necessary to disassemble the engine for service, it must be removed from the car on all models.

### Engine R & R

First, remove the hood, then drain the cooling system and disconnect the battery. While not strictly necessary, it is better to remove the battery completely to prevent breakage by the engine as it is lifted out.

Remove the fan shroud, radiator and disconnect all heater hoses and oil cooler lines. Remove air cleaner and all fuel, vacuum and oil hoses (e.g., power steering and power brakes). Plug all openings to keep out dirt.

*CAUTION: Air conditioner lines should not be indiscriminately disconnected without taking proper precautions. It is best to swing the compressor out of the way while*

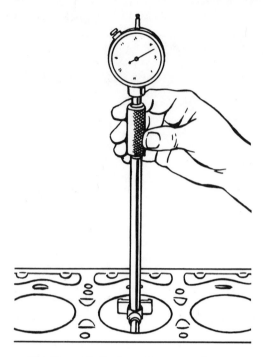

Checking cylinder bores for wear and taper.

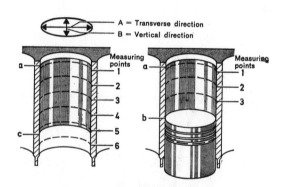

a. Top reversal point of first ring
b. Bottom dead center
c. Bottom reversal point of scraper ring

Cylinder bore measuring points.

*still connected to its hoses. Never do any welding around the compressor—heat may cause an explosion. Also, the refrigerant, while inert at normal room temperature, breaks down under high temperature into hydrogen fluoride and phosgene (among other products), which are highly poisonous.*

Remove the viscous coupling and fan and, on four-cylinder engines, disconnect the carburetor choke cable. On diesel engines, disconnect the idle control and starting cables. On all engines, disconnect accelerator linkage. On six-cylinder engines with three-groove crankshaft pulley, remove the heater pipe on the firewall. Disconnect all ground straps and electrical connections. It is a good idea to tag each wire for easy reassembly.

Detach the gearshift linkage and the exhaust pipes from the manifolds. Loosen the steering relay arm and pull it down out of the way, along with the center steering rod and hydraulic steering damper. The hydraulic engine shock absorber should be removed. Remove hydraulic line from clutch housing and the oil line connectors from automatic transmission (see illustration). Remove the exhaust pipe bracket attached to the transmission and place a wood-padded jack under the bellhousing, or place a cable sling under the oil pan, to support the engine.

Mark the position of the rear engine support and unbolt the two outer bolts, then remove the top bolt at the transmission and pull the support out. Disconnect speedometer cable and the front driveshaft U-joint. Push the driveshaft back and wire it out of the way.

Unbolt the engine mounts on both sides, and, on four-cylinder engines, the front limit stop. Unbolt the power steering fluid reservoir and swing it out of the way; then, using a chain hoist and cable as illustrated, lift the engine and transmission upward and outward. An angle of about 45° will allow the car to be pushed backwards while the engine is coming up.

Reverse the procedure to install, making sure to bleed the hydraulic clutch, power steering, power brakes and fuel system.

### Bearings, Pistons and Piston Rings

With the engine removed and the cylinder head off, support the engine on an engine stand, or from each end, with the oil pan facing upwards. Remove the oil pan bolts and the pan and, on most models, the lower crankcase section. Remove the oil pump.

Remove the connecting rod nuts, after first marking the rod caps and rods with punchmarks to indicate proper assembly, then remove the caps and lower bearing shells.

1. Steering relay arm
2. Tie-rods
3. Steering shock absorber

Lowering transmission.

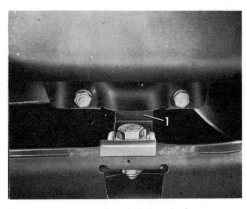

Front limit stop used with four-cylinder engines.

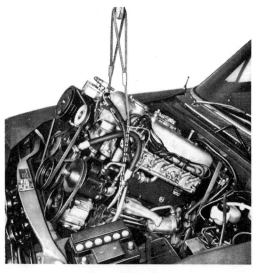

Removing engine.

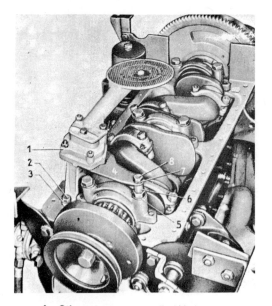

1. Oil pump
2. Hex screw
3. Spring washer
4. Bracket
5. Washer
6. Screw
7. Lockwasher
8. Hex screw

Underside of engine with oil pan removed—190 illustrated.

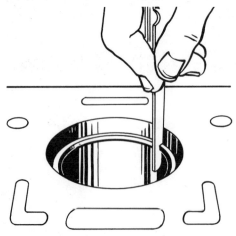

Checking piston ring end gap.

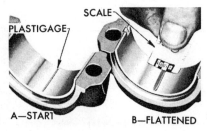

Checking bearing clearance using Plastigage.

Place plastic tubing on rod bolts to prevent crankshaft damage. Inspect the crankshaft journals for nicks and roughness and measure diameters. Turn the engine over and ream the ridge from the top of the cylinders. With a hammer handle or other piece of hard wood, gently tap the pistons and rods out from the bottom. The cylinder bores can be inspected at this time for taper and general wear. Check the pistons for proper size and inspect the ring grooves. If any rings are cracked, it is almost certain that the grooves are no longer true, because broken rings work up and down. Worn grooves can be recut and ring spacers used to maintain proper side clearance, but it is best to replace any such worn pistons.

The pistons, pins and connecting rods are marked with a color dot assembly code. Only parts having the same color may be used together.

If the cylinders are bored, make sure the machinist has the pistons beforehand—cylinder bore sizes are nominal, and the pistons must be individually fitted to the block. Maximum piston weight deviation in any one engine is 4 grams.

With the block completely disassembled, inspect the water passages and bearing webs for cracks. If the water passages are plugged with rust, they can be cleaned out by boiling the block at a radiator shop. *CAUTION: Aluminum parts must not be boiled out—they will be eaten away by chemicals.*

Measure piston ring end gap by sliding a new ring into the bore and measuring as illustrated. Measure the gap at both top, bottom and midpoint of piston travel, and correct by filing or grinding the ring ends.

To check bearing clearances, use either Plastigage or brass shim stock inserted between the oil-free bearing and the crankshaft journal. Blow out all crankshaft oil passages before measuring; torque the rod bolts to specification.

If shim stock is used, be careful not to score the bearings. Try to turn the crankshaft by hand. If the crank turns with slight resistance, clearance is equal to the shim stock thickness. If the crankshaft spins freely, check again with thicker shims; if it won't turn at all, use thinner shims.

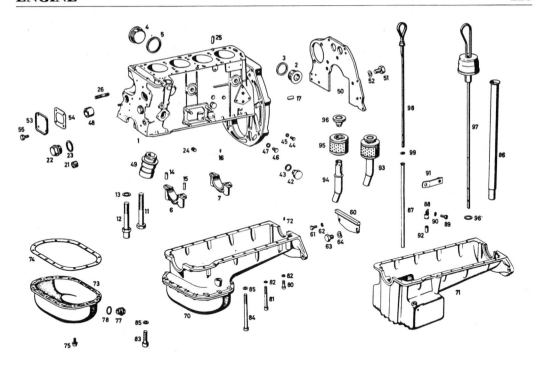

Four-cylinder engine block and associated parts.

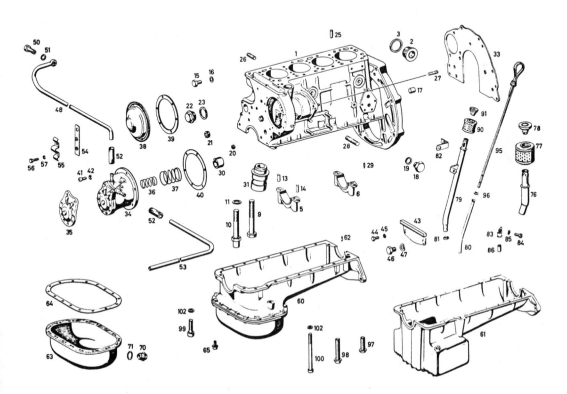

Diesel engine block and associated parts.

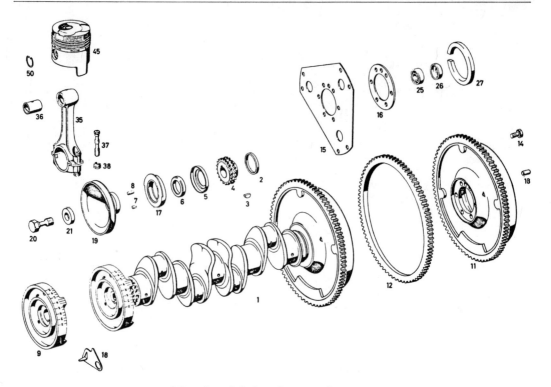

Diesel crankshaft and associated parts.

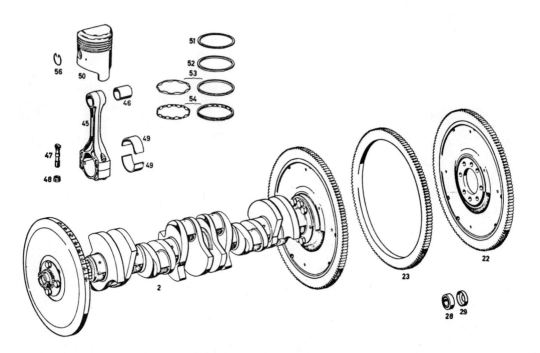

Type 300SE crankshaft and associated parts.

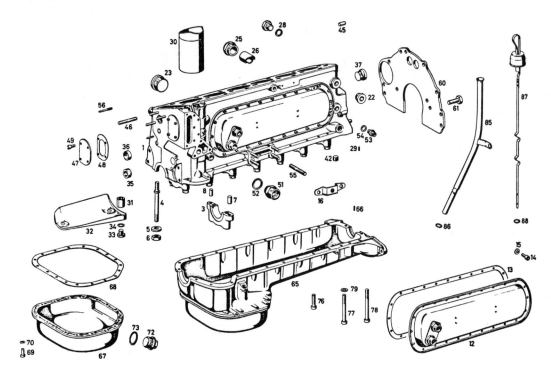

Type 300SE engine block and associated parts.

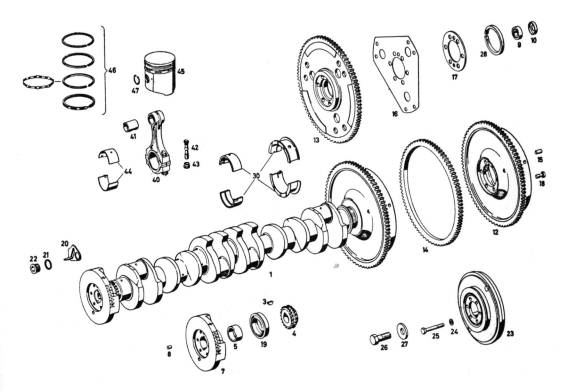

Six-cylinder crankshaft and associated parts—250, 280 illustrated.

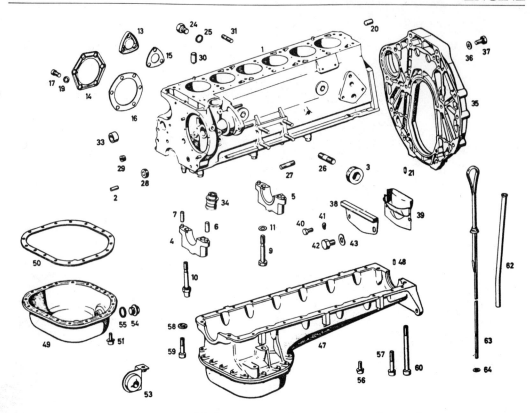

Six-cylinder engine block and associated parts—250, 280 illustrated.

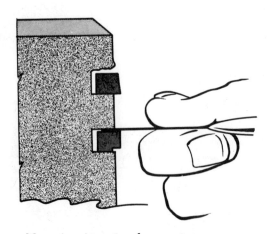

Measuring piston ring clearance in groove.

Plastigage is a thin plastic strip that is crushed by the bearing and cap and spreads out an amount in proportion to clearance. After torquing the bearing cap, remove the cap and compare the width of the Plastigage with the scale. *NOTE: Do not rotate crankshaft.*

Bearing shells of various thicknesses are available, and should be used to correct

clearance; it may be necessary to machine the crankshaft journals undersize to obtain the proper oil clearance. *CAUTION: Use of shim stock between bearings and caps to decrease clearance is not good practice.* Now, check crankshaft end-play, using a feeler gauge.

When installing new piston rings, follow the instructions on the package for best results. The ring grooves must be cleaned out, preferably using a special groove cleaner, although a broken ring will work as well. After installing the rings, check ring side clearance as illustrated.

**Flywheel**

The flywheel and crankshaft are balanced together as a unit, therefore disassembly must be preceded by matchmarking these components for correct assembly positioning.

Stretch bolts are used to hold some newer flywheels in place. These are easily identified by their "hourglass" shape (see illustrations). These bolts are deformed, or stretched, when tightened, and their use-

Standard Transmission                                                    Automatic Transmission

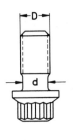
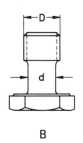
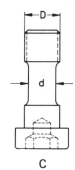

|   A   |   B   |   C   |

| Part No. | 615 032 05 71 | 621 032 00 71 | 108 032 01 71 | 108 990 03 19 | 108 990 04 19 |
|---|---|---|---|---|---|
| Thread Diameter | M 10 x 1 | M 10 x 1 | M 12 x 1 | M 10 x 1 | M 12 x 1 |
| Diameter "d" of Stretch Bolt When New (mm.) | .33"-.01" (8.5-0.2) | .31"-.01" (8.0-0.2) | .36"-.01" (9.2-0.2) | .31"-.01" (7.7-0.2) | .36"-.01" (9.2-0.2) |
| Minimum Diameter | .31" (8.1 mm.) | .30" (7.6 mm.) | .34" (8.8 mm.) | .29" (7.3 mm.) | .34" (8.8 mm.) |
| Installed in Engines of Models: | 220/8 220D/8 | 230/8 | 250/8 280S/8 280SE/8 280SE/8 Cp/Cv. 300SEL/8 280SL/8 | 220/8 220D/8 230/8 | 250/8 280S/8 280SE/8 280SE/8 Cp/Cv. 300SEL/8 280SEL/8 |

Stretch bolts used on Mercedes-Benz flywheels.

fulness must be determined by measuring their diameter at the stretch point.

Stretch bolts must be torqued to the prescribed "preload" initial reading, then the wrench turned through a certain number of degrees rotation. This method ensures that the bolts will not loosen in service.

After pretightening, do not slack up on the wrench, but immediately turn the required number of degrees. While not strictly accurate, the number of degrees can be estimated.

**Engine Assembly**

Assemble the engine using all new gaskets and seals, and make sure all parts are properly lubricated. Bearing shells and cylinder walls must be lubricated with engine oil before assembly. Make sure no

Flywheel matchmarks (arrows) and angle of rotation tightening—four-cylinder illustrated.

metal chips remain in cylinder bores or crankcase.

To install piston and rod, turn engine right side up and insert rod into cylinder.

Clamp the rings to the piston, with their gaps equally spaced around the circumference, using a piston ring compressor. Gently tap the piston into the bore, using a hammer handle or similar hard wood, making sure the rings clear the edge.

Torque the rod and main caps to specification and try to turn the crankshaft by hand. It should turn with moderate resistance, not spin freely or be locked up.

Disassemble the oil pump and check the gear backlash as illustrated. Place a straightedge on the cover and check for warpage. Deep scoring on the cover usually indicates that metal or dirt particles have been circulating through the oil system. Covers can be machined, but it is best to replace them if damaged.

Install the oil pan and lower crankcase and tighten bolts evenly all around, then turn the engine right side up and install the cylinder head gasket and head. Make sure the gasket surfaces are clean before installation—a small dirt particle could cause gasket failure. Tighten the cylinder head bolts in sequence, in stages, to insure against distortion. Don't forget the small bolts at the front of the head.

Install intake and exhaust manifolds, tightening all bolts evenly, then install engine into vehicle.

*NOTE: See Chapter 1 concerning break-in oils.*

*NOTE: It is good practice to retighten all bolts after about 500 miles of running, although this is not absolutely necessary. The cylinder head is the only exception to this and should be retightened to specifications after 500 miles.*

Stretch bolts are used for the connecting rods of some of the phase II models, the 280 SL/8 and 300 SEL/8 in particular. These bolts are tightened by angle of rotation rather than by use of a torque wrench. Make sure the stretch section diameter is greater than 0.35″ (−.003″). Remove the bolt from the rod and measure the diameter at the point normally covered by the rod—it should be at least 0.31″.

### Front Seal Installation

Most leaky front seals can be replaced with the engine in the car. An exception is the silicone rubber seal used in 230, 230 S, 230 SL, 250 S, 250 SE and 250 SL models.

Measuring oil pump gear backlash (.12–.16 mm.).

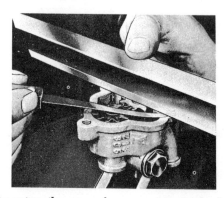
Measuring oil pump surface gap using straightedge.

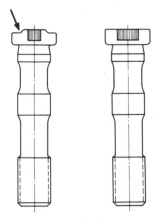
Connecting rod stretch bolts.

This seal, white-yellow in color, should be replaced only with the engine disassembled, because the sealing surface would be scraped off as the seal was installed into the housing. A new seal, however, was

Driving out cylinder liner—300SE.

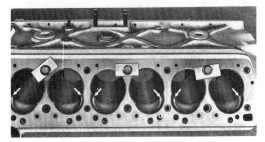

Retaining plates to hold liners if only one liner is to be replaced.

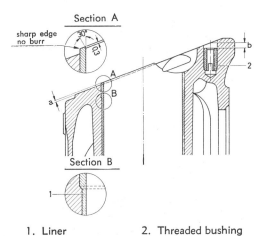

1. Liner       2. Threaded bushing

Machining 300SE liners.

developed so that replacement is possible with the engine in place; it can be used on these older engines as well.

## Special Diesel Engine Service

When overhauling an older OM621 se-

ries engine, many components from the OM615 engine can be used to help increase reliability. The injection timer from the OM615 often helps reduce diesel knock, and also increases chain and slide rail life. The newer camshaft has wider lobes and rocker arms and can be used if the complete rocker assembly is installed. Always check valve timing after effecting such a change.

It is also possible to use the stronger OM615 valve springs. This is especially desirable in older engines that have had several valve jobs; the valves seat deeper in the head and reduce spring tension.

## Cylinder Liner Removal and Replacement

Some aluminum block engines, the 300 SE for example, have thin grey iron liners installed into the bores. When these liners become worn or damaged, they must be replaced, because boring is not feasible.

Obviously, this job is not one for the home mechanic, but it is included for the sake of machine shops and garages not familiar with the Mercedes-Benz.

If only one cylinder is to be relined, anchor the remaining liners using small retainers similar to those illustrated.

Completely strip the block and degrease it using Gunk or kerosene. Heat the block evenly for 30–45 minutes at a temperature of 575–640° F. in an oven.

After removal from the oven, drive the liners out from the bottom using a suitable drift. If the liner will not move, it can be split, or bored, but care must be taken not to damage the block.

After the block has cooled to room temperature, carefully clean the bores in the block and measure their diameter. Measure the O.D. of the new cylinder liners and compare with specifications.

Ideally, the block should be pressure checked before installing new liners. Oil galleries should withstand 90 psi, water jackets 30 psi, without leaking.

Heat the block again and insert the liners from the top, being careful of alignment. After cooling, the projecting liners must be milled square with relation to the block (see illustration). The liners must then be honed to final finish tolerances and the valve recesses re-machined.

# Chapter Five
# Electrical System

## Starter

All Mercedes-Benz passenger cars are equipped with 12-volt Bosch electric starters of various rated outputs. The starter motor is actually nothing but a simple series-wound electric motor of high torque output, fitted with a drive pinion and a device to mesh the pinion with the flywheel ring gear. The carrier, which is connected to the pinion through the over-running clutch, runs in splines machined in the armature shaft. When the armature rotates, these splines force the pinion into mesh. When the engine starts, the over-running (one-way) clutch releases the

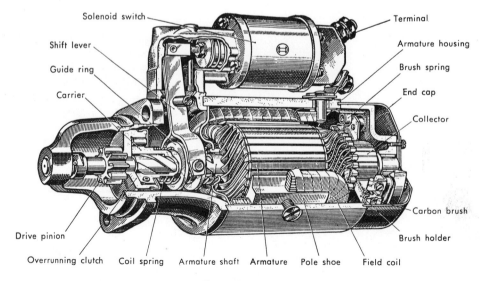

Starter motor.

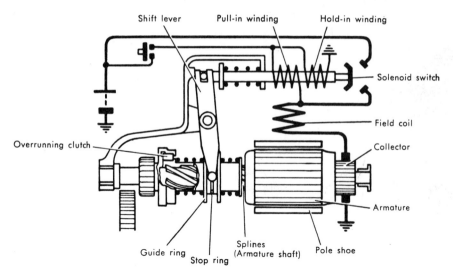

Shift lever    Pull-in winding    Hold-in winding

Solenoid switch

Field coil

Collector

Overrunning clutch

Armature

Guide ring    Stop ring    Splines (Armature shaft)    Pole shoe

Starter motor in schematic form.

pinion and the unit disengages. The starter is actuated and the pinion engaged by an electric solenoid mounted on top of the starter motor.

After performing in-car tests as described in Chapter 2, the starter motor must be removed, if judged faulty, and tested further.

## Starter Removal

Disconnect the ground cable at the battery, then disconnect wires at the solenoid. *NOTE: Tag wires for ease in installation.*

Unbolt the starter from the bellhousing and remove the ground cable, then remove starter from beneath the car.

## Starter Disassembly and Assembly

Remove the end cap (4) and lift out the brushes. Disconnect the cable that runs between the field coil and the solenoid (at the solenoid end). Unscrew the nut in front of commutator bearing and remove washers. Unscrew the nuts from the armature housing bolts and remove drive bearing end frame and armature. *NOTE: Lay armature brake components on bench, in order, for easy assembly.*

Remove the bolts that hold the solenoid, then remove solenoid. Disassemble shift lever mechanism, knocking the pin out with a drift. Then remove shift lever and armature from drive bearing end frame. Inspect the overrunning clutch; it should turn clockwise only (seen from drive pinion end), then check the pinion gear itself for

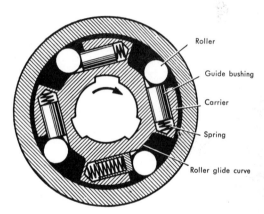

Roller

Guide bushing

Carrier

Spring

Roller glide curve

Overrunning clutch.

1. Ground strap
2. Hexagon screws
3. Solenoid switch
4. Connecting bolt
5. Starter
6. Connecting cable
7. Hexagon nut
8. Hexagon screws

Starter motor installed.

# Electrical Specifications
## Starter Specifications

| Model | Type Starter (Bosch) | Short Circuit Test Amps. | volts | Load Test Amps. | volts | Speed (rpm) | Idling Test Amps. | volts | Speed (rpm) | Solenoid Yoke Length (mm.) | Generator Type Used |
|---|---|---|---|---|---|---|---|---|---|---|---|
| 190c | EF(R)12V0, 8PS 0 001 208 003 | 250—285 | 6 | 165—200 | 9 | 1,100—1,450 | 35—45 | 12 | 6,400—7,900 | 19±.1 | LJ/GG 240/12/2400/AR8, LJ/GK 300/12/1450 AR2, LJ/GEG 160/12/2500 R8, G 1 14 V 30 A 25 or K 1 14 V 38 A 15 |
| 200 | EF(R)12V0, 8PS 0 001 208 025 | 250—285 | 6 | 165—200 | 9 | 1,100—1,450 | 35—45 | 12 | 6,400—7,900 | 19±.1 | K 1 14 V 35 A 20 |
| 190Dc | JD(R)12V1, 8PS 0 001 354 064 | 670—750 | 6 | 310—350 | 9 | 1,250—1,450 | 60—80 | 11.5 | 6,000—7,100 | 49±.2 | same as 190c |
| 200D | JD(R)12V1, 8PS 0 001 354 064 | 670—750 | 6 | 310—350 | 9 | 1,250—1,450 | 60—80 | 11.5 | 6,000—7,100 | 49±.2 | K 1 14 V 35 A 20 |
| 230 | EF(R)12V0, 8PS 0 001 208 003 | 250—285 | 6 | 165—200 | 9 | 1,100—1,400 | 35—45 | 12 | 6,400—7,900 | 19±.1 | K 1 14 V 35 A 20 |
| 220b | EED 0.8/12 R 45 | 340—400 | 8.5 | 180 | 10 | 1,100—1,400 | 30—50 | 11.5 | 5,000—7,500 | 32.4±.1 | |
| 220Sb | EF(R)12V0, 8PS 0 001 208 003 | 250—285 | 6 | 165—200 | 9 | 1,100—1,450 | 35—45 | 12 | 6,400—7,900 | 19±.1 | same as 190c |
| 230S | EF(R)12V0, 8PS 0 001 208 003 | 250—285 | 6 | 165—200 | 9 | 1,100—1,450 | 35—45 | 12 | 6,400—7,900 | 19±.1 | K 1 14 V 35 A 20 |
| 250S | EF(R)12V0, 8PS 0 001 208 026 | 250—285 | 6 | 165—200 | 9 | 1,100—1,450 | 35—45 | 12 | 6,400—7,900 | 19±.1 | K 1 14 V 35 A 20 |
| 220SEb | EF(R)12V0, 8PS 0 001 208 003 | 250—285 | 6 | 165—200 | 9 | 1,100—1,450 | 35—45 | 12 | 6,400—7,900 | 19±.1 | same as 190c |
| 250SE | EF(R)12V0, 8PS 0 001 208 026 | 250—285 | 6 | 165—200 | 9 | 1,100—1,450 | 35—45 | 12 | 6,400—7,900 | 19±.1 | K 1 14 V 35 A 20 |
| 230SL | EF(R)12V0, 8PS 0 001 208 009 | 250—285 | 6 | 165—200 | 9 | 1,100—1,450 | 35—45 | 12 | 6,400—7,900 | 19±.1 | K 1 14 V 35 A 20 |
| 250SL | EF(R)12V0, 8PS 0 001 208 026 | 250—285 | 6 | 165—200 | 9 | 1,100—1,450 | 35—45 | 12 | 6,400—7,900 | 19±.1 | K 1 14 V 35 A 20 |
| 300SE, 300SEb, 300SEL | GE(R)12V1, 3PS 000 1 307 019 | 500—550 | 7 | 270—310 | 9 | 1,200—1,400 | 40—60 | 11.5 | 6,500—8,000 | 32.2±.1 | LJ/GK 300/12/1450/AR53 K 1 14 V 38 A 15 |
| 220D/8 | 2.5/12 | 1,000—1,200 | 6 | 650—750 | 9 | 1,000—1,200 | 80—95 | 12 | 7,500—8,500 | | K 1 14 V 35 A 20 |
| 220/8 | EF 0.8/12 | 250—285 | 6 | 165—200 | 9 | 1,100—1,450 | 35—45 | 12 | 6,400—7,900 | | K 1 14 V 35 A 20 |
| 230/8 | EF 0.8/12 | 250—285 | 6 | 165—200 | 9 | 1,100—1,450 | 35—45 | 12 | 6,400—7,900 | | K 1 14 V 35 A 20 |
| 250/8 | EF 0.8/12 | 250—285 | 6 | 165—200 | 9 | 1,100—1,450 | 35—45 | 12 | 6,400—7,900 | | K 1 14 V 35 A 20 |

## Generator and Regulator Specifications

### Generator Specifications / Regulator Specifications

| Generator Type | Setting Load (Watts/Amps) | Rated Voltage Speed (rpm) | Test Speed (rpm) cold | Test Speed (rpm) warm | Resistance of Exciter Coil | Associated Regulator Bosch RS/… | Cut-In Voltage (volts) | Return Current (Amps.) | Regulating Voltage (without load) | Load at Double Rated Speed (Starting of reg. Amps.) cold | Load at Double Rated Speed warm |
|---|---|---|---|---|---|---|---|---|---|---|---|
| LJ/GEG 160/12/2500R8 | 160/30 | 1,900 | 2,500 | 2,600 | 4.8 +0.5 ohms | UA 160/12/15 | 12.7–13.4 | 2.5–6.6 | 13.8–14.6 | 19.5–22.5 | 17.5–20.5 |
| LJ/GG 240/12/2400R8 | 240/30 | 1,700 | 2,300 | 2,500 | 4.8 +0.5 ohms | UA 240/12/38 | 12.7–13.4 | 5.0–9.0 | 13.8–14.6 | 30.0–34.0 | 27.0–31.0 |
| LJ/GG 240/12/2400AR8 | | | | | | UAA 240/12/43 | 12.5–13.2 | 5.0–11.5 | 13.5–14.5 | 29.0–33.0 | 27.5–32.0 |
| G 1 14 V 30 A 25 0 101 302 023 | –/30 | 1,700 | 2,300 | 2,500 | 4.8 +0.5 ohms | 0 190 309 002 UAA 240/12/43 | 12.5–13.2 | 5.0–11.5 | 13.5–14.5 | 29.0–33.0 | 27.5–32.0 |
| LJ/GK 300/12/1450AR53 | 300/38 | 1,150 | 1,450 | 1,500 | 5.2 +0.5 ohms | UA 300/12/43 | 12.5–13.2 | 5.0–11.5 | 13.5–14.5 | 37.0–41.0 | 35.5–40.0 |
| K 1 14 V 38 A 15 0 101 402 076 | –/38 | 1,100 | 1,450 | 1,500 | 5.2 +0.5 ohms | UAA 300/12/43 0 190 309 010 | 12.5–13.2 | 5.0–11.5 | 13.5–14.5 | 37.0–41.0 | 35.5–40.0 |
| LJ/GK 300/12/1450AR2 | 300/38 | 1,100 | 1,450 | 1,500 | 5.2 +0.5 ohms | UA 300/12/43 | 12.5–13.2 | 5.0–11.5 | 13.5–14.5 | 37.0–41.0 | 35.5–40.0 |
| K 1 14 V 38 A 15 0 101 402 071 | –/38 | 1,100 | 1,450 | 1,500 | 5.2 +0.5 ohms | UA 300/12/43 0 190 300 079 | 12.5–13.2 | 5.0–11.5 | 13.5–14.5 | 37.0–41.0 | 35.5–40.0 |
| K 1 14 V 35 A 20 0 120 400 504 ④ | –/35 | 2,000 | | | 4.0 +0.4 ohms ③ | AD 1/14/1 ADN 1/14 V ① | N.A. | | 13.5–14.2 13.9–14.8② | | 28.0–30.0 |

① Suppressed version.
② With load.
③ Between slip rings.
④ Do not test without regulator—see text.

## Starter Diagnosis

| Condition | Probable Cause | Correction |
|---|---|---|
| Starter does not crank or cranks sluggishly | 1. Battery discharged. <br> 2. Battery defective. <br> 3. Battery terminals loose or corroded; defective cables. <br> 4. Starter terminals or brushes shorted to ground. <br> 5. Carbon brushes in starter not contacting commutator, oily or broken. <br> 6. Defective solenoid switch. <br> 7. Excessive voltage drop in cables, damaged cables, loose connections. | 1. Charge battery. <br> 2. Test and/or replace battery. <br> 3. Tighten, clean and grease terminals. <br> 4. Fix short. <br> 5. Check brushes, clean and/or replace; check for free movement in holders. <br> 6. Replace solenoid. <br> 7. Check leads and connections. |
| Starter turns but does not engage | 1. Pinion binding. <br> 2. Teeth on pinion or ring gear damaged. | 1. Disassemble and clean pinion. <br> 2. Remove burrs, replace ring gear or pinion. |
| Starter turns but stalls when pinion is engaged | 1. Battery discharged. <br> 2. Brush spring tension inadequate. <br> 3. Solenoid defective. <br> 4. Excessive voltage drop in cables. | 1. Charge battery. <br> 2. Check and/or replace brushes/ springs. <br> 3. Replace solenoid. <br> 4. Check leads and terminals. |
| Starter turns after ignition switch released | 1. Ignition switch faulty. <br> 2. Solenoid sticking. | 1. Replace switch. <br> 2. Replace solenoid or free up. |
| Pinion does not engage, starter spins freely | 1. Pinion or ring gear damaged or dirty. <br> 2. Solenoid spring weak or broken. | 1. Clean gears or replace. <br> 2. Replace spring. |
| Pinion engages but starter breaks free and spins | 1. Overrunning clutch slipping. | 1. Replace pinion and clutch. |

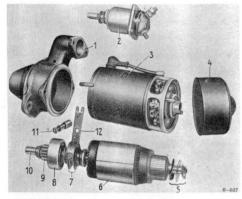

1. Drive bearing
2. Solenoid switch
3. Armature housing
4. End cap
5. Parts of armature brake
6. Armature
7. Guide ring
8. Overrunning clutch
9. Pinion
10. Armature shaft
11. Pivot pin
12. Shift lever

Starter disassembled.

chipped or broken teeth. Remove the armature shaft snap-ring and inspect the bearings. New bearings must be pressed into the housing ends. The brushes must be washed in carbon tet to remove all grease and replaced if worn badly. New brushes can be lightly sanded with emery cloth so that they slide freely in their holders. If brushes are replaced, it is a good idea to replace the brush springs as well.

Clean the commutator with carbon tet and check for burned areas. The commutator can be turned down on a lathe to make it perfectly round. The segments then must be undercut to a depth of .024″–.032″ using a suitably ground hacksaw blade. *NOTE: Do not sand armature with emery paper, because metallic particles in paper may short out segments.*

Check solenoid yoke length "a" and ad-

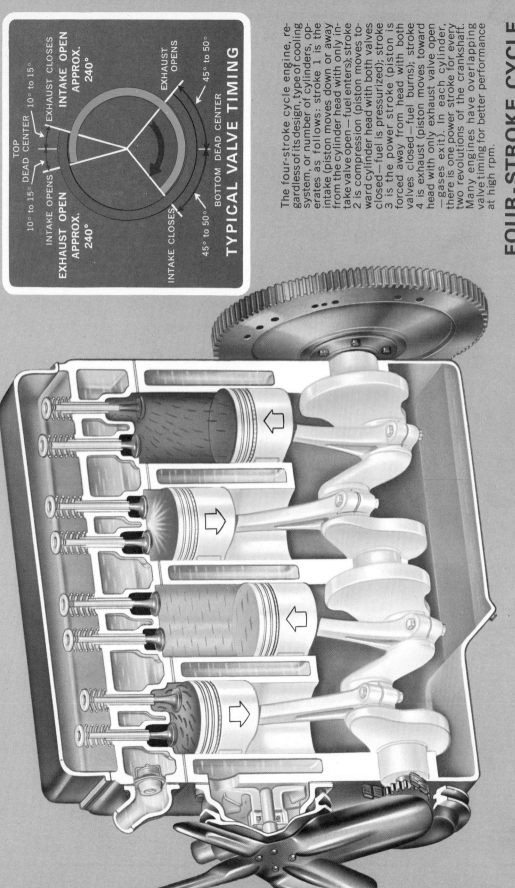

# FOUR-STROKE CYCLE

The four-stroke cycle engine, regardless of its design, type of cooling system, or number of cylinders, operates as follows: stroke 1 is the intake (piston moves down or away from the cylinder head with only intake valve open — fuel enters); stroke 2 is compression (piston moves toward cylinder head with both valves closed — fuel is pressurized); stroke 3 is the power stroke (piston is forced away from head with both valves closed — fuel burns); stroke 4 is exhaust (piston moves toward head with only exhaust valve open — gases exit). In each cylinder, there is one power stroke for every two revolutions of the crankshaft. Many engines have overlapping valve timing for better performance at high rpm.

## TYPICAL VALVE TIMING

TOP
DEAD CENTER

10° to 15°    10° to 15°

INTAKE OPENS
EXHAUST CLOSES

EXHAUST OPEN
APPROX.
240°

INTAKE OPEN
APPROX.
240°

EXHAUST
OPENS

45° to 50°

INTAKE CLOSES

45° to 50°

BOTTOM DEAD CENTER

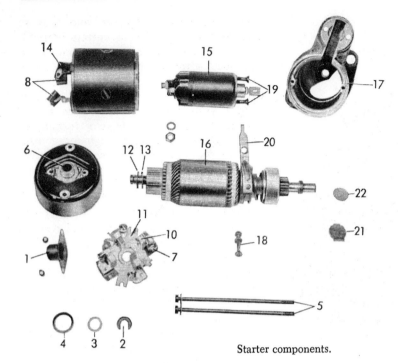

1. Protective cover
2. Locking plate
3. Compensating washer
4. Seal
5. Armature housing screws
6. Collector
7. Brush springs
8. + Carbon brushes
10. Guides
11. Brush holder
12. Thrust washer
13. Compensating washer
14. Connection exciter coil
15. Solenoid switch
16. Armature
17. Driving end shield
18. Bolt with nut
19. Fixing screws
20. Shift fork
21. Rubber seal
22. Steel washer

Starter components.

just, if necessary, by loosening locknut and screwing shaft in or out. Assembly is the reverse of disassembly.

### Armature Testing—Starter Disassembled

Lay the disassembled armature in the jaws of an armature growler and turn on the current. Slowly rotate the armature while holding a 6″ length of hacksaw blade against the metal segments. If the blade is

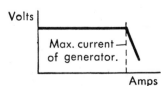

magnetically attracted to any part of the armature (buzzes), the armature must be replaced.

Use the test prods to test pairs of commutator segments. If the light goes on it indicates a short circuit in the commutator.

### Field Coil Testing— Starter Disassembled

Connect the prods from the armature growler between ground and the lead that normally goes to the solenoid (or use an ohmmeter). If the light goes on, or the ohmmeter indicates continuity. the field coil is grounded and must be replaced.

## Generator and Regulator

The generator is actually a DC shunt-wound electric motor operating in a manner opposite to that of a normal motor. Instead of current being supplied to the unit and mechanical power being "generated", mechanical power is supplied to the unit via a V-belt driven by the engine, and the resultant generated current used to recharge the battery and power the various electrical subsystems of the vehicle. En-

Armature testing. Top—using armature growler; Bottom—using 40-watt bulb. Dampness sometimes causes slight illumination.

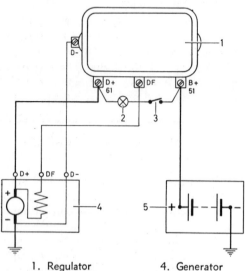

1. Regulator
2. Charging light
3. Ignition switch
4. Generator
5. Battery

Generating circuit.

gine speed varies, however, and thus so does generator speed (and current output). In order to keep the current constant for a fixed load, a regulator is utilized. In effect, this acts as an electrical "switch" to cut off current at a predetermined value, thus preventing system damage from "too much" current. *NOTE: This is why turning on the headlights on long, high-speed runs does nothing to prevent overcharging.*

### In-Car Generator Testing—Models with Three-Element Regulator

Hold the positive lead of a voltmeter to terminal #51 at the regulator and connect the negative lead to ground. The rated battery voltage should be indicated (12 volts). Turn on the ignition switch and check that the charging light goes on. Disconnect the blue wire from terminal D+ (#61) at the regulator; the charging light should now go out. If the light stays on, the blue wire is grounded somewhere along its length.

To test the regulator, connect a voltmeter between terminal D+ (#61) and the D— terminal at the regulator. Start the engine and disconnect the red wire from terminal B+ (#51) at the regulator and tape its end. Increase the engine speed and watch the voltmeter; when the needle no longer rises the regulating voltage has been achieved. No voltage indicates a maladjusted or malfunctioning regulator. In this case, sometimes polarizing the generator solves the problem. Disconnect the fan belt and connect a jumper wire between terminal DF and regulator terminal D—. Connect a jumper between regulator terminals B+ (#51) and D+ (#61). The generator should now spin (working like an electric motor) in its normal direction of

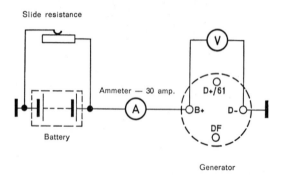

Alternator test.

# Generator Diagnosis

| Condition | Probable Cause | Correction |
|---|---|---|
| Battery not charging or not charging enough | 1. Brushes not touching commutator, sticking, worn, broken or oil-fouled.<br>2. Commutator oily.<br>3. Commutator worn.<br>4. Faulty connections<br>5. Defective battery.<br>6. Generator windings shorted.<br>7. Defective voltage regulator.<br>8. Fanbelt too loose; pulleys worn. | 1. Clean or replace brushes.<br>2. Clean commutator.<br>3. Machine commutator and undercut segments.<br>4. Tighten connections or replace wires.<br>5. Check battery and/or replace.<br>6. Test generator and repair.<br>7. Replace regulator.<br>8. Tighten fanbelt; replace pulleys. |
| Ammeter light does not light with engine off and ignition on | 1. Ammeter light bulb burnt out.<br>2. Battery discharged.<br>3. Defective battery.<br>4. Loose connections.<br>5. Defective voltage regulator. | 1. Install new bulb.<br>2. Charge battery.<br>3. Test and/or replace battery.<br>4. Tighten connections.<br>5. Replace regulator. |
| Ammeter light does not go out at high engine speed | 1. Wire at terminal No. 61 shorted.<br>2. Defective voltage regulator.<br>3. Defective generator. | 1. Replace wire or fix short.<br>2. Replace regulator.<br>3. Test and/or repair generator. |
| Ammeter light flickers | 1. Loose fanbelt.<br>2. Pulleys worn.<br>3. Generator brushes sticking. | 1. Tighten fanbelt.<br>2. Replace pulleys.<br>3. Check brushes and replace if necessary. |

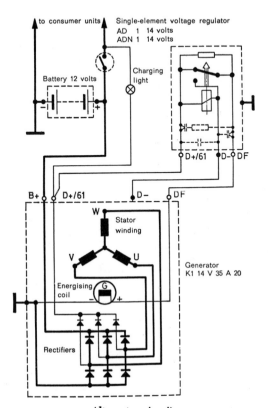

Alternator circuit.

rotation. Repeat the regulating voltage test. If the voltage is too low (see table), either the generator or regulator is faulty; if voltage is too high, usually only the regulator is at fault.

Test the regulator current regulation next. Disconnect the battery ground cable and the red wire from regulator terminal B+ (#51). Connect an ammeter between terminal #51 and the wire just removed, then reconnect the battery ground cable. Turn on all accessories and start the engine. Speed up the engine and check the ammeter reading; it now should indicate the regulating current. No current indicates a defective regulator, which must be replaced as a unit. Allow the engine to slow to idle speed. The ammeter should now indicate a slight *discharge* (reserve current).

### In-Car Generator Testing—Models with Three-Phase Generator (Alternator) and Single-Element Regulator

*CAUTION: On this model, never disconnect the generator leads or battery cables with the engine running, as induced peak voltage will destroy the sensitive* diode rectifiers. *Never short terminals to ground for the same reason (polarization). Always observe battery polarity when jump-starting and never use a battery charger as a "hot shot". Charge batteries with cables disconnected.*

To test regulation, connect a voltmeter between the generator B+ terminal and ground, after disconnecting battery ground cable. Disconnect the red wire at the B+ generator terminal and connect an ammeter (30–0–30) between the terminal and the wire just disconnected. Reconnect the battery ground cable and start the engine; turn on all electrical accessories (headlights on high beam, radio, air conditioner, etc.). Run the engine at 2,200 rpm and check the meter readings, comparing them to the specifications table.

If the voltage falls outside the specified limits, connect the voltmeter between the generator D+ and D− terminals and repeat the test. If the difference in the two voltmeter readings is greater than 0.5 volt,

the alternator is at fault; if less than 0.5 volt, the regulator. *NOTE: Remember, loose connections can result in false readings.*

### Generator Removal and Installation

Disconnect the battery ground cable and the wires at the generator. Tag the wires for easy assembly. Loosen the generator

1. Annular grooved
   bearing
2. Splash disc
3. Collector
4. Armature
5. Splash disc
6. Cover disc
7. Annular grooved
   bearing
8. Splash disc
9. Spacer ring

Generator armature.

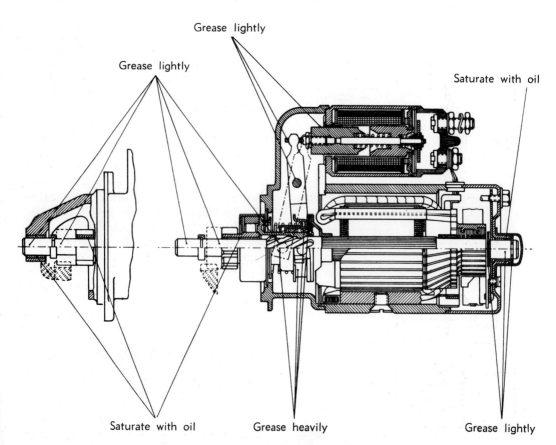

Lubrication points on Bosch starter.

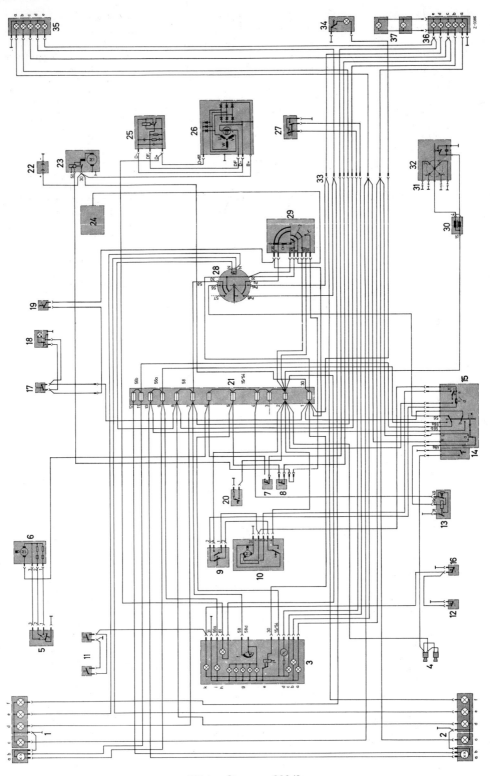

Wiring diagram—220/8.

*See overleaf for Key*

1. Right lighting unit
2. Left lighting unit
   a. Upper beam
   b. Lower beam
   c. Flash signal
   d. Parking light
   e. Fog light
   f. Clearance light
3. Instrument cluster
   a. Left signal indicator
   b. Right signal indicator
   c. Fuel reserve warning light
   d. Fuel level indicator
   e. Electric clock
   f. Control resistance for
       instrument lighting
   g. Instrument lighting
   h. Charging light
   i. Upper beam indicator
   k. Brake control
       Choke control indicator
4. Two-tone horn system
5. Blower switch (air intake)
6. Blower motor (air intake)

7. Stop light switch
8. Reversing light switch
9. Foot pump (windshield
    washer)
10. Wiper motor
11. Control switch for brake
    fluid
12. Control switch for parking
    brake
13. Flash signal mechanism
14. Horn ring
15. Combination switch
    a. Flash signal switch
    b. Flash approach signal
        switch
    c. Hand dimmer
    d. Windshield wiper switch
    e. Wiper speed switch
16. Choke cable control switch
17. Front left door contact
18. Reading light
19. Front right door contact
20. Cigar lighter

21. Fuses
22. Battery
23. Starter
24. Lead for optional extra
    (radio)
25. Voltage regulator
26. Generator
27. Fuel level indicator
28. Rotary light switch
29. Ignition starter switch
30. Ignition coil
31. Spark plugs
32. Distributor
33. Sleeve union for tail light
    wiring harness
34. Trunk compartment light
35. Right tail light
36. Left tail light
    a. Flash signal
    b. Tail light
    c. Reversing light
    d. Clearance light
    e. Stop light
37. License plate light

*Opposite*

1. Right lighting unit
2. Left lighting unit
   a. Upper beam
   b. Lower beam
   c. Flash signal
   d. Parking light
   e. Fog light
   f. Clearance light
3. Instrument cluster
   a. Left signal indicator
   b. Right signal indicator
   c. Fuel reserve warning light
   d. Fuel level indicator
   e. Electric clock
   f. Control resistance for
       instrument lighting
   g. Instrument lighting
   h. Charging light
   i. Upper beam control
   k. Brake control
4. Two-tone horn system
5. Blower switch (air intake)
6. Blower motor (air intake)

7. Stop light switch
8. Reversing light switch
9. Foot pump windshield
    washer
10. Wiper motor
11. Control switch for brake
    fluid
12. Control switch for parking
    brake
13. Flash signal mechanism
14. Horn ring
15. Combination switch
    a. Flash signal switch
    b. Flash approach signal
        switch
    c. Hand dimmer
    d. Windshield wiper switch
    e. Wiper speed switch
16. Cigar lighter
17. Front left door contact
18. Reading light
19. Front right door contact
20. Fuses

21. Lead for optional extra
    (radio)
22. Battery
23. Starter
24. Rotary light switch
25. Steering lock
26. Glow starter switch
27. Glow plug resistance control
28. Glow plugs
29. Sleeve union for tail light
    wiring harness
30. Fuel level indicator
31. Generator
32. Voltage regulator
33. Trunk compartment light
34. Right tail light
35. Left tail light
    a. Flash signal
    b. Tail light
    c. Reversing light
    d. Clearance light
    e. Stop light
36. License plate light

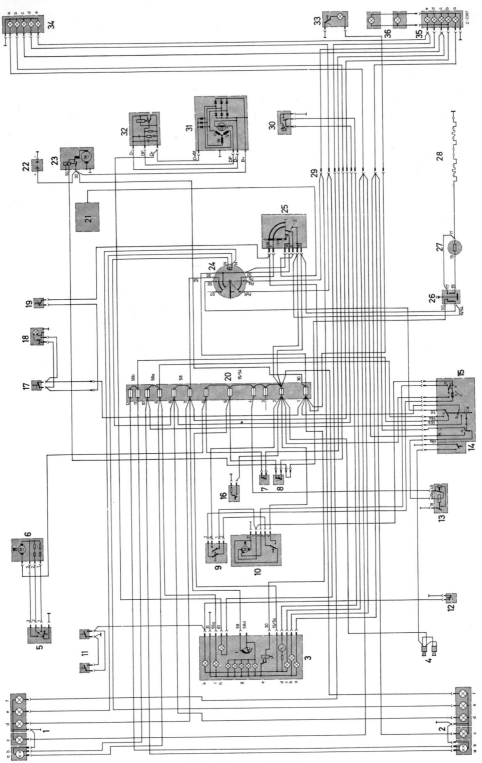

Wiring diagram—220D/8.

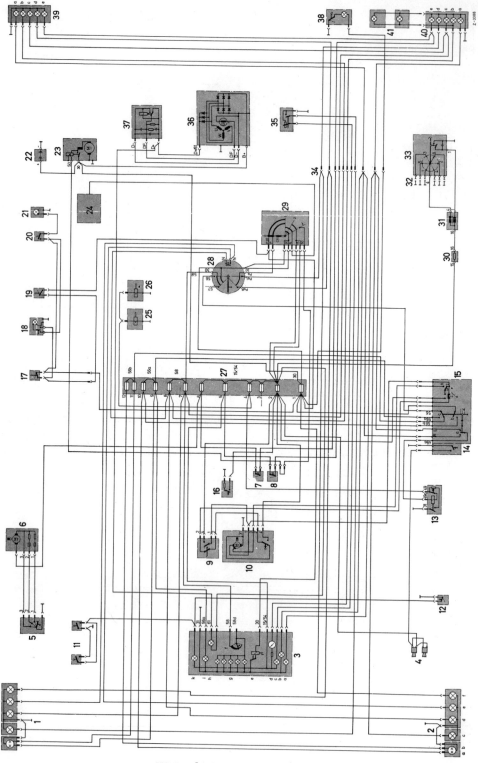

Wiring diagram—230/8, 250/8.

1. Right lighting unit
2. Left lighting unit
   a. Upper beam
   b. Lower beam
   c. Flash signal
   d. Parking light
   e. Fog light
   f. Clearance light
3. Instrument cluster
   a. Left signal indicator
   b. Right signal indicator
   c. Fuel reserve warning light
   d. Fuel level indicator
   e. Electric clock
   f. Control resistance for
      instrument lighting
   g. Instrument lighting
   h. Charging light
   i. Upper beam control
   k. Brake control
4. Two-tone horn mechanism
5. Blower switch (air intake)
6. Blower motor (air intake)
7. Stop light switch
8. Reversing light switch
9. Foot pump windshield
   washer
10. Wiper motor
11. Control switch for brake
    fluid
12. Control switch for parking
    brake
13. Flash signal mechanism
14. Horn ring
15. Combination switch
    a. Flash signal switch
    b. Flash approach signal
       switch
    c. Hand dimmer
    d. Windshield wiper switch
    e. Wiper speed switch
16. Cigar lighter
17. Front left door contact
18. Reading light
19. Front right door contact
20. Roof-light switch (on
    Model 250 only)
21. Rear roof light (on Model
    250 only)
22. Battery
23. Starter
24. Lead for optional extra
    (radio)
25. Automatic start mechanism
    on rear carburetor
26. Automatic start mechanism
    on front carburetor
27. Fuses
28. Rotary light switch
29. Ignition starter switch
30. Series resistance
31. Ignition coil
32. Spark plugs
33. Distributor
34. Sleeve union for tail light
    wiring harness
35. Fuel level indicator
36. Generator
37. Voltage regulator
38. Trunk compartment light
39. Right tail light
40. Left tail light
    a. Flash signal
    b. Tail light
    c. Reversing light
    d. Clearance light
    e. Stop light
41. License plate light

bracket pivot bolts, then loosen the swing bracket bolt and move the generator inward to remove the V-belt. Remove all bolts and remove generator. Installation is the reverse of removal. *NOTE: Fanbelt tension should be such that thumb pressure on the longest belt section results in .25"–.50" belt deflection.*

### Generator Service

Service procedures vary in detail. but in general are the same as for starter motors. Armature and field coil testing is identical, as is brush replacement and cleaning procedures. Disassembly and assembly is *basically* the same.

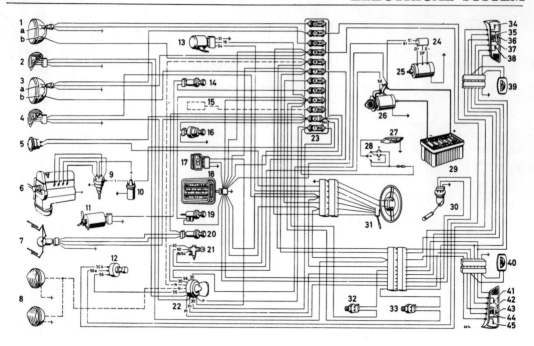

| | | | | | |
|---|---|---|---|---|---|
| 1a. | Headlight left, upper beam and lower beam | 12. | Foot dimmer switch | 29. | Battery |
| 1b. | Headlight left, parking light | 13. | Flash signal mechanism | 30. | Fuel level indicator |
| | | 14. | Heater blower switch | 31. | Flash signal switch with upper beam flash signal switch |
| 2. | Clearance and flash signal lights left | 15. | Free for optional extra | | |
| | | 16. | Cigar lighter | | |
| 3a. | Headlight right, upper beam and lower beam | 17. | Clock | 32. | Stop light switch |
| | | 18. | Instrument cluster | 33. | Reversing light switch |
| 3b. | Headlight right, parking light | 19. | Choke control | 34. | Flash signal right |
| | | 20. | Windshield wiper switch | 35. | Clearance light right |
| 4. | Clearance and flash signal lights right | 21. | Ignition starter switch | 36. | Reversing light right |
| | | 22. | Light switch with additional positions for clearance light and pull switch for fog lights | 37. | Tail light right |
| 5. | Horn | | | 38. | Stop light right |
| 6. | Engine | | | 39. | License plate light right |
| 7. | Windshield wiper | | | 40. | License plate light left |
| 8. | Fog light (optional extra) | 23. | Fuses | 41. | Stop light left |
| 9. | Distributor | 24. | Regulator | 42. | Tail light left |
| 10. | Ignition coil | 25. | Generator | 43. | Reversing light left |
| 11. | Heater blower motor | 26. | Starter | 44. | Clearance light left |
| | | 27. | Reading light | 45. | Flash signal left |
| | | 28. | Door contact switch | | |

Wiring diagram—190c.

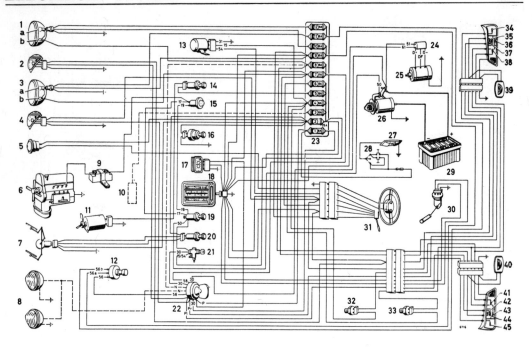

| | | |
|---|---|---|
| 1a. Headlight left, upper beam and lower beam | 12. Foot dimmer switch | 29. Battery |
| 1b. Headlight left, parking light | 13. Flash signal mechanism | 30. Fuel level indicator |
| 2. Clearance and flash signal lights left | 14. Heater blower switch | 31. Flash signal switch with upper beam flash signal switch |
| 3a. Headlight right, upper beam and lower beam | 15. Glow plug indicator resistor | |
| | 16. Cigar lighter | |
| 3b. Headlight right, parking light | 17. Clock | 32. Stop light switch |
| | 18. Instrument cluster | 33. Reversing light switch |
| 4. Clearance and flash signal lights right | 19. Glow plug starter switch | 34. Flash signal right |
| | 20. Windshield wiper switch | 35. Clearance light right |
| 5. Horn | 21. Steering lock | 36. Reversing light right |
| 6. Engine | 22. Light switch with additional positions for clearance light and pull switch for fog lights | 37. Tail light right |
| 7. Windshield wiper | | 38. Stop light right |
| 8. Fog light (optional extra) | | 39. License plate light right |
| 9. Glow plug resistance | | 40. License plate light left |
| 10. Free for optional extra | 23. Fuses | 41. Stop light left |
| 11. Heater blower motor | 24. Regulator | 42. Tail light left |
| | 25. Generator | 43. Reversing light left |
| | 26. Starter | 44. Clearance light left |
| | 27. Reading light | 45. Flash signal left |
| | 28. Door contact switch | |

Wiring diagram—190Dc.

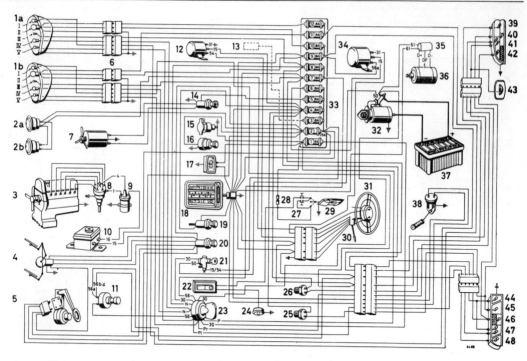

| | | |
|---|---|---|
| 1a. Lighting unit left | 10. Series resistance | 29. Reading light |
| I. Flash signal light | 11. Foot dimmer switch | 30. Flash signal switch and |
| II. Upper beam and lower | 12. Flash signal mechanism | upper beam signal |
| beam | 13. Automatic clutch | switch |
| III. Parking light | (optional) | 31. Steering wheel with horn |
| IV. Fog light | 14. Heater blower switch | ring |
| V. Clearance light | 15. Socket | 32. Starter |
| 1b. Lighting unit right | 16. Cigar lighter | 33. Fuses |
| I. Flash signal light | 17. Clock | 34. Upper beam flash |
| II. Upper beam and lower | 18. Instrument cluster | mechanism |
| beam | 19. Choke control | 35. Regulator |
| III. Parking light | 20. Windshield wiper switch | 36. Generator |
| IV. Fog light | 21. Ignition starter switch | 37. Battery |
| V. Clearance light | 22. Roof light switch | 38. Fuel level indicator |
| 2a. Horn right | (220 Sb) | 39. Flash signal right |
| 2b. Horn left | 23. Rotary light switch with | 40. Reversing light right |
| 3. Engine | positions for clearance | 41. Clearance light and tail |
| 4. Windshield wiper, two- | light left and right and | light right |
| stage | pull switch for fog lights | 42. Stop light right |
| 5. Foot pump with switch for | 24. Roof light | 43. License plate light right |
| windshield washer | 25. Reversing light switch | 44. License plate light left |
| 6. Plug connections | 26. Stop light switch | 45. Stop light left |
| 7. Heater blower motor | 27. Door contact switch | 46. Reversing light left |
| 8. Distributor | 28. Plug connections | 47. Tail and clearance light left |
| 9. Ignition coil | | 48. Flash signal left |

Wiring diagram—220b, 220Sb (first version).

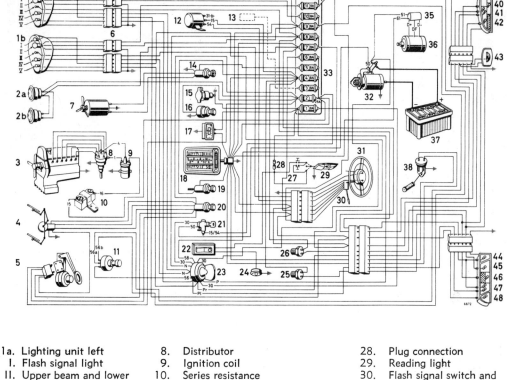

| 1a. | Lighting unit left | 8. | Distributor | 28. | Plug connection |
| I. | Flash signal light | 9. | Ignition coil | 29. | Reading light |
| II. | Upper beam and lower beam | 10. | Series resistance | 30. | Flash signal switch and upper beam flash signal switch |
| III. | Parking light | 11. | Foot dimmer switch | | |
| IV. | Fog light | 12. | Flash signal mechanism | | |
| V. | Clearance light | 13. | Free for optional extra | 31. | Steering wheel with horn ring |
| 1b. | Lighting unit right | 14. | Heater blower switch | | |
| I. | Flash signal light | 15. | Socket | 32. | Starter 12 volts |
| II. | Upper beam and lower beam | 16. | Cigar lighter | 33. | Fuses |
| | | 17. | Clock | 35. | Regulator |
| III. | Parking light | 18. | Instrument cluster | 36. | Generator 12 volts |
| IV. | Fog light | 19. | Choke control | 37. | Battery 12 volts |
| V. | Clearance light | 20. | Windshield wiper switch | 38. | Fuel level indicator |
| 2a. | Horn right | 21. | Steering lock | 39. | Flash signal right |
| 2b. | Horn left | 22. | Roof light switch | 40. | Reversing light right |
| 3. | Engine | | (only Model 220 S) | 41. | Clearance light and tail light right |
| 4. | Windshield wiper (two-stage in 220 S) | 23. | Light switch with additional positions for clearance light and pull switch for fog lights | 42. | Stop light right |
| 5. | Foot pump for windshield washer with switch for windshield wiper | | | 43. | License plate light right |
| | | 24. | Roof light (only Model 220 S) | 44. | License plate light left |
| | | | | 45. | Stop light left |
| | | 25. | Reversing light switch | 46. | Reversing light left |
| 6. | Plug connections | 26. | Stop light switch | 47. | Tail and clearance light left |
| 7. | Heater blower motor | 27. | Door contact switch | 48. | Flash signal left |

Arrangement Model 220 S Model 220 / Model 220 S applies to items 39–48.

Wiring diagram—220b, 220Sb (second version).

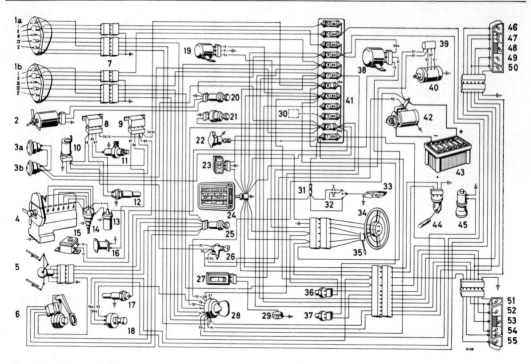

1a. Lighting unit left
  I. Flash signal light
  II. Upper beam and lower beam
  III. Parking light
  IV. Fog light
  V. Clearance light
1b. Lighting unit right
  I. Flash signal light
  II. Upper beam and lower beam
  III. Parking light
  IV. Fog light
  V. Clearance light
2. Heater blower motor
3a. Horn right
3b. Horn left
4. Spark plugs (engine)
5. Windshield wiper
6. Foot pump and switch for windshield washer
7. Plug connection
8. Relay for electromagnetic starting valve
9. Relay for automatic starter aid
10. Time switch

11. Electro-magnetic starting valve
12. Thermo time switch
13. Ignition coil
14. Distributor
15. Series resistance for ignition coil
16. Magnet for mixture control
17. Thermo switch
18. Foot dimmer switch
19. Flash signal mechanism
20. Switch for heater blower motor
21. Cigar lighter
22. Socket
23. Electric clock
24. Instrument cluster
25. Windshield wiper switch
26. Steering lock
27. Roof light switch
28. Rotary light switch
29. Roof light
30. Free for optional extra
31. Plug connection
32. Door contact switch left and right
33. Reading light

34. Steering wheel with horn ring
35. Flash signal switch and upper beam flash signal switch
36. Stop light switch
37. Reversing light switch
38. Beam flash signal
39. Regulator (Lima)
40. Generator
41. Fuses
42. Starter
43. Battery
44. Fuel level indicator
45. Electric fuel feed pump
46. Flash signal right
47. Tail light and clearance light right
48. Reversing light right
49. Stop light right
50. License plate light right
51. Licnse plate light left
52. Stop light left
53. Reversing light left
54. Tail light and clearance light left
55. Flash signal left

Wiring diagram—220b, 220Sb (first version).

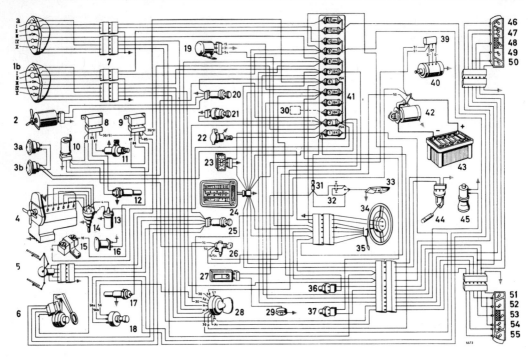

| | | |
|---|---|---|
| 1a. Lighting unit left | 11. Electromagnetic starting valve | 33. Reading light |
|   I. Flash signal light | 12. Thermo time switch | 34. Steering wheel with horn ring |
|   II. Upper beam and lower beam | 13. Ignition coil | 35. Flash signal switch and upper beam flash signal switch |
|   III. Parking light | 14. Distributor | |
|   IV. Fog light | 15. Series resistance for ignition coil | |
|   V. Clearance light | 16. Magnet for mixture control | 36. Stop light switch |
| 1b. Lighting unit right | | 37. Reversing light switch |
|   I. Flash signal light | 17. Thermo switch | 39. Regulator (Lima) |
|   II. Upper beam and lower beam | 18. Foot dimmer switch | 40. Generator |
|   III. Parking light | 19. Flash signal mechanism | 41. Fuses |
|   IV. Fog light | 20. Switch for heater blower motor | 42. Starter |
|   V. Clearance light | 21. Cigar lighter | 43. Battery |
| 2. Heater blower motor | 22. Socket | 44. Fuel level indicator |
| 3a. Horn right | 23. Electric clock | 45. Electric fuel feed pump |
| 3b. Horn left | 24. Instrument cluster | |
| 4. Spark plugs (engine) | 25. Windshield wiper switch | 46. Flash signal right |
| 5. Windshield wiper, two-stage | 26. Steering lock | 47. Tail light and clearance light right |
| 6. Foot pump and switch for windshield washer | 27. Roof light switch | 48. Reversing light right |
| | 28. Rotary light switch | 49. Stop light right |
| 7. Plug connection | 29. Roof light | 50. License plate light right |
| 8. Relay for electromagnetic starting valve | 30. Free for optional extra | 51. License plate light left |
| | 31. Plug connection | 52. Stop light left |
| 9. Relay for automatic starter aid | 32. Door contact switch left and right | 53. Reversing light left |
| | | 54. Tail light and clearance light left |
| 10. Time switch (delay switch) | | 55. Flash signal left |

Wiring diagram—220SEb sedan (second version).

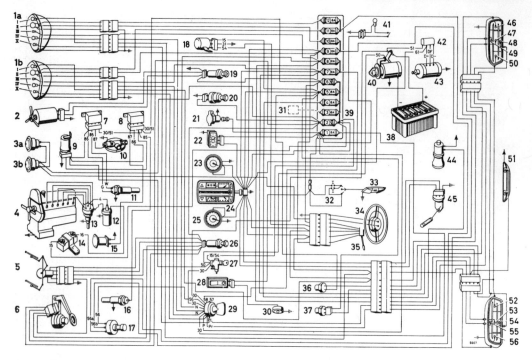

| 1a. | Lighting unit left |
| I. | Flash signal light |
| II. | Upper beam and lower beam |
| III. | Parking light |
| IV. | Fog light |
| V. | Clearance light |
| 1b. | Lighting unit right |
| I. | Flash signal light |
| II. | Upper beam and lower beam |
| III. | Parking light |
| IV. | Fog light |
| V. | Clearance light |
| 2. | Heater blower motor |
| 3a. | Horn right |
| 3b. | Horn left |
| 4. | Spark plugs (engine) |
| 5. | Windshield wiper, two-stage |
| 6. | Foot pump for windshield washer with switch for windshield wiper |
| 7. | Relay for electromagnetic starting valve |
| 8. | Relay for automatic starter aid |
| 9. | Time switch for automatic starter aid |
| 10. | Electromagnetic starting valve |
| 11. | Thermo time switch (for para 10) |
| 12. | Ignition coil |
| 13. | Distributor |
| 14. | Series resistance for ignition coil |
| 15. | Solenoid switch for mixture control |
| 16. | Thermo switch (for para 15) |
| 17. | Foot dimmer switch |
| 18. | Flash signal mechanism |
| 19. | Blower switch with pilot light |
| 20. | Cigar lighter |
| 21. | Socket |
| 22. | Electric clock |
| 23. | Speedometer |
| 24. | Instrument cluster |
| 25. | Revolution counter |
| 26. | Windshield wiper switch |
| 27. | Steering lock |
| 28. | Roof light switch |
| 29. | Rotary light switch |
| 30. | Roof light |
| 31. | Optional extra |
| 32. | Door contact switch left and right |
| 33. | Reading light |
| 34. | Steering wheel with horn ring |
| 35. | Flash signal switch and upper beam flash signal switch |
| 36. | Reversing light switch |
| 38. | Battery |
| 39. | Fuses |
| 40. | Starter |
| 41. | Glove compartment light |
| 42. | Regulator (generator) |
| 43. | Generator |
| 44. | Electric fuel feed pump |
| 45. | Fuel level indicator |
| 46. | Flash signal right |
| 47. | Tail light right |
| 48. | Reversing light right |
| 49. | Clearance light right |
| 50. | Stop light right |
| 51. | License plate light |
| 52. | Stop light left |
| 53. | Tail light left |
| 54. | Reversing light left |
| 55. | Clearance light left |
| 56. | Flash signal left |

Wiring diagram—220SEb Coupe.

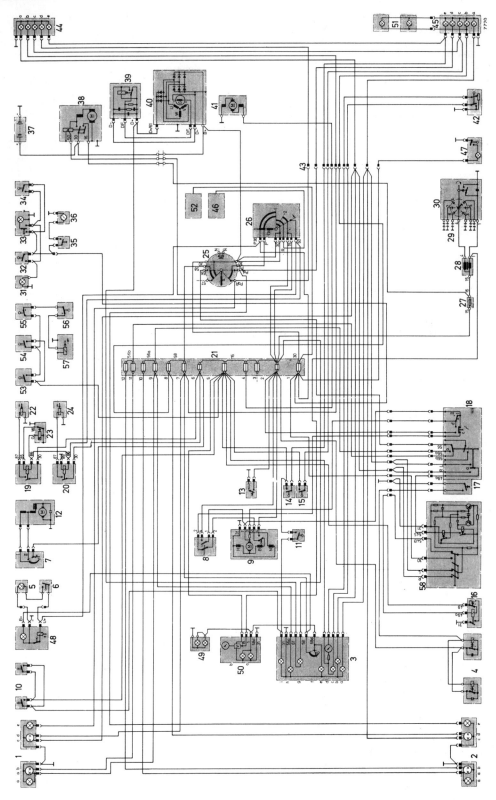

Wiring diagram—280SE/8 Coupe and Conot.

*See overleaf for Key*

1. Light assembly (right side)
2. Light assembly (left side)
 a. High beam
 b. Low beam
 c. Turn signal light
 d. Parking light
 e. Side light
3. Instrument cluster
 a. Turn signal light indicator, left
 b. Turn signal light indicator, right
 c. Low fuel level warning light
 d. Fuel gauge
 e. Instrument illumination
 f. Instrument illumination rheostat
 g. Generator (alternator) charge warning light
 h. High beam indicator
 i. Parking brake and brake fluid level warning light
4. Horn system
5. Glove compartment light
6. Switch for glove compartment light
7. Heater blower switch
8. Windshield washer foot pump
9. Wiper motor
10. Brake fluid level warning light control element
11. Parking brake warning light control element

12. Heater blower motor
13. Cigar lighter
14. Stop light switch
15. Back-up light switch
16. Sending unit for turn signal light
17. Horn ring
18. Combination switch
 a. Turn signal light switch
 b. Headlight dimmer switch
 c. Windshield wiper switch
 d. Windshield wiper speed control switch
19. Relay for starter valve
20. Relay for mixture control
21. Fuses
22. Magneto for starter valve
23. Thermo time switch
24. Magneto for mixture control
25. Headlight switch
26. Ignition starter switch
27. Series resistance
28. Ignition coil
29. Spark plugs
30. Distributor
31. Entrance light
32. Courtesy light switch, left door
33. Reading light
34. Courtesy light switch, right door
35. Switch for dome light, rear
36. Dome light, rear

37. Battery
38. Starter
39. Voltage regulator
40. Alternator
41. Fuel feed pump
42. Fuel gauge sending unit
43. Rear light unit wiring harness connecting plug
44. Rear light unit (right side)
45. Rear light unit (left side)
 a. Turn signal light
 b. Tail light
 c. Back-up light
 d. Side light
 e. Stop light
46. Spare wire for extras (radio)
47. Trunk light
48. Electric clock
49. Speedometer light
50. Tachometer
 a. Tachometer light
 b. Electric indicating system
51. License plate light
52. Automatic antenna (optional)
53. Switch, 3rd gear
54. Switch, 4th gear
55. Switch, clutch pedal
56. Switch, accelerator pedal shaft
for exhaust emission control system
57. Magneto
58. Hazard warning light transmitter

*Opposite*

1. Light assembly (right side)
2. Light assembly (left side)
 a. High beam
 b. Low beam
 c. Turn signal light
 d. Parking light
 e. Side light
3. Instrument cluster
 a. Turn signal light indicator, left
 b. Turn signal indicator, right
 c. Low fuel level warning light
 d. Fuel gauge
 e. Electric clock
 f. Instrument illumination rheostat
 g. Instrument illumination
 h. Generator (alternator) charge warning light
 i. High beam indicator
 k. Parking brake and brake fluid level warning light
4. Dual horn system
5. Glove compartment light
6. Switch for glove compartment light
7. Heater blower switch
8. Windshield washer foot pump
9. Wiper motor
10. Brake fluid level warning light control element

11. Parking brake warning light control element
12. Heater blower motor
13. Cigar lighter
14. Stop light switch
15. Back up light switch
16. Sending unit for turn signal light
17. Horn ring
18. Combination switch
 a. Turn signal light switch
 b. Headlight dimmer switch
 c. Windshield wiper switch
 d. Windshield wiper speed control switch
19. Relay for starter valve
20. Relay for mixture control
21. Fuses
22. Magneto for starter valve
23. Thermo time switch
24. Magneto for mixture control
25. Headlight switch
26. Ignition starter switch
27. Series resistance
28. Ignition coil
29. Spark plugs
30. Distributor
31. Entrance light
32. Courtesy light switch, left front door
33. Reading light
34. Courtesy light switch, right front door
35. Switch for dome light

36. Dome light, rear
37. Battery
38. Starter
39. Voltage regulator
40. Alternator
41. Fuel feed pump
42. Fuel gauge sending unit
43. Rear light unit wiring harness connecting plug
44. Rear light unit (right side)
45. Rear light unit (left side)
 a. Turn signal light
 b. Tail light
 c. Back up light
 d. Side light
 e. Stop light
46. Spare wire for extras (radio)
47. Trunk light
48. License plate light
49. Door contact, rear, right
50. Door contact, rear, left
51. Switch, accelerator pedal shaft
52. Switch, clutch pedal
53. Solenoid, injection pump
54. Switch, gear-shift position (in 3rd and 4th gear closed)
for exhaust emission control system
55. Hazard warning light transmitter

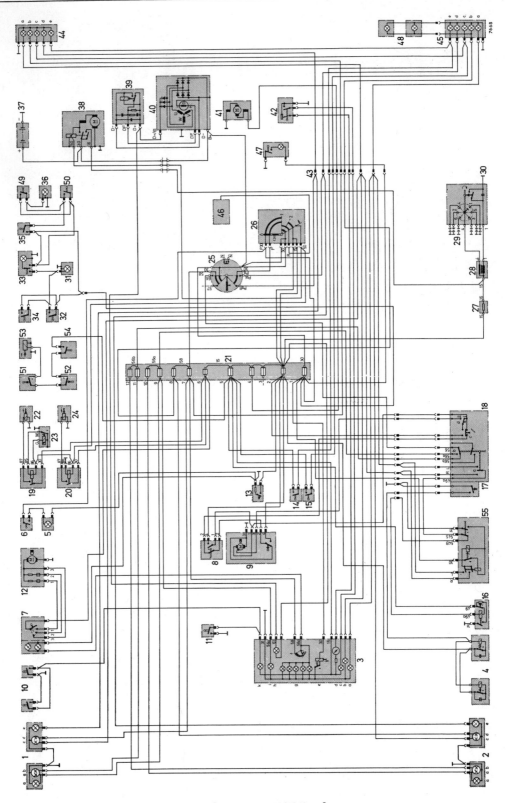

Wiring diagram—280SE/8 sedan.

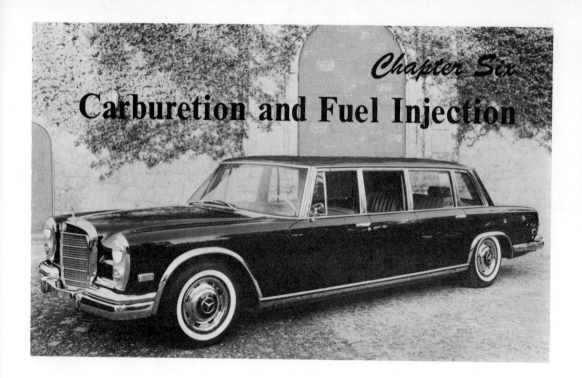

# Chapter Six
# Carburetion and Fuel Injection

## Part I
## Carburetion

### Idle and Linkage Adjustment—190c

The 190c is equipped with one Solex 34 PICB carburetor. To adjust, first check the throttle butterfly shaft for ease of movement. Detach pushrod (9) from lever (11) and disconnect return spring (1). Turn out the idle screw (8) until the butterfly is completely closed, then turn the screw in until the butterfly is almost ready to open. From this position, turn screw in exactly one turn. Open the butterfly all the way and make sure the limit screw (12) contacts the full load stop on the housing, then reconnect the pushrod (9) and return spring (1). Press the accelerator pedal to the floor and make sure the butterfly opens fully.

To adjust idle speed, screw in the idle mixture screw (7) until it seats, then back it out exactly two turns. *NOTE: Do not overtighten—which would damage the needle seat.*

Start the engine and allow it to warm up, connect a tachometer between the distributor-to-coil *primary* wire and ground, and adjust idle speed to 750–800 rpm. Adjust

the *mixture* screw until the highest, smoothest idle speed is attained, then re-adjust screw (8) to get 750–800 rpm idle speed again.

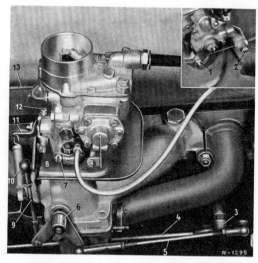

| | |
|---|---|
| 1. Clamp screw | 8. Idle adjustment |
| 2. Clamp screw |    screw |
| 3. Control lever | 9. Pushrod |
| 4. Rod | 10. Return spring |
| 5. Rod | 11. Throttle valve lever |
| 6. Control lever | 12. Aperture limiting |
| 7. Idle mixture ad- |    screw |
|    justment screw | 13. Choke control |

Type 190c carburetor.

## Carburetor Specifications

| Model | Carb. Type | Air Horn Ø (mm.) | Main Jet | Air Correct. Jet | Mixing Tube | Emuls. Chamber Vent | Idle Fuel Jet | Idle Air Jet Bore | Enrich. Valve | Acceler- ator Pump | Inject. Amt. (cc./stroke) | Pump Jet | Inject. Tube | Choke Fuel Jet | Choke Air Bore (mm.) | Float Needle | Float Wt. (gm.) | Fuel Level (mm.) | Bypass Bores (mm.) |
|---|---|---|---|---|---|---|---|---|---|---|---|---|---|---|---|---|---|---|---|
| 190c | S 34PICB | 28 | 0145 | 170 | 49 | | 50 | 1.5 | | No. 72 neutral | 1.0–1.2 | 80 | high .5 graded | 230[3] | 6.5[5] | 2.0 | 5.7 | 17–19 | 1.2 |
| 200 | S 38PDSI | 28 | 137.5 | 80 | N.R. | 0.5 | 62.5[4] | 1.6 | | neutral | 0.7–1.0[6] | | high .5 graded | | | 2.0 | 8.5 | [6] | 1.5/1.3 |
| 220b | S 34PICB | 24 | 0120 | 200 | 44 | | 50 | 1.0 | | No. 72 neutral | 0.9–1.2 | 50 | high .5 graded | 180 | 4.0 | 1.5 | 5.7 | 17–19 | 1.25 |
| 230 | S 38PDSI | 26 | 135 | 180 | N.R. | 0.5 | 50 | 1.6 | 90[7] | neutral | 1.0–1.3[5] | | high .4 graded* | | | 2.0 | 8.5 | [6] | 1.5/1.3 |
| 220Sb [11][12] | Front / Rear | 23 / 27 | 0115[8] / 135 | 200 / 190 | 44 | | 50 | 1.4[9] | 60[8] | No. 831 neutral | 1.3–1.7 / 1.3–1.7 | 80 | high .5 graded | 90 [10] | 2.0 [10] | 2.0 / 2.0 | 7.3 | 19–21 | 1.2/1.8 |
| 220Sb [12] | Front / Rear | 23 / 27 | 112.5 / 120 | 100 / 150 | 4S / 4N | | 45 | 1.5 | | | 0.8–1.2 | | .5 graded | | | 2.0 / 2.0 | 8.5 / 8.5 | 18–20 / 18–20 | |
| 230, 230S | Front / Rear | 24 / 28 | 115 / 120 | 100[12] / 130 | 4S / 4N | | 45 | 1.3 | | | 0.7–1.0 | | .5 graded | | | 2.0 / 2.0 | 8.5 / 8.5 | 21–23 / 21–23 | |
| 250S | Front / Rear | 24 / 28 | 120 / 120 | 110 / 120 | 4S / 4N | | 45 | 1.3 | | | 0.7–1.0 | | .5 graded | | | 2.0 / 2.0 | 8.5 / 8.5 | 21–23 / 21–23 | |

NOTE: For late-model carburetors modified for U.S. market (exhaust emission control), see Appendix.

1. Solex 34PAITA carburetors.
2. Zenith 35/40 INAT carburetors.
3. Up to chassis No. 10—105281 or 12—107377—choke air bore 4.0 and jet 180.
4. Up to chassis No. 161599—idle fuel jet 55, idle air bore 1.0 and bypass bores 1.3/1.0.
5. Automatic transmission front carburetor—0.6–0.9 cc./stroke.
6. Float level O.K. if 1.0 mm. (0.039") seal ring installed under float needle.
7. Up to chassis No. 006122—100.
8. Some models with carburetor No. 4 413 610 had 0112.5 main jet and No. 50 enrichment jet (front carburetor).
9. Up to engine No. 10—068125, 11—004644 and 12—000390—1.5 with bypass bores 1.15/1.15.
10. Up to engine No. 10—031160 and 11—003114— 100 with 3.0 mm. choke air bore.
11. Pump diaphragm bolt length – 18.7–18.9 mm., plate diameter 32 mm. (22 mm. on carburetor No. 4 509 149).
12. Up to chassis No. 019242 (230) and 094927 (230S) — 90.

* Front carburetor, automatic transmission – .5 graded.

NOTE: Carburetor repair kits are of three basic types—repair, Vit, and gasket. The following summarizes the parts in each type:

**Repair kits**
all jets and gaskets
all diaphragms
float needle value
volume control screw
spring for pump diaphragm
pump ball value
main jet carrier
float
complete intermediate rod
intermediate pump lever
complete injector tube
some cover hold-down screws and washers

**Vit kits**
all gaskets
float needle value
volume control screw
all diaphragms
spring

**Gasket kits**
all needed gaskets

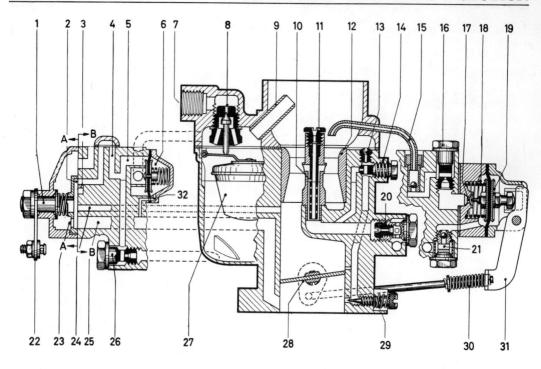

1. Starter rotary slide valve
2. Graded intake bore in starter flange for fuel canal (4)
3. Graded intake bore in starter flange for fuel slot
4. Fuel canal to starter system
5. Air canal from starter air valve to fuel canal (4)
6. Starter air valve
7. Fuel-line connection in carburetor cover
8. Float needle valve
9. Vent tube for float chamber
10. Mixing tube holder with mixing tube
11. Air correction jet
12. Air horn
13. Idle air jet
14. Idle fuel jet
15. Injection tube
16. Pump jet
17. Bore
18. Diaphragm spring
19. Pump diaphragm
20. Main jet plug with main jet
21. Ball valve
22. Starter lever
23. Starter air bore in starter rotary slide valve
24. Additional air canal
25. Starter mixture canal
26. Starter fuel jet
27. Float
28. Throttle valve
29. Idle mixture adjustment screw
30. Connecting rod with compression spring
31. Pump arm
32. Vacuum canal for starter air valve

Solex 34PICB carburetor.

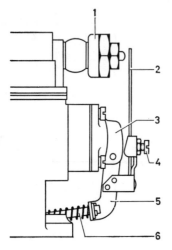

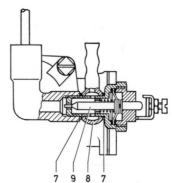

1. Return valve
2. Spring-loaded the pump arm head
3. Accelerator pump
4. Adjusting screw
5. Pump arm
6. Connecting rod
7. Fiber gasket
8. Ring connector
9. Valve pin

Scavenging device on 190c.

| | | |
|---|---|---|
| 1. Double lever | 7. Relay lever | 17. Fuel line |
| 2. Pushrod | 8. Spring-loaded pushrod | 18. Idle fuel jet |
| 3. Eccentric screw | 9. Throttle valve lever | 19. Pump jet |
| 4a. Ball socket, left-hand thread | 10. Return spring | 20. Idle mixture adjustment screw |
| 4b. Ball socket, right-hand thread | 11. Idle adjustment screw | 21. Main jet |
| 5a. Hexagon nut, left-hand thread | 12. Aperture limiting screw | 22. Union for tester |
| 5b. Hexagon nut, right-hand thread | 13. Coil spring for choke control | 23. Screw plug |
| 6. Pushrod | 14. Choke control | 24. Vacuum line distributor |
| | 15. Clamping screw for choke control | 25. Pump arm |
| | 16. Connecting rod | 26. Accelerating pump |

Type 220b with Solex 34PICB carburetors.

During idling or low speed operation, the engine needs little fuel and, as a consequence, the danger of vapor lock under high temperature conditions is increased. To compensate for this, a fuel return valve is incorporated into the carburetor. This valve is operated by the spring-loaded accelerator pump arm to allow excess fuel to run back through the valve and return line to the fuel tank, thus cooling the fuel and preventing vapor lock.

To adjust the valve, push the accelerator linkage until the accelerator pump lever (5) is fully against its stop, then turn adjusting screw (4) until return valve (1) is completely closed.

## Idle and Linkage Adjustment— 220b and 220Sb

Early models of the 220 b series used two Solex 34 PICB carburetors with "straight" linkage, while later models used progressive linkage. The 220 Sb used two Solex 34 PAITA carburetors with both "straight" and progressive linkage, while later models used two Zenith 35/40 INAT carburetors with progressive linkage. (See Chapter 1 for ending chassis numbers.)

1. Double lever
2. Pushrod
3. Eccentric screw
4a. Ball socket, left-hand thread
4b. Ball socket, right-hand thread
5a. Hexagon nut, left-hand thread
5b. Hexagon nut, right-hand thread
6. Pushrod
7. Relay lever
8. Spring-loaded pushrod
9. Throttle valve lever

10. Return spring
11. Idle adjustment screw
12. Return spring
13. Clamp
14. Relay lever
15. Connecting rod (to starter lever)
16. Connecting rod
17. Fuel pressure line
18. Idle fuel jet
19. Pump jet
20. Idle mixture adjustment screw
21. Main jet of stage 1
22. Union for tester
23. Screw plug

24. Vacuum line, distributor
25. Pump arm
26. Accelerating pump
27. Adjustment screw and lock nut
28. Spring-loaded pump arm head
29. Fuel return valve
30. Fuel return line
31. Coil spring for choke control
32. Rubber bushing
33. Adjusting nut
34. Choke control
35. Clamping screw for choke control

Type 220Sb with Solex 34PAITA carburetors.

To adjust the linkage on both 220 b and 220 Sb models using Solex carburetors, first detach pushrods (2) and (6) (or (3) and (5) for progressive linkage) and check their length. Pushrod (2) should be 3.34″ long (center to center of ball sockets); pushrod (5) should be 3.86″ long; pushrods (6) and (3) should be 7.41″ long. Pack the ball sockets with chassis grease and re-install, then detach pushrods (8), or (1), from the front and rear carburetors and check the linkage and carburetor butterflies for ease of movement; oil if necessary.

Operate pushrod (8) to open the butter-fly and make sure the limit screw (12) contacts the full load stop with the butterfly fully open (220 b).

On 220 Sb models, the limit stop on the second carburetor must contact the housing with the butterflies of *both* carburetors fully open. Unscrew the idle screw (11) on both carburetors until the butterflies are completely closed, then turn them in until the butterflies are just ready to open. From this point, turn the screws in one turn.

On cars having "straight" linkage, adjust eccentric screw (3) so that the slot is at

1. Spring-loaded
   pushrod
2. Relay lever
3. Pushrod
4. Adjustment screw
   or fillister
   head screw
   M 8 DIN 85
5. Pushrod
6. Adjusting ring
7. Relay lever
8. Roller
9. Quadrant lever
10. Cylinder cover
11. Threaded bolt
12. Bearing bracket

Type 220Sb with Solex 34PAITA carburetors and progressive linkage.

| | | |
|---|---|---|
| 1. Connecting rod | 7. Reversing lever | 11. Lever |
| 2. Throttle valve lever | 8. Float chamber vent valve | 12. Fuel return valve |
| 3. Quadrant lever | 9. Pushrod | 13. Pushrod |
| 4. Idle adjustment screw | 10. Adjustment screw | 14. Relay lever |
| 5. Pump arm | | 15. Adjusting ring |
| 6. Idle mixture adjustment | | 16. Roller |
|     screw | | 17. Quadrant lever |

Type 220Sb with Zenith 35/40 INAT carburetors.

right angles to the front relay lever, with the eccentric pointing upward. On cars having progressive linkage, install a screw (4), similar to the one shown, having a ⅝" diameter head. Pull back on the bellcrank until it contacts the eccentric screw (3) or the homemade screw (4) and make sure that the butterfly lever is resting against the idle adjustment screw. Adjust the pushrods so that, in this position, it is possible to snap them over their ball sockets without forcing. Remove screw (4) and depress the accelerator pedal to the floor to make sure the butterflies open fully.

In the case of the 220 Sb having INAT carburetors, disconnect pushrods (9) and (13) and check linkage for ease of movement, then check that bellcrank (7) contacts the housing with the butterfly fully open. Adjust idle screws (4), after unloading chokes, by unscrewing until the butterflies are fully closed, then turning in until the butterflies are just ready to open and continuing exactly one turn more after that point.

The connecting rods (1) then must be adjusted to 1.58" in length and the pushrod (9) adjusted so that, with the butterfly levers resting against idle stop screws, it can be pushed onto its ball sockets without forcing.

Idle speed adjustment is the same for both the 220 b and 220 Sb. First screw in the idle mixture screws (20) or (6) until bottomed, then back out 1½ turns on 220 b and two turns on 220 Sb. Start the engine and allow it to warm up, then, on engines having progressive linkage, disconnect pushrods (5) or (13). On engines having "straight" linkage, turn the eccentric screw (13) to gain enough clearance between the screw and bellcrank (7) for idle adjustment.

Connect a tachometer between the coil-to-distributor primary wire and ground, then evenly adjust idle speed screws (11) or (4) on *both* carburetors to attain 750–800 rpm idle speed. Now adjust the idle *mixture* screws, evenly, to attain the smoothest, fastest idle speed possible, then readjust idle speed screws evenly to get 750–800 rpm engine speed.

On 220 Sb models having INAT carburetors, check the float chamber vent. With the butterfly in idle position, the lever (7) should lift the valve pin (8) .060"–.080";

adjust by carefully bending lever (7). On engines having progressive linkage, attach pushrods (5) or (13) and adjust the knurled nuts (6) or (15) so that the roller (8) or (16) rests against the limit stop without tension. On engines having "straight" linkage, adjust eccentric screw (3) to give .008" clearance between it and the bellcrank (7). Make sure the chokes operate in synchronization.

The 34 PAITA carburetors have a fuel return valve incorporated into the accelerator pump system in the same manner as on 190 c models. To adjust this valve, depress the spring-loaded pushrod at the butterfly lever of the front carburetor and

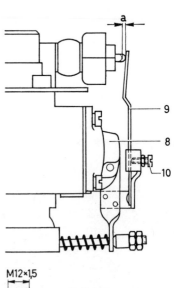

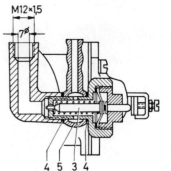

3. Valve pin
4. Fiber gasket
5. Ring connector
8. Accelerating pump
9. Spring-loaded pump arm head
10. Adjusting screw
a. = 0.4—0.6 mm. (.016-.024")

Scavenging device on 220b and 220Sb.

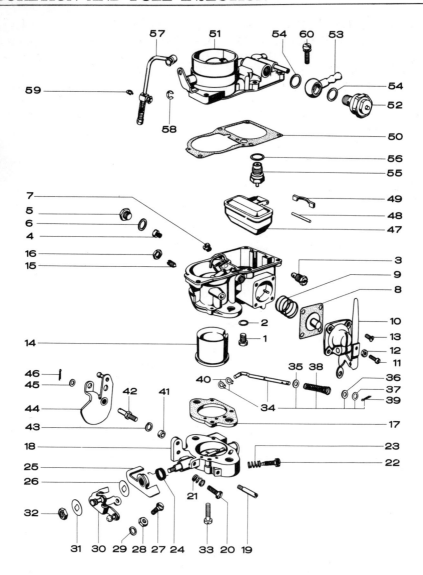

| | | |
|---|---|---|
| 1. Cheesehead screw | 21. Pressure spring | 41. Washer |
| 2. Seal ring | 22. Idle volume control screw | 42. Bearing bolt |
| 3. Idle jet | 23. Pressure screw | 43. Lockwasher |
| 4. Main jet | 24. Return spring | 44. Choke lever |
| 5. Plug screw | 25. Operating lever | 45. Washer |
| 6. Seal ring | 26. Spacer washer | 46. Cotter pin |
| 7. Air correction jet | 27. Choke adjustment screw | 47. Complete float |
| 8. Diaphragm | 28. Hex head nut | 48. Float pin |
| 9. Diaphragm spring | 29. Lockwasher | 49. Hold-down |
| 10. Pump cover | 30. Throttle lever | 50. Seal ring |
| 11. Cheesehead screw | 31. Safety washer | 51. Carburetor top |
| 12. Hex head nut | 32. Hex head nut | 52. Fuel return valve |
| 13. Countersunk screw | 33. Cheesehead screw | 53. Ring hose piece |
| 14. Venturi | 34. Pump connecting rod | 54. Seal ring |
| 15. Venturi lockscrew | 35. Flat washer | 55. Needle valve |
| 16. Hex head nut | 36. Flat washer | 56. Seal ring |
| 17. Isolation gasket | 37. Flat washer | 57. Choke connecting rod |
| 18. Complete throttle valve | 38. Pressure spring | 58. Safety washer |
| 19. Connection tube | 39. Cotter pin | 59. Expansion ring |
| 20. Idle adjustment screw | 40. Expansion ring | 60. Cheesehead screw |

Solex 36/40 PDSI carburetor (U. S. version).

back out the idle speed screw until the throttle butterfly is completely closed. Now, screw in adjusting screw (10) on the accelerator pump arm until the return valve is completely closed, then back out the adjusting screw to the point where the return valve pin has covered a distance ("a") of .016″–.024″; lock the adjusting screw. Improper adjustment of the return valve often results in a lack of fuel at high speeds.

### Idle and Linkage Adjustment—200, 230, 230S and 250S with Solex 36/40 PDSI Carburetors

These models use two Solex 36/40 PDSI-2 carburetors. Since the advent of the closed crankcase breather system in 1965, it is sometimes difficult to attain smooth idle speed. (The engine sucks in unburnt crankcase vapor, which impairs combustion efficiency at low speeds.) Before adjusting carburetors, adjust the ignition timing and check the spark plugs. Start the engine and allow it to come to operating temperature, then remove the air cleaner.

To adjust carburetors, disconnect pushrods (1) and (15) and turn in the idle mixture screws (8) until they seat (don't overtighten). Turn the screws out ¾ turn for 200 and 230 models, 1¼ turns for 230 S

and 250 S. Check that, as accelerator pedal is depressed, both throttle butterflies open fully and together. Re-adjust pushrod length to achieve this.

Connect a tachometer between engine ground and the distributor-to-coil primary wire and adjust idle speed screws (6) evenly to obtain specified idle speed (see Chapter 2). Now, adjust idle mixture screws (8) evenly to attain the smoothest, fastest idle speed possible, then re-adjust idle speed screws evenly to specified idle speed again. *NOTE: On 230 S and 250 S models, idle speed is adjusted by turning the knurled screws on the plastic connecting rods.*

Recheck throttle butterfly synchronization and check length of pushrod (1); it should be equal in length to the distance between bearing bolts (3) on 200 and 230 models. *NOTE: It must be possible to connect all pushrods without binding or forcing.*

Adjust pushrod (15) so that roller (18) contacts the limit stop at (17) without tension, then check that the accelerator pedal is fully against its stop with both throttle butterflies fully open. If not, adjust linkage at firewall.

Reconnect all pushrods and recheck idle speed, then install air cleaner.

1. Thrust rod
2. Angular lever
3. Bearing bolt
4. Thrust rod
6. Idling adjusting screw
8. Idling mixture control screw
15. Thrust rod

Type 220 carburetor linkage.

# Troubleshooting Guide—
## Solex Carburetors

| PROBLEM | SOLUTION |
|---|---|
| **Hard cold start** | |
| Choke valves do not move easily. | Free up choke valves. |
| Choke valves not closing properly. | Adjust starter cable. |
| Throttle valve opening angles too small. | Check throttle valve angle. |
| **Rough running of engine during warm-up** | |
| Starter valve vacuum diaphragm defective. | Replace diaphragm. |
| Vacuum bore for starter valve clogged. | Check performance of starter valve; blow out bore with compressed air. |
| Compression springs at starter connecting rod not adjusted correctly. | Adjust compression springs. |
| Throttle valve opening angle out of synchronization. | Adjust and synchronize throttle valve opening angle. |
| **Rough idle** | |
| Idle fuel jet or idle air bore clogged. | Clean jet and bore. |
| Idle canal and by-pass bores clogged. | Clean bores and canal. |
| Float leaks. | Replace float. |
| Float adjustment wrong. | Adjust float. |
| Damaged idle mixture adjustment screw or damaged seat in chamber. | Replace idle mixture adjustment screw and/ or throttle valve assembly. |
| Injection tube dripping after fuel injection. | Check relief bores for clogging and clean relief bores. |
| Gaskets leaking at carburetors, at suction tube, or at vacuum connections. | Find leaks by pressure test and stop them. |
| **Idle speed too high** | |
| Throttle valve jammed. | Free up valve. |
| Ball heads on control linkage sticking. | Replace ball heads. |
| Dashpot too far out. | Adjust dashpot. |
| **Poor acceleration** | |
| Injection tube clogged. | Clean injection tube. |
| Pump diaphragm faulty. | Replace diaphragm. |
| Injection amount wrong; injection angle wrong. | Adjust injection amount and direction. |
| Baffle plate incorrectly installed. | Install baffle plate properly. |
| **Engine stalls when engaging gear.** | |
| Dashpot maladjusted. | Adjust dashpot. |
| **High fuel consumption** | |
| Float needle valve leaking; wrong float adjustment. | Replace float needle valve and gasket. |
| Loose idle or main jet. | Tighten jets. |
| Injection amount too large. | Adjust injection amount. |
| Wrong type of jets installed. | Install proper jets. |

# Troubleshooting Guide—
## Zenith Carburetors

| PROBLEM | SOLUTION |
|---|---|
| **Hard cold start** | |
| Choke valves sticking. | Free up valves. |
| Choke valves do not close. | Free up valves. |
| Bi-metal spring in starter cover defective. | Replace bi-metal spring. |
| Starter cover has insufficient preload. | Increase starter cover preload. |
| Throttle valve opening angle insufficient. | Adjust cold start idle increase. |
| **Engine stalls after cold start** | |
| Starting mixture too rich or too lean. | Adjust pilot throttle gap. |
| Starter valve vacuum diaphragm defective. | Replace vacuum diaphragm. |
| **Rough idle** | |
| Choke valves do not open. | Replace fuse. |
| Fuse for automatic choke blown. | Replace heater coil. |
| Heater coil in starter cover burnt. | Replace heater coil. |
| Choke valves jam. | Free up choke valves. |
| Idle fuel jet or idle air bore clogged. | Clean jet or bore. |
| Idle canal and/or by-pass bores clogged. | Clean idle canal and/or bypass bores. |
| Floats leak. | Replace floats. |
| Float adjustment wrong. | Adjust float. |
| Damaged idle mixture adjustment screw or damaged seat in chamber. | Replace idle mixture adjustment screw and/ or throttle valve component. |
| Gaskets leaking at carburetors, at intake manifold, or at vacuum connections. | Use new gaskets. |
| **Idle speed too high** | |
| Throttle valve jammed. | Free up valve. |
| Ball heads at control linkage sticking. | Replace ball heads. |
| Vacuum control too far out. | Adjust vacuum control. |
| Float chamber vent valves do not move easily. | Replace vent valves. |
| **Poor acceleration** | |
| No injection or injection amount too small. | Clean injection tube. |
| Injection tube clogged. | Slide sleeve back over and make sleeve smoother. |

| Accelerating pump sleeve has too little preload. | Clean intake valve. |
| Injection amount too large. | Adjust injection amount. |
| Injection angle wrong | Bend injection tube to proper angle. |

### Hard hot starting

| Float chamber vent valve does not open far enough. | Adjust vent valve. |
| Vent valve blocked. | Clean vent valve. |

### High fuel consumption

| Float needle valve leaking. | Replace float needle valve and gasket. |
| Float adjustment wrong. | Adjust float. |
| Injection amount too large. | Adjust injection amount. |
| Wrong type of jets installed. | Install proper jets. |
| Choke valves do not open all the way. | Check choke valves for ease of movement. Check performance of heater coil in starter cover. |

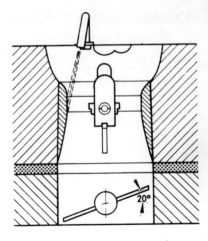

Bending injection tube—type 200 front carburetor.

## Carburetor Modifications—200

To obtain the best performance possible without stalling, some modifications to the model 200 carburetor were made in production. Cars not having these modifications can be improved in the following manner:

On automatic transmission models, carefully bend the injection tube of the front carburetor toward the venturi wall, as illustrated. This helps to eliminate flat spots. In serious cases of hesitation when starting out from rest, modify the rear carburetor in the same manner.

On all cars, the lower bypass bore (3) can be enlarged to 1.5 mm. (from 1.3 mm.); the upper bypass bore (2) enlarged to 1.3 mm. (from 1.0 mm.); the idle bore (1) enlarged to 1.6 mm. (from 1.0 mm.); the idle fuel jet (7) changed from 55 to 62.5 and a fuel deflector plate (4) installed. *NOTE: The carburetors must be removed and disassembled.*

Use a No. 52 drill for enlarging bore (1), a No. 53 drill for bore (3) and a No. 55 drill for bore (2). *CAUTION: Use a hand drill only; turn drill very slowly and determine proper drill angle before starting.*

## Idle and Linkage Adjustment—230, 230S, 250S with Zenith INAT Carburetors

The basic set-up is similar to the one pictured for 220 Sb models having Zenith

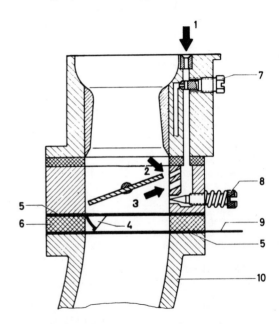

| | | | |
|---|---|---|---|
| 1. | Idle air bore | 7. | Idle fuel jet |
| 2. | Bypass bore | | (nozzle) |
| 3. | Bypass bore | 8. | Mixture adjustment |
| 4. | Deflector plate | | screw |
| 5. | Gasket (seal) | 9. | Screening plate |
| 6. | Gasket (seal) | 10. | Suction tube |

Carburetor modifications to type 200.

carburetors. First check the spark plugs and ignition timing, then start the engine and allow it to warm up. Remove the air cleaner and disconnect the pushrod and bellcrank linkage from front carburetor, then connect rubber hose (⅜" inside diameter) between camshaft cover and intake manifold bypass connector. Connect a tachometer between engine ground and the distributor-to-coil primary wire and adjust carburetor idle speed screws evenly to obtain 800–850 rpm. Adjust mixture screws evenly, after seating fully (without overtightening) to get the smoothest, fastest possible idle speed, then readjust idle speed screws evenly to 800–850 rpm. Connect the pushrods, making sure they seat properly with no tension or binding and reconnect bellcrank linkage to front carburetor. There should be .004"–.008" clearance between the bellcrank and roller.

If car is equipped with automatic transmission, place selector lever in "D" and adjust spring (7) by turning nut (8) to obtain an idle speed of 650–700 rpm. Then, shift transmission into neutral and check that actuating lever (10) contacts the idle stop screw (1). If the lever rests against the hex screw (9), turn the screw clockwise and shift the selector lever to "D" position. Readjust the spring (7) to obtain 650–700 rpm.

If car is equipped with manual transmission, emission control system and air conditioning, adjust spring (7) to obtain a clearance of .004" between the hex screw (9) and actuating lever (10).

With the above adjustments completed, disconnect tachometer and breather hose and reinstall air cleaner. *NOTE: Remember to reconnect hose to intake manifold.*

## Choke, Pre-Throttle and Fast Idle Adjustment—230, 230S, 250S with Zenith INAT Carburetors

Check that the choke butterflies operate smoothly, then check the alignment of the index marks on the choke housing. The choke springs are preloaded .196" normally, although in cases of stalling during warmup a preload of .118" may be required.

To adjust the pre-throttle gap, first warm up the engine, then lift the accelerator linkage slightly and place a screwdriver between the choke housing and throttle lever. Lift connecting rod (5) to the stop position of diaphragm rod and release linkage. The clearance at this point between the throttle butterfly and carburetor throat should be .079"–.083". Clearance is measured by inserting the shank of a No. 47 or No. 45 drill. If necessary, adjust setscrew (5) on the starter valve. Repeat procedure for the other carburetor.

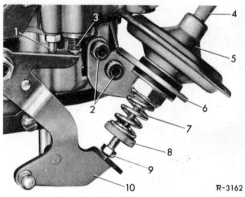

R-3162

| | |
|---|---|
| 1. Idle stop screw | 7. Compression |
| 2. Allen head screw | spring |
| 3. Vent valve | 8. Knurled nut |
| 4. Vacuum hose | 9. Hex head screw |
| 5. Idle compensator | 10. Actuating lever |
| 6. Bracket | |

Dashpot adjustment—230, 230S, 250S with INAT carburetors.

1. Marking for cars up to 3,000 miles
2. Choke housing marking
3. Choke housing cover marking
4. Choke housing cover

Choke adjustment—230, 230S, 250S with INAT carburetors.

| | |
|---|---|
| 1. Choke housing cover | 4. Throttle lever |
| 2. Choke housing | 5. Connecting rod |

Adjusting pre-throttle gap—230, 230S, 250S with INAT carburetors.

1. Control lever
2. Control lever (hot start)
3. Adjusting screw
4. Step cam
5. Diaphragm control rod
6. Return spring

Adjusting pre-throttle gap—230, 230S, 250S with INAT carburetors.

To adjust fast idle, first warm up engine, then, with engine not running, lift accelerator linkage and insert a screwdriver between the choke housing and throttle lever. Lift the connecting rod (5) and release accelerator linkage. This should place the adjusting screw on the highest point of the cam.

Start engine, after connecting a tachometer, and check engine speed; it should be 2,400–2,600 rpm. Repeat procedure for the other carburetor. *NOTE: Turning adjusting screw clockwise increases engine speed and vice-versa. If engine is cold, fast idle speed should be 1,800 rpm.*

### Carburetor Accelerator Lever Modifications—230, 230S, 250S with INAT Carburetors

If the engine stalls or hesitates during acceleration, a modified accelerator cam lever can be installed and the accelerator pump fuel delivery volume increased. First remove the air cleaner, then the carburetor tops and pre-atomizers (3). Remove the hold-down screw from each inner pump lever and push outer pump levers and shafts out.

Remove accelerator pump plungers and inspect the leather washers; replace if necessary. Clean the pump cylinders with alcohol, then reinstall pump plungers and check the pump injection action. *NOTE: Depressing the pump lever slowly should result in 0.7–1.0 cc. fuel injection per stroke. If less than this, bend inner pump lever to increase pump plunger stroke.*

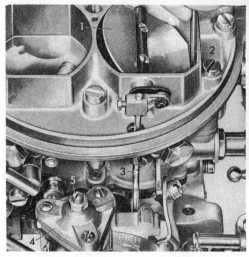

1. Choke valve
2. Measuring pin (pre-throttle gap)
3. Connecting rod
4. Starter valve
5. Set screw

Adjusting pre-throttle gap—230, 230S, 250S with INAT carburetors.

1. Choke housing cover
2. Choke housing
3. Adjusting screw

230, 230S, 250S choke housing showing adjusting screw.

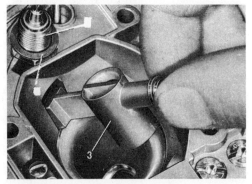

Removing atomizers—230, 230S, 250S with INAT carburetors.

1. Fastening screw
2. Fastening screw
3. Plunger assembly
4. Cam lever
5. Outer pump lever

Bending lever—230, 230S, 250S with INAT carburetors.

Check that the fuel discharge tube directs the fuel spray to a point .39″–.59″ below the upper edge of the intermediate plate block. Carefully, bend the tube, without crushing it, to adjust.

Reassemble carburetors, using the modified cam lever (as illustrated), then adjust carburetor synchronization and idle speed as described previously.

## Idle Speed and Linkage Adjustment—220/8

The 220/8 uses two 36/40 PDSI Solex

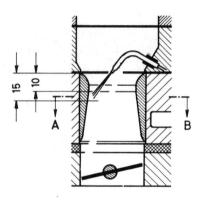
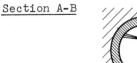
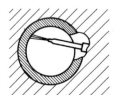

Section A-B

Fuel discharge tube modifications.

carburetors in a set-up quite similar to that used on early 230 models.

First warm up engine, then detach pushrods (15) and (4). Adjust pushrod (1) so that its length equals the distance between the lever pivot pins (3). Adjust idle speed by turning screws (6) evenly, then adjust idle mixture screws (8) evenly for the fastest, smoothest idle. Readjust idle speed screws to obtain specified idle speed, then

1. Push rod
2. Angle relay lever
3. Pivot pin
4. Pushrod
5. Throttle lever
6. Idle adjustment screw
7. Starter adjustment screw
8. Idle fuel adjustment screw
9. Starter link rod
10. Fuel return valve
11. Flat spring
12. Adjustment screw of fuel return valve
13. Angle relay lever stop
14. Adjusting ring
15. Pushrod
16. Angle relay lever
17. Quadrant lever
18. Roller

Carburetor adjustment—type 220/8.

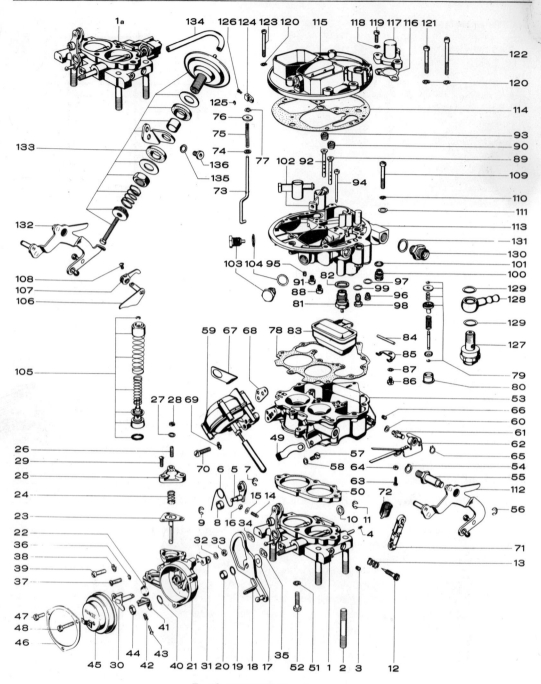

Zenith 35/40 INAT carburetor.

2. Pin screw
3. Screw
5. Joint lever
6. Return spring
7. Safety washer
8. Roller
9. Safety washer
10. Flat washer
11. Safety washer
12. Idle mixture screw
13. Pressure spring
14. Adjustment screw
15. Spring washer
16. Hex head nut
17. Flat washer
18. Throttle lever
19. Safety washer
20. Spacer
21. Choke body
22. Return spring
23. Diaphragm spring
24. Pressure spring
25. Valve cover
26. Screw
27. Seal ring
28. Hex head nut
29. Countersunk screw
30. Operating lever
31. Transfer lever

32. Spring washer
33. Hex head nut
34. Gasket
35. Gasket
36. Star washer
37. Countersunk screw
38. Spring washer
39. Screw
40. Safety washer
41. Stop lever
42. Pressure spring
43. Stop screw
44. Hex head nut
45. Choke cover
46. Stop ring
47. Hex head nut
48. Hex head nut
49. Clamp
50. Isolation flange
51. Spring washer
52. Screw
53. Float bowl
54. Spring washer
55. Bearing bolt
56. Safety washer
57. Cheesehead screw
58. Spring washer
59. Vacuum chamber
60. Seal ring

69. Spring washer
70. Cheesehead screw
71. Connecting rod
72. Return spring
73. Connecting rod
74. Flat washer
75. Pressure spring
76. Washer
77. Tension ring
78. Seal ring
79. Air valve
80. Bushing
81. Needle valve
82. Seal ring
83. Float
84. Shaft
85. Bracket
86. Cheesehead screw
87. Spring washer
88. Main jet
89. Mixture tube
90. Air correction jet
91. Main jet
92. Mixture tube
93. Air correction jet
94. Idle jet
95. Jet
96. Pump suction valve
97. Seal ring

98. Pump pressure valve
99. Seal ring
100. Jet
101. Seal ring
102. Sprayer
103. Pressure screw
104. Seal ring
105. Pump piston
106. Pump lever
107. Inner pump lever
108. Countersunk screw
109. Cheesehead screw
110. Lockwasher
111. Spring washer
114. Carburetor body gasket
115. Carburetor top
116. Seal ring
117. Cover
118. Lockwasher
119. Cheesehead screw
120. Lockwasher
121. Cheesehead screw
122. Cheesehead screw
123. Cheesehead screw
124. Joint piece
125. Safety washer
126. Cheesehead screw

### Additional parts for carburetor 000.120-13 DB 16

1. Throttle valve
60. Lockwasher
61. Bearing bolt
62. Operating lever

63. Cheesehead screw
64. Hex head nut
65. Expansion ring
112. Complete operat-

ing lever
113. Complete platin block
127. Fuel return valve

128. Ring hose piece
129. Seal ring
130. Threaded fitting
131. Seal ring

### Additional parts for carburetor 000.120-14 DB 17

1. Throttle valve
4. Screw
66. Threaded pin
67. Cable holder

112. Complete operat- ing lever
113. Platin block

### Additional parts for carburetor 000.120-23 DB 27

1. Throttle valve
67. Cable holder
113. Platin block
132. Operating lever

133. Vacuum regulator
134. Rubber hose
135. Lockwasher
136. Cheesehead screw

### Additional parts for carburetor 000.120-15 DB 18

1a. Throttle valve
60. Lockwasher
61. Bearing bolt
62. Operating lever

63. Cheesehead screw
64. Hex head nut
65. Expansion ring
67. Cable holder

112. Complete operat- ing lever
113. Platin block
127. Fuel return valve

128. Ring hose piece
129. Seal ring
130. Threaded fitting
131. Seal ring

place pushrod (4) in such a position that the bellcrank (2) is .040″ from the limit tab on the intake manifold. Install pushrod (4), after adjusting it to a length where it goes onto its ball sockets without binding or tension.

Adjust pushrod (15) by turning the knurled nut (14) so that the roller rests in its slot without tension (on cars with manual transmission) or so that the lever (5) is against the idle stop (on cars with automatic transmission).

**Vacuum Control Valve Adjustment—220/8**

AUTOMATIC TRANSMISSION MODELS

Loosen bolt (6) to give .040″ clearance between it and the bellcrank (7). *NOTE: In "D" range.*

AUTOMATIC TRANSMISSION MODELS
WITH NO ACCESSORIES
OR AIR CONDITIONED MODELS,
ANY TRANSMISSION

Place selector lever in "D" or, if equipped with manual transmission, turn on air conditioner. Adjust bolt (6) to obtain specified idle speed, then adjust nut (4) to rest against stop (5).

MODELS WITH TWO OR
MORE ACCESSORIES

Place car in "D" or, if equipped with manual transmission, turn on one accessory (air conditioning, full lock on power steering, etc.). Adjust bolt (6) to obtain specified idle speed, then adjust nut (4) to give .080″ clearance between it and stop (5).

**Accelerator Pump Adjustment—220/8**

Check the accelerator pump in the same manner as with Zenith INAT carburetors. On the front carburetor used in automatic transmission applications, the fuel spray must hit the side of the venturi, not shoot directly into the carburetor throat. On both carburetors used in manual transmission applications, and on the rear carburetor in automatic transmission applications, the fuel spray must be parallel to the venturi axis and go through the gap between the venturi and throttle butterfly when the butterfly is opened 20°.

1. Vacuum hose
2. Closing damper
3. Bracket
4. Polystop nut
5. Stop
6. Hexagon bolt
7. Angle relay lever
8. Pushrod
9. Starter adjustment screw
10. Idle adjustment screw
11. Mixture adjustment screw

Dashpot adjustment—220/8.

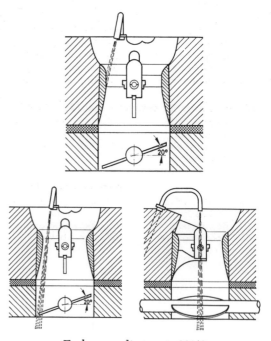

Fuel spray adjustment—220/8.

The amount (volume) of fuel delivered by the accelerator pump is adjusted by adding or removing shims (4) between the pump lever (5) and the cotter pin on the pump rod (6). Adding shims increases volume, and vice-versa.

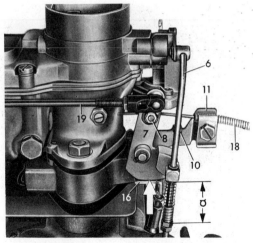

| | |
|---|---|
| 1. Fuel return valve | 4. Shim |
| 2. Flat spring | 5. Pump lever |
| 3. Adjusting screw | 6. Connecting rod |

Accelerator pump adjustment—220/8.

| | |
|---|---|
| 6. Starter link rod | 11. Bowden cable |
| 7. Starter lever | clamp |
| 8. Clamping screw | 16. Follower link lever |
| 10. Stop | 18. Starter cable coil |
| | 19. Connecting rod |

Choke adjustment—220/8.

## Cut-Off Valve Installation—220/8

If the engine "overruns" after shutting off the ignition, electric fuel cut-off valves can be installed in place of the existing idle jets. Replace both idle jets with the new cut-off valves, connect the valves together and route the wire to the fuse box. Loosen the fuse box mounting and connect wire to Terminal No. 3 (output side), then re-install fuse box. *NOTE: Needed are two cut-off valves, part No. 000 072 00 17; one wiring harness, part No. 110 540 28 09.*

## Choke Adjustment—220/8

Adjust idle speed and check throttle linkage for ease of movement. Detach pushrod (19) at rear carburetor and clamp choke cable (18) so that its end is in alignment with clamp (11). Push choke lever (7) forward against stop (10), then press choke control in until there is .040″ clearance between it and dashboard. Tighten choke cable at lever (7) by tightening screw (8).

Turn the shoulder nut (8) on the choke link (1) so that distance "a" equals 1.12″ at the rear carburetor. Set lever (7) as illustrated (arrow) by adjusting connecting link (19).

## Idle Speed and Linkage Adjustment—230/8, 250/8 with INAT Carburetors

Warm up engine, remove air cleaner and detach control rods (11) and (16). Adjust idle speed screws (1) evenly to obtain specified idle speed, then turn mixture screws (7) in until they seat (do not over-tighten) and adjust outwards evenly to obtain the fastest, smoothest idle speed. Re-check idle speed and adjust screws (1) if necessary.

On cars having manual transmission, adjust length of control rod (16) so that the roller rests against the end of the slot without tension. On cars having automatic transmission, hold throttle butterfly lever (8) against the idle stop and adjust control rod (16) so that it can be easily hooked up without binding.

## Dashpot Adjustment—230/8, 250/8 with INAT Carburetors

If car is equipped with automatic transmission, place selector lever in a drive range and, with engine not running, back out hex bolt (9) until vent valve (3) is raised .020″–.040″. Then start engine and adjust compression spring (7) by turning nut (8) to obtain specified idle speed. *NOTE: With parking brake locked.*

Place selector lever in "N" and check that the lever (10) is against the idle stop. If the lever touches hex bolt (9), back out the bolt and readjust spring (7) with car in "D".

1. Idle adjustment screw
2. Throttle valve lever
3. Test union
4. Pump lever
5. Idle stop screw
6. Float chamber vent valve
7. Idle mixture adjustment screw

8. Actuating lever
9. Hexagon bolt
10. Adjustment nut
11. Connecting rod
12. Adjustment screw
13. Return valve lever

14. Fuel return valve
15. Hexagon nut
16. Control rod
17. Lever
18. Lever
19. Adjustment screw

Carburetor adjustment—types 230/8, 250/8, 280S/8.

If car is equipped with manual transmission, start engine, make sure all accessories are turned off, and adjust nut (8) to give .004″ clearance between hex bolt (9) and the actuating lever (10).

**Automatic Choke Adjustment—
230/8, 250/8 with INAT Carburetors**

Check that the choke butterflies operate without binding, then check the choke housing cover; the marks must line up. NOTE: The spring is preloaded .20″.

Turn on the ignition switch and make sure the throttle butterflies open after a few minutes (engine cold). To adjust the pilot throttle gap with the engine running, lift accelerator linkage and insert a screwdriver between the choke housing (2) and the throttle lever (4). Press the relay lever (5) upwards until it touches the stop on the diaphragm rod, then release linkage. Measure the clearance between the choke butterfly and the carburetor bore; it should

be .096″. If necessary, adjust by turning screw (5) on the starter valve.

Start the engine and allow it to warm up. Shut off the engine, raise the accelerator linkage and insert a screwdriver between the starter housing (2) and the throttle lever (4) of one carburetor. Press the relay lever upward and release linkage. This should cause the adjustment screw (3) inside the choke housing to come to rest on the top notch of the cam (4).

Hook up a tachometer and start the engine; adjust screw (3) to obtain proper fast idle. Adjust the other carburetor in the same manner.

**Exhaust Emission Control System
Modifications—230/8**

The 230/8 is equipped with two emission control systems, one using a Saginaw air pump and injection tubes and another that superseded the Saginaw type after chassis number 018 018 (January, 1969).

The new system complies with Federal standards through engine modifications rather than use of an air pump system. During deceleration, the rear carburetor vacuum control unit (dashpot) is governed to hold the throttle butterfly open above 1,800 rpm engine speed. This is accomplished through use of a relay and solenoid valve connected to a vacuum hose that runs between the intake manifold and the vacuum control valve on the rear carburetor. At engine speeds in excess of 1,800 rpm, the relay activates the solenoid valve to shut off intake manifold vacuum and expose the control valve diaphragm to atmospheric pressure. Without vacuum, a spring pushes adjustment screw (7) outward to hold the throttle butterfly slightly open. *NOTE: The idle speed adjustment procedure described previously for the 230/8 is still valid.*

To adjust the vacuum control valve properly, turn the hex screw (7) to lift the vent valve (2) .020"–.040" (engine not running). Start the engine and make sure all power accessories are shut off. Adjust spring (5) by turning nut (6) to give .004" clearance between screw (7) and lever (8). When the engine is warmed up, remove vacuum hose (4) and check engine speed; it should not exceed 1,750 rpm. Adjust by turning screw (7).

To test the relay, first connect a tachometer, then pull off the connector at the solenoid valve and hook a 12-volt test light to the connector. Start the engine and gradually increase speed; test light should go on at 2,000 $^{+50}_{-30}$ rpm and should go off when speed drops below 1,750–1,800 rpm.

## Service Note—Synchronizing Multiple Carburetors

Carburetor synchronization is greatly simplified by use of one of the various devices made for the purpose. A Moto Meter unit is illustrated, but a similar device is readily available in this country under the name Uni-Syn.

To use this unit, warm up the engine, then remove air cleaner and disconnect the linkage between the carburetors. Adjust the idle speed as previously described, then place the synchronizing device on the air venturi of one of the carburetors. Adjust the air intake on the measuring unit until

1. Idle stop screw
2. Vent valve
3. Vacuum hose to valve
4. Vacuum hose connecting valve
   and vacuum control unit
5. Compression ring
6. Knurled nut
7. Hex head adjustment screw
8. Actuating lever

Dashpot adjustment—230/8 with emission control.

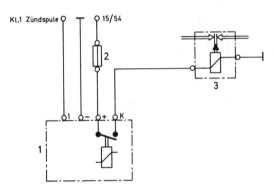

1. Speed relay switch
2. Fuse #5
3. Solenoid valve
K1. 1 Zündspule = Terminal 1 - ignition coil

Fuel cut-off valve—230/8 with emission control.

1. Mounting bracket
2. Electrical speed relay
3. Solenoid valve
50 mm. = 2"

Solenoid valve—230/8 with emission control.

the ball float is somewhere in the center of
the tube. Now simply transfer the unit to
the other carburetor and note how far the
ball rises. Adjust carburetors until the ball
rises equally for both. *NOTE: A grease
pencil is handy for marking the ball position in the tube. The tube must be vertical
to allow free movement of the ball.*

# Part II
# Fuel Injection

Mercedes-Benz passenger cars use intermittent intake pipe fuel injection units
with mechanical two- or six-element
pumps. An electric fuel pump draws fuel
from the supply tank and forces it through
a filter into the suction chamber of the
injection pump. Excess fuel flows back to
the fuel tank via fuel return lines. The injection pump plungers force the fuel
through the pressure valves into the fuel
distribution lines and injection valves. The
injection valves spray atomized fuel into
the intake ports in the cylinder head, where
it is mixed with air from the air venturi.
The fuel-air mixture then enters the combustion chambers, where it is ignited by a
conventional electric ignition system.

The injection pump and its attendant
control linkage can only be accurately
tested and adjusted using special test apparatus and tools not readily available. For
this reason it is recommended that all work
on the fuel injection system be carried out
by an authorized Mercedes-Benz dealer.

Many troubles in starting can be traced
to the cold start electrical system incorporated. A study of the wiring diagrams, and
use of an ohmmeter or other continuity
tester, will often help isolate problem components.

Idle speed can be adjusted by turning
the idle screw on the air venturi and the
spring-loaded idle control knob on the injection pump to obtain smooth operation.
*NOTE: The knob must be pushed in
against spring pressure. Turning counterclockwise leans the mixture and vice-versa.
Do not exceed three notches in either
direction.*

It must be emphasized, however, that
adjustments of this nature are extremely

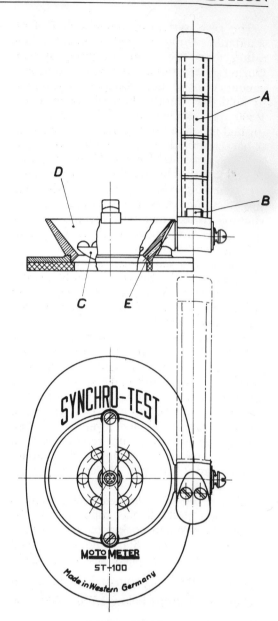

Synchronizing device.

critical in light of emission control regula-
tions, and that the use of a CO meter is
necessary to obtain best operation. *NOTE:
CO values, where applicable, are given in
the Appendix.*

Other simple service procedures include
checking the linkage for ease of movement
and the injection control rod for binding.
Detach the pushrod at the adjustment lever
and push the lever to the full load stop
position. Allow the lever to return slowly
until it rests against the idle stop, making

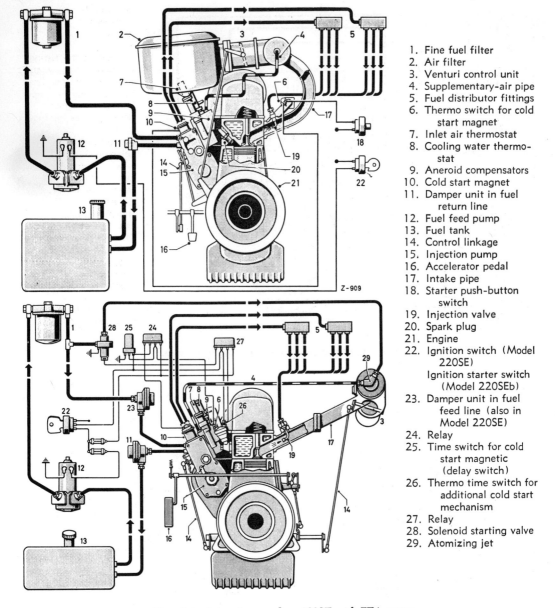

1. Fine fuel filter
2. Air filter
3. Venturi control unit
4. Supplementary-air pipe
5. Fuel distributor fittings
6. Thermo switch for cold start magnet
7. Inlet air thermostat
8. Cooling water thermostat
9. Aneroid compensators
10. Cold start magnet
11. Damper unit in fuel return line
12. Fuel feed pump
13. Fuel tank
14. Control linkage
15. Injection pump
16. Accelerator pedal
17. Intake pipe
18. Starter push-button switch
19. Injection valve
20. Spark plug
21. Engine
22. Ignition switch (Model 220SE)
    Ignition starter switch (Model 220SEb)
23. Damper unit in fuel feed line (also in Model 220SE)
24. Relay
25. Time switch for cold start magnetic (delay switch)
26. Thermo time switch for additional cold start mechanism
27. Relay
28. Solenoid starting valve
29. Atomizing jet

Top—injection system used on 220SE with ZEA pump.

Bottom—Injection system used on 220SEb with ZEA pump.

sure there is no binding in the system.

To check the fuel control rod, start the engine and allow it to warm up. If, after operating the adjusting lever, the idle speed can be *considerably* increased by backing out the idle air screw on the air venturi, the fuel control rod is probably binding and the injection pump must be replaced.

## Exhaust Emission Controls

In order to meet Federal standards for hydrocarbon emission for 1968 import, some modifications were necessary on models imported to the United States. The type 200 carburetor and distributor were

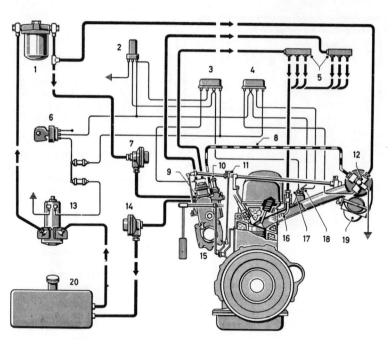

1. Fine fuel filter
2. Time switch
3. Relay
4. Relay
5. Fuel distributor fittings
6. Ignition starter switch
7. Damper unit (feed line)
8. Supplementary air pipe
9. Cold start magnet
10. Cooling water thermo-stat
11. Control linkage
12. Solenoid starting valve with atomizing jet
13. Fuel feed pump
14. Damper unit (return line)
15. Injection pump
16. Injection valve
17. Thermo switch in cooling water circulation system
18. Thermo time switch in cooling water circulation system
19. Venturi control unit
20. Fuel tank

Injection system used on 300SE with ZEA pump.

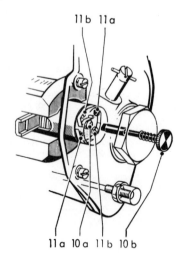

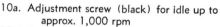

10a. Adjustment screw (black) for idle up to approx. 1,000 rpm
10b. Spring-loaded idle control knob
11a. Adjustment screw (black) for partial load or medium engine speed range from approx. 700 to approx. 4,000 rpm
11b. Adjustment screw (white) for partial load or upper engine speed range from approx. 2,000 rpm

ZEA pump adjustment screws.

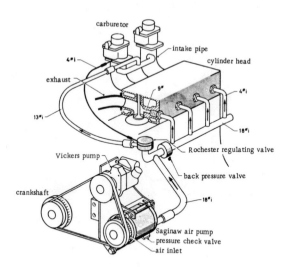

Manifold Air Oxydation System—230, 230S, 250S.

1. Inlet air thermostat (no longer installed on the ZEB Injection pump)
2. Cold start magnet
3. Pin
4. Guide pin for cam lever
5. Reversing lever
6. Starting delivery lever
7. Fuel control rod head
8. Relay lever
9. Eccentric bushing
10a. Idle adjustment screw (black) up to appr. 1,000 rpm
10b. Spring-loaded idle control knob
11a. Adjustment screw (black) for partial load or medium speed range of appr. 700 to appr. 4,000 rpm
11b. Adjustment screw (white) for partial load or top speed range as from appr. 2,000 rpm
12. Dipstick
13. Governor sleeve stop screw
14. Joint
15. Governor springs
16. Flyweights
17. Supporting lever
18. Governor sleeve
19. Sliding piece
20. Plug with lubricating plate
21. Camshaft
22. Fixing screw for roller tappet
23. Roller tappet
24. Plunger spring
25. Control sleeve
26. Mobile toothed quadrant

27. Fixing screw for pump element
28. Fuel return pipe
29. Pump element
30. Pipe union
31. Clamping jaws
32. Pressure pipe
33. Fuel feed pipe
34. Fuel control rod
35. Drive lug
36. Cam plate
37. Cam lever
38. Air filter
39. Cooling water thermostat

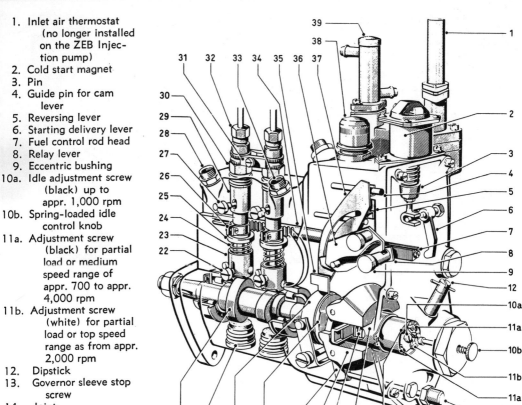

ZEA injection pump.

modified so that vacuum control works only during idling and deceleration, when the throttle is contacting the idle stop, to retard the ignition spark. The carburetor was modified so that, even with the ignition timing maladjusted, the mixture cannot become too rich.

The 230, 230 S and 250 S presented a more difficult emission problem. As a result, in addition to carburetor and distributor modifications, similar to those used on the 200, a port burning (afterburner) system was incorporated. This system, known as the "Manifold Air-Oxydation System", should be familiar to American mechanics, for it utilizes many U.S.-made components. A V-belt driven air pump forces clean air, under slight pressure, to the exhaust ports. This air combines with the hot exhaust gases and "afterburning", or more complete combustion, takes place.

The distributor was modified by increasing the advance range of the centrifugal advance mechanism and incorporating a

S = Starting position of fuel
       control rod
V = Full load position
L = Idle position
  2. Cold start magnet
  3. Pin
  4. Guide from cam lever
  5. Reversing lever
  6. Starting delivery lever
  7. Fuel control rod head
  8. Relay lever
  9. Eccentric axle
10a. Idle adjustment screw
       (black) for up to appr.
       1,000 engine rpm
11a. Adjusting screw (black)
       for partial load or
       medium speed range of
       appr. 700 to appr.
       4,000 engine rpm
11b. Adjusting screw (white)
       for partial load or top
       speed range as from
       appr. 2,000 engine rpm
13. Governor sleeve stop screw
14. Joint
15. Governor springs
16. Flyweights
17. Supporting lever
18. Governor sleeve
19. Sliding piece
34. Fuel control rod
35. Drive lug
36. Camshaft

37. Cam lever
63. Venturi control unit
64. Throttle valve
65. Throttle valve lever

66. Control lever
67. Adjustment lever
68. Pushrod
69. Axle
70. Pullrod

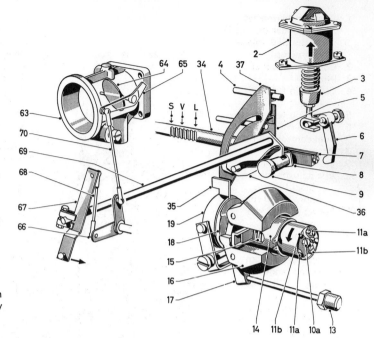

ZEA injection pump control linkage.

device to retard the ignition spark at idle and under deceleration. The carburetors were essentially unchanged, although some models were rejetted and on all models manufacturing tolerance limits tightened up.

The illustration shows the afterburner system in schematic form. The Saginaw rotary vane air pump, driven at 0.94 engine speed, draws fresh air, through a centrifugal air filter, into a chamber. This chamber is vented to the atmosphere by a pressure check valve, which protects the pump by allowing excess pressure to escape. The air is compressed by the rotary vanes and is forced through a pipe and one-way (back pressure) valve into the air distribution manifold, thence into each exhaust port.

The back pressure valve allows the air from the pump to flow only one way, thus acting as a pump protective device in the event that exhaust pressure exceeds pump

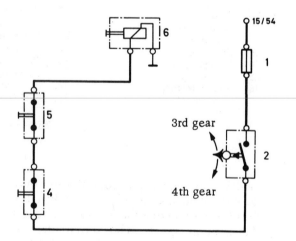

1. Fuse
2. Operating contact switch on jacket tube, third and fourth gear
4. Contact switch on clutch pedal
5. Micro-switch on control shaft
6. Stop solenoid on injection pump

Stop solenoid—columnshift manual transmission.

output (as it would if the V-belt broke).

In addition, an air regulating valve (Rochester) is incorporated into the system. During deceleration, a vacuum forms in the intake manifold. This vacuum evaporates the fuel drops adhering to the inside of the manifold and enriches the mixture. The air regulating valve supplies air from the pump to the intake manifold to compensate for this. A control mechanism for the air regulating valve, similar to a standard vacuum advance unit, meters air with relation to the intake manifold vacuum.

Fuel injected models required little modification. The three-dimensional cam on the injection pump was changed slightly and the full-load adjustment capability increased. In addition, an electric solenoid switch was incorporated to stop fuel delivery under deceleration.

The air venturi throttle butterfly setting was closed down to 4° from the previous 7°.

## Troubleshooting the Port Injection System

Start the engine and allow it to idle. The pressure check valve should be noise-free. Now, remove the hose from the air pump outlet fitting and make sure air is being expelled. Hold the outlet fitting closed and check that the pressure check valve operates.

Disconnect the hose in front of the back pressure valve. With the engine idling, no exhaust should escape from the valve. Now, remove the hose in front of the Rochester valve. With the engine idling, the valve should not suck in air (a small amount is, however, permissible if idling is unaffected). Speed the engine up and allow it to come back to idle speed. During deceleration the valve should open for about one second to suck in air.

## Troubleshooting Fuel Shut-Off Valve— Injected Engines

### Manual Transmission

Connect a 12-volt test light between the solenoid and ground, then switch on the ignition. The light should go on in first and fourth gears without touching the accelerator pedal.

Now, to check the switches on the trans-

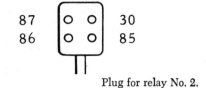

Plug for relay No. 2.

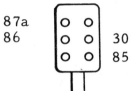

Plug for relay No. 1.

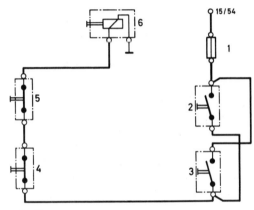

1. Fuse
2. Operating contact switch on gearbox cover (3rd gear)
3. Operating contact switch on gearbox cover (4th gear)
4. Contact switch on clutch pedal
5. Micro-switch on control shaft
6. Stop solenoid on injection pump

Stop solenoid—floorshift manual transmission.

mission cover or column jacket, move shift lever to neutral, first, second and reverse positions *without* touching the clutch or accelerator pedals; the test light should go out.

To check the switch on the clutch pedal, place lever in third *or* fourth gear and depress clutch pedal *without* touching the accelerator pedal; the test light should go out.

To check the micro-switch on the throttle linkage, engage third *or* fourth gear and depress the accelerator pedal *without* touching the clutch pedal; the test light should go out in this position as well.

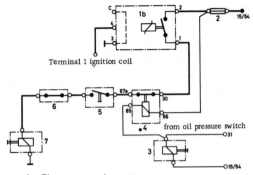

Terminal 1 ignition coil

from oil pressure switch

1. Electronic tachometer
2. Fuse
3. Solenoid for idle speed compensator
4. Dual circuit relay
5. Starter locking and back-up light switch
6. Micro-switch on control shaft
7. Stop solenoid in injection pump

Stop solenoid—automatic transmission.

### AUTOMATIC TRANSMISSION

Connect a tachometer between ground and the coil-to-distributor primary wire, then connect a 12-volt test light between the stop solenoid and ground. Place the instruments inside the passenger compartment, then start the engine and test drive the car on a level road. To check the micro-switch on the throttle linkage, accelerate in lever position "4" until the transmission shifts into fourth gear, then let off the accelerator pedal and watch the test light and tachometer. The test light must remain lit until the speed drops to 1,150 rpm.

To check the oil pressure switch on the transmission, place the lever in "3" and accelerate in third gear to 1,600 rpm. At this point, shift the lever into "2" and let off the accelerator pedal; the light should go out.

To check the "tachometer" sending unit, switch on the ignition and disconnect the plug and hook the 12-volt lamp between terminal No. 1 (black wire) and ground. Start the engine and check the lamp; at 1,400 rpm it must go on. *NOTE: To adjust the micro-switch on the throttle linkage, remove the plug on the dual-circuit relay and connect the 12-volt light between terminals No. 87a and No. 86. Shift lever into "2", "3", "4" or "R" and adjust micro-switch adjusting screw so that, when actuating linkage, light goes out before throttle butterfly moves.*

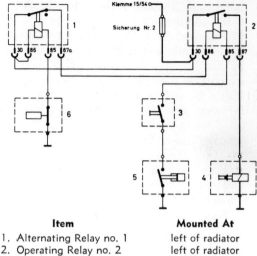

| Item | Mounted At |
|---|---|
| 1. Alternating Relay no. 1 | left of radiator |
| 2. Operating Relay no. 2 | left of radiator |
| 3. Micro-switch | firewall |
| 4. Stop solenoid switch | injection pump |
| 5. Oil pressure switch | transmission |
| 6. Temperature switch | engine block |

Klemme = Terminal
Sicherung = Fuse

Stop solenoid—after August, 1969.

The introduction of a new automatic transmission in mid-1969 necessitated a modification of the stop solenoid circuit. On models 280 SE/8, 280 SEC/8 and 300 SEL/8, the oil pressure switch on the transmission controls the solenoid. The switch does not operate at coolant temperature below +62° F.

To test the "62° F." switch. remove the plug from relay No. 1 and connect a 12-volt test light between terminals No. 30 and No. 85. The test light should go on below 62° F. temperature.

To test the micro-switch on the throttle linkage, connect the oil pressure switch terminal to ground, then remove the four-prong plug from relay No. 2 and connect the test light between the brown-white wire (No. 85) and the red-black wire (No. 30). Turn on the ignition switch and depress the accelerator pedal; the light should go out. Reconnect the terminal to the oil pressure switch.

To test the oil pressure switch, remove the plug from relay No. 2 and connect the test light between terminals No. 30 and No. 85. Test drive the car on a level road. Accelerate to 25 mph, then release the accelerator pedal; the light should stay lit while decelerating above 15 mph.

## General

The brake systems used on Mercedes-Benz automobiles are of three basic types: drums front and rear, discs front and drums rear, and discs front and rear. The drum brakes are manually adjusted or automatically adjusted, while the disc brakes are all automatically adjusted.

Disc brakes have certain advantages over drum types. They are not as sensitive to heat build-up, thus they don't "fade" as quickly. Also, dirt and water do not affect brake action, because such contaminants are thrown off by centrifugal force or scraped off by the pads.

Most models imported into this country have one of the disc brake arrangements, the more recent models having the four-wheel discs exclusively.

The drum brake system is of conventional construction, utilizing two hydraulic wheel cylinders operating leading and trailing brake shoes.

The front disc/rear drum system has a master hydraulic cylinder with a special

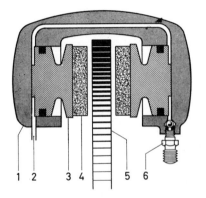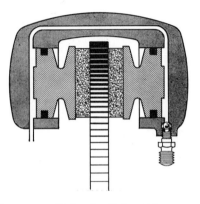

Girling disc brake. Left—Non-applied position. Right—Applied position.

# Brake System Diagnosis

| Condition | Probable Cause | Correction |
|---|---|---|
| Brake pedal soft or "spongy" | 1. Air in hydraulic system.<br>2. Brake fluid low.<br>3. Brake fluid boiling.<br>4. Leaking master cylinder.<br>5. Worn friction pads or linings.<br>6. Leaking wheel or pressure cylinder.<br>7. Damaged check valve. | 1. Bleed hydraulic system.<br>2. Top up fluid; bleed system.<br>3. Let system cool down; bleed if necessary.<br>4. Check and replace master cylinder seals or master cylinder.<br>5. Replace pads or linings.<br>6. Replace units or damaged seals.<br>7. Replace check valve. |
| Brakes heat up or fail to release | 1. Clogged compensating port in master cylinder.<br>2. Pushrod/piston clearance too small (single circuit).<br>3. Sticking wheel or pressure cylinder piston.<br>4. Rubber seals swollen by use of incorrect brake fluid.<br>5. Parking brake cables sticking.<br>6. Drum-brake self-adjusters binding.<br>7. Brake shoe return springs weak.<br>8. Rear drum-brake (aluminum shoes) pushrod clearance too small.<br>9. Check valve sticking, allowing residual pressure in system.<br>10. T-50 power brakes—vacuum piston or check ball in slave cylinder sticking.<br>11. T-51 power brakes—brake pushrod and master cylinder piston bind. | 1. Clean port with stiff wire.<br>2. Adjust brake pedal free-play.<br>3. Repair wheel or pressure cylinder.<br>4. Clean and rebuild entire system.<br>5. Readjust parking brake; lube cable.<br>6. Check for wear; lining/shoe clearance.<br>7. Replace return springs.<br>8. Adjust pushrod clearance.<br>9. Replace check valve.<br>10. Replace damaged components.<br>11. Replace power brake unit. |
| Brakes do not stop car fast enough (normal pedal travel, hard pedal) | 1. Brake linings or friction pads oily or greasy.<br>2. Brake linings or friction pads heat glazed.<br>3. Friction pads worn.<br>4. Brake discs or drums worn or dusty. | 1. Replace linings or pads; replace rear grease seals or front hub seals.<br>2. Replace linings or friction pads.<br>3. Replace friction pads.<br>4. Replace or clean discs or drums. |
| Brakes do not stop car fast enough (long pedal travel and hard pedal) | 1. Vacuum hose or connections leaking.<br>2. Damaged seal between master cylinder and vacuum unit.<br>3. Damaged master cylinder seals.<br>4. Damaged or leaking control valve.<br>5. Low engine vacuum.<br>6. Check valve sticking.<br>7. T-50 power brakes—leaking check valve in slave cylinder.<br>8. T-50 power brakes—vacuum piston sticking.<br>9. Diesel only—defective vacuum pump. | 1. Tighten or replace hose.<br>2. Replace seal.<br>3. Replace seals or master cylinder.<br>4. Replace power brake unit.<br>5. Check manifolds and valves for leaks.<br>6. Replace vacuum line and check valve.<br>7. Replace power brake unit.<br>8. Replace power brake unit.<br>9. Repair vacuum pump. |

# Brake System Diagnosis *(Continued)*

| Condition | Probable Cause | Correction |
|---|---|---|
| Brakes rattle or chatter | 1. Rear shock absorbers worn.<br>2. Rear suspension/spring broken.<br>3. Excessive wheel wobble/bent rim/tires out of round. | 1. Replace shock absorbers.<br>2. Repair faulty components.<br>3. Replace rims/tires. |
| | Disc Brakes<br>1a. Excessive disc runout.<br>2a. Friction pads wearing unevenly.<br>3a. Brake discs uneven thickness.<br>4a. Brake discs grease-coated, rusty. | 1a. Correct runout.<br>2a. Replace pads; break in carefully.<br>3a. Install new disc so that difference does not exceed 0.0012".<br>4a. Clean brake discs. |
| | Drum Brakes<br>1b. Brake drums out of round.<br>2b. Brake drum wall thickness unequal.<br>3b. Unequally worn brake linings. | 1b. Replace or machine drums; must be less than 0.0008" variation.<br>2b. Replace brake drums if variation exceeds 0.040".<br>3b. Replace brake linings |
| Brakes dragging on one side (drum brakes) | 1. Brake linings worn unevenly.<br>2. Brake shoes on one side too large in diameter.<br>3. Brake drums out of round or scored.<br>4. Internal diameter of drums unequal.<br>5. Brake linings oily or greasy.<br>6. One shoe sticking on anchor pin.<br>7. Wheel cylinder sticking.<br>8. Brakes unequally adjusted.<br>9. Dust in brake drums.<br>10. Heat glazed linings. | 1. Replace linings.<br>2. Replace shoes.<br>3. Replace or machine.<br>4. Equalize diameter by grinding.<br>5. Replace linings; replace grease seals or front hub seals.<br>6. Clean and lubricate pin.<br>7. Recondition or replace wheel cylinder.<br>8. Adjust brakes or check self-adjuster operation.<br>9. Blow out dust with compressed air.<br>10. Replace or sand linings. |
| Brakes dragging on one side (disc brakes) | 1. Friction pads oily or greasy.<br>2. Friction pad on one side worn.<br>3. Brake caliper not parallel to disc.<br>4. One friction pad heat glazed.<br>5. Clearance in one caliper insufficient. | 1. Replace pads and seals.<br>2. Replace pads, both sides.<br>3. Adjust caliper using shims.<br>4. Replace all pads.<br>5. Dunlop—check clearance, replace pressure cylinder if necessary. Girling/Teves—check pistons for ease of movement. |
| Brakes squealing | Disc Brakes<br>1. Friction pad loose on piston guide (Dunlop).<br>2. Piston cocked in caliper (Teves).<br>3. Friction pad has insufficient play in caliper gap.<br><br>Drum Brakes<br>1a. Faulty shoe-to-anchor contact.<br>2a. Too much clearance between brake shoe eye and anchor pin.<br>3a. Unequally worn or glazed linings.<br>4a. Dust in brake drums. | 1. Reseat pad.<br>2. Check piston position.<br>3. Grease rear and side pad surfaces with Molykote.<br><br>1a. Straighten contact plates.<br>2a. Adjust clearance.<br>3a. Replace brake linings.<br>4a. Blow out dust and sand linings. |

1. Front wheel hub
2. Brake disc
4. Connecting line
   with pipe clip
6. Friction pad with
   fitting plate
9. Brake caliper
10. Stirrup
11. Brake line
18. Bleed screw

Dunlop front disc brake.

1. Brake caliper
2. Stirrup
3. Hexagon screw
   with hexagon
   nut and serrated
   lockwasher
4. Friction pad with
   fitting plate
   (foot brake)
12. Pressure cylinder
19. Brake disc
20. Connecting line
   with pipe clip
24. Locking plate
25. Swing bolt
26. Leg spring
27a. Outer lining
    carrier
27b. Inner lining
    carrier
29. Friction pad with
   fitting plate
   (handbrake)
31. Adjustment screw
34. Tension lever
38. Brake line
40. Wheel fixing disc
41. Brake support
   lever
42. Rear axle shaft

Dunlop rear disc brake.

check valve and a power brake unit to supply the increased hydraulic pressure needed to actuate this design. There is also a pressure valve that maintains a residual pressure of 7.4–11.8 psi in the rear brake hydraulic system.

When the brake pedal is depressed, the master cylinder piston is forced forward, displacing hydraulic fluid. Since the volume of the system is constant, this displacement results in increased pressure,

1. Brake caliper
2. Stirrup
4. Friction pad
5. Fitting plate
6. Lining pressure plate
7. Dust cap
8. Piston
9. Piston seal
10. Piston plate
12. Pressure cylinder
15. Return pin
16. Friction spring
17. Spring plate
18. Retaining plate
22. Ball
23. Bleed screw

Dunlop disc brake caliper components.

which is exerted on the front caliper pistons and/or wheel cylinders, thus forcing the friction pads or brake shoes against the disc or drums.

Pressure is in direct proportion to the effort applied to the brake pedal, although disc/drum systems utilize a proportioning valve to maintain a front/rear pressure ratio, thereby reducing the possibility of premature wheel lock-up.

When the pedal is released, hydraulic pressure drops and the brake return springs (on drum brakes) and wobbling action of the disc (on disc brakes) return the shoes/pads to their proper positions and force the displaced fluid back into the master cylinder.

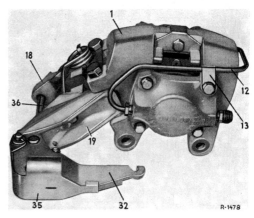

| 1. Brake caliper | 19. Inner lining carrier |
| 12. Connecting line | 32. Tension lever |
| 13. Pipe clip | 35. Cover plate |
| 18. Outer lining carrier | 36. Adjustment screw |

Rear parking brake mechanism—Dunlop.

## Brake Types

### Girling Disc Brakes

There are three versions of this brake system. On the first and second versions, the steering knuckle bracket is riveted to the knuckle and the caliper is aligned with the disc by shims. The third version has a combination bracket and knuckle and no shims are used to locate the calipers.

The first and second versions can be distinguished from the third version by the external hydraulic line that connects the inner and outer pistons. The third version has an internal passage connecting the pistons.

### Dunlop Disc Brakes

This type brake is used at both front and rear wheels. The caliper is attached to the steering knuckle bracket (or to rear axle housing) and fits around the rotating brake disc. Pistons on each side of the disc keep tension constant and prevent any distortion.

As with the other disc systems, the Dunlop brake is self-adjusting and maintains a good pedal regardless of pad wear.

There is an automatic adjustment mechanim within the caliper pistons but it cannot be disassembled, nor does it require any maintenance.

The rear wheel discs require a separate mechanism to provide parking brake action.

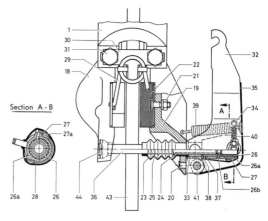

Section A - B

| 1. Brake caliper | 28. Rubber cap |
| 18. Outer lining carrier | 29. Leg spring |
| 19. Inner lining carrier | 30. Locking plate |
| 20. Bearing bracket | 31. Swing bolt |
| 21. Cheesehead screw | 32. Tension lever |
| with hexagon | 33. Driving block |
| nut and crimped | 34. Pin on tension |
| washer | lever |
| 22. Friction pad with | 35. Cover plate |
| mounting plate | 36. Adjustment screw |
| 23. Rubber grommet | 37. Retaining spring |
| 24. Plastic bushing | 38. Cup |
| 25. Pressure spring | 39. Return spring |
| 26. Adjusting nut | 40. Return spring |
| 26a. Adjusting sleeve | 41. Collar bolt |
| 26b. Snap-ring | 43. Brake disc |
| 27. Flat spring | 44. Cotter pin |
| 27a. Pin | |

Rear brake caliper and parking brake mechanism—Dunlop.

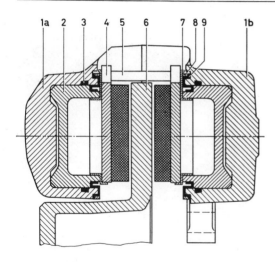

1a. Outer brake caliper half
1b. Inner brake caliper half
2. Piston
3. Piston seal
4. Friction pad
5. Lock pin
6. Brake disc
7. Heat screening plate
8. Clamp ring
9. Dust cap

Friction pad and caliper piston location—Teves.

As with drum brakes, a separate handbrake is used to mechanically activate the brake linings or, in this case, friction pads.

The illustrations show how the system works. When the lever (32) is activated by the handbrake, lining carriers (18) and (19) are pivoted on the caliper assembly (1) and the pads are pressed against the disc. The pads are also automatically adjusted in this application.

When the clearance of the pads becomes greater than .008", the pin (27a) advances into the next notch of adjusting nut (26). When the handbrake is released, the adjustment is completed.

### Teves Disc Brakes

The operation and construction of this type system is similar to the third version Girling disc brakes. At the front, the caliper is attached to the steering knuckle/caliper bracket without use of aligning

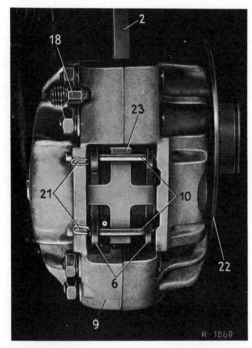

2. Brake disc
6. Friction pad
9. Brake caliper
10. Lock pin
18. Bleed screw
21. Locking clip
22. Front wheel hub
23. Cross leaf spring

Teves disc brake.

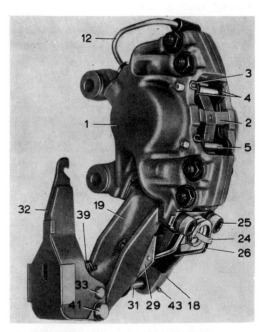

1. Brake caliper
2. Cross leaf spring
3. Locking clip
4. Friction pad (service brake)
5. Lock pin
12. Connecting line
18. Outer lining carrier
19. Inner lining carrier
24. Retaining plate for leg spring
25. Swing bolt
26. Leg spring
29. Friction pad (parking brake)
31. Adjustment screw
32. Tension lever
33. Crosshead
39. Return spring
41. Collar bolt
43. Cotter pin

Rear brake caliper and parking brake mechanism—Teves.

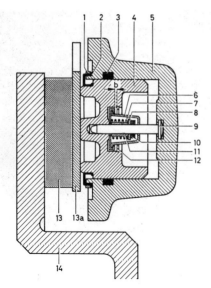

| 1. | Clamp ring | 9. | Guide pin |
| 2. | Dust cap | 10. | Clamp rings |
| 3. | Piston seal | 11. | Spacer sleeve |
| 4. | Piston | 12. | Lock ring |
| 5. | Pressure cylinder | 13. | Friction pad |
| | of brake cali- | 13a. | Base plate |
| | per | 14. | Brake disc |
| 6. | Stop cap | b. | Clearance be- |
| 7. | Pressure spring | | tween stop cap |
| 8. | Spacer washer | | and lock ring |

Caliper piston and associated parts—Teves.

1. Hexagon screw
2. Locking plate
3. Anchor pin

Typical drum brake.

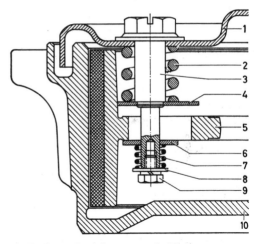

| 1. Brake anchor plate | 6. Washer |
| 2. Pressure spring | 7. Pressure spring |
| 3. Adjustment bolt | 8. Washer |
| 4. Eccentric plate | 9. Hexagon screw |
| 5. Brake shoe | 10. Brake drum |

Guide pin and components—mechanical adjusters.

shims. The two halves of the caliper are bolted together permanently. *NOTE: These bolts should never be removed for any reason.*

The rear calipers are equipped with an automatic adjusting mechanism and, in addition, a disc-wobble compensator. This last feature is required because of the large movement of the axle shafts, especially on turns. Without the compensator, the pistons would be required to move a longer distance to press the pads against the disc, thus increasing brake pedal travel.

## Lining Replacement

### Front Lining Replacement—Drum Brakes with Mechanical Adjustment

Jack up the car and remove the brake drum. Using brake spring pliers, or a screwdriver, remove the two return springs. If pliers are used, always place a piece of

rubber tile, or equivalent, on the lining for protection.

Remove the hold-down bolts, washers and coil springs, then unscrew the stop bolts from the rear of the wheel cylinder. Bend the lock tabs back and unscrew the anchor pins from the wheel cylinder. *NOTE: One version has the anchor pin*

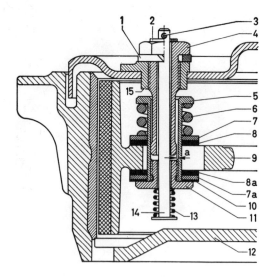

1. Lockwasher
2. Washer
3. Cotter pin
4. Bolt
5. Adjusting sleeve
6. Pressure spring
7. and 7a. Thrust
　　washers

8 and 8a. Friction
　　washers
9. Brake shoe
10. Washer
11. Tensioning screw
12. Brake drum
13. Pressure spring
14. Guide pin
a. clearance

Guide pin and components—self-adjusters.

1. Guide pin
2. Brake wheel cylinder
3. Locking plate
4. Anchor pin

Lining installed.  Note chamfered lining edges.

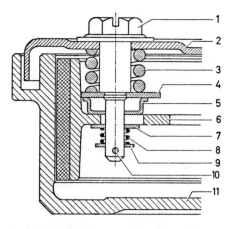

1. Adjustment bolt
2. Brake anchor plate
3. Pressure spring
4. Eccentric plate
5. Cup washer
6. Brake shoe
7. Washer
8. Pressure spring
9. Washer
10. Cotter pin
11. Brake drum

Guide pin and components used on 2″ wide shoes
—rear mechanical.

*screwed directly into the wheel cylinder, therefore the rear bolt does not need loosening.*

Remove the brake shoes and blow the backing plates off with compressed air. The edges of new brake shoes should be chamfered before installation to allow faster lining break-in without dust build-up.

Install the new brake shoes and all other components. Then adjust the brakes as outlined later in this chapter.

**Front Lining Replacement—Drum Brakes with Self-Adjusters**

Jack up the car and remove brake drum and return springs. Remove the cotter pins (3) on guide pin (14) from behind the backing plate, then remove the washer, guide pin and spring (13).

Loosen the bolts (4) from behind the backing plate and remove along with lockwashers. Then remove the stop bolts (2) and lockwashers. *NOTE: Some versions do not require removal of the stop bolts.*

Bend the lock tabs (6) away from the

anchor pins and remove the pins, then the brake shoes. Remove the retaining pins from the wheel cylinder, blow the backing plate off with compressed air and install the new shoes, first chamfering the edges of the lining. *CAUTION: The automatic self-adjusters must be checked before installing the brake drums. Using a large*

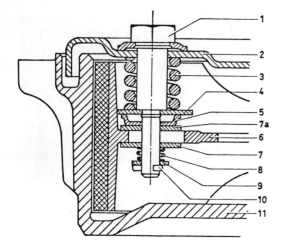

1. Adjustment bolt
2. Brake anchor plate
3. Pressure spring
4. Eccentric plate
5. Cup washer
6. Brake shoe
7. Washer
7a. Washer
8. Pressure spring
9. Washer
10. Cotter pin
11. Brake drum

Guide pin and components used on 2.6" wide shoes—rear mechanical.

*screwdriver, work the brake shoes outward and inward as far as they will go. The brake shoes must remain in any position they are placed, even when gently tapped. Before installing the drums, force the shoes to their innermost position and, before driving the car, pump the brake pedal a few times to adjust the brakes.*

### Rear Lining Replacement—Drum Brakes with Mechanical Adjustment

There were three versions used—two with cast-iron shoes 2" and 2.6" lining width and one with cast aluminum shoes having 2.6" linings.

To replace lining on models with cast-iron shoes, jack up car and remove brake drum and return spring. Remove the cotter pin, washer, spring and rear washer. Remove the hex bolt from the anchor pin and remove all washers. The brake shoes and parking brake cable now can be removed, as well as the spring. Clean the backing plate with compressed air and install new shoes, first chamfering the lining edges. Coat the anchor pins with a light coat of grease, then reinstall all components. Adjust the brakes as outlined later in this chapter. *NOTE: The washer arrangements on the 2" and 2.6" brakes differ—see illustrations.*

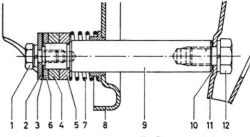

1. Hexagon screw
2. Washer
3. Brass washer
4. Outer brake shoe
5. Inner brake shoe
6. Washer
7. Pressure spring
8. Brake anchor plate
9. Anchor pin
10. Shim
11. Bracket
12. Hexagon screw

Anchor pin and components—rear mechanical.

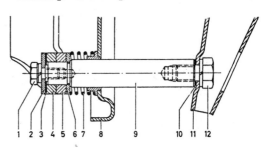

1. Hexagon screw
2. Washer
3. Brass washer
4. Outer brake shoe
5. Inner brake shoe
6. Washer
7. Pressure spring
8. Brake anchor plate
9. Anchor pin
10. Shim
11. Bracket
12. Hexagon screw

Anchor pin and components—rear mechanical.

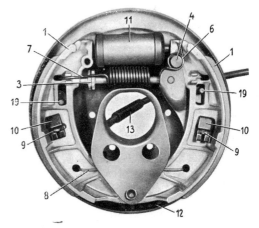

1. Brake shoes
3. Pushrod
4. Collar bolt
6. Brake lever spring
7. Upper return spring
8. Lower return spring
9. Retaining pin
10. Flat spring
11. Wheel cylinder
12. Brake anchor plate
13. Brake cable
14. Eccentric plate

Aluminum 2.6" wide shoes.

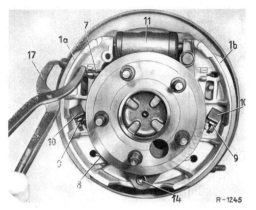

| | | | |
|---|---|---|---|
| 1a. | Front brake shoe | 10. | Flat spring |
| 1b. | Rear brake shoe | 11. | Wheel cylinder |
| 7. | Upper return spring | 14. | Brake shoe anchor pin |
| 8. | Lower return spring | 17. | Brake spring pliers |
| 9. | Retaining pin | | |

| | |
|---|---|
| 1b. | Rear brake shoe |
| 2. | Brake lever |
| 16. | Pry bar 1 ½" wide |

Removing rear brake shoe.

Shoe removal. Note pad under pliers to protect
linings.

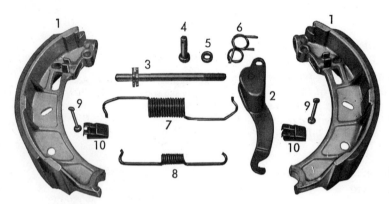

1. Brake shoes
2. Brake lever
3. Pushrod
4. Collar bolt
5. Sleeve
6. Return spring
7. Upper return spring
8. Lower return spring
9. Retaining pin
10. Flat spring

Brake components.

The aluminum brake shoes require a slightly different replacement procedure. After removing the brake drum, detach the upper and lower return springs, then, using a screw driver, press off the two shoe retaining clips and remove the associated pins.

Rotate the two eccentrics (19) until the shoes are out to the end of their travel, then insert a suitable piece of flat steel between the brake cable lever and the rear shoe and remove the shoe. Now remove the front shoe and disconnect the rear shoe from the brake lever. Unscrew the pushrod from the brake lever and remove the upper return spring from the pushrod.

To install new shoes, first coat the pushrod threads with a good graphite grease or Molykote, then hook the return spring to the pushrod, with the long end toward the thread. Screw the pushrod into the brake lever and attach the lever, pushrod and *both* return springs to the rear brake shoe. Place a punch through one retaining hole to lock the return spring in position, insert the flat steel pry bar between the brake shoe and lever, attach the brake cable and install the shoe to the backing plate. Install the front shoe, after coating the anchor pins and pivot points with grease, then turn the two eccentrics to adjust the brakes inward. Insert the re-

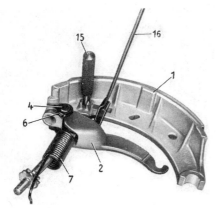

1. Brake shoes
2. Brake lever
4. Collar bolt
6. Brake lever spring
7. Upper return spring
15. Retaining pin
16. Spreader

Retaining pin (punch) placement.

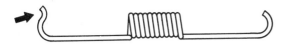

Spring used with rear drums having self-adjusters.

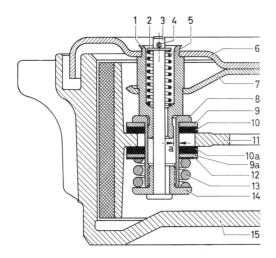

1. Bolt
2. Washer
3. Guide pin
4. Cotter pin
5. Pressure spring
6. Brake anchor plate
7. Bow
8. Adjusting sleeve
9. and 9a. Thrust washer
10. and 10a. Friction washer
11. Brake shoe
12. Washer
13. Pressure spring
14. Tensioning screw
15. Brake drum
a. Clearance

Guide pin and components. Pin can be reversed for ease in installation, with cotter pin end facing forward—self-adjusters.

taining pins through the backing plate and shoes and snap the clips onto the ends of the pins. Attach the upper return spring and remove the punch from the retaining hole. Attach the lower return spring so that the end with the kink in its hook is attached to the front brake shoe. Install the brake drums and adjust the brakes as outlined later in this chapter.

## Rear Lining Replacement—Drum Brakes with Self-Adjusters

Jack up the car, remove the brake drums, then detach the brake shoe and brake lever return springs. Remove the cotter pins from the automatic adjusters, then the washers, pins and springs. Remove the brake shoes and detach the handbrake cable, then remove the washer and spring from the anchor pin. Remove the spring-loaded pins from one wheel cylinder, then remove the activating pin (2) from the guide pin (5) and check the springs (3) for tension. Clean the backing plate with compressed air, chamfer the edges of the new lining, and install. It will be necessary to compress the pressure spring during installation using a small C-clamp. *NOTE: The left- and right-hand return springs are different—see illustration. Check the auto-*

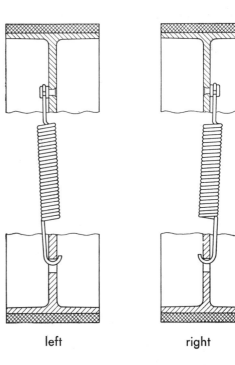

left                    right

Return springs—self-adjusters.

1. Front wheel hub
2. Brake disc
3. Brake caliper
4. Connecting line
5. Bleed screw
6. Friction pad
7. Spring clip

Girling disc brakes.

1. Friction pad
2. Brake caliper
3. Brake disc

Pad removal—Girling.

*matic adjusters as outlined in Front Lining Replacement—Drum Brakes With Self-Adjusters, then adjust the handbrake as outlined later in this chapter.*

**Pad Replacement—Girling Disc Brakes**

The construction of this type brake allows complete pad inspection without disassembly. Check the pads and replace only if worn to .080″ or less, or if the disc and pads are oil-coated.

To remove, pull the spring clips (7) out of the retaining pins and remove the pins. Using a wire hook, bent from 3/16″ welding rod, pull the pads from the calipers. Blow off the brake assembly with compressed air and push the pistons back out of the way. *NOTE: This sometimes forces fluid from the master cylinder reservoir.*

Before pushing the pistons back, remove the inner heat shield, if present, to prevent damage. These shields, by the way, can be replaced with anti-squeak plates, available at authorized dealers, if brake squealing is a problem.

Making sure the dust caps are properly seated by pressing them back with a screwdriver, install new pads, then insert retaining pins and clips. Pump the brake pedal a few times to seat the pads, then

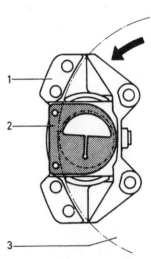

1. Calipers
2. Anti-squeal plate
3. Brake disc

Girling anti-squeal plate installation.

check the master cylinder reservoir and fill if necessary.

As with all new brakes, disc brake pads should be carefully broken in or they will become heat glazed and useless. In other words, *no hard stops* for several hundred miles.

| 1. | Front wheel hub | 9. | Brake caliper |
|----|-----------------|-----|---------------|
| 2. | Brake disc | 10. | Stirrup |
| 4. | Connecting line | 11. | Brake line |
| 6. | Friction pad | 18. | Bleed screw |

| 1. | Brake caliper | 19. | Brake disc |
|----|---------------|-----|------------|
| 4. | Friction pad | 47. | Hook |
| 12. | Pressure cylinder | | |

Pad removal using hook (47)—Dunlop.

Dunlop disc brake configuration. Stirrup (10) must be removed before pads can be replaced.

## Pad Replacement—Dunlop Disc Brakes

### A. FOOT BRAKE

Dunlop pads should be replaced if worn to .24″ or less in thickness, or if oil covered. To check, unbolt the retainer (10) and remove it and the bolt. If worn, remove pads with a hook, then blow off the brake assembly with compressed air.

Before installiing new pads, push the pistons back into their bores. The illustration shows this being done using special piston pliers, but, if care is exercised, a piece of steel will serve the same purpose.

Check the guide for the pad pressure plate and remove all dirt and score marks with emery paper. *NOTE: Pushing pistons back may displace brake fluid from master cylinder reservoir.*

Install pad onto piston guide bolt, making sure it is properly engaged. Attach the pad retainer and bolt and pump the brake pedal to seat the pads. Do not abuse the brakes for several hundred miles; otherwise, the pads will become heat glazed.

### B. PARKING BRAKE

The parking brake (handbrake) pads must be replaced if worn to .18″ or less, or if oil covered.

To remove, pull the cotter pin on the outer lining carrier (27a) and back out the adjustment screw (31) a few turns. Detach

| 1. | Brake caliper |
|----|---------------|
| 4. | Connecting line |

Holding caliper pistons in retracted position using special tool (48a)—Dunlop.

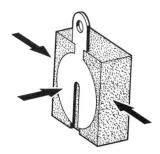

Dunlop friction pad lubrication points. Even one drop of grease on pad friction surface will result in erratic brake action.

1. Brake caliper     26. Leg spring
12. Pressure cylinder     27. Lining carrier
19. Brake disc     29. Friction pad
24. Locking plate     47. Removal hook

Removing rear friction pads—Dunlop.

| | |
|---|---|
| 1. Brake caliper | 26. Leg spring |
| 2. Stirrup | 27a. Outer lining |
| 3. Hexagon screw | carrier |
|     with hexagon | 27b. Inner lining |
|     nut and ser- | carrier |
|     rated lock- | 29. Friction pad with |
|     washer | fitting plate |
| 4. Friction pad with | (handbrake) |
|     fitting plate | 31. Adjustment screw |
|     (service brake) | 34. Tension lever |
| 12. Pressure cylinder | 38. Brake line |
| 19. Brake disc | 40. Wheel fixing |
| 20. Connecting line | disc |
|     with pipe clip | 41. Brake support |
| 24. Locking plate | lever |
| 25. Swing bolt | 42. Rear axle shaft |

Rear brake caliper and disc arrangement—Dunlop.

1. Rear brake cables     6. Center brake cable
2. Return spring     7. Relay lever guide
3. Equalizer     8. Wingnut for hand-
4. Tensioning screw        brake adjust-
5. Relay lever        ment

Parking brake cables must be slackened—Dunlop.

the hairpin spring (26) and loosen the nut that holds the pads to the lining carriers. Pull the pad from the carrier using a hook, then clean the pad guide on the lining carrier with emery paper.

Loosen the parking brake cables by backing out the wingnut at the relay lever, then install the new friction pads. Install the hairpin spring and adjust the pads by turning screw (31) until a clearance of .020″ exists between the pads and disc. Lock the adjusting screw with a cotter pin, then seat the pads by pulling the handbrake on a few times. Adjust the handbrake cables as outlined later in this chapter.

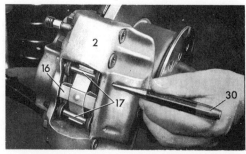

2. Brake caliper     17. Retaining pin
16. Cross-leaf spring     30. Drift

Driving out retaining pin—Teves.

1. Brake caliper
18. Friction pad

Holding pistons in retracted position using special pliers (31)—Teves.

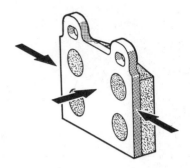

Friction pad lubrication points—Teves.

## Pad Replacement—Teves Disc Brakes

Pads must be replaced if worn to .080" or less, or if oil covered. Remove the cover plate (front only) and drive the retaining pins out of the caliper, using a drift. Remove the "cross" spring, then remove one pad by pulling out on both tabs with bent pieces of welding rod. Blow off the brake assembly with compressed air and clean the pad guide in the caliper. Check the dust covers for cracks. If cracks exist, the caliper must be disassembled and the cover replaced.

Press one piston back into its bore, using special pliers or a flat piece of steel bent to fit. *NOTE: Fluid may be displaced from the master cylinder reservoir.*

Install one friction pad, then push the other piston back and install the other pad. *NOTE: One pad must always remain in caliper, because pushing one piston back would bring the other forward too far.*

Install the "cross" spring and retaining pins, then seat the pads by pumping the brake pedal a few times.

Hard stopping for the first few hundred miles could ruin the new pads by causing heat glazing.

## Lining Replacement—
## Teves Drum Parking Brake

To replace rear parking brake lining, first remove the brake caliper and disc (as described later in this chapter), then detach the lower return spring (31), using brake spring pliers. Turn the axle flange

| | |
|---|---|
| 15. Rear axle shaft flange | 31. Lower return spring |
| 20. Brake shoes | 39. Brake spring pilers |
| 24. Compression spring | |

Removing parking brake linings—Teves.

| | |
|---|---|
| 13. Support web | 20. Brake shoes |
| 15. Rear axle shaft flange | 24. Compression spring |

Removing retaining springs using special tool (40) —Teves.

R-325?

| | |
|---|---|
| 11. Cover plate | 20. Brake shoes |
| 13. Support web | 22. Adjustment device |
| 15. Rear axle shaft | 29. Upper return |
| flange | spring |

Lifting parking brake shoes over axle flange—
Teves.

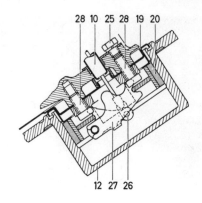

| | |
|---|---|
| 10. Brake cable | 26. Pin |
| 12. Brake disc | 27. Expansion lock |
| 19. Cover plate | 28. Hexagon socket |
| 20. Brake shoes | screw |

Cross-section of parking brake assembly—Teves.

so that a threaded bolt hole aligns with a retainer spring (24). Depress the spring as illustrated, then turn 90° and remove. Remove the other spring in the same manner, then pull the brake shoes apart at the lower end and remove upward. Detach the upper return spring and star wheel adjuster, then press out pin (26) from the expansion lock (27) and remove lock from brake cable.

Coat all moving surfaces with Molykote paste, then attach the expansion lock to the brake cable and press the lock into the backing plate. Adjust the star wheel to its innermost position, after lubricating threads, and install it and the upper return spring onto the new shoes. Slip the shoes over the axle and hook them to the expansion lock, then hook up the retainer spring and lower return spring. The long-hooked end is attached last. Install brake disc, caliper and adjust parking brake. (Brake adjustment is found later in this chapter.)

## Disc Brake Caliper Replacement

To remove the caliper, first remove the brake line (11) from the caliper (9). *NOTE: Plug the line to prevent fluid loss.* The lines are arranged as follows:

*Girling (1st version)*—line is attached to inner position bore by a hollow bolt. The brake hose connector points upward and

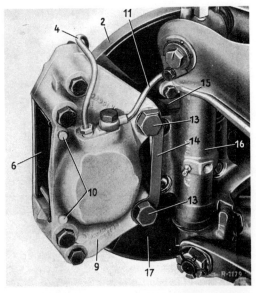

| | |
|---|---|
| 2. Brake disc | 13. Hexagon fitting |
| 4. Connecting line | screw |
| 6. Friction pad | 14. Locking plate |
| 9. Brake caliper | 15. Steering knuckle |
| 10. Locking pin | bracket |
| 11. Brake line with | 16. Steering knuckle |
| connector | 17. Cover plate |

Girling disc brake (first version).

the bleed screw is in the outer caliper half.

*Girling (2nd version)*—line is attached to outer piston bore. Hose connector is connected behind steering knuckle and bleed screw is on inner cylinder.

# BRAKES 187

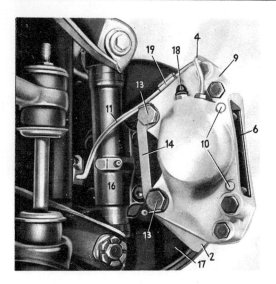

1. Feeler gauge    3. Brake caliper
2. Brake disc    M = Measuring point

Measuring caliper to disc clearance on Girling brakes.

2. Brake disc
4. Connecting line
6. Friction pad
9. Brake caliper
10. Locking pin
11. Brake line with connector

13. Hexagon fitting screw
14. Locking plate
16. Steering knuckle
17. Cover plate
18. Bleed screw
19. Rubber lug

Girling disc brake (second version).

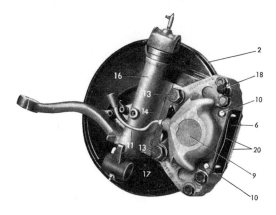

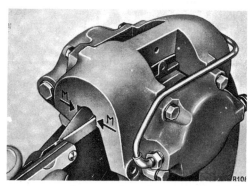

Measuring caliper to disc clearance on Dunlop brakes. M = Measuring point.

2. Brake disc
6. Friction pad
9. Brake caliper
10. Locking pin
11. Brake line with connector
13. Hexagon fitting screw

14. Locking plate
16. Steering knuckle
17. Cover plate
18. Bleed screw with rubber cap
20. Heat screening plate

Girling disc brake (third version).

*Girling (3rd version)*—line is connected to inner piston bore and there is no external connecting line.

*Teves*—same as 3rd version Girling.

*Dunlop*—the brake line is attached to the outer piston bore.

*NOTE: The caliper need not be removed unless the disc or hub must come off.*

Next, bend back the lock tabs (14) and remove the hold-down bolts (13). The caliper can be removed at this time. Any shims should be taped together and their positions noted.

To install, reverse the removal procedure, paying special attention to shim placement. Always use a new lock tab—bending weakens the metal.

It is extremely important that the brake disc be exactly parallel to the caliper. Using a feeler gauge, measure the clearance

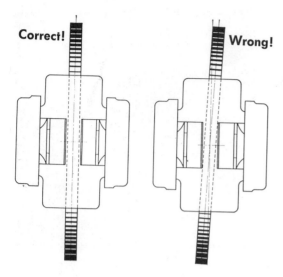

| | |
|---|---|
| 1. Brake caliper | 25. Hexagon screw |
| 2. Hexagon screw | 32. Brake line |
| 3. Locking plate | 33. Bracket for brake |
| 10. Brake cable | cable with rub- |
| 11. Cover plate | ber grommet |

Teves rear brake caliper used on phase II models.

If the caliper and disc are misaligned uneven friction pad wear will result.

at the top and bottom of the caliper (between disc and caliper) and on both sides of the disc (see illustrations). If the clearance varies beyond specifications, position the brake caliper by adding or subtracting shims as required.

Tighten all bolts to proper torque specifications, then install the lock tabs. Connect the brake line, using new copper gaskets, then bleed the system as outlined later in this chapter.

Before test driving the car, turn the steering wheel to the extreme left and right positions and make sure that the brake lines do not rub anywhere. Pump the brake pedal to seat the pads and check for "sponginess". If the pedal is spongy, bleed the brakes again.

## Brake Disc Removal

### Front

Removal for the various types is similar. First, remove the brake caliper, then the front hub (see Chapter 1). Fasten the hub in a vise or holding fixture (be careful not to distort the housing), matchmark the disc and hub, then unbolt the brake disc.

Inspect the disc for burning (blue color), cracks and scoring. The disc becomes scored slightly in normal service; therefore,

| | | | |
|---|---|---|---|
| 1. | Brake caliper | 26. | Leg spring |
| 2. | Stirrup | 27a. | Outer lining |
| 3. | Hexagon screw | | carrier |
| | with hexagon | 27b. | Inner lining |
| | nut and ser- | | carrier |
| | rated washer | 29. | Friction pad with |
| 4. | Friction pad with | | mounting plate |
| | mounting plate | | (handbrake) |
| | (service brake) | 31. | Adjustment screw |
| 12. | Pressure cylinder | 34. | Tension lever |
| 19. | Brake disc | 38. | Brake line |
| 20. | Connecting line | 40. | Wheel fixing disc |
| | with pipe clip | 41. | Brake support |
| 24. | Locking plate | | lever |
| 25. | Swing bolt | 42. | Rear axle shaft |

Dunlop rear brake caliper used on 300SE models.

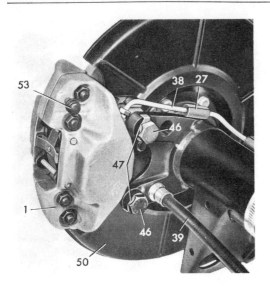

1. Brake caliper
27. Rubber ring
38. Brake line
39. Brake cable
46. Hexagon fitting screw
47. Locking plate
50. Cover plate
53. Bleed screw with rubber cap

Rear brake caliper as used on 250S, 250SE and 300SEb models.

1. Brake disc
2. Dial gauge
3. Dial gauge holder
4. Hexagon bolt
5. Distance sleeve
6. Cover plate

Checking runout of brake disc using a dial indicator.

Brake disc, showing unacceptable level of damage.

1. Brake caliper
12. Brake disc
14. Fitting pin
15. Rear axle shaft flange
16. Cross-leaf spring
17. Retaining pin
18. Friction pad

Teves rear disc replacement.

1. Outer caliper half
2. Piston
3. Piston seal
4. Dust cap
5. Friction pad
6. Connecting line
7. Bleed screw
8. Hexagon screw
9. Hexagon screw
10. Spring clip
11. Retaining pin
12. Inner caliper half
13. Piston
14. Piston seal
15. Dust cap

Girling caliper components (first and second versions).

replace it only if the depth of individual scores exceeds .020″.

To ensure proper alignment, clean the hub and disc with emery paper to remove all rust and/or burrs, then bolt the disc to the hub. It is a wise precaution to use new lockwashers under the bolts. Install the hub and disc, then check the disc for run-out (wobble), using a dial indicator as illustrated. If runout is excessive, it sometimes helps to remove the disc and reseat it on the hub. *Never hammer on the disc.* Install the caliper assembly and bleed the brakes.

### Rear

Remove the brake caliper and unbolt disc from rear axle flange. *NOTE: The parking brake must be released.*

Discs that will not come off can be gently tapped with a fiber hammer. Before installing, coat the axle flange with Moly-kote grease, then install disc and caliper and check runout. Bleed the brakes before moving the car.

## Piston Seal Replacement— Girling Disc Brakes

*CAUTION: Although exploded views show caliper halves disassembled, the two halves should NEVER be unbolted.*

Remove brake caliper and friction pads, as previously described. On versions having an external connecting line, insert a wood block about ¾″ thick into the caliper gap and force the piston out using compressed air (7–8 psi). Remove the wood and the piston. On versions having an internal connecting passage, clamp the inner piston and force the two outer pistons out using compressed air. Remove the clamp, block the outer caliper passage, and blow out the inner piston.

Remove the dust boots and remove the piston seals. Check the cylinder bores for wear or corrosion. If the bores are scored, do *not* hone them—replace the entire caliper assembly.

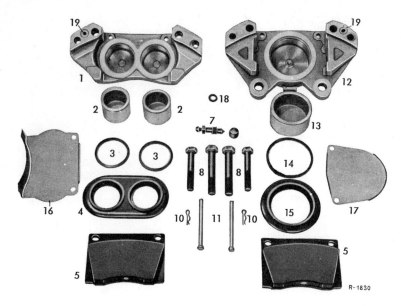

1. Outer caliper half
2. Piston
3. Piston seal
4. Dust cap
5. Friction pad
7. Bleed screw
8. Hexagon screw
10. Spring clip
11. Retaining pin
12. Inner caliper half
13. Piston
14. Piston seal
15. Dust cap
16. Heat screening plate
17. Heat screening plate
18. Rubber sealing ring
19. Connecting passage in caliper halves

Girling caliper components (third version).

Before installing new seals, clean all passages with brake fluid and compressed air. Install the seals, dust caps and pistons, coating everything with brake fluid before assembly. Install the connecting line (if present) and brake caliper, then bleed the brakes.

# Piston Seal Replacement— Teves Disc Brakes

*CAUTION: Do not unbolt the two caliper halves for any reason. NOTE: Remove the brake caliper for easier service.*

Remove the friction pads, brake line and dust cap, then pry the clamp ring from the housing. Using a rubber-backed piece of flat steel, hold one piston in place while blowing the other one out with compressed air (7–8 psi). *NOTE: If a piston is stuck, clamp the other piston in place and pump the brake pedal. The hydraulic pressure will force the piston out. This is a messy operation, so protect exterior paint from splashing brake fluid.*

Remove the piston seals from the cylinder bores and examine the bores. Scored bores necessitate replacement of the entire caliper, since the inner surface is chrome plated and cannot be honed. Clean the

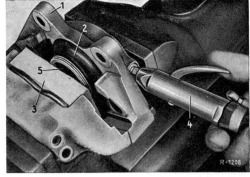

1. Brake caliper      4. Compressed air
2. Dust cap          5. Piston
3. Piece of wood

Removing caliper piston—Girling.

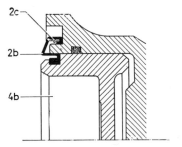

2b. Dust cap        4b. Piston
2c. Closed clamp ring

Piston seal and dust cover—Teves.

bores with crocus cloth only, never emery paper.

Install the new seals, coating them with brake fluid beforehand, then install the piston so that the projection points downward. *NOTE: If the projection is in any other position, the brakes may squeal badly.*

Install the dust cap, clamp ring and heat shield. The recess in the heat shield must fit the piston projection, but be above the shield level by about .004″. *NOTE: The heat shields differ for inner and outer pistons.*

Install the friction pads and the caliper assembly, then bleed brakes. *IMPORTANT: The rear brake pistons must be installed with the piston projection facing upward.*

## Wheel Cylinder Service— Drum Brakes

Any time the brakes are inspected, the wheel cylinders should also be inspected. Wheel cylinder malfunctions usually fall into two general categories—leakage and sticking or binding.

The best leakage check is simply to peel back the rubber dust cover. If fluid seeps out, or if the cover is wet on the inside, the wheel cylinders should be rebuilt. It is best to rebuild all wheel cylinders at once, for if one is leaking, the rest are sure to follow. Use new seals throughout.

**Front Wheels**

To disassemble, unscrew the bleed screw and remove actuating pin (8), metal boot (6) and rubber dust cover (7). Remove the piston (5), cap (4), cap expander (3) and stop spring (2) from the housing.

Clean the cylinder bore with alcohol or brake fluid, then examine the bore. Scored or rusted wheel cylinders are normally replaced. Honing destroys the surface and, with the single-end design of these cylinders, is difficult to do properly. Assembly is the reverse of disassembly. *NOTE: Coat all parts with brake fluid.*

**Rear Wheels**

To replace wheel cylinders, remove the brake shoes, disconnect brake lines and un-

1. Brake caliper          23. Holding fixture
2. Piston

Holding fixture in place—Teves.

Double-end wheel cylinder installed.

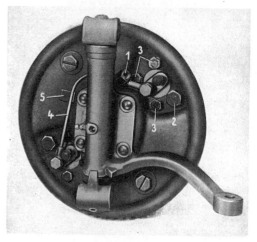

1. Square socket at the       3. Hexagon screw
   brake line                 4. Brake line
2. Stop screw or hexa-        5. Rubber pad
   gon screw

Rear of backing plate.

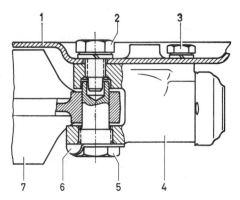

1. Brake anchor plate
2. Stop screw
3. Hexagon screw
4. Brake wheel cylinder
5. Anchor pin
6. Locking plate
7. Brake shoe

First version wheel cylinder mounting—front.

1. Pressure bolt
2. Rubber cap
3. Piston
4. Blind hole cup
6. Pressure spring
7. Wheel brake
cylinder

Wheel cylinder components—rear.

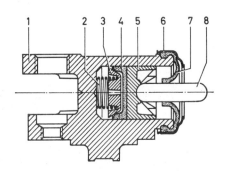

1. Brake wheel cylinder
housing
2. Spring
3. Piston cup expander
4. Cup
5. Piston
6. Metal boot
7. Rubber boot
8. Actuating pin

Wheel cylinder internal parts—front.

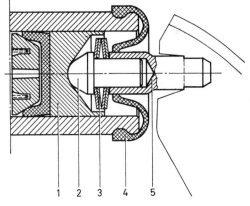

1. Piston
2. Bolt
3. Cup spring
4. Rubber boot
5. Guide pin

Wheel cylinder with spring-loaded pin—rear.

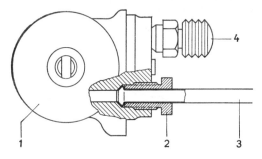

1. Wheel cylinder
housing
2. Cap screw
3. Brake line
4. Bleed screw

Wheel cylinder external parts—front.

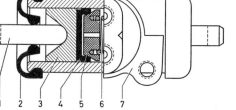

1. Actuating pin
2. Rubber boot
3. Piston
4. Cup
5. Piston cup expander
6. Spring
7. Wheel cylinder

Wheel cylinder with rigid pin—rear.

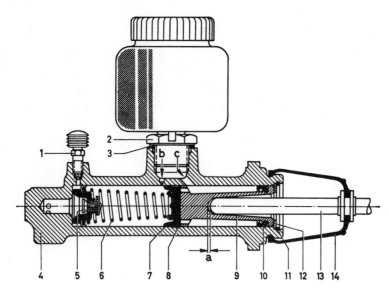

1. Bleed screw
2. Tubular screw
3. Sealing ring
4. Housing
5. Check valve
6. Pressure spring
7. Primary cup
8. Piston cup washer
9. Piston
10. Secondary cup
11. Piston stop ring
12. Piston stop washer
13. Piston pushrod
14. Boot
a = Clearance between piston and pushrod
b = Compensating ports
c = Connecting ports

Single circuit master cylinder.

bolt cylinder from the rear. Bleed brakes after installing new cylinders.

Inspection and disassembly is essentially the same and, while it is *possible* to hone wheel cylinder bores, it is recommended that the entire cylinder be replaced. Coat all parts with brake fluid before assembly.

## Single Master Cylinder Service

The function of the master cylinder is to convert the mechanical action of the foot pedal into hydraulic pressure, which acts on the wheel cylinders (caliper pistons) to actuate the brake shoes (pads) and stop the car. The basic design of all master cylinders is the same, whether single or dual type. Operation is very similar to that of the wheel cylinder in reverse. A push-rod moves a piston against spring pressure, displacing hydraulic fluid in a closed system. Since the volume is constant, pressure rises. This pressure serves to operate the wheel cylinders of drum brakes or caliper pistons of disc brakes.

The master cylinder should be checked if fluid loss is experienced, or if the fluid constantly becomes aerated.

To remove, first drain the master cylinder

1. Screw cap (master cylinder)
2. Screw cap (supply cylinder)
3. Bleed screw (supply cylinder)
4. Bleed screw (master cylinder)
5. Brake line
6. Brake line
7. Brake line
8. Brake line
9. Brake line
10. Line from supply cylinder to extraction cylinder
11. Stop light switch
12. Plug connection
13. Flash signal mechanism
14. Plug connection
15. Upper beam flash mechanism
16. Plug connection

Master cylinder installed.

4. Master cylinder
5. Check valve
6. Pressure spring
7. Primary cup
8. Piston cup washer

9. Piston
10. Secondary cup
11. Piston stop ring
12. Piston stop washer
14. Boot

Single circuit master cylinder components.

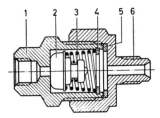

1. Housing
2. Check valve
3. Pressure spring

4. Piston stop ring
5. Sealing ring
6. Threaded union

Check valve.

1. Screw cap
   (master cylinder)
2. Screw cap
   (supply cylinder)
3. Bleed screw
   (master cylinder)
4. Bleed screw
   (supply cylinder)
5. Brake line
6. Brake line
7. Brake line
8. Brake line
9. Brake line
10. Line from supply

cylinder to ex-
traction cylinder
11. Stop light switch
12. Plug connection
13. Primary pressure
valve
14. Relay
15. Relay
16. Assembly plate
17. Relay
18. Relay
19. Inspection lamp
socket

Master cylinder installation—front disc/rear drum system.

by opening the bleed screw, then disconnect all brake levers and the stop light switch. On cars with front disc/rear drum systems, first disconnect the brake line at the primary pressure valve, then unscrew the valve from the master cylinder.

To install, reverse removal procedure, making sure that stop light switch and primary pressure valve threads seal tightly. The master cylinder pushrod clearance must be maintained by adjusting the pedal freeplay—see section on brake adjustment in this chapter.

To bleed the master cylinder, pump the pedal and maintain pressure while having the bleed screw cracked open. When the pedal goes to the floor, hold it there and tighten the bleed screw (to prevent sucking air into hydraulic system). Continue this procedure until no more air bubbles issue from the bleed screw opening, then top up the fluid level and bleed the brakes at the wheels.

Disassembly is simple, just remove the dust boot and the snap-ring, then pull out

all internal parts. While it is possible to hone rusted or corroded bores, it is not recommended, because this destroys the surface and a lasting repair is not usually achieved. If the cylinder bore is good, replace the rubber sealing caps with new components, clean all passages and parts with brake fluid and reassemble the master cylinder. It is a good idea to replace the check valve at this time, as well as the pressure spring.

## Dual Master Cylinder Service

The dual master cylinder operates in the same manner as the single piston model. It, however, has a safety feature which the single unit lacks—if a leak develops in one brake circuit (rear wheels, for example),

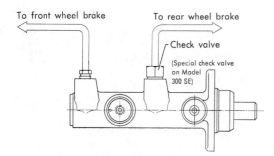

Tandem master cylinder.

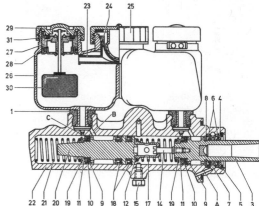

the other circuit will still operate.

Failure of one system is immediately obvious—the pedal travel increases appreciably and a warning light is activated. This warning light is operated by a simple switch attached to a float in the reservoir/s. When the fluid falls below a certain level, the switch activates the circuit. *CAUTION: This design was not intended to allow driving the car for any distance with, in effect, a two-wheel brake system. If one brake circuit fails, braking action is correspondingly lower. Front circuit failure is the more serious, however, since the front brakes contribute up to 75% of the braking force required to stop the car. Repair any leaks immediately!*

| | | |
|---|---|---|
| 1. Plug | 20. | Piston (intermediate piston) |
| 3. Piston (pushrod circuit) | 21. | Pressure spring |
| 4. Piston stop washer | 22. | Housing |
| 5. Piston stop ring | 23. | Splash guard |
| 6. Vacuum seal | 24. | Strainer |
| 7. Spacer ring | 25. | Screw cap |
| 8. Support ring | 26. | Reservoir |
| 9. Piston cup washer | 27. | Contact insert |
| 10. Primary cup | 28. | O-ring |
| 11. Thrust ring | 29. | Cover cap |
| 12. Spring retainer | 30. | Float |
| 14. Connecting screw | 31. | Sealing ring |
| 15. Stop screw | A. | Leak port |
| 17. Pressure spring | B. | Connecting port |
| 18. Ring cup | C. | Compensating port |
| 19. Spring retainer | | |

Tandem master cylinder internal parts.

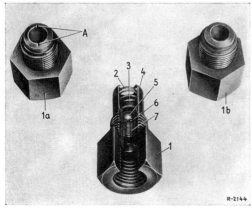

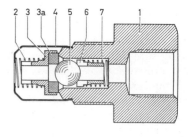

| Left | | | |
|---|---|---|---|
| 1. | Connector with check valve | 4. | Metal sleeve |
| | | 5. | Ball |
| 1a. | Connector for special check valve | 6. | Spring sleeve |
| | | 7. | Pressure spring |
| 1b. | Connector for check valve | A. | Notches in the connector for the special check valve |
| 2. | Pressure spring | | |
| 3. | Spring retainer | | |

| Right | | | |
|---|---|---|---|
| 1. | Connector | 4. | Metal sleeve |
| 2. | Pressure spring | 5. | Ball |
| 3. | Spring retainer | 6. | Spring sleeve |
| 3a. | Rubber ring | 7. | Pressure spring |

Check valves used in first version Tandem master cylinders.

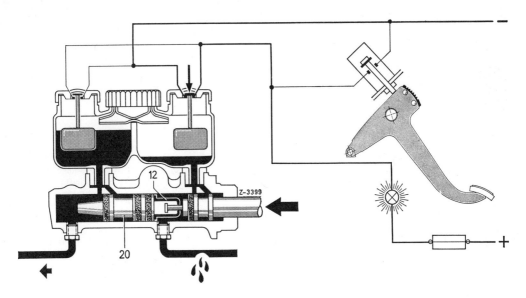

Tandem master cylinder warning light circuit indicates a leak in any one circuit.

To remove the master cylinder, first open a bleed screw at one front, and one rear, wheel. Pump the pedal to empty the reservoir completely, then disconnect the switch connectors using a small screwdriver. Disconnect the two brake lines and plug the ends with bleed screw caps or equivalent. Unbolt the master cylinder from the power brake unit and remove.

To disassemble, pull the reservoir out of the top of the cylinder, then remove screw cap (25), strainer (24) and splash shield (23). Unscrew the cover caps (29) and take out inserts (27) and O-rings (28). Push the piston inward slightly and remove the stop screw (15). Remove the piston stop ring (5) in the same manner, then pull out the piston and other components. The spring must be unscrewed from the piston.

Assembly precautions are similar to that of single master cylinder. *NOTE: Do not hone the cylinder bore. If slight rust marks do not come out with crocus cloth, replace the master cylinder.*

*CAUTION: Always use a new O-ring between the master cylinder and power brake unit.*

1. Tandem master cylinder
2. Reservoir
3. Plug connection
4. Screw cap
5. Cover cap
6. Power brake
7. Reservoir for supply cylinder
8. Vacuum line
9. Brake line to right front wheel brake

Tandem master cylinder installation.

attached brackets and cables, then detach the pushrod from the brake pedal and unbolt the brake unit from the firewall. Installation is the reverse of removal; make sure to use a new O-ring seal between the master cylinder and power brake unit.

## Power Brake Unit Replacement

Remove the master cylinder and the vacuum line at the brake unit. Remove all

## Bleeding Brakes

Always bleed the brakes after performing any service, or if the pedal seems

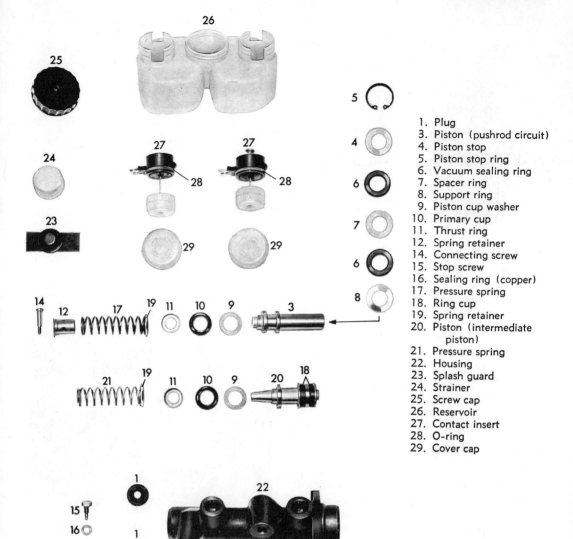

1. Plug
3. Piston (pushrod circuit)
4. Piston stop
5. Piston stop ring
6. Vacuum sealing ring
7. Spacer ring
8. Support ring
9. Piston cup washer
10. Primary cup
11. Thrust ring
12. Spring retainer
14. Connecting screw
15. Stop screw
16. Sealing ring (copper)
17. Pressure spring
18. Ring cup
19. Spring retainer
20. Piston (intermediate piston)
21. Pressure spring
22. Housing
23. Splash guard
24. Strainer
25. Screw cap
26. Reservoir
27. Contact insert
28. O-ring
29. Cover cap

Exploded view of tandem master cylinder.

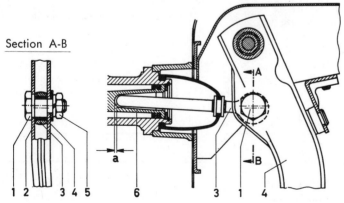

Section A-B

1. Adjusting screw
2. Polyamide bushing
3. Pushrod
4. Brake pedal
5. Hexagon nut
6. Piston
a. = Clearance between pushrod and piston

Adjustment of brake pedal free-play on models with single circuit master cylinder.

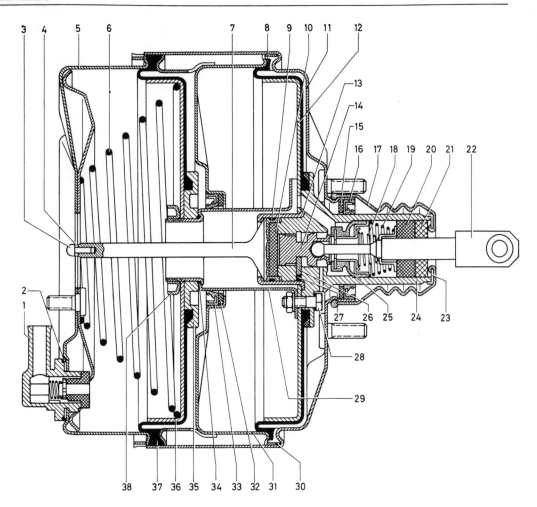

T 51/200 power brake unit.

| | | |
|---|---|---|
| 1. Check valve | 14. Valve plunger | 27. Seal |
| 2. O-ring | 15. Guide ring | 28. Hexagon screw with washer |
| 3. Pressure button | 16. Sealing ring | and hexagon nut |
| 4. Compensating washer | 17. Boot | 29. Spacer tube |
| 5. Front vacuum cylinder | 18. Poppet return spring | 30. Ring |
| 6. Pressure spring (piston | 19. Valve rod return spring | 31. Center vacuum cylinder |
| return spring) | 20. Air cleaner | 32. Guide ring |
| 7. Pushrod | 21. Muffler | 33. Sealing ring |
| 8. Roller-type diaphragm | 22. Valve operating rod | 34. O-ring |
| 10. Reaction disc | 23. Muffler bracket | 35. Support |
| 11. Rear vacuum cylinder | 24. Control housing | 36. Diaphragm retainer |
| 12. Diaphragm retainer | 25. Poppet assembly | 37. Roller-type diaphragm |
| 13. Guide bushing | 26. Stop disc | 38. Sheet-metal nut |

spongy ("soft"). The location of the bleed screws can be seen by consulting the illustrations throughout this chapter. The procedure is simple, first have an assistant pump the brakes and hold the pedal. Then, starting at the point farthest from the master cylinder, slightly open the bleed screw. When the pedal hits the floor, close the bleed screw before allowing pedal to return (to prevent air from being sucked into the system). Continue this procedure until no more air bubbles exit from bleed screw hole, then go to the next wheel. To prevent fluid splashing on car (it eats

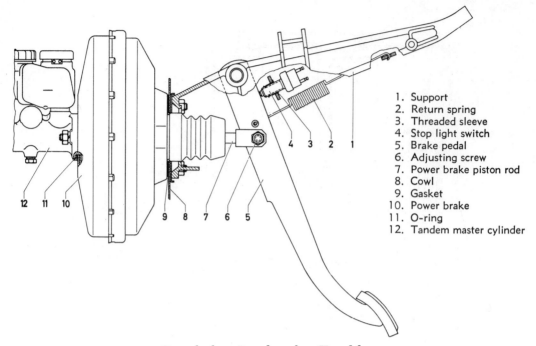

1. Support
2. Return spring
3. Threaded sleeve
4. Stop light switch
5. Brake pedal
6. Adjusting screw
7. Power brake piston rod
8. Cowl
9. Gasket
10. Power brake
11. O-ring
12. Tandem master cylinder

Power brake unit used on phase II models.

paint), place one end of a section of hose on the bleed screw and the other in an open jar of brake fluid. This fluid is filled with microscopic air bubbles after bleeding

Section A-B

2. Piston rod of power brake
3a. Adjusting screw with hexagon nut and lockwasher
4. Pivot pin with hexagon nut and lockwasher
12. Clutch pedal
13. Brake pedal
14. Supply cylinder
17. Pedal support
21. Bushings in the pedals
25. Bushings in the brake pedal
26. Hexagon screw with hexagon nut and lockwasher

Adjustment of brake pedal free-play on models with tandem master cylinder (all except 230SL).

process is completed, therefore it should be discarded.

### Sequence of Bleeding Operations

A. *Single master cylinder, drum brakes or four-wheel discs.* First bleed the master cylinder, then the power brake (if installed). Start bleeding at right rear wheel and work toward master cylinder.

B. *Single master cylinder, discs front/drums rear.* First bleed the master cylinder, then the power brake unit. Bleed the brake caliper farthest from master cylinder (depending on model), then the other brake caliper. Bleed the drum brakes last, again starting with the brake farthest from master cylinder.

C. *Dual master cylinder.* Bleed only the circuit that has been opened. If both circuits have been opened, first bleed the circuit connected to the pushrod bore, then the other circuit.

## Brake Adjustment

### Drum Brakes

To adjust the brakes, turn the cam bolts until definite drag is felt, then back off the

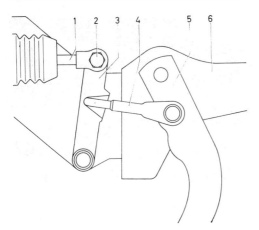

1. Piston rod of power brake
2. Adjusting screw with hexagon nut and lockwasher
3. Relay lever
4. Pushrod
5. Brake pedal
6. Pedal support

Adjustment of brake pedal free-play on type 230SL.

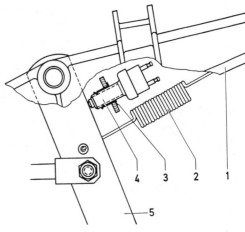

1. Pedal support
2. Return spring
3. Threaded sleeve
4. Switch
5. Pedal

Adjustment of stop light switch.

bolts until the wheel turns freely again.

### SINGLE CIRCUIT BRAKE PEDAL FREE-PLAY

Check the brake pedal free-play—it should be .16″–.20″. If adjustment is necessary, loosen hex nut (5) on the pedal and turn the adjustment bolt (1). (The .16″–.20″ free-play should equal .20″–.28″ pushrod/master cylinder clearance.)

*NOTE: Some cases of locked brakes are caused by insufficient pushrod/master cylinder clearance. If the master cylinder piston cannot return fully, the compensating port in the master cylinder is not uncovered and residual hydraulic pressure holds the brake shoes against the drums.*

*NOTE: Disc brakes require no adjustment.*

### DUAL-CIRCUIT BRAKE PEDAL FREE-PLAY

The brake pedal travel should be 6.08″ on all models. To adjust on all models except 230 SL, turn adjusting bolt (3a) until the notch on the bolt head points rearwards. This gives maximum travel, and adjustment is made from this point. *NOTE: If pedal hits brass threads of stop light switch, use shims under switch so that switch button protrudes 0.16″.*

On the 230 SL, remove the plastic ring from the bolt head and remove the stop light switch. Turn adjusting bolt (2) on the relay lever until the notch on the bolt head faces rearward. Adjust the stop light switch so that the button protrudes 0.16″ and the brake lights operate with a pedal depression of 0.8″. Now, pump the brake pedal a few times and jack up the front of the car. Spin one wheel and open the bleed screw of the brake caliper on that wheel. If this results in a freer-spinning wheel, the stop light switch must be further adjusted, because it is holding the brake pedal forward and allowing residual pressure to stay in the system.

### Parking Brake Adjustment

On cars equipped with cast-iron brake shoes (rear), tighten wingnut (1) on brake lever (3) or the wingnut (8) on relay lever (5) until the brake holds when the handle is pulled out 2.4″–2.6″. If the rear wheels do not spin free with the handbrake all the way in, readjust until they do spin.

On cars equipped with aluminum rear brake shoes, the distance is 2.4″.

If adjustment is not possible by this method, adjust the rear wheel brakes, then back out the cable wingnut at the relay lever and allow the cables to hang loosely. Adjust pushrod (3) by turning adjustment wheel (2) to give .040″ clearance at "b". It is advisable to remove the brake drum

1. Wingnut
2. Front brake cable
3. Brake lever
4. Support rod
5. Cotter pin
6. Pivot pin
7. Center brake cable

Parking brake linkage—first version.

1. Front brake cable
2. Hexagon screw with locking plate
3. Pull rod for supporting the handbrake lever mounting
4. Handbrake lever
5. Center brake cable
6. Cotter pin

Parking brake linkage—second version.

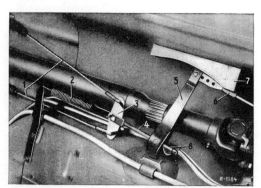

1. Rear brake cables
2. Return spring
3. Equalizer
4. Tensioning screw
5. Relay lever
6. Center brake cable
7. Guide for relay lever
8. Wingnut for adjusting the handbrake

Parking brake linkage—second version.

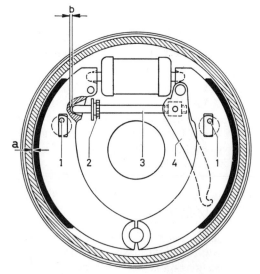

1. Eccentric
2. Adjusting star wheel
3. Pushrod
4. Brake lever

Parking brake pushrod adjustment—drum brakes with aluminum shoes.

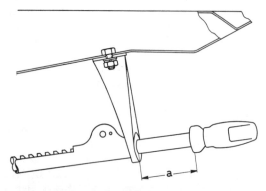

Handbrake travel—drum brakes (see text).

for this job. The brakes, if correctly adjusted, should not touch the pushrod, and there should be .010"–.012" clearance between the linings and drums.

The relay lever should be adjusted to give 0.8"–1.6" at "a".

LEVER HANDBRAKE—SL MODELS

Adjust the drilled adjustment wheel (10) by inserting a drill rod into the holes. The

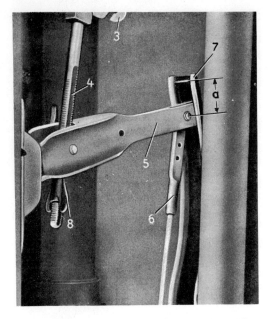

3. Equalizer
4. Tensioning screw
5. Relay lever
6. Center brake cable
7. Guide for relay lever
8. Wingnut

Relay lever adjustment.

lever should have to come up only three notches in order to hold the car on a slight grade.

TEVES DRUM-TYPE PARKING BRAKE

If the floor pedal can be depressed more than two notches before actuating the brakes, adjust by jacking up the rear of the car, then removing one lug bolt and adjusting the star wheel with a screwdriver. Move the screwdriver upward on left (driver's) side, downward on right (passenger's) side to tighten the shoes. When the wheel is locked, back off about 2–4 "clicks". With this type system, the adjusting bolt on the cable relay lever only serves to equalize cable length; therefore, do not attempt to adjust brakes by turning this bolt.

**Parking Brake Warning Light—220/8 to 250/8**

The red parking brake warning light should go out when the brake is released. If the master cylinder reservoirs are full,

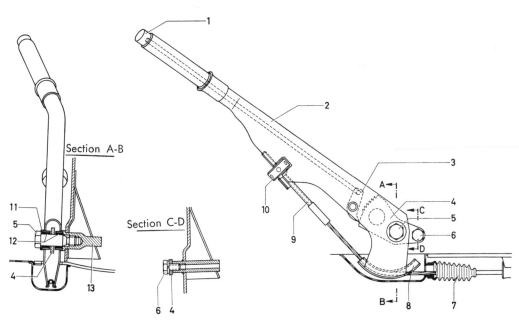

Section A-B

Section C-D

1. Push button
2. Handbrake lever
3. Pawl
4. Toothed segment
5. Pivot pin
6. Hexagon screw with lockwasher
7. Rubber sleeve
8. Brake cable guide
9. Front brake cable
10. Circular four-hole nut
11. Washer
12. Bearing bushing
13. Threaded member for fastening brake lever to chassis base panel

Handbrake lever adjustment—SL models.

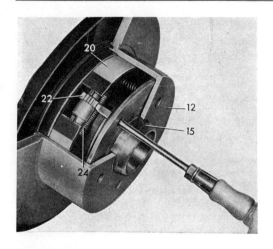

1. Disc wheel                3. Screwdriver
2. Rear axle shaft           F = Direction of travel

12. Brake disc              22. Adjustment device
15. Rear axle shaft         24. Upper return
    flange                      spring
20. Brake shoes

Parking brake shoe adjustment—wheel installed—
Teves.

Adjusting parking brake shoes—wheel removed—
Teves.

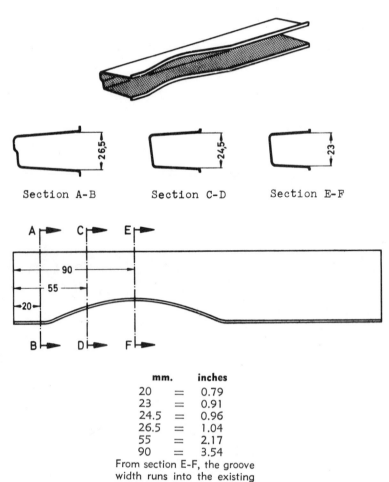

Section A-B          Section C-D          Section E-F

| mm. | | inches |
|---|---|---|
| 20 | = | 0.79 |
| 23 | = | 0.91 |
| 24.5 | = | 0.96 |
| 26.5 | = | 1.04 |
| 55 | = | 2.17 |
| 90 | = | 3.54 |

From section E-F, the groove
width runs into the existing
width.

Parking brake modifications necessary if warning light doesn't go out—220/8 to 250/8.

and the light still does not go out, check the intermediate relay lever and its guide rail for binding. Working from underneath the car, clean the guide rail thoroughly, then remove the cotter pin and bend the rail to conform with the measurements illustrated. Grease the guide rail and re-assemble.

If the light still does not go out, bend the switch contact carrier slightly to the left, making sure that the switch itself is not acting as a stop for the pedal linkage.

## Brake Pressure Regulator

The brake pressure regulator serves to "split" the hydraulic pressure in the brake system in proportion to the braking requirement at the front and rear wheels. This prevents premature lock-up with attendant loss of braking control.

To check the unit for proper operation, jack up the car and, with normal vacuum in the brake booster, depress the pedal with about 65 lbs. force. Have an assistant hold a hand on the pressure regulator while the

1. Brake force regulator
2. Bracket
3. Brake line from tandem brake master cylinder
4. Brake hose to left rear wheel brake
5. Bracket at frame floor

Brake pressure regulator.

pedal is slowly released. A distinct "knock" will be felt in the regulator if it is working properly. *CAUTION: The unit cannot be serviced with any degree of success, or safety. Always replace malfunctioning regulators, not forgetting to bleed the brakes after doing so.*

# Chapter Eight
# Clutch and Transmission

## Part I
## Manual Transmission

The Mercedes-Benz manual transmission can be either a four- or five-speed unit, floorshift or columnshift actuated. If major internal repairs are necessary, the normal procedure is to replace the entire unit, although individual parts replacement is certainly possible.

With this in mind, this chapter is devoted to inspection, adjustment, and removal and replacement procedures, although exploded diagrams of a few various transmission types are included for reference. Assembly and disassembly procedures are basically the same as those for American-made four-speed transmissions.

Clutch problems, being more common than transmission failures, are covered in more detail in Part II of this chapter.

### Removal and Replacement

To remove, first jack up the car at all four corners and place on axle stands. Remove the negative battery cable and unhook all shift rods. With column-mounted gearshift lever, remove rods (2) and (1) at the relay arm from under the hood. On floorshift models, unhook the rods (1) and (2) at the transmission side cover by prying upwards on the clips from the open

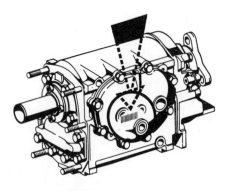
Transmission identification numbers—side cover.

Transmission identification numbers—top cover.

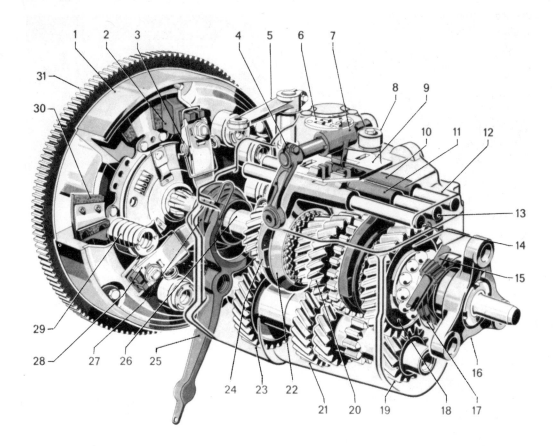

Transmission internal parts—top cover model illustrated.

1. Flywheel
2. Clutch pressure plate
3. Spring
4. Lever (for shifter shaft)
5. Selector lever
6. Gate plate
7. Shifter dog
8. Vent
9. Guide plate
10. Shifter head (reverse gear)
11. Shifter fork (1st and 2nd gear)
12. Shifter rod (reverse gear)
13. Shifter rod (1st and 2nd gear)
14. Shifter rod (3rd and 4th gear)
15. Speedometer drive
16. Three-armed flange
17. Helical gear
18. Helical gear (1st gear)
19. Countershaft
20. Helical gear (2nd gear)
21. Countershaft gear (3rd gear)
22. Sliding sleeve (3rd and 4th gear)
23. Countershaft gear (4th gear)
24. Shifter fork (3rd and 4th gear)
25. Release fork
26. Drive shaft
27. Release body (with release bearing)
28. Lever
29. Clutch spring
30. Clutch lining
31. Starter ring gear

end with a screwdriver. On models having a top cover shift mechanism, the floor tunnel must be removed to reach the shift rods. On older models having the clutch slave cylinder held to the clutch housing with two bolts, remove the cylinder completely and swing it out of the way. On newer models it is sufficient to remove the hose at point "A" (see illustration) and plug it to prevent fluid loss.

Remove the speedometer cable and the exhaust pipe bracket and wire them out of the way. Now, on pre-1965 models, disconnect the driveshaft by unbolting the center bearing support and the front U-joint plate at the transmission, then sliding the shaft back and out of the way. On later models, a double nut configuration is used. Holding one nut with a wrench, loosen the other, then unbolt the shaft from the transmission tailshaft. Remove the center bearing support on these models as well.

1. Selector rod
2. Shift rod
3. Cover
4. Relay lever
5. Fixing clip
6. Selector lever
7. Flexible speedometer drive
8. Spring-loaded ball connector

Columnshift levers.

1. Shift rod for 1st and 2nd gear
2. Shift rod for 3rd and 4th gear
3. Shift rod for reverse gear
4. Shift lever for reverse gear
5. Flexible speedometer driveshaft
7. Pressure hose for clutch actuation
8. Pressure line for clutch actuation
13. Clamping screws for exhaust pipe support
A. Pressure hose fitting to pressure line

Transmission and clutch linkage must be disconnected.

5. Flexible speedometer drive shaft
6. Clamp screw
7. Pressure hose for clutch mechanism
8. Pressure line for clutch actuating mechanism
9. Propeller shaft bolt
10. Fixing screw for fastening crossmember to chassis base panel
11. Fixing screw for fastening crossmember with rubber mounting to transmission
12. Fixing nuts (covered) for exhaust pipe strut
13. Bolts for exhaust pipe clamping bracket
14. Clamping bracket
A. Pressure hose fitting to pressure line

Crossmember must be unbolted before removing transmission.

1. Pushrod
2. Hexagon nut
3. Pressure pin
4. Hexagon screw
5. Extraction cylinder
6. Bleed screw
7. Rubber cover cap
8. Line
9. Hose
10. Return spring
11. Throwout fork
12. Cuff

Clutch slave cylinder.

NOTE: *It is a good idea to scribe marks on the center bearing support bracket for ease in assembly.*

Mark the position of the rear crossmember and slightly jack up the engine with a block of wood between the jack and the oil pan. This serves to take the weight off the crossmember bolts during removal and prevents stripped threads. Unscrew all crossmember bolts that hold it to the body and transmission and remove the crossmember. Unbolt the bellhousing and

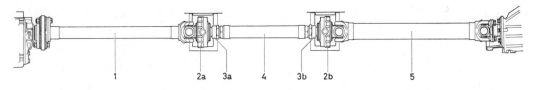

1.      Front driveshaft         4.  Intermediate bearing
2a., 2b. Intermediate bearing      5.  Rear driveshaft
3a., 3b. Clamp nut

Three-piece driveshaft.

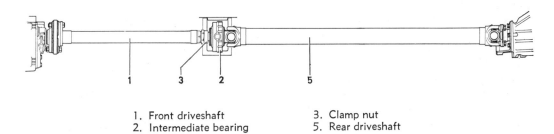

1. Front driveshaft            3. Clamp nut
2. Intermediate bearing      5. Rear driveshaft

Two-piece driveshaft.

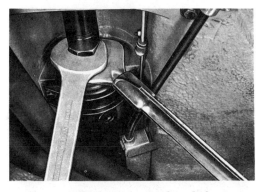

Double clamp nuts on driveshaft.

starter bolts and pull the transmission straight backward, while rotating clockwise 90° to clear obstructions. Make absolutely sure the mainshaft is out of the clutch before lowering the transmission, otherwise the clutch hub will be damaged.

Installation is the reverse of removal except that the rear U-joint must be split on some models and the driveshaft pushed further back for clearance. Always coat the mainshaft splines and pilot bushing surfaces with Vaseline or Molykote grease

1. Shift rod for 1st and 2nd gear
2. Shift rod for 3rd and 4th gear
4. Shift rod for reverse gear

Side cover shift linkage rods.

Lowering transmission.

before installing. Don't forget the ground cables under the nuts, and take care that all bolts are tightened evenly and the 300 SE dowel pins properly lined up. The center bearing support must not be cocked or it will soon disintegrate under torque loads, so tighten its mounting bolts finger tight until everything else is torqued, then tighten them. The driveshaft double clamp nuts get torqued to about 140 ft.-lbs. Bracing the hold-down wrench on the body pan is not recommended without some insulation to distribute the load.

Use a 24″ section of pipe on the wrench handle, but don't put full weight on it or the nut might be distorted. *CAUTION: On all Allen-head bolts, use the proper size key with a short extension. Use of too small American keys may round the bolt heads to such a degree that removal without drilling is impossible. Unfortunately, Allen bolts are extremely hard, and almost impossible to drill out with any success if they are in an awkward position. Grinding an oversize American key to fit is O.K. if the grinding is done slowly so as not to destroy the temper of the steel from frictional heating.*

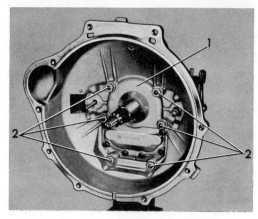

Bolts (2) that secure bellhousing (1) to transmission.

## Separating Transmission and Bellhousing

The reason for removing both the transmision and bellhousing together is immediately obvious when the unit is out: the transmission hold-down bolts can be reached only from the inside. Bolt configurations vary slightly with the different models, but, in general, removal procedure is identical. The exception is the 300 SE with manual transmission. This model was usually equipped with an automatic transmission quite sensitive to misalignment, therefore the bellhousing was aligned at the factory and stamped with the car engine number for identification. Since the manual transmission-equipped cars used the same bellhousing, it is necessary to use the old bellhousing with any replacement transmission, or it is necessary to realign the new housing.

To remove the housing, pull off the throwout bearing, then the throwout fork. The non-anchored end of the fork must be pulled outward, then to the left to disengage the ball socket pivot. (Directions "A" and "B" in illustrations.) Unscrew the

Throwout bearing (1) and fork (2).

Removing throwout fork (2) from ball pin (3).

bolts that hold the transmission to the housing, then tap the housing lightly with a fiber hammer to separate it from the transmission nose piece. The housing is easily distorted, so never use a steel hammer.

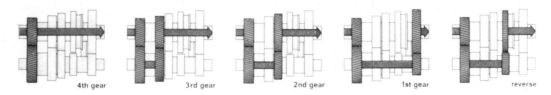

4th gear 3rd gear 2nd gear 1st gear reverse

Power flow in four-speed transmission.

## Transmission Inspection

"Locked-up" transmissions or shifting problems may be caused by defective parts in the shifting mechanism of the transmission itself. After making sure that the shift rods are all in proper adjustment, check the first and second gear shift yoke needle bearings and the shift detent mechanism.

Drain the transmission oil and remove the clamp bolt and reverse shift lever at the transmission. Remove the lock tab from the reverse shift shaft and unscrew the cover hold-down bolts. Tap the cover with a fiber hammer to loosen it, while driving the reverse shift shaft upward with another fiber hammer. When the cover is off about ¾", reach in and slide the shift forks out of shift yokes, then pull the cover downward and upward.

The transmission gears are now visible for inspection, as is the shift mechanism.

1. Transmission cover
2. Shift lever for 1st and 2nd gear
3. Shift lever for 3rd and 4th gear
4a. Shift lever finger for reverse gear
8. Fixing bolt for detent cage
9. Locking plate
10. Transmission vent
12. Clamp screws

Side shift cover.

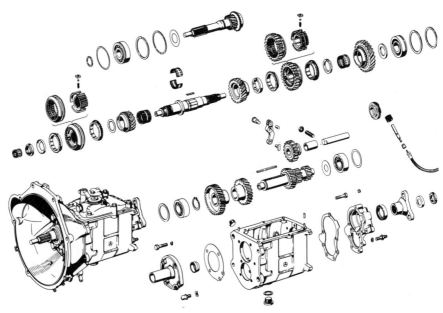

Internal transmission parts—220SEb, 190c, 190Dc, 200, 200D, 230, 300SE, 250S, 250SE, 280S, 280SE, 300SEb, 230SL, 250SL, 280SL.

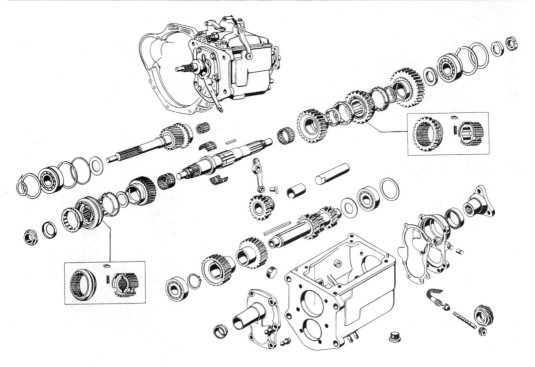

Internal transmission parts—top cover.

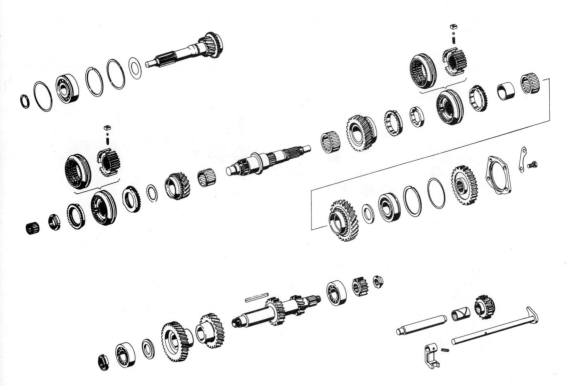

Internal transmission parts—side cover used on phase II models.

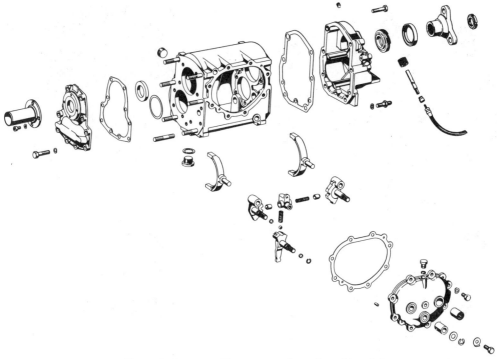

Transmission case—side cover used on phase II models.

When inspecting gear teeth, rotate all the gears to make sure no part has been missed. A chipped tooth is as bad as a broken tooth, for it weakens the entire gear and can lead to transmission failure. Work the gears by hand and check the synchronizers. Badly burred or worn synchronizing rings usually cause "grinding" during shifting.

To disassemble the shift mechanism, loosen the clamp bolts and remove the shift levers from the outside of the cover. Going to the inside, remove the circlips from the shafts and pull out shift yokes (2a) (3a) and the reverse detent lever (4a). Using a screwdriver, bend back the lock tab on bolt (8) and unbolt the detent cage (7) and locating pin. The detent balls should not be scarred and should move in and out easily, although under spring tension. If they are immovable even under pressure, or if they flop in and out with ease, the detent cage should be replaced. The shift yokes then must be checked for wear, as a burred shift yoke will more than likely ruin a new detent cage in a short time.

Check the bearings where the shift rods pass through the cover. If the caged needle bearings are scored or broken, new ones must be pressed into place. Use of an arbor press is recommended, although some inge-

Synchronization

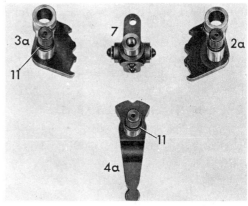

| | |
|---|---|
| 2a. Shift yoke for 1st and 2nd gear | 4a. Shift lever finger for reverse gear |
| 3a. Shift yoke for 3rd and 4th gear | 7. Detent cage |
| | 11. O-ring |

Shifter components—side cover (showing detent ball and cage).

1.   Transmission cover
2.   Shift lever for 1st and 2nd gear
2a.  Shift yoke for 1st and 2nd gear
3.   Shift lever for 3rd and 4th gear
3a.  Shift yoke for 3rd and 4th gear
4.   Shift lever for reverse gear
4a.  Shift lever finger for reverse gear
5.   Shaft circlip
6.   Washer (only for 1st and 2nd gear)
7.   Detent cage
8.   Fixing screw
9.   Locking plate
10.  Transmission vent
Note: A taller vent is available to prevent water
   leaking into transmission.)

Side cover shift linkage and internal parts.

nuity and a large bench vise can be utilized
in an emergency. Don't forget to replace
the O-rings, because they will almost always leak after once being disturbed. Adjustment of the levers is described later in
this chapter.

**Replacing Front and Rear Seals**

Fluid leaking from the front seal is usually visible in the clutch housing and can
cause clutch slippage if allowed to progress
too far. In any case, it is good practice to
replace the front and rear seals while the
transmission is out, just on general prin-
ciples.

After the clutch housing is removed, unscrew the front cover bolts and remove the
cover. The thrust washers must be replaced in exactly the same position, so note
their order when removing.

Unbolt the nose piece from the front

Transmission front cover installed.

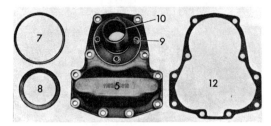

5.   Transmission front cover
7.   Spacer washer for driveshaft
8.   Spacer washer for countershaft
9.   Fixing bolts
10.  Mounting tube
12.  Paper gasket

Transmission front cover removed.

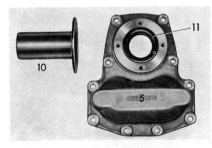

Transmission front cover (5), showing seal (11)
and installation tool (10).

cover, then press the old seal out. It is
recommended that an arbor press with a
1¾″ adapter be used, but a slide hammer
with a screw attachment can be used for
this job. It is important, however, that the
new seal is *pressed* into the cover, not
hammered. The thrust washers can be held
in place with wheel bearing grease during
installation of the cover. *NOTE: Use non-
hardening Permatex on the cover and bolt
threads to prevent leaks.*

7. Spacer washer for driveshaft
8. Spacer washer for countershaft

Front transmission bearings.

| 1. Transmission case | 9. Seal |
|---|---|
| rear cover | 10. Paper gasket |
| 8. Fitting sleeve | |

Transmission rear cover and gasket.

Rear transmission cover (1) must be aligned with keyed portion of reverse shaft (11) and sleeve (8).

To remove the rear seal, insert a bar through the rear flange and remove the lock tab and nut. Remove the flange, then remove the cover bolts and cover. The gear train can now be inspected for wear and the seal replaced. *CAUTION: When installing, the reverse shaft must be properly aligned with the keyed portion of the cover or breakage of the cover will result.*

**Linkage Adjustments—Columnshift**

Proper adjustment of the columnshift linkage is dependent on both the position of the levers at the transmission and the length of the shift rods.

TOP COVER TRANSMISSION

Check that the levers are not binding anywhere in their travel, then place the

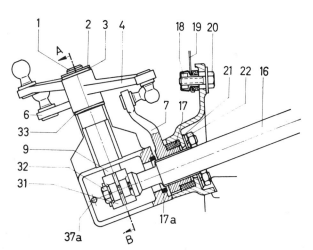

1. Relay lever shaft
2. Snap-ring
3. Washer
4. Relay lever
6. Selector lever
7. Lever on shift tube
9. Selector shaft
16. Shift tube
17. Vulkollan bushing
17a. Spacer ring
18. Cage nut
19. Front panel
20. Hexagon screw with washer
21. Washer
22. Hexagon nut with lockwasher
31. Selector lever on shift tube
32. Hexagon screw (clamp screw)
33. Spring washer
37a. Water outlet bore

Second version columnshift linkage.

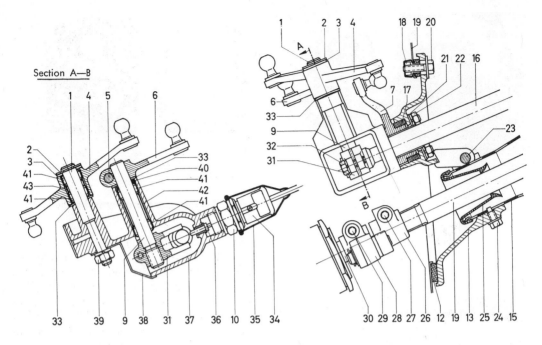

Section A—B

First version columnshift linkage.

1. Relay lever shaft
2. Snap-ring
3. Washer
4. Relay lever
5. Hexagon screw (clamp screw)
6. Selector lever
7. Lever on shift tube
9. Selector shaft
10. Reversing light switch
12. Rubber gasket
13. Cover plate
15. Steering column jacket
16. Shift tube
17. Vulkollan bushing
18. Cage nut
19. Steering tube
20. Hexagon screw with washer
21. Washer
22. Hexagon nut with lockwasher
23. Hexagon screw (clamp screw)
24. Stud screw with lockwasher
25. Rubber sleeve
26. Upper flange
27. Hexagon socket screw
28. Lower flange (clamp screw)
29. Hexagon socket screw (clamp screw)
30. Steering worm
31. Selector lever on shift tube
32. Hexagon screw
33. Spring washer
34. Plug connection
35. Protective cap
36. Pressure pin
37. Bearing assembly
38. Cover
39. Hexagon nut with lock-washer
40. Sealing ring
41. Needle bearing
42. Spacer sleeve
43. Spacer sleeve

1. Shift tube
2. Hexagon nuts for attaching the bearing assembly of the steering wheel shift system
3. Cover plate
4. Cable for reversing light switch
5. Steering column jacket
6. Tightening strap for steering column jacket

Columnshift lower bearing assembly.

shift lever in neutral and loosen the clamp bolt (5) at the selector lever (6). Then pull the selector lever forward in the direction of travel and pull the relay lever (4) forward by the lower leg. This should engage fourth gear.

Remove the rubber cover on the shift lever at the steering column and have a helper pull the shift lever upward until about .080″ separates the shift tube collar and the recess in the steering tube jacket. Tighten the clamp bolts (5) on the selector lever, preloading the spring washer (33) while doing so.

Now, try shifting through all the gears, using the clutch of course. When engaging reverse, a resistance should be felt. If not, the reverse gear interlock on the top cover probably is weak and a new spring should be installed. When the shift lever is in second or fourth gear, it should vary only about ⅝″ from the horizontal. Small corrections to this can be made by shortening or lengthening the shift rod.

If shifting is hard, the shift tube (16) may be touching the steering column passage or, in first version units. the lever (7) may be binding in its bearing. To correct the latter condition, loosen the steering column strap (6) (see illustration) and the firewall cover plate and correct any misalignment.

If the selector lever (31) binds in the shift tube (16), it must be removed and checked for straightness. The selector lever dogs may be bent apart or ground down to fit. Grease all the ball sockets and check that the lower bearing assembly at the bottom of the steering column hasn't pulled off its studs.

The spring-loaded ball connector in the bearing assembly often wears and causes hard shifting. Replace it with the newer type connecting rod and adjust length to 67 mm. (2⅝″).

### SIDE COVER TRANSMISSION

Check the positioning of the shift levers at the transmission (see illustration) and correct by loosening clamp bolts. The diagram shows the levers in neutral.

Next, go to the lower steering column and lock the three levers by inserting a .2156″ rod (a No. 3 drill will do) through the levers and the hole in the bearing block.

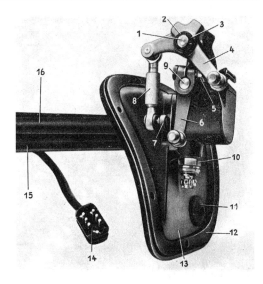

1. Shaft
2. Snap-ring
3. Spring washer
4. Relay lever
5. Hexagon nut
6. Selector lever
7. Lever on shift tube
8. Spring-loaded ball connector
9. Selector shaft
10. Backup light switch
11. Rubber grommet
12. Rubber gasket
13. Cover plate
14. Plug connection
15. Steering column jacket
16. Shift tube

Columnshift lower bearing assembly.

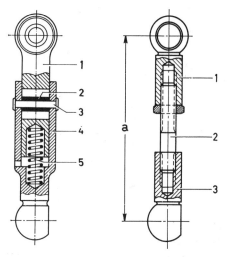

Left
1. Spring-loaded ball connector
2. Polyamide bushing
3. Cylindrical pin
4. Spring-loaded ball connector (outer part)
5. Pressure spring

Right
1. Ball connector
2. Stud bolt
3. Ball connector
a = Adjusting dimension

Spring-loaded ball connector and new-type connecting rod which replaces it.

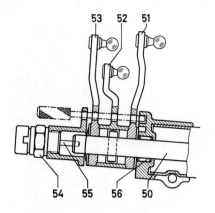

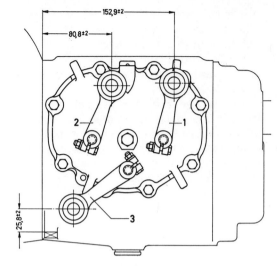

51. Reverse lever
52. 1st and 2nd gear lever
53. 3rd and 4th gear lever

Columnshift levers—phase II models (side cover).

1. 1st and 2nd gear lever
2. 3rd and 4th gear lever
3. Reverse lever

Side cover columnshift transmission levers—phase II models.

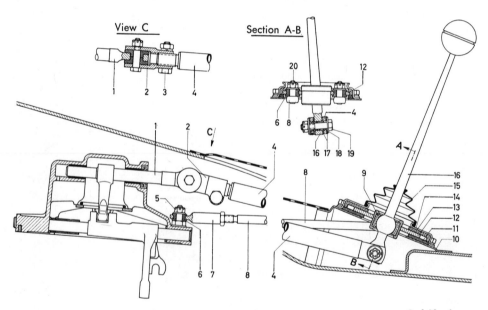

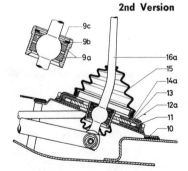

**2nd Version**

| | | |
|---|---|---|
| 1. | Shifting shaft | |
| 2. | Yoke end | |
| 3. | Hexagon screw | |
| 4. | Shift tube | |
| 5. | Castle nut | |
| 6. | Bushing | |
| 7. | End piece | |
| 8. | Pushrod | |
| 9. | Ball socket (vulcollan) | |
| 9a. | Split ball socket | |
| 9b. | Internal circlip | |
| 9c. | Corrugated washer | |
| 10. | Transmission tunnel | |
| 11. | Lower bearing cover | |

12. Shift lever bearing
12a. Shift lever bearing, new version
13. Upper bearing cover
14. Cover plate 1st version, sheet metal
14a. Cover plate 2nd version, vulcollan
15. Cuff
16. Shift lever
17. Bushing
18. Washer
19. Hexagon screw
20. Castle nut

Floorshift lever—top cover transmission.

With the shift levers at the lower steering column locked and the levers at the transmission adjusted, try hooking the shift rods into their respective levers. If they are too long or short, adjust their length by loosening the locknuts and turning the ball socket ends. Remove the locking rod and try shifting through the gears. Very slight further adjustments may clear up any binding.

### Linkage Adjustments—Floorshift

#### TOP COVER TRANSMISSION

To adjust, move the shift shaft (1) against the reverse gear stop and engage second gear by actuating the shaft. Then move the shift lever (16) into the first or second gear shifting plane and insert the shift tube (4) into the yoke serrations at least ⅝″ and tighten the clamp bolt. Try shifting through all the gears. If the shift lever hits the bearing (12), adjust both pushrods (8) an *equal* amount.

#### SIDE COVER TRANSMISSION

The adjustment procedure is the same as that for side cover column shift transmissions, with the exception of the lever positioning at the transmission. The three shift levers and bearing block (where the locking rod is inserted) are found underneath the floor tunnel, which must be removed.

*CAUTION: On all types of transmissions, never hammer or force a new shift knob on with the shift lever installed, as the plastic bushing connected to the lever will be destroyed and cause hard shifting.*

---

## Part II
## Clutch

---

### Removal and Installation

To remove the clutch, first remove the transmission and bellhousing. On 300 SE models, place hold-down clamps, or equivalent, as illustrated. Now, loosen the clutch pressure plate hold-down bolts evenly, 1–1½ turns at a time, until tension is relieved. Never remove one bolt at a time, as damage to the pressure plate is

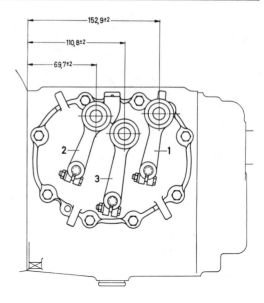

1. 1st and 2nd gear lever
2. 3rd and 4th gear lever
3. Reverse lever

Floorshift transmission levers—phase II (side cover).

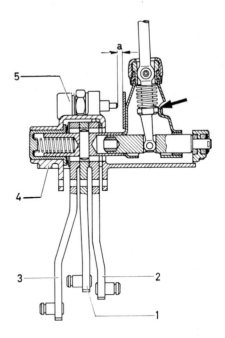

1. Shift lever for 1st and 2nd gear
2. Shift lever for 3rd and 4th gear
3. Shift lever for reverse gear
4. Bearing block
5. Backup light switch
6. Adjusting dimension for reversing light switch, 4±1 mm. – gearshift lever in shifting plane 1st or 2nd gear

Floorshift lever—phase (side cover).

Clutch hold-down device—300SE models.

Diaphragm spring clutch pressure plate.

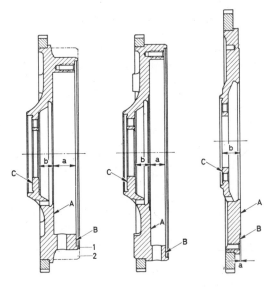

| 1. | Throwout unit with bearing | 5. | Return spring |
| 3. | Transmission case front cover | 6. | Spring retainer |
| | | 7. | Snap-ring |
| | | 8. | Snap-ring pliers |

Removing throwout bearing—300SE models.

| | Left | Middle | Right |
|---|---|---|---|
| 1. | 190c, 200 | 220b, 220Sb | 300SE manual transmission |
| 2. | 190Dc, 200D | 220SEb, 230SL | 300SEb |
| | | 230, 230S, 250S 250SE | 300SEL manual transmission |

Flywheel tolerances.

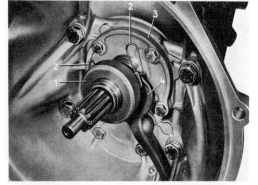

| 1. | Throwout unit and bearing | 3. | Transmission case front cover |
| 2. | Spring clip | 4. | Throwout fork |

Removing throwout bearing.

possible. Examine the flywheel surface for blue heat marks, scoring or cracks. If the flywheel is to be machined, always machine an equal amount from surfaces "A" and "B" in order to maintain distance "a".

# Clutch Pressure Plate Specifications

## Clutch Pressure Plate—Coil Spring Type

| Specification | | | 190c 190Dc 200 200D | 220b 220Sb 220SEb Sedan | 220 SEb/C | 230 230S 230SL 250S 250SE | 300SE 300SEb 300SEL |
|---|---|---|---|---|---|---|---|
| Control dimension "e" between cover plate and release levers with new driven plate installed | (mm.) | | 17.5±0.2 | | 7.0±0.2 | | 18±0.2 |
| Resulting adjusting dimension of worn-out driven plate | (mm.) | | 24.5 | | 14 | | 11 |
| Adjusting dimension "d" for clutch assembly | (mm.) | | 41.4 | | 36.8 | | 42.5 |
| Travel "i" of release levers because of permissible wear of driven plate | (mm.) | | | | 7 | | |
| Throwout travel "h" of release levers | (mm.max.) | | | | 10 | | 10.6 |
| Free-play "g" between throwout bearing and release levers (clutch free-play) | (mm.) | | | | 2 | | |
| Maximum permissible difference between the release levers ① | (mm.) | | | | 0.3 | | |
| Thickness "c" of pressure plate | (mm.) | | 15 | | 16.5 | | 14.5 |
| Regrind dimension of the pressure plate ② | (mm.max.) | | | | 1 | | |
| Maximum permissible unbalance of the pressure plate | (cmg.) | | 20 | | 15 | | |
| Contact pressure | (pounds) | | 1045 | | 1185±55 | | 1360 |
| Clutch springs | Number | | | | 9 | | |
| | Color code | | colorless and gold | | yellow and gold | | light blue and gold |
| | External diameter | (mm.) | 29 | | 28.6 | | 27.4 |
| | Wire gauge | | 4 | | 4.1 | | 4.2 |
| | Free length | (mm.) | 50 | | 55.1 | | 58.5 |
| | Length under load | (mm.) | 32.4 | | 37.2 | | 39.5 |
| | Load | (kg.) | 53+6 | | 61.5±2.5 | | 69±3.5 |

① *Press down the release levers several times before measuring.*
② *If the reduction in thickness exceeds .020", shims corresponding in thickness to the total amount of material removed should be placed between the clutch springs and the cups to restore the total spring pressure.*

# Clutch Pressure Plate Specifications

## Clutch Pressure Plate—Diaphragm Spring Type

| Specification | | 220D/8 220/8 | 230/8 250/8 |
|---|---|---|---|
| Contact pressure | (pounds) | 1080—1235 | 1185—1320 |
| Max. permissible unbalance | (cmg.) | 15 | 20 |
| Throwout travel "e" at thrust ring | (mm.) | | 9 |
| Travel "f" of thrust ring due to permissible wear of driven plate | (mm.) | | 8 |
| Control dimension "d" for new driven plate | (mm.) | 48 | 47.9 |
| for driven plate with max. wear | (mm.) | 56 | 55.9 |

# Clutch Plate Specifications
## Clutch Plate—Coil Spring Type

| Specification | | | 190c 190Dc 200, 200D | 220b 220Sb 220SEb | 230, 230S 230SL 250S, 250SE | 300SE 300SEb 300SEL |
|---|---|---|---|---|---|---|
| Thickness of the driven plate "f" | | | | | | |
| | released | (mm.) | 10.3+0.3 | | 10.3+0.4 | 10.6+0.4 |
| | compressed | (mm.) | 9.1+0.3 | | +0.4 9.1-0.1 | +0.4 9.3-0.1 |
| Thickness of facing | | (mm.) | 3.5 | | 3.8 | 3.5 |
| Permissible wear of facing thickness on either side | | (mm.) | | 1 | | |
| Permissible unbalance | | (cmg.) | | 5 | | |
| Permissible runout | | (mm.) | | 0.5 | | |
| Permissible radial play on driveshaft | | (mm.) | | 0.04±0.01 | | |
| Torsion damper — Free motion torque, traction side | | (mkg.) | 17.3 | | 20 | 30 |
| Torsion damper — Stop angle | | (deg.) | 8°30' | | 5° | 4° |
| Torsion damper — Friction torque | | (mkg.) | 0.6—0.9 | | 1.4—1.7 | 0.9—1.2 |

# Clutch Plate Specifications
## Clutch Plate—Diaphragm Spring Type

| Specification | | | 220D/8 220/8 | 230/8 250/8 |
|---|---|---|---|---|
| Thickness of driven plate "c" | | | | |
| | released | (mm.) | 10.3 | |
| | compressed | (mm.) | 8.9 | |
| Thickness of lining | | (mm.) | 3.8 | |
| Permissible wear on lining thickness (per side) | | (mm.) | 1 | |
| Permissible unbalance | | (cmg.) | 5 | |
| Permissible runout | | (mm.) | 0.5 | |
| Permissible radial play on driveshaft | | (mm.) | 0.04 ±0.01 | |
| Torsion damper — Free motion torque traction side | | (mkg.) | 17 | 20 |
| Torsion damper — Stop angle | | (deg.) | 8°30' | 5° |
| Torsion damper — Friction torque | | (mkg.) | 0.6—0.9 | 1.4—1.7 |

To reinstall, coat splines with high temperature grease and place clutch disc against flywheel, centering it with a clutch pilot shaft. A wooden shaft, available at automotive jobbers, is satisfactory, but an old transmission mainshaft works best. Tighten the pressure plate hold-down bolts evenly 1–1½ turns at a time until tight, then remove pilot shaft.

CAUTION: Most clutch plates have the flywheel side marked as such, (Kupplungsseite). Do not assume that the pressure springs always face the transmission, since some do not (e.g., 300 SE, 230, 230 S, 230 SL, 250 S and 250 SE).

### Diagnosis

The most common problems with both the coil and diaphragm spring type clutches concern "sticking" or "squealing".

# Throwout Bearing Specifications

## Throwout Bearing—Coil Spring Clutches

| Specification | | 190c to 230SL | 300SE |
|---|---|---|---|
| Internal diameter of the throwout bearing | (mm.) | 39.988 / 40.000 | 49.988 / 50.000 |
| External diameter of the throwout bearing | (mm.) | 40.006 / 39.995 | 50.006 / 49.995 |
| Oversize (+) or play (−) of the throwout bearing on the throwout unit | (mm.) | −0.005 | +0.018 |
| Internal diameter of the throwout unit | (mm.) | 35.600 / 35.639 | 40.100 / 40.139 |
| External diameter of the transmission case front cover | (mm.) | 35.500 / 35.438 | 40.000 / 39.938 |
| Clearance between throwout unit and neck at transmission case front cover | (mm.) | 0.1—0.2 | |

# Throwout Bearing Specifications

## Throwout Bearing—Diaphragm Spring Clutches

| Specification | | 220D/8—250/8 |
|---|---|---|
| Internal diameter of throwout bearing | (mm.) | 41.6 |
| External diameter of throwout bearing | (mm.) | 68.000 / 67.987 |
| Internal diameter of bearing seat within throwout unit | (mm.) | 67.970 / 68.000 |
| Seat tolerance between throwout bearing external dia. and throwout unit internal dia. Force fit (+); play (−) | (mm.) | +0.030 to −0.013 |
| Internal diameter of throwout unit | (mm.) | 34.050 / 34.112 |
| External diameter of guide tube at transmission case front cover | (mm.) | 34.000 / 33.938 |
| Play between throwout unit and guide tube at transmission case front cover | (mm.) | 0.050—0.174 |

If the clutch pedal itself is not hitting anything, the problem may be in the clutch master cylinder or the hydraulic slave cylinder. Disassemble these units and check their cylinder walls. Binding is evidenced by shiny, worn spots, and the application of a special grease (available at the dealer) will usually stop the problem. Score marks, however, require cylinder replacement.

To bleed the hydraulic clutch, remove the caps from both the brake and clutch reservoirs and connect a section of hose to a bleed screw on one of the front brake calipers (or drums). Open the bleed screw and pump the brakes in order to fill the hose with fluid. When this is accomplished, connect the hose to the bleed screw on the clutch slave cylinder, open that bleed screw, top up the reservoirs and pump the brakes slowly. As the pedal is pumped, air bubbles should escape from the system, but it is extremely important that the brake fluid

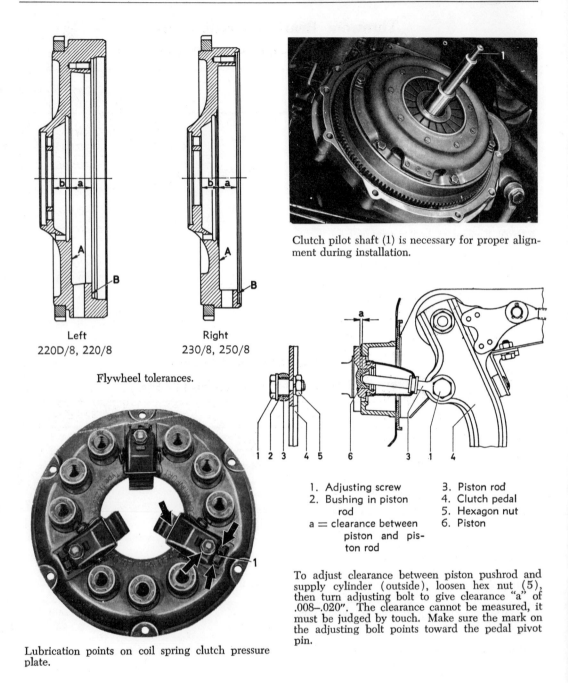

Clutch pilot shaft (1) is necessary for proper alignment during installation.

Left
220D/8, 220/8

Right
230/8, 250/8

Flywheel tolerances.

1. Adjusting screw
2. Bushing in piston
   rod
a = clearance between
   piston and pis-
   ton rod

3. Piston rod
4. Clutch pedal
5. Hexagon nut
6. Piston

To adjust clearance between piston pushrod and supply cylinder (outside), loosen hex nut (5), then turn adjusting bolt to give clearance "a" of .008–.020". The clearance cannot be measured, it must be judged by touch. Make sure the mark on the adjusting bolt points toward the pedal pivot pin.

Lubrication points on coil spring clutch pressure plate.

reservoir never run dry. If it does, the brakes must be bled as well.

When no more air bubbles come out of the clutch fluid reservoir, close the clutch bleed screw, then the brake bleed screw. Test both pedals for proper operation. If the clutch pedal feels spongy or low, repeat the procedure until all air is evacuated. Remember to top up both brake and clutch reservoirs with a recommended fluid.

*NOTE: It may be necessary to bleed the clutch master cylinder as well.*

A sticking pedal on a 250 S–300 SE might be caused by a blocked valve in the hydraulic line. This valve may be drilled out to 0.118″ (3 mm.), but all metal chips must be carefully removed or clutch operation will be impaired.

Squealing and sticking may also be caused by the pressure plate lugs binding

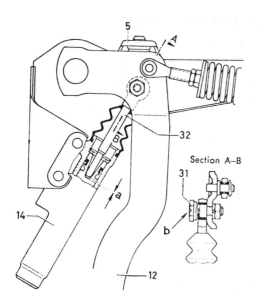

| | |
|---|---|
| 1. Pushrod | 8. Line from supply |
| 2. Hexagon nut | cylinder |
| 3. Pressure pin | 9. Pressure hose |
| 4. Hexagon screw | 10. Return spring |
| 5. Extraction cylinder | 11. Throwout fork |
| 6. Bleed screw | 12. Cuff |
| 7. Protective cap | |

First version clutch slave cylinder. The pushrod length can be adjusted by removing the spring and loosening the locknut.

| | |
|---|---|
| 5. Rubber stop for | nut and lock- |
| clutch pedal | washer |
| 12. Clutch pedal | 32. Piston rod |
| 14. Supply cylinder | a = Clearance between |
| 31. Adjusting screw | piston and pis- |
| with hexagon | ton rod |
| | b = Line marking |

Inside clutch supply cylinder. Clearance is adjusted in the same way as for outside cylinder, except that the mark on the adjusting bolt must point toward the rear.

against the openings in the cover plate. The arrowed points in the illustration show the lubrication points. Use Molykote paste on these areas, as well as on the throwout bearing surface and transmission nose piece. If lubrication does not stop the noise, filling the affected parts is O.K. if too much material is not removed.

The normal adjustment of the pedal over-center spring is 2.64″ (67 mm.). Increasing this to 2.83″ (72 mm.) also helps alleviate sticking. The reason for clutch slippage is usually pretty easy to spot—oil on the clutch plate. This can be either transmission oil from a leaking front transmission seal, or engine oil from a leaking rear main bearing oil seal. Never just replace the disc; find the leak and fix it or the new clutch will be ruined in a short time.

A clutch worn down near the rivets must be replaced or flywheel and/or pressure plate damage is certain. Check the clutch plate linings for looseness. If they can be

| | |
|---|---|
| 1. Pushrod | 8. Line from supply |
| 4. Stud screw | cylinder |
| 5. Extraction cylinder | 9. Pressure hose |
| 6. Bleed screw | 10. Return spring |
| 7. Protective cap | 11. Throwout fork |
| | 12. Cuff |

Second version clutch slave cylinder. The pushrod length can be adjusted in the same way as for the first version cylinder.

slid back and forth on the rivets, the plate must be discarded no matter how little wear is in evidence.

# Hydraulic Automatic (Hydrak) Clutch

### Operation

This type of clutch is an interim step between a straight mechanical set-up and

# Hydrak Hydraulic Automatic Clutch Diagnosis

| Condition | Probable Cause | Correction |
|---|---|---|
| Slow acceleration, engine races during shifting | 1. Insufficient oil in torque converter.<br>2. Driven plate of clutch oily. | 1. Check stall speed and refill.<br>2. Replace driven clutch plate. |
| Clutch slips too long after shifting | 1. Coasting—adjusting screw on reducing valve screwed in too far.<br>2. With accelerator pedal depressed—adjusting screw on rear axle switch screwed in too far.<br>3. With accelerator pedal partly depressed—spring-loaded diaphragm incorrectly adjusted. | 1. Adjust control element.<br>2. Adjust rear axle switch.<br>3. Replace control element. |
| Coasting downshift too harsh | 1. Adjusting screw on reducing valve unscrewed too far. | 1. Adjust control element. |
| Shifting harsh during acceleration | 1. Rear axle switch adjusting screw unscrewed too far.<br>2. Defective rear axle switch.<br>3. Limit switch in servo jammed "off". | 1. Adjust rear axle switch.<br>2. Replace rear axle switch.<br>3. Free up or replace switch. |
| Intermittent harsh shifting (down-shift) | 1. Reducing valve plugged or dirt at valve head. | 1. Remove and clean valve. |
| Clutch slips under acceleration or on hills | 1. Driven plate of clutch oily.<br>2. Servo pull rod incorrectly adjusted. | 1. Replace driven clutch plate.<br>2. Adjust pull rod. |
| Driven clutch plate continues spinning at idle speed | 1. Driven plate hub jammed in splines.<br>2. Broken or warped linings on clutch plate.<br>3. Defective needle bearing in Hydrak unit. | 1. Free up and install new driven plate if necessary.<br>2. Replace clutch driven plate.<br>3. Replace Hydrak unit. |
| Clutch does not disengage during shifting | 1. Servo pull rod incorrectly adjusted.<br>2. Lines leaking; supply cylinder leaking.<br>3. Bellows in servo defective.<br>4. Needle bearing in Hydrak unit broken.<br>5. Broken electrical circuit.<br>6. Shift lever switch contacts burned or corroded.<br>7. Control valve electromagnet defective. | 1. Adjust pull rod.<br>2. Repair leak.<br>3. Replace servo assembly.<br>4. Replace Hydrak unit.<br>5. Trace circuit and repair break.<br>6. Clean contact points in switch.<br>7. Replace electromagnet. |
| Clutch does not engage after shift. | 1. Contact of shift lever switch sticking. | 1. Clean contact points in switch and adjust switch. |

**Driven Plate**

**Pressure Plate**

Models 190 c,
190 Dc, 200
and 200 D

Models 220 b,
220 Sb
and 220 SEb

with single
spring-loaded
facing

Models 220 b,
220 Sb, 220 SEb
and 230 SL

with double
spring-loaded
facing

Models 230,
230 S, 250 S,
250 SE and
230 SL

with double
spring-loaded
facing

1 Sheet-metal ring for better engine speed adaptability

Clutch types used in various models.

**Driven Plate**

**Pressure Plate**

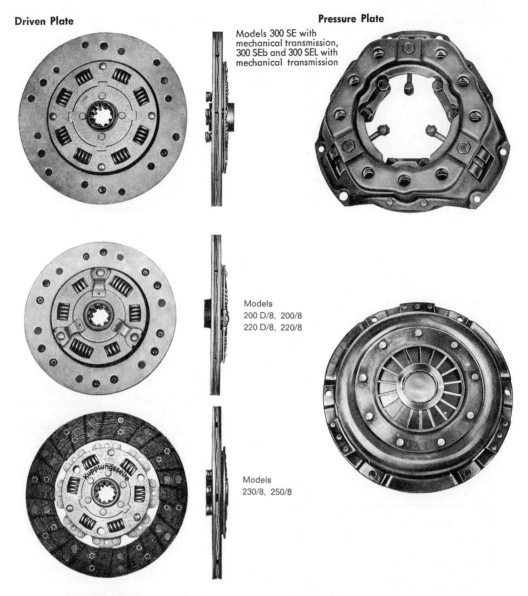

Models 300 SE with
mechanical transmission,
300 SEb and 300 SEL with
mechanical transmission

Models
200 D/8, 200/8
220 D/8, 220/8

Models
230/8, 250/8

Clutch types used in various models.

an automatic transmission. It is similar in operation to some Chrysler Corporation units of the early fifties and the Volkswagen automatic stickshift.

The clutch consists of four main groups:

1. A hydraulic coupling (i.e. torque converter).
2. A conventional clutch.
3. A servo assembly for operating clutch.
4. A servo control unit.

Actually, the car is driven in the same manner as a standard transmission car

except that there is no clutch pedal and the car may be left in gear while idling.

When the shift lever is touched, an electrical circuit is actuated that operates the clutch servo through a control valve. All this valve does is open one side of the servo diaphragm to manifold vacuum, leaving the other side exposed to normal 14.7 psi atmospheric pressure. The resultant movement of the diaphragm is transmitted mechanically to a normal clutch throwout arm to release the clutch. To overcome one of the hazards of this type system, a free-

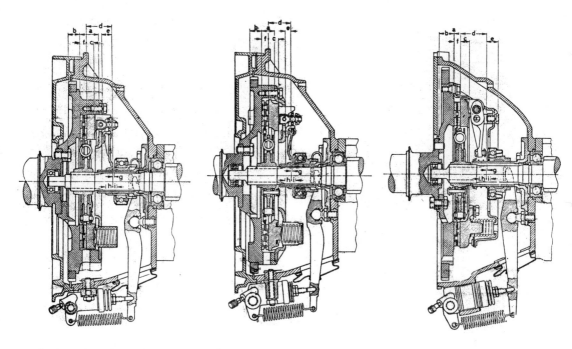

Clutch used on 190c, 190Dc, 200 and 200D models.

Clutch used on 220b, 220Sb, 220-SEb, 230SL, 230, 230S, 250S, and 250SE models.

Clutch used on 300SE and 300-SEL with manual transmission and on 300SEb.

a = Clearance between clutch face and clutch clamping face on the flywheel
b = Clearance between clutch face and flywheel attaching flange
c = Thickness of clutch pressure plate
d = Adjusting dimension for clutch assembly
e = Control dimension between cover plate and release levers for new driven plate

f = Thickness of new driven plate compressed
g = Free-play between throw-out bearing and release levers (clutch free-play)
h = Throwout travel
i = Travel of release levers because of driven plate wear

## Hydrak Automatic Hydraulic Clutch Specifications

### Drive Plate for Clutch

| Specification | | 220b 220Sb | 220SE 220SEb |
|---|---|---|---|
| Clearance "a" between the clutch face and the clamping face for the pressure plate ① | (mm.) | 1.5+0.1 | 19.4±0.1 |
| Thickness "b" of drive plate | | | |
| new | (mm.) | 14.5 | 31.0 |
| when repaired | (mm.) | 13.5 | 30.0 |
| Permissible runout of mounted drive plate | (mm.) | 0.05 | |

① *If the clutch face "A" is being reconditioned, the drive plate at the clutch clamping face "B" for the pressure plate should be machined so that the dimension "a" is maintained.*

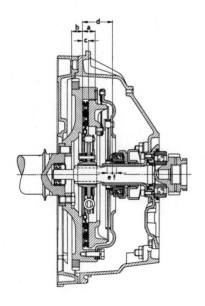

a. Indicates the distance between the clutch face and the contact face at the flywheel;

b. Indicates the distance between the clutch face and the flywheel attaching flange;

c. Indicates the thickness of the new driven plate in compressed condition (clutch contact pressure);

d. Indicates a control dimension between the clutch face at the flywheel and the external thrust ring face at the clutch with new driven plate.

e. Indicates the throwout travel

f. Indicates the thrust ring travel due to permissible wear of the driven plate.

Diaphragm spring clutch used on phase II models.

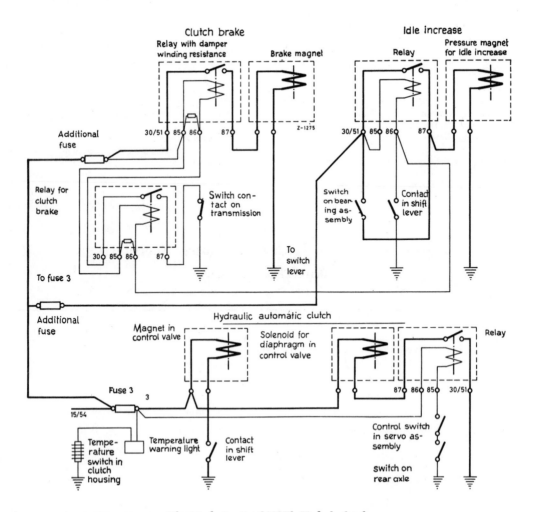

Electrical circuits—220SEb Hydrak clutch.

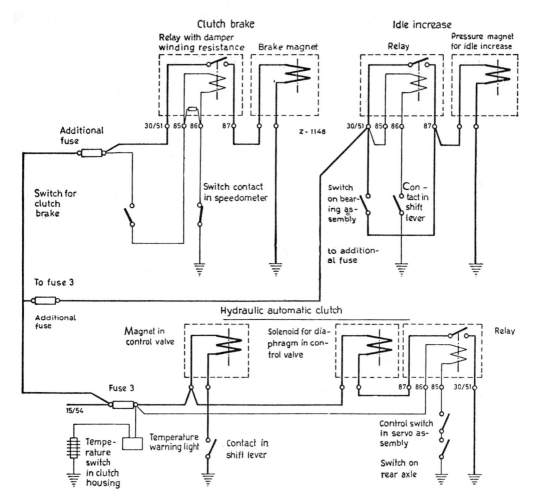

Electrical circuits—220SE Hydrak clutch.

# Hydrak Automatic Hydraulic Clutch Specifications

## Clutch Driven Plate

| Specification | | 220b 220Sb | 220SE 220SEb |
|---|---|---|---|
| Thickness of the driven plate "c" | | | |
| released | (mm.) | 8.8+0.3 | 9.8+0.3 |
| compressed | (mm.) | 7.8+0.3 | 9.1+0.3 |
| Thickness of facing | (mm.) | 3.5 | 4.2 |
| Permissible wear of facing thickness on either side | (mm.) | 1 | |
| Permissible unbalance | (cmg.) | 5 | |
| Permissible runout | (mm.) | 0.5 | |
| Permissible radial play on the drive shaft | (mm.) | 0.04±0.01 | |
| Torsion damping | | | |
| Free motion torque, traction side | (mkg.) | 17.5 | 20 |
| Stop angle | (degrees) | 3°15' | 5° |
| Friction torque | (mkg.) | 0.4—0.8 | 0.9—1.3 |

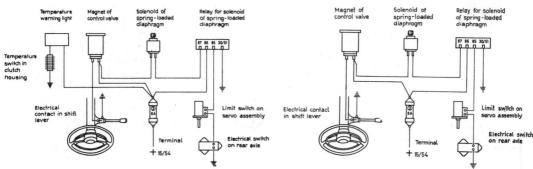

Electrical circuits—220b, 220Sb Hydrak clutch.     Electrical circuits—219, 220S, Hydrak clutch.

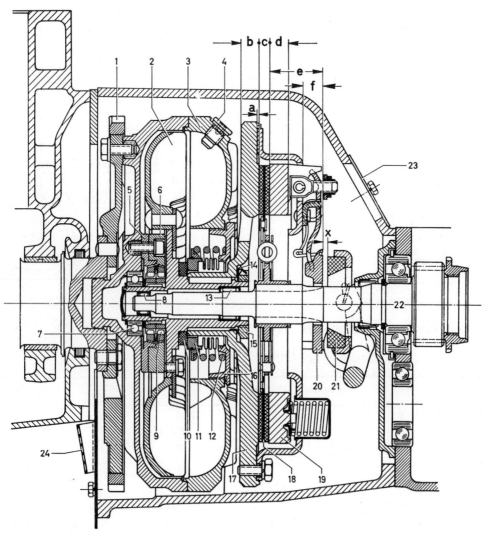

a = Clearance between clutch face and clutch
    clamping face for the clutch pressure plate
b = Thickness of drive plate
c = Thickness of driven plate
d = Thickness of pressure plate

e = Adjusting dimension of release levers between
    clutch face and contact ring
f = Adjusting dimension between cover plate and
    contact ring
x = Clutch free-play

Hydrak clutch.

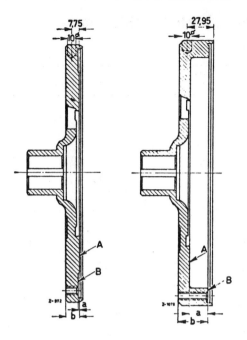

Left—220b, 220Sb    Right—220SE, 220SEb
A = Clutch face
B = Clutch clamping face for pressure plate
a = Clearance between clutch face and clutch
    clamping face
b = Thickness of drive plate

Hydrak drive plates.

1.  Screw plug
2.  Hydraulic coupling
3.  Mechanical clutch

KFX 12 Hydrak clutch unit.

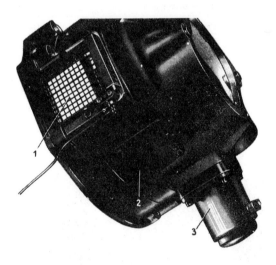

1.  Cover plate with temperature switch
2.  Cover plate
3.  Clutch brake

Underside of Hydrak clutch husing.

wheeling device automatically locks the engine and differential together during coasting, thus allowing the driver to use engine compression for slowing down, as well as allowing the car to be pushstarted.

The torque converter consists of two units, the primary unit, which is bolted to the crankshaft, and the secondary unit, to which the clutch and transmission is attached. The power loss through the coupling is negligible for all practical purposes, being around 2%.

The clutch itself consists of a drive plate, a driven plate and a contact plate. The drive plate is bolted to the flanged shaft of the secondary converter unit with a grooved nut, further located with a Woodruff key. The transmission mainshaft is centered in two needle-type pilot bearings in the shaft of the secondary converter unit.

The clutch housing has a temperature controlled flap that allows cooling air to circulate when the coupling oil temperature reaches about 180° C. (356° F.).

The servo assembly is pretty straight-forward; a limit switch on the servo breaks the circuit to the control element solenoid when the clutch is engaged. In addition, the control element is influenced by a switch on the rear axle via a relay.

The 220 SE and SEb, the last models to have the Hydrak clutch, had a larger clutch

# Hydrak Automatic Hydraulic Clutch Specifications

## Clutch Pressure Plate

| Specification | | | 220b 220Sb | | 220SE 220SEb | |
|---|---|---|---|---|---|---|
| Adjusting dimension "f" for new driven plate with clutch installed ① | (mm.) | | 15.5 | | | |
| Resulting adjusting dimension of worn-out driven plate | (mm.) | | 23.5 | | | |
| Thickness "d" of the pressure plate ② | (mm.) | | 15 | | 16.5 | |
| Regrind dimension of pressure plate | (mm.) | | 1 | | | |
| Permissible unbalance of pressure plate | (cmg.) | | 15 | | | |
| Thrust pressure | (pounds) | | 1055 | | 1155 | |
| Clutch springs | Number | | 3 | 6 | 3 | 6 |
| | Color code | | white with gold line | yellow with gold line | brown with gold line | yellow with gold line |
| | External diameter | (mm.) | 25.6 | 25.75 | 29.0 | 28.6 |
| | Wire gauge | (mm.) | 3.6 | 3.75 | 3.8 | 4.1 |
| | Free length | (mm.) | 44 | 45 | 58.7 | 55.5 |
| | Length under load | (mm.) | | 29.2 | | 37.2 |
| | Load | (kg.) | 45+4 | 56+4 | 46±3 | 61.5±2.5 |

① Press down the release levers several times before measuring. It is important that the distance from the cover plate should be identical for all three release levers and that the difference should not exceed .012".

② If the reduction in thickness exceeds .020", shims corresponding in thickness to the total amount of material removed should be placed between the clutch springs and the cups and/or the pressure plate to restore the total spring pressure. The selection and the color designation of the springs can be seen from the table. The tolerance of pressure springs of the same color designation within a clutch should be as small as possible.

1. Cover plate
2. Cover plate for cooling air inlet
3. Clutch brake
4. Cable connection at clutch brake
5. Clutch housing
6. Jointing flange
7. Cover plate for cooling air outlet

Underside of Hydrak clutch installed in 220SE.

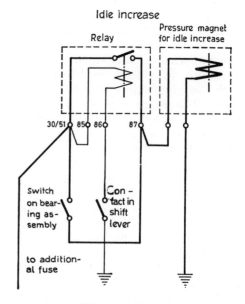

Idle speed circuit.

plate to handle the additional power of their fuel-injected engines. In order to eliminate rough engagement on starting, with attendant chattering, an electric brake located on the clutch housing serves to stop the disc as soon as the gearshift lever is touched. To make sure the clutch brake is never actuated except when stopped or creeping slowly, an additional switch in the speedometer breaks the circuit to the unit at speeds above 5 mph. The 220 SEb has a somewhat different setup, and above 5 mph an eddy current switch on the transmission case breaks the circuit to the clutch brake.

In addition, the 220 SE and 220 SEb have a device to increase the idle speed by 40–60 rpm when a gear is engaged. Touching the gearshift lever causes a solenoid to energize which, through a pushrod, opens the throttle a slight amount. When the gear is fully engaged, the solenoid deactivates and speed returns to normal.

## Maintenance

The oil level in the converter can be determined by making a stall speed test. Hook up a tachometer and start the engine. If the oil level is correct, the stall speed will be 1,600–1,800 rpm for carbureted versions and 1,750–1,950 rpm for 220 SE and 220 SEb models. The test is made with the brakes on, fourth gear engaged and the accelerator floored. If the stall speed is too high, there is too little oil in the converter or the clutch is slipping.

To check the oil level or refill the unit,

lift the carpet from the floor tunnel and remove the plug from the right-hand side. The engine should be turned over by hand until one of the coupling plugs is visible. It's a good idea to let the coupling cool down before opening the plug, as pressure build-up may force a stream of hot oil out the hole. Always replace the gaskets and torque to no more than 21 ft.-lbs. The filling capacity is 1.5 liters ATF Type A.

The cooling air cover plates should be cleaned every 5,000 miles at least, because a blocked plate will cause the converter to overheat badly.

## Adjustments

### CLUTCH FREE-PLAY

Measured at the pull rod, the free-play should be .39"–.47" for the 220 S, .23"–.31" for the 220 b, 220 Sb, 220 SE, and 220 SEb. On the 220 SE, only the long pull rod may be adjusted.

### CONTROL ELEMENT

The control element can be adjusted to regulate the "harshness" of the shift by turning screw (2). Screwing inward makes shifting smoother and screwing outward roughens the shift. If shifting is irregular in spite of adjustment, there could be dirt in the reducing valve (18).

To disassemble, unscrew the threaded

1. Turnbuckle
2. Adjusting clamps (180 589 12 23) for adjusting the free-play
3. Pull rod
4. Connector head
5. Throwout lever
6. Limit switch

Hydrak linkage as installed on 219 and 220S.

1. Relay
2. Threaded ring
3. Screw plug
4. Adjusting screw and locknut
5. Hose to servo assembly
6. Hose to vacuum supply reservoir
7. Screw plug
8. Servo assembly
9. Control element
10. Vacuum tube from intake manifold

Control element installation—220SE.

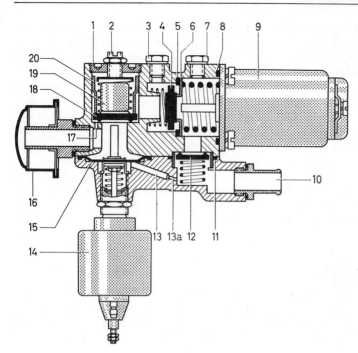

1. Threaded ring
2. Adjusting screw with lock-nut
3. Screw plug
4. Control valve
5. Rubber washer
6. Valve head
7. Screw plug
8. Rubber washer
9. Electromagnet for control valve
10. Vacuum union for intake manifold
11. Rubber washer
12. Check valve
13. Vacuum canal
13a. Throttle in vacuum canal
14. Solenoid for spring-loaded diaphragm
15. Spring-loaded diaphragm
16. Air cleaner
17. Jet in reducing valve
18. Reducing valve
19. Damper weight
20. Damper sleeve

Control element.

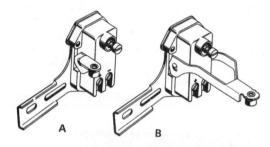

Rear axle switches.

1. Bearing for relay lever
2. Relay lever
3. Pinion rim grease fitting
4. Graduated disc
5. Turnbuckle
6. Long pull rod
7. Spring for the switch of the clutch brake
8. Pointer
9. Short pull rod

Adjusting linkage.

lock ring and carefully remove the spring (6), damper sleeve (4), damper weight (5) and the valve head.

### Electrical Switch at Rear Axle

Remove the cover plate from inside the trunk. With the car level, the handbrake released and the shift lever in neutral, hook a test light between the positive battery terminal and the "+" terminal of the switch.

Adjust the spring-loaded screw until the light just comes on. Backing the screw out causes harsher shifts, and vice-versa.

Switches with longer transmission arms ("B" in illustration) require a further screw adjustment of ½–¾ turn inward after the light comes on.

### Shift Lever Switch

Connect a test light between the positive battery terminal and the black wire at the control element solenoid. Loosen the lock-nut and screw the cover cap in until the two contacts touch and the light comes on. Back the cap off to give .008″–.012″ (.2–.3 mm.) clearance.

### CLUTCH BRAKE

Using a protractor and a piece of heavy cardboad, make a gauge and pointer similar to the one illustrated. Press the gauge onto the relay lever, then unscrew the grease fitting and attach the pointer.

1. Bearing for relay lever
2. Long pull rod
3. Turnbuckle
4. Relay lever
5. Spring for clutch brake switch
6. Short pull rod
7. Bracket for servo assembly
8. Servo assembly

Linkage as installed on 220SE.

Push either the short or long pushrod forward until the throwout bearing contacts the clutch. Zero the gauge and pointer and detach the long pull rod. Connect a test light between the clutch brake switch and ground, then move the relay lever (2) forward until the pointer is opposite the 11° mark on the gauge (that is, the pointer moves through 11° of arc). At this point, the test light should come on. If not, adjust the switch bracket—forward if the brake engages early, rearward if it engages late.

## Part III
## Automatic Transmission

Due to the complexity of this automatic transmission, and the special tools needed for any practical service, it is recommended that any work other than simple adjustment of the shift linkage be done by an authorized Mercedes-Benz dealer.

Even such a job as removal and replacement requires a special jack, and hydraulic pressure testing and troubleshooting require instruments not easily obtainable.

### Shift Linkage Adjustment—Columnshift

With the full weight of the car on its suspension, remove shift rod (7) and set

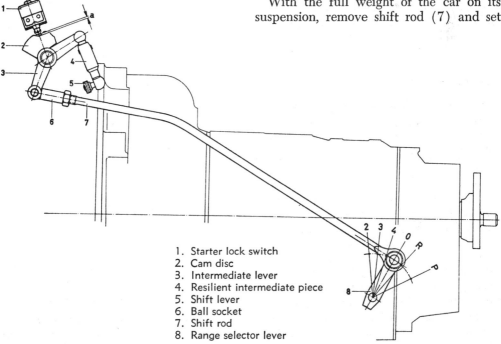

1. Starter lock switch
2. Cam disc
3. Intermediate lever
4. Resilient intermediate piece
5. Shift lever
6. Ball socket
7. Shift rod
8. Range selector lever

Automatic transmission columnshift linkage.

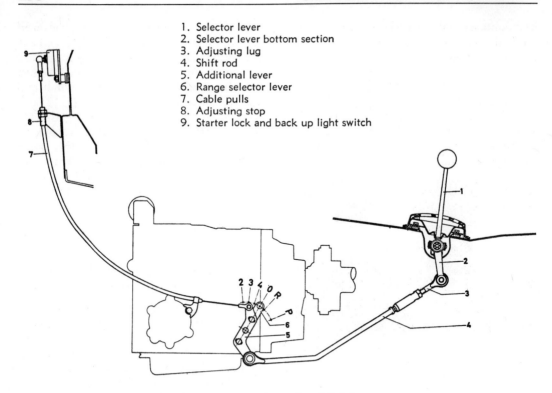

1. Selector lever
2. Selector lever bottom section
3. Adjusting lug
4. Shift rod
5. Additional lever
6. Range selector lever
7. Cable pulls
8. Adjusting stop
9. Starter lock and back up light switch

Automatic transmission floorshift linkage.

the range selector lever (at transmission) and gearshift lever in neutral. The shift rod (7) should be exactly the right length so that it fits on the ball sockets at intermediate lever (3) and lever (8) without any tension. On models with neutral safety switch set up as illustrated, clearance "a" should be .040".

### Shift Linkage Adjustment—Floorshift

Remove shift rod (4) and set the range selector lever (6) and the gearshift lever (1) in neutral. There should be about .040" play between the lever and the sleeve neutral detent.

At the transmission, loosen the bolts that told the extra lever to the selector lever and align the adjusting mark on the upper oblong hole with the centerline of the selector lever. On the 230 SL, the centerlines of both levers should coincide. Tighten bolts, hook up shift rod, and test through all gearshift lever positions.

The cable attached to the extra lever operated the back-up light and neutral safety switch. It can be adjusted at point (8) if required.

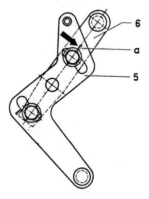

5. Additional lever
6. Range selector lever
▲ Adjusting mark

Additional lever arrangement.

### Column Shift Range Indicator

Place the gearshift lever in neutral, loosen locknut (5) and adjust the knurled nut (4) to bring the pointer into the proper position.

## Kickdown Switch

Unscrew the kickdown switch (4) from cover plate (2) on the steering column jacket. Check operation of throttle linkage and screw the switch back into the cover plate until the throttle valve lever is ³⁄₁₆″ from the full-load stop screw (2) when the gas pedal rests against the switch (position "B"). When the pedal is depressed to position "C", there should be ³⁄₆₄″ between the throttle valve lever and the full load stop on the venturi housing. On fuel injected models, the injection pump adjusting lever should rest against the full load stop.

## Control Pressure Linkage

On the 220/8, detach the pull rod (7) from the socket (11) and push the control pressure lever (8) so that it contacts the stop. Adjust the pull rod length so that it may be connected without tension.

On the 230/8 and 250/8, detach the linkage at the rear carburetor and detach the pull rod (7) from the ball head (11), pressing the control pressure lever (8) against the stop at the same time.

Loosen the two clamp bolts at lever (4) and turn adjusting lever (3) until the ball socket can be hooked up without forcing it.

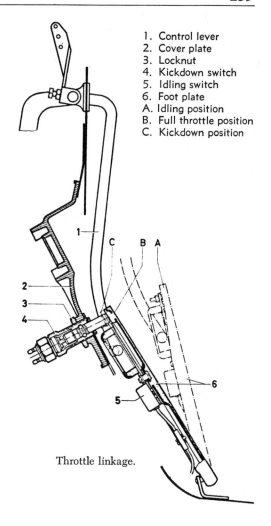

1. Control lever
2. Cover plate
3. Locknut
4. Kickdown switch
5. Idling switch
6. Foot plate
A. Idling position
B. Full throttle position
C. Kickdown position

Throttle linkage.

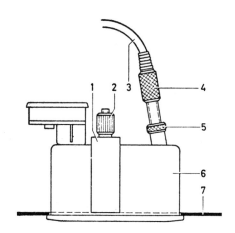

1. Clamp
2. Clamp nut
3. Bowden cable
4. Knurled nut

5. Locknut
6. Housing
7. Instrument panel

Adjusting selector lever pointer.

1. Pushrod
2. Intermediate lever
3. Adjusting lever
4. Clamp screw
5. Bearing bracket
6. Intermediate rod
7. Control pressure pull rod
8. Control pressure lever
9. Accelerator pedal
10. Kickdown switch
11. Ball head
A. Idling position
B. Full-throttle position
C. Kickdown position

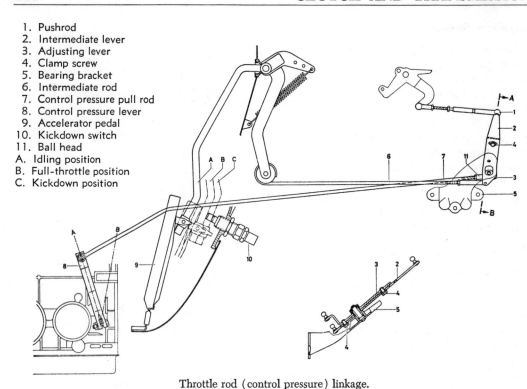

Throttle rod (control pressure) linkage.

1. Spring-loaded pull linkage
2. Intermediate lever
3. Ball head
4. Bore fore setting gauge
6. Intermediate rod
7. Control pressure pull rod
8. Control pressure lever
9. Accelerator pedal
10. Kickdown switch
A. Idling position
B. Full-throttle position
C. Kickdown position

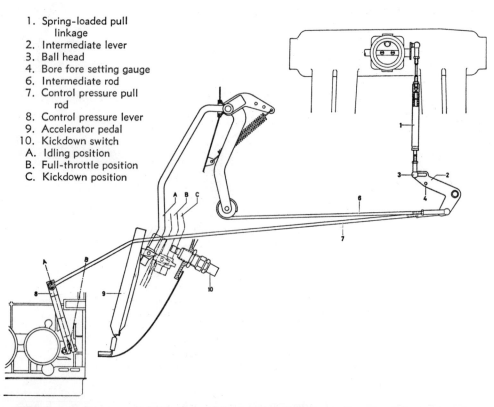

220D/8 control pressure linkage. A special gauge is required to adjust this linkage properly.

1. Spring-loaded connecting rod
2. Angle lever
3. Pushrod
4. Ball head
5. Control rod
6. Spring-loaded stop (kick-down change-down)
7. Accelerator pedal
8. Modulating pressure transmitter
9. Test connection for modulating pressure
10. Basic adjustment screw

Positions of accelerator pedal
A. Idling
B. Full throttle
C. Kickdown
a. Kickdown travel
b. Non-extended length of connecting rod

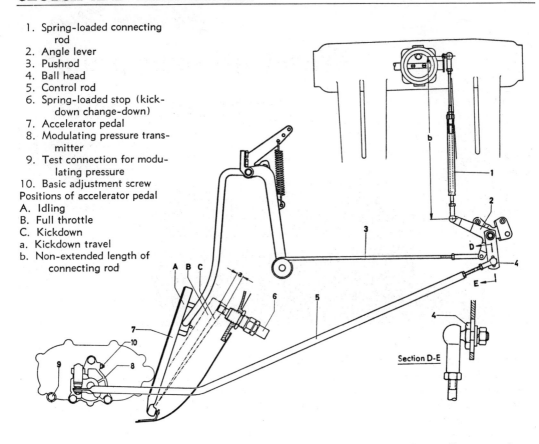

Section D-E

190Dc and 200D control pressure linkage. It is difficult to adjust this linkage without special gauges.

# Chapter Nine
# Wheel Alignment and Front Suspension

In order for an automobile to have safe, easy steering with minimal tire wear, there are certain adjustable angles incorporated into front suspension design. The relationship of each of these angles to all the others is called steering geometry.

*Camber angle* is the amount the front wheels are inclined outward at the top, expressed in degrees. The purpose of camber angle is to take some of the load from the outer wheel bearings.

*Caster angle* is the amount that the king pins, or knuckle support pivots, are tilted toward the rear of the car. Caster angle is also measured in degrees. Positive caster means that the top of the king pin is tilted toward the rear of the car, while negative caster is the reverse. Positive caster tends to allow the car to steer the path of least resistance, down off a crowned road for example, or with a crosswind.

*King pin slant* is the angle assumed by the tops of the king pins, or knuckle supports, as they incline toward each other. This inclination tends to make the automobile steer in a straight line regardless of outside forces acting upon it. As the wheels are turned from right to left, the spindle scribes an arc, apparently rising to its highest point when the wheels are straight ahead, then gradually falling off. In actual operation, the spindle cannot physically rise and fall because the wheel is in contact with the road, therefore the car itself will rise in a turn of either direction, assuming its lowest position when steered straight ahead. It is easy to see then, that the weight of the car itself will tend to keep the car in a straight line.

*Included angle* is the sum total of king pin slant and camber, expressed in degrees. This angle should remain constant for the

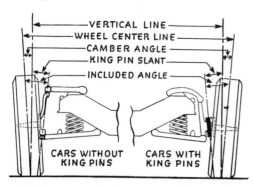

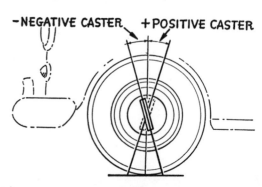

242

life of the car, assuming the spindle itself is undamaged. When checking the included angle, it must be kept in mind that the totals for both sides of the car should be exactly the same, regardless of variance from specifications.

For example, if the left side of the car has 5½° king pin slant and 1° positive camber, included angle is 5½° + 1° = 6½°. If the right side of the car has 6½° king pin slant, and 0° camber, the included angle is also 6½°. Both sides check out the same, and since it is highly unlikely that both spindles would be bent at exactly the same angle, it can be safely assumed that correcting the camber angle will also correct the king pin slant proportionately.

A bent spindle might show up like this: left side of car has ¾° positive camber + 5¼° king pin slant = 6° included angle. Right side has 1¼° positive camber + 6° king pin slant = 7¼° included angle. One of these spindles is bent, and correcting for camber only will never bring the king pin slant along in the same proportion.

Since the most common cause of a bent spindle is striking the curb while parking, which bends the spindle downward, the side having the greater included angle is usually the side with the bent spindle. Always replace a bent spindle, never try to bend it back into shape using heat, for the steel will be weakened.

*Toe-in* is the amount that the front wheels are closer to each other at the front of the wheel than they are at the rear. This dimension is usually given in millimeters or inches.

Generally, the wheels are toed-in due to camber influence. If a car has 0° camber it will have 0 mm./in. toe-in. As camber increases, so does the toe-in. The cambered wheel tends to steer in the direction it is cambered, therefore this tendency must be overcome by compensating very slightly in the direction opposite to that in which it tends to roll. Since caster and camber both have an effect on toe-in, toe-in is usually the last job done on a front end alignment.

### TRACKING

While tracking is more a function of the rear axle and frame than it is of the front axle, it is difficult to align the front suspension properly if the car does not track correctly. Therefore, the car must be checked for tracking before any attempt is made to correct difficulties in the front suspension.

Tracking means that the centerline of the rear axle follows exactly the path of the centerline of the front axle, when the car is moving in a straight line. With cars which have equal tread, front and rear, the rear tires will follow in exactly the tread of the front tires when the car is moving in a straight line. However, there are many cars with a rear tread wider than the front tread; on such cars the rear axle tread will straddle the front axle tread an equal amount on both sides when the car is moving in a straight line.

Perhaps the easiest way to check tracking is to park the car on a level floor, drop a plumb bob from the extreme outer edge of the front suspension lower A-frame, using the same drop point on each side of the car. Make a chalk mark where the plumb bob strikes the floor. Do the same with the rear axle, selecting a point on the rear axle housing for the plumb bob and being certain that the same point is selected on both sides of the rear axle.

Now measure diagonally from the left

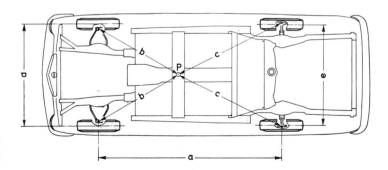

a. Wheelbase
b. Front axle positioning distance
c. Rear axle positioning distance
d. Front axle track
e. Rear axle track
P. Check bore in the second crossmember on the chassis base panel

Frame alignment.

rear mark to the right front mark and from the right rear mark to the left front mark. These two diagonal measurements should be exactly the same. However, a difference of approximately ¼″ would be acceptable.

If the measurements taken diagonally are not the same for both sides, measure from the right rear to the right front and from the left rear to the left front. These two measurements should also be the same within ¼″.

If the diagonal measurements are different but the longitudinal measurements are the same on both sides, the frame is swayed (diamond-shaped). However, in the event that the diagonal measurements are uneven and the longitudinal measurements are also uneven, and the car is tracking incorrectly, the rear axle is misaligned. If the diagonal measurements are uneven and the longitudinal measurements are also uneven, but the car tracks correctly as observed on the street, a "kneeback" is indicated; in other words, the entire front suspension is bent back on one side. This is often caused by "crimping" the front wheels against the curb when parking the vehicle and then starting up without straightening out the front wheels. This causes full power to be applied against the wheel which is crimped against the curb, bending the front suspension unit back.

It is possible to have caster, camber, toe-in, king pin slant and included angle exactly correct and, if the car has a kneeback or does not track properly, have it handle very poorly.

## Diagnosis

### STEERING WHEEL SPOKE POSITION NOT CENTERED

1. Start with steering gear set on high-spot.
2. Check for proper toe-in.
3. Check for proper relation between lengths of each tie-rod.

### FRONT END RIDES HARD

1. Improper tires.
2. Improper air pressure.
3. Shock absorbers too "hard" or malfunctioning.

### RIDES TOO SOFT

1. Improper air pressure.
2. Loss of spring load-rate, (weak-springs).
3. Weak or leaking shock absorbers.

### CAR STEERS TO ONE SIDE AT ALL TIMES

1. Incorrect caster angle.
2. Incorrect camber angle.
3. Incorrect king pin or wheel support angle.
4. Unequal air pressure, or unequal tire tread.
5. Unequal or one-side brake drag.
6. Unequal shock absorber control.
7. Bent or damaged steering or suspension components.
8. Uneven or weak spring condition, front or rear, causing car to sit unevenly.
9. Improper tracking.

### CAR STEERS TO ONE SIDE, ONLY WHEN BRAKES ARE APPLIED

1. Improper brake adjustment, shoes or anchors.
2. Grease or foreign substance (dust) on brake lining.
3. Excessive wear or bent condition in suspension components.

### CAR STEERS DOWN OFF CROWNED ROAD BUT NORMALLY ON FLAT ROAD

1. Excessive positive camber at one or both sides.
2. Weak or uneven shock absorber action.
3. Excessive or unequal wear in suspension components.

### CAR WANDERS—STEERS ERRATICALLY

1. Incorrect caster.
2. Improper tire pressure or unequal tire tread.
3. Excessive wear or damaged suspension components.
4. Power steering gear condition causing power operation to function when not in normal operation.

### CAR STEERS HARD

1. Binding steering or suspension parts.
2. Improper lubrication.
3. Improper (too large) tires.
4. Low air pressure.

### Tires Cup on Outside Edge with Ripple Wear Pattern

1. Generally incorrect camber or toe-in.

### Tires Wear Unevenly in Center and Faster than Outer Edges

1. Generally too much air pressure.

### Tires Wear and Scuff on Both Outer Edges, Not in Center

1. Generally low air pressure.

### Uneven Outer Edge Wear—Center and Inner Edge Wear Normal

1. With adjustments normal, this is generally caused by driving into turns at too-high speed. Do not confuse with OUTER EDGE CUPPING mentioned above.

### Unequal Tire Wear Between Front Wheels

1. Unequal air pressure.
2. Unequal tire quality or size.
3. Bent or worn steering suspension components.
4. Improper tracking.

### Tire Squeal on Turns

1. Low air pressure.
2. Driving at too-high speed going into turn.
3. Damaged or misaligned parts causing improper front wheel toe-out—steering radius.
4. Improper camber adjustment.

---

## Front Wheel Camber and Caster

---

On older models, camber is adjusted by turning an eccentric bolt on the steering knuckle. Newer phase II models have a provision for adjusting both camber and caster at the same time. This is accomplished by turning two eccentric pins on the lower control arm mountings—the front pin changes caster, the rear changes camber. *NOTE: Vehicles must be fully loaded. This is especially important on phase II models, as the rubber mountings may twist in the control arm if load is too light.*

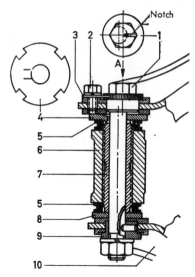

1. Eccentric bolt for camber adjustment
2. Hexagon screw with lockwasher
3. Locking plate
4. Adjusting washer

for caster adjustment
5. Rubber sealing ring
6. King pin
7. Threaded bolt
8. Eccentric bushing with drive pin
10. Upper control arm

Camber and caster adjustment.

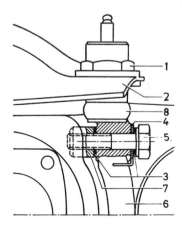

1. Threaded bushing
2. Upper control arm
3. Shim
4. Lock plate
5. Bolt
6. Pivot pin
7. Front axle support
8. Rubber seal

Upper control arm bushings.

To adjust camber on older models, loosen the hex bolt (2) and remove it and the lock plate (3). The camber can be adjusted by turning the eccentric thus exposed. In some cases, camber cannot be adjusted using the eccentric alone. Install or remove shims (3) between pivot pin (6) and upper control arm (2) and front axle support (7). If a shim is removed from between the front axle support and the pivot pin, it must be reinstalled between the locking plate and the hex bolt.

On phase II models, caster and camber are interrelated. When caster is increased, the camber is changed in a positive direction; when caster is decreased, the reverse is true. When camber is adjusted in the positive direction, caster is changed negatively.

Changing camber by 0°15′ results in 0°20′ caster change; changing caster by 1° results in a 0°7′ camber change. The diagram illustrates this relationship between caster and camber. For example, x = measured caster of 3°30′, measured camber of +1°. Set correction camber to +0°14′ (A1) and/or +0°8′ (B1), then adjust caster (A2) and/or (B2).

Adjustment of front wheel caster on older models is accomplished by swiveling the front axle support on the eccentric bolts at the flat springs on the longitudinal front axle support. Differences in caster between the left and right sides can be minimized by turning the threaded bolt (7) on top of the steering knuckle.

| | |
|---|---|
| 1. Front axle sub-frame | 27. Torsion bar connecting linkage |
| 3. Lower control arm | 29. Torsion rubber mounting |
| 7. Suspension joint | 30. Eccentric bolt |

Lower control arm, showing eccentric adjusters.

First, loosen the four bolts that hold the rear motor mount. This relieves any tension on the mount during adjustment. Loosen the hex bolts (10) and (13) on the right and left of the flat spring, then loosen the locknut (15) for eccentric bolt (14). Remove the support strut which goes to the front axle support, then matchmark the flat spring and the chassis. Adjust the eccentric evenly on both sides. If left- and right-side

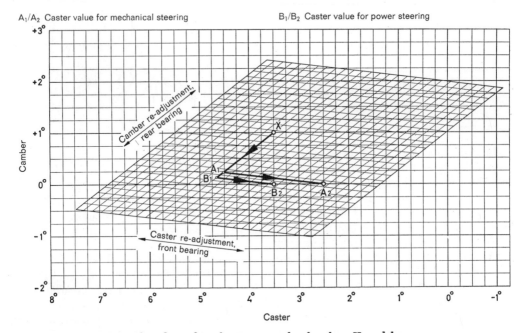

The relationship of caster to camber for phase II models.

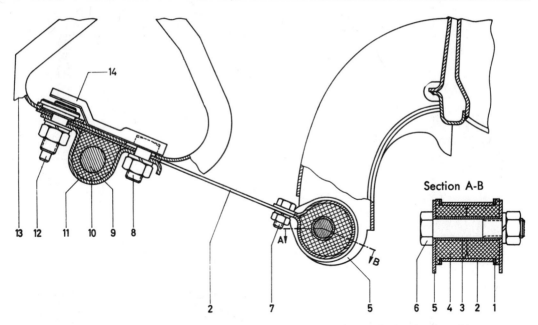

Section A-B

1. Spacer ring
2. Flat spring
3. Spacer tube
4. Rubber mounting
5. Bearing bracket at front axle support
6. Hexagon screw with nut and lockwasher
7. Hexagon screw (clamping screw) with nut and lockwasher
8. Square screw with nut and lockwasher
9. Torsion bar
10. Rubber mounting for torsion bar
11. Bracket for rubber mounting
12. Eccentric with nut, lockwasher, and washer
13. Bearing bracket on chassis base panel
14. Cage for square screw and eccentric

Longitudinal support (flat spring) on second version front axle.

caster differs, loosen the hex nut of the eccentric bolt and turn the threaded bolt. *CAUTION: Never alter caster by turning the upper control arm pivot pin.*

20. Tie-rod
20a. Clamp
21. Center tie-rod
24. Steering relay lever

Tie-rod adjustment.

## Front Wheel Toe-In

Toe-in is adjusted by changing the length of the two tie-rods with the wheels in the straight ahead position. The illustration shows one tie-rod and its adjusting points. Some older models have a hex nut locking arrangement rather than the newer clamp (20a), but adjustment is the same. *NOTE: Install new tie-rods so that the left-hand thread points toward left-hand side of car.*

## Front End Service

### Steering Knuckle/Ball Joint Replacement

To check the steering knuckles or ball joints, jack up the car, placing the jack directly under the front spring plate. This unloads the front suspension to allow the

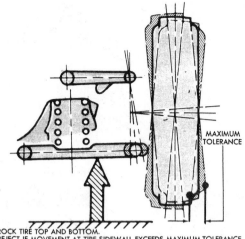

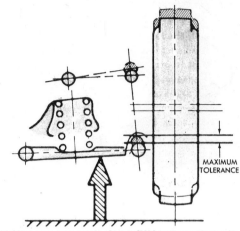

ROCK TIRE TOP AND BOTTOM.
REJECT IF MOVEMENT AT TIRE SIDEWALL EXCEEDS MAXIMUM TOLERANCE,
BUT DO NOT CONFUSE WHEEL BEARING LOOSENESS WITH BALL JOINT
WEAR.

REJECT IF AXIAL PLAY IN BALL JOINT EXCEEDS MAXIMUM TOLERANCE.

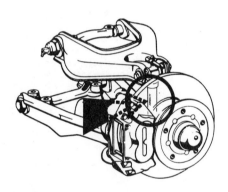

Front suspension identification number location.

1. Supporting fixture
2. Eccentric bolt of upper steering knuckle
   mounting
3. Threaded pin of lower mounting

Steering knuckle removal.

maximum play to be observed. On older
models having king pins, the maximum
allowable play between the king pin and
bearing bushing is 0.016″; the king pin
end-play is the same. Late model ball
joints need be replaced only if dried out
with plainly visible wear and/or play.

To replace steering knuckles on cars
equipped with drum brakes, first remove
the brake drum, then disconnect the brake
hose where it hooks to the steel line. On
cars with disc brakes, remove the brake
caliper and unscrew the brake hose and
line from the steering knuckle.

Disconnect the tie-rod from the knuckle
arm and, on older models, remove the shock
absorber.

Referring to the two illustrations, on
models having king pins, place a support
rod (1) in position (or place a screw jack
under the lower control arm), then loosen

bolt (2) and remove. Remove the cotter
pin and castle nut (3) from the lower control arm and unscrew the threaded pin,
then remove the entire knuckle assembly.
On models having ball joints, remove the
nuts at the ball joints (7) and (6), then
press the ball joints from the knuckle from
the inside. The upper joint can be re-

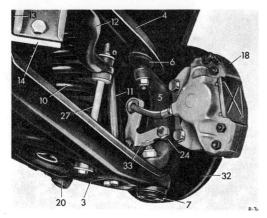

| | |
|---|---|
| 1. Hexagon nut | 6. Thrust washer |
| 2. Locking plate | 7. Dust cover |
| 3. King pin | 8. Threaded pin top |
| 4. Steering knuckle | 9. Threaded pin bottom |
|    support | |
| 5. Shim | |

Steering knuckle components.

| | |
|---|---|
| 3. Lower control arm | 14. Bracket |
| 4. Upper control arm | 18. Caliper |
| 5. Steering knuckle | 20. Tie-rod |
| 6. Guide joint | 24. Steering relay lever |
| 7. Suspension joint | 27. Torsion bar connecting linkage |
| 10. Front spring | 32. Cover plate |
| 11. Front shock-absorber | 33. Bracket for brake hose |
| 12. Torsion bar | |
| 13. Rubber mounting for torsion bar | |

Ball joint suspension.

| |
|---|
| 1. Wheel spindle |
| 2. Contact surface for seal |
| 3. Steering arm |

Checking spindle runout.

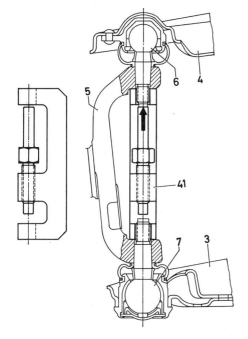

| | |
|---|---|
| 3. Lower control arm | 7. Suspension joint |
| 4. Upper control arm | 41. Puller (115 589 |
| 5. Steering knuckle | 02 33 00) |
| 6. Guide joint | |

Ball joint removal.

moved without special tools by striking the knuckle support with a hammer at point (5) (see illustration). Then, after the upper joint is disconnected, strike the knuckle support at the corresponding lower ball joint in the same manner.

To disassemble, remove front brake shoes and wheel cylinders (if so equipped), then the front wheel hub. *NOTE: It may be necessary to remove the disc brake dust cover as well.*

Unscrew the threaded pin from the upper knuckle support and the hex nut (1) from the king pin. Strike the king pin sharply with a hammer to unseat the lower

Reaming king pin bushings.

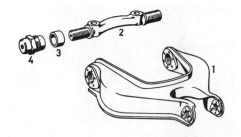

1. Upper control arm    3. Rubber sealing ring
2. Pivot pin           4. Threaded bushing

Upper control arm and shaft.

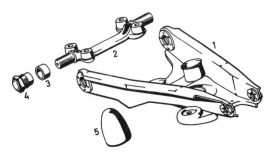

1. Lower control arm    4. Threaded bushing
2. Pivot pin           5. Additional rubber
3. Rubber sealing ring      buffer

Lower control arm and shaft.

knuckle support (4), then remove the lower support and shim washer.

Check the spindle for runout (wobble) by suspending it in the jaws of a lathe and checking with a dial indicator, then check the knuckle arm for distortion and the knuckle support for internal wear and cracks. The king pin bushings can be driven out using a drift. New bushings are *pressed* in, then reamed to size.

| | |
|---|---|
| 3. Lower control arm | 13. Rubber mounting |
| 4. Upper control arm | 14. Bracket |
| 5. Steering knuckle | 18. Brake caliper |
| 6. Ball joint | 20. Tie-rod |
| 7. Suspension joint | 24. Steering relay lever |
| 10. Front spring | 27. Torsion bar con- |
| 11. Front shock- | necting linkage |
| absorber | 32. Cover plate |
| 12. Torsion bar | 33. Bracket |

Front suspension components (ball joint).

## Control Arm Replacement

On models having threaded control arm supports, first remove the steering knuckle, then unscrew the threaded bushings (4) and the pivot pin (2). Remove the rubber seals (3) and the control arm.

On models having hex bolt supports, support the control arm with a jack, then disconnect the sway bar (27) and shock absorber. Remove the front coil spring, then disconnect the brake hose from the steel line, plug the line to prevent fluid loss and unscrew the hex bolts. *NOTE: The bolts are installed from the inside—the nut always goes on the outside of the control arm.*

To install, reverse removal procedure. On models having threaded bushings, make sure the bushing rotates freely on the pivot pin.

## Front Shock Absorber Replacement

Shock absorbers are normally replaced only if excessively leaking (oil visible on

1. Threaded bushing
1a. Groove
2. Code number on control arm
3. Pivot pin

Threaded pivot pin bushing.

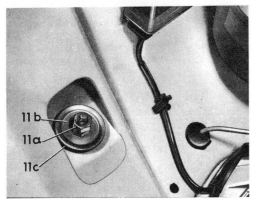

11a. Hexagon nuts
11b. Cup
11c. Rubber ring

Shock absorber upper mounting.

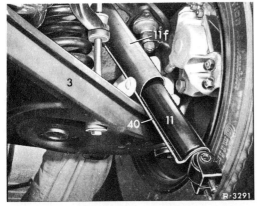

3. Lower control arm    11f. Protective sleeve
11. Shock-absorber     40. Stirrup

Shock absorber removal.

outside cover) or if internally worn to a point where the car no longer rides smoothly and rebounds after hitting a bump. A good general test of shock absorber condition is made by bouncing the front of the car by standing on the bumper. If the car rebounds more than two or three times after jumping off the bumper, it can be assumed that the shock absorbers need replacement.

To replace, jack up the car and support the lower control arm with a jack stand. Remove the upper and lower mounting bolts, compress the shock absorber and remove. On some early models it may be necessary to remove the battery and air cleaner to gain access to the upper bolts. *NOTE: The steel stirrups must be removed and changed over to the new shock absorbers. Use new rubber bushings throughout.*

## Front Spring Replacement

Jack up the front of the car and remove the front wheels. On cars having drum brakes, remove the brake drum. Remove the front shock absorber and disconnect the sway bar. On cars having pivot pins and threaded bushings, unscrew the two outer bolts that attach the pivot pin to the frame. Place a jack under the inner control arm, then remove the two inner bolts and gradually lower the jack and arm. When

3. Lower control arm    12. Torsion bar
4. Upper control arm    29. Rubber mounting
6. Guide joint          44. Jack cradle
7. Suspension joint     47. Angled intermediate brace
10. Front spring
11. Front shock-absorber

Removing front coil spring—phase II models.

the spring tension is relieved, remove spring and its rubber bumpers.

On cars having eccentric adjusters, first punchmark the position of the adjusters, then loosen the hex bolts. Support the lower control arm with a jack, then knock out the eccentric pins and gradually lower the arm until spring tension is relieved. The spring can now be removed. *NOTE: Check caster and camber after installing new spring.*

## Wheels and Tires— Balance and Runout

Vibration problems can be caused by many things: weak shock absorbers, incorrect or uneven tire pressure, vertical or lateral wobbling of front hubs or rear axle shafts. The most common cause of vibration, however, is tires or wheels being unbalanced and/or out of round. *NOTE: Radial tires are especially susceptible to unbalance.*

To check wheel runout, jack up the car and rig a piece of chalk as illustrated. Rotate the tire with the chalk not quite touching the wheel rim. Bent wheels will be indicated by a chalk mark at the bent portion. *NOTE: Up to 0.040" out of round is acceptable. The same set-up can be used to check the tires. Conventional tires may be .047" out of round; radial tires may be .040" out of round (measured at center of tread).*

*NOTE: Tires must be warmed up by driving at least five miles before checking.*

Wheel balance can be accomplished in several ways. If the car is equipped with drum brakes, jack up the car and loosen the brake adjusters and/or wheel bearings so that the tire rotates freely without drag. Spin the tire by hand and allow it to come to rest naturally. Mark the lowest spot on the tire with chalk (the "down" side) and repeat the test four or five times. If the tire rotates freely, the "low" spot should be the same for each test within 1–1½". This "low" spot is the heaviest point of the tire/wheel combination, the highest spot being the lightest.

Using the proper wheel weights, temporarily fix a weight on the "high" (lightest)

1. Front spring
2. Lower control arm
3. Jack cradle
4. Pivot pin for lower control arm

Removing front coil spring—early models.

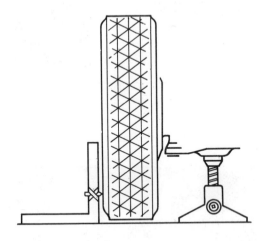

spot and repeat the test. Add weights until the tire no longer returns to any *one* low point, but stops spinning at random locations around its circumference. Attach one weight, equal to the total weight necessary, to the rear of the rim (at the lightest spot).

*NOTE: The magnitude of wheel/tire unbalance can be determined, with practice, by observing how fast the tire comes to rest on the "low" spot. It sometimes helps to rotate the tire on the rim so that the valve stem is opposite the heaviest portion of the tire.*

Cars having disc brakes present a special problem. Since the pads are always in contact with the disc it is impossible to obtain perfectly free rotation. In this case, tires and wheels must be balanced either dynamically, or statically using a "bubble" balancer.

If tire pressure, shock absorbers, wheels and tires are all within tolerance, but vibration still exists, check the front and rear axle mounting flanges using a dial indicator.

## Front Axle

Maximum vertical deviation—.0012″
Maximum lateral deviation (runout) at flange—.0012″

## Rear Axle

Maximum vertical deviation—.0039″
Maximum lateral deviation (runout) at flange—.0047″
*CAUTION: Tighten wheel lug bolts to 65–72 ft.-lbs. (wheels cold) using a hand wrench. Always check torque reading if air or electric impact wrenches are used, as they may overtighten bolts to the point where the lug wrench supplied with the car will not be capable of loosening the bolts.*

## Tire Rotation

Assuming wheel alignment and tire pressure is correct, tires still will wear unevenly between front and rear. At high speeds, front tires will wear more rapidly on the shoulder than rear tires; rear tires will show more rapid center tread wear than front tires. Normally, city driving results in more rapid front tire wear, although the tires will wear more evenly all around.

For this reason, tire life can be greatly extended by rotating tires from front to rear, and vice-versa, every 3,000 miles or so. Don't rotate the tires in an "X" pattern, as wear may become uneven.

Studded snow tires *never* must have their direction of rotation reversed, as the studs will be loosened and thrown off. If four studded snow tires are used, rotate them every 1,500 miles.

## Conventional Bias-Ply Tires

With conventional tires, the cords of the tire carcass run at a rather upright angle, as shown, from bead to bead. The permis-

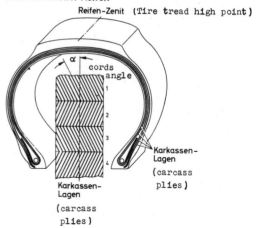

Conventional Tire
**Konventioneller Reifen**
Reifen-Zenit (Tire tread high point)
α cords angle
1 2 3 4
Karkassen-Lagen (carcass plies)
Karkassen-Lagen (carcass plies)

sible maximum speed for a tire is determined mainly by the angle of cords and carcass material. On standard conventional tires for speeds up to 95 mph, rayon cords are generally used. Racing tires for speeds up to 110 mph usually have nylon cords. These cords run at a more upright angle with respect to the tire centerline.

## Radial-Ply Tires

The classic radial-ply tire is the Michelin-X. Its carcass consists of two plies, the rayon cords of which run at a very flat angle, i.e., almost radially from bead to bead. On top of these is the so-called "brace", which in this brand consists of three superimposed layers of steel wire fabric. Because of this construction, the tread is very firm, although, because of its soft walls, there is sufficient flexibility for acceptable driving comfort. A variation is the Michelin-XAs. Properly inflated radial tires look almost "flat". Under no circumstances exceed maximum allowable tire pressure.

## Semi-Radial-Ply Tires

In order to obtain a more comfortable radial-ply tire and to achieve smoother transition when taking sharp curves, the "semi-radial-ply tire" (radial-ply tire with semi-radial carcass) has been developed. It is applicable to Mercedes-Benz cars having 14″ wheels. The Continental Radial, Dunlop Sp, and Firestone-Phoenix P 110 (size 185 HR 14) belong to this group. The nylon carcass (two plies) is enclosed by a rayon brace having four plies. The

Michelin-X Tire with
Radial Carcass
Michelin-X-Reifen
mit radialer Karkasse

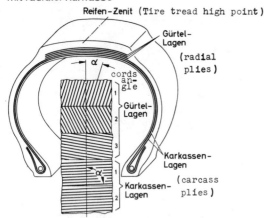

Michelin-XAs Tire with
Radial Carcass
Michelin-XAs-Reifen
mit radialer Karkasse

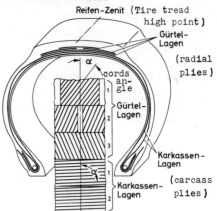

driving characteristics of these tires are midway between those of the conventional tires and those of the radial-ply tires with radial carcasses.

### Advantages of Radial-Ply Tires

The firm tread gives better resistance to wear and somewhat reduced rolling friction, thereby giving longer service life and reduced fuel consumption. Generally, higher curve speeds are possible; however, the lateral stability generally diminishes faster than with conventional tires. This tendency to "breakaway" suddenly is increased on cars having swing axles. For this reason, it is not recommended that radial-ply tires be used on cars of "prephase II" vintage. Their winter properties are slightly better, but they are not as good as snow tires.

### Disadvantages of Radial-Ply Tires

On cobble-stone roads, they are noisier at speeds less than 40 mph, and they may vibrate at higher speeds. Under certain driving conditions, they may cause jolting, as they have little dampening ability. In crosswinds, most radial-ply tires behave like conventional tires, although there are some makes which react more sensitively. When mounted on the front wheels, some radial-ply tires tend toward higher shoulder wear, whereas on the rear they show higher center tread wear.

### Changing to Radial-Ply Tires

When changing to radial-ply tires, use only tires of the same make and same model. Do not use them in combination with conventional tires. In special cases, conventional tires may be mounted *temporarily* on the front and radial-ply tires on the rear, but never vice-versa. Of course, the tire pressure of the respective tire type must be observed. Combinations of summer and winter tires are not recommended.

## Wheel Alignment Specifications

| Model | Front Camber | | Front Caster | | Front Toe-in (in.) | King Pin Inclination | Rear Toe-in (in.) |
|---|---|---|---|---|---|---|---|
| | Curb ▲ | Test ★ | Manual | Power | | | |
| 190c | +0°30′ ± 10′ | 0°20′ −20′ | 3°30′ ± 15′ | 4° ± 15′ | .080 ± .040 | 5°30′ ± 10′ | ± .080 |
| 200 | +0°30′ ± 10′ | 0°20′ −20′ | 3°30′ ± 15′ | 4° ± 15′ | .080 ± .040 | 5°30′ ± 10′ | ± .080 |
| 190Dc | +0°30′ ± 10′ | 0°20′ −20′ | 3°30′ ± 15′ | 4° ± 15′ | .080 ± .040 | 5°30′ ± 10′ | ± .080 |
| 200D | +0°30′ ± 10′ | 0°20′ −20′ | 3°30′ ± 15′ | 4° ± 15′ | .080 ± .040 | 5°30′ ± 10′ | ± .080 |
| 230 | +0°30′ ± 10′ | 0°20′ −20′ | 3°30′ ± 15′ | 4° ± 15′ | .080 ± .040 | 5°30′ ± 10′ | ± .080 |
| 220b | +0°30′ ± 10′ | 0°20′ −20′ | 2°45′ ± 15′ | 4° ± 15′ | .080 ± .040 | 5°30′ ± 10′ | ± .080 |
| 220Sb | +0°30′ ± 10′ | 0°20′ −20′ | 2°45′ ± 15′ | 4° ± 15′ | .080 ± .040 | 5°30′ ± 10′ | ± .080 |
| 230S | +0°30′ ± 10′ | 0°20′ −20′ | 3°30′ ± 15′ | 4° ± 15′ | .080 ± .040 | 5°30′ ± 10′ | ± .080 |
| 250S | +0°30′ ± 10′ | 0°20′ −20′ | 3°30′ ± 15′ | 4° ± 15′ | .080 ± .040 | 5°30′ ± 10′ | ± .080 |
| 220SEb | +0°30′ ± 10′ | 0°20′ −20′ | 2°45′ ± 15′ | 4° ± 15′ | .080 ± .040 | 5°30′ ± 10′ | ± .080 |
| 220SEb/C | +0°30′ ± 10′ | 0°20′ −20′ | 3°30′ ± 15′ | 4° ± 15′ | .080 ± .040 | 5°30′ ± 10′ | ± .080 |
| 250SE | +0°30′ ± 10′ | 0°20′ −20′ | 3°30′ ± 15′ | 4° ± 15′ | .080 ± .040 | 5°30′ ± 10′ | ± .080 |
| 230SL | +0°10′ ± 20′ | 0° + 20′ | 3°30′ ± 15′ | 4° ± 15′ | .080 ± .040 | 5°30′ ± 10′ | ± .080 |
| 250SL | +0°10′ ± 20′ | 0° + 20′ | 3°30′ ± 15′ | 4⓺ ± 15′ | .080 ± .040 | 5°30′ ± 10′ | ± .080 |
| 300SE, SEL | +0°20′ − 20′ | | | 4° ± 15′ | .080 ± .040 | 5°30′ ± 10′ | ± .080 |
| 300SEb | +0°30′ ± 10′ | 0°20′ −20′ | 3°30 ± 15′ | 4° ± 15′ | .080 ± .040 | 5°30 ± 10′ | ± .080 |
| 220D/8 | 0° ± 10′ | 0° ± 10′ | 2°30′ ± 20′ | 3°30′ ± 20′ | .200 ± .040 | 6° ± 10′ | .040 +.080 −.040 |
| 220/8 | 0° ± 10′ | 0° ± 10′ | 2°30′ ± 20′ | 3°30′ ± 20′ | .200 ± .040 | 6° ± 10′ | .040 +.080 −.040 |
| 230/8 | 0° ± 10′ | 0° ± 10′ | 2°30′ ± 20′ | 3°30′ ± 20′ | .200 ± .040 | 6° ± 10′ | .040 +.080 −.040 |
| 250/8 | 0° ± 10′ | 0° ± 10′ | 2°30′ ± 20′ | 3°30′ ± 20′ | .200 ± .040 | 6° ± 10′ | .040 +.080 −.040 |
| 280S/8 | 0° ± 10′ | 0° ± 10′ | 2°30′ ± 20′ | 3°30′ ± 20′ | .200 ± .040 | 6° ± 10′ | .040 +.080 −.040 |
| 280SE/8 | 0° ± 10′ | 0° ± 10′ | 2°30′ ± 20′ | 3°30′ ± 20′ | .200 ± .040 | 6° ± 10′ | .040 +.080 −.040 |
| 280SL/8 | 0° ± 10′ | 0° ± 10′ | 2°30′ ± 20′ | 3°30′ ± 20′ | .200 ± .040 | 6° ± 10′ | .040 +.080 −.040 |
| 300SEL/8 | 0° ± 10′ | 0° ± 10′ | 2°30′ ± 20′ | 3°30′ ± 20′ | .200 ± .040 | 6° ± 10′ | .040 +.080 −.040 |
| 300SEL/8 6.3 | 0°20′ −20′ | +0°20′ −20′ | | 6° ± 15′ | .080 ± .040 | 5°30′± 10′ | ± .080 |

▲  Check in this attitude.
★  Adjust in this attitude, with proper test load.
①  Station wagon — +2° ± 30′.
②  Station wagon — +1° ± 30′.
③  Coupe and Convertible — +0°30′ ± 1°.
④  Station wagon — +0°30′ ± 1°.
⑤  Operate level valve connecting rods at left and right front and center rear (by hand) until specified level reached.
⑥  With air suspension — -0°45′ ± 15′ curb, -0°45′ ± 1° test.


TEST LOADS: Sedan, Coupe, Convertible — 286 lbs. front seat, 143 lbs. rear seat
                    Sports cars — 330 lbs. front seat, 88 lbs. in trunk
                    Station Wagon — same as sedan

## Wheel Alignment Specifications *(Continued)*

| | Rear Wheel Camber | | | | | | | |
| | Without Level Control | | | | With Level Control | | | |
| | Standard Suspension | | H.D. Suspension | | Standard Suspension | | H.D. Suspension | |
| Model | Curb ▲ | Test ★ | Curb ▲ | Test ★ | Curb ▲ | Test ★ | Curb ▲ | Test ★ |
|---|---|---|---|---|---|---|---|---|
| 190c | +1°30'±30' | −0°45'±30' | +2°15'±30'① | +0°30'±30'② | +0°30'±1° | −0°45'±30' | +1°±1°④ | +0°30'±1°④ |
| 200 | +1°30'±30' | −0°45'±30' | +2°15'±30' | +0°30'±30' | +0°30'±1° | −0°45'±30' | +1°±1°④ | +0°30'±1°④ |
| 190Dc | +1°30'±30' | −0°45'±30' | +2°15'±30'① | +0°30'±30'② | +0°30'±1° | −0°45'±30' | +1°±1°④ | +0°30'±1°④ |
| 200D | +1°30'±30' | −0°45'±30' | +2°15'±30' | +0°30'±30' | +0°30'±1° | −0°45'±30' | +1°±1°④ | +0°30'±1°④ |
| 230 | +1°30'±30' | −0°45'±30' | +2°15'±30' | +0°30'±30' | +0°30'±1° | −0°45'±30' | +1°±1° | +0°30'±1° |
| 220b | +1°30'±30' | −0°45'±30' | +2°15'±30' | +0°30'±30' | +0°30'±1° | −0°45'±30' | +1°±1° | +0°30'±1° |
| 220Sb | +1°30'±30' | −0°45'±30' | +2°15'±30' | +0°30'±30' | 0°±1° | −0°45'±30' | +0°45'±1° | +0°30'±1° |
| 230S | | | | | 0°±1° | −0°45'±30' | +0°45'±1°④ | +0°30'±1°④ |
| 250S | | | | | 0°±1° | −0°45'±30' | +0°45'±1° | +0°30'±1° |
| 220SEb | +1°30'±30' | −0°45'±30' | +2°15'±30' | +0°30'±30' | 0°±1° | −0°45'±30' | +0°45'±1° | +0°30'±1° |
| 220SEb/C | +1°30'±30' | −1°15'±30' | +1°30'±30' | +0°30'±30' | 0°±1° | −0°45'±30' | +0°30'±1° | +0°30'±1° |
| 250SE | | | | | 0°±1° | −0°45'±30' | +0°45'±1°③ | +0°30'±1° |
| 230SL | +1°45'±30' | −1°45'±30' | +1°30'±30' | +1°30'±30' | | | | |
| 250SL | +1 30'±30' | −1 45'±30' | +1 30'±30' | +1 30'±30' | | | | |
| 300SE, SEL | | | | | ⑤ ⑥ | ⑤ ⑥ | | |
| 300SEb | | | | | 0°±1° | −0°45' | +0°45' | +0°30'±1° |
| 220D/8 | −0°45'±20' | −0°45'±20' | −0°5'±20' | −0°5'±20' | −1°15'±20' | −1°15'±20' | −0°5'±20' | −0°5'±20' |
| 220/8 | −0°45'±20' | −0°45'±20' | −0°5'±20' | −0°5'±20' | −1°15'±20' | −1°15'±20' | −0°5'±20' | −0°5'±20' |
| 230/8 | −0°45'±20' | −0°45'±20' | −0°5'±20' | −0°5'±20' | −1°15'±20' | −1°15'±20' | −0°5'±20' | −0°5'±20' |
| 250/8 | −0°45'±20' | −0°45'±20' | −0°5'±20' | −0°5'±20' | −1°15'±20' | −1°15'±20' | −0°5'±20' | −0°5'±20' |
| 280S/8 | −0°45'±20' | −0°45'±20' | −0°5'±20' | −0°5'±20' | −1°15'±20' | −1°15'±20' | −0°5'±20' | −0°5'±20' |
| 280SE/8 | −0°45'±20' | −0°45'±20' | −0°5'±20' | −0°5'±20' | −1°15'±20' | −1°15'±20' | −0°5'±20' | −0°5'±20' |
| 280SL/8 | −0°45'±20' | −0°45'±20' | −0°5'±20' | −0°5'±20' | −1°15'±20' | −1°15'±20' | −0°5'±20' | −0°5'±20' |
| 300SEL/8 | −0°45'±20' | −0°45'±20' | −0°5'±20' | −0°5'±20' | −1°15'±20' | −1°15'±20' | −0°5'±20' | −0°5'±20' |
| 300SEL/8 6.3 | | | | | −0°45'±15' | −0°45'±1° | | |

*Chapter Ten*

# Rear Suspension and Differential

## Rear Suspension

### Rear Shock Absorber Replacement

Jack up the car and support the axle tube or the lower control arm. From inside the trunk, remove the rubber cap, locknut and hex nut. Then, from underneath the car, remove the lower mounting nut (or bolt), lockwasher and associated components. The shock absorber can now be removed.

*NOTE: Use new rubber bushings throughout.*

On cars with automatic level control, open the bleed screw (11a) in the line to the rear suspension units and drain about a pint of hydraulic fluid into a clean jar. Remove the back seat and the two cover plates. Seal off hydraulic line (B2) on the suspension unit and plug the banjo fitting with a bolt and nut, then unscrew nuts (5a) and remove washer and rubber gasket. Unbolt the lower bolts on the trailing arm (19) and remove the suspension unit.

*NOTE: Use new gaskets throughout. Use only special fluid for level system. See Chapter 1.*

### Rear Spring Replacement

Jack up the car, place on stands and remove the rear wheel, then support the con-

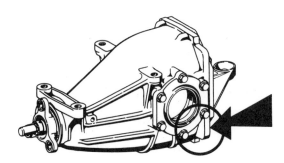

Differential identification number location.

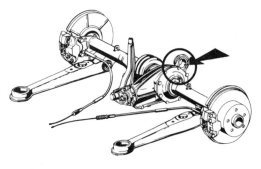

Differential identification number location.

1. Upper spring plate on chassis base panel
2. Upper rubber mounting
3. Rear spring
4. Lower rubber mounting
5. Lower spring plate
6. Torque arm
7. Support for lower shock-absorber suspension
8. Lower shock absorber suspsenion
9. Rear shock absorber

Rear coil spring and trailing arm.

5. Suspension unit
5a. Hexagon nuts
5b. Washer
5c. Upper rubber ring
B3. Hydraulic fluid line from spring accumulator
    to suspension unit

Level control removal (shock absorber unit).

trol arm on a jack. Install two spring compressors similar to those illustrated and jack up the control arm to compress the spring. Tighten the spring compressors, then lower the jack and control arm gradually until the spring and rubber mounting pads can be removed. *NOTE: Fasten the*

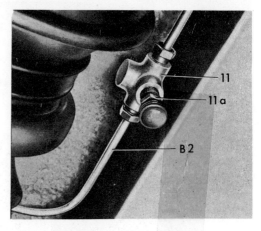

11.   Coupling
11a. Bleed screw
B2.   Hydraulic fluid line from level control to
      spring accumulator

Level control system fitting and bleed screw.

4.  Spring accumulator
5.  Suspension unit
10. Torsion bar
18. Rear spring
19. Oblique control arm
B2. Hydraulic fluid line from level control to
    spring accumulator
B3. Hydraulic fluid line from spring accumulator
    to suspension unit

Level control and rear suspension—phase II models.

*rubber mounting plate to the spring, using masking tape for easy installation.*
    *NOTE: On phase II models, the shock absorber must be removed.*

**Compensating Spring Replacement**

STEEL COIL-TYPE

Jack up the car from the rear and support on jack stands. Compress the spring as

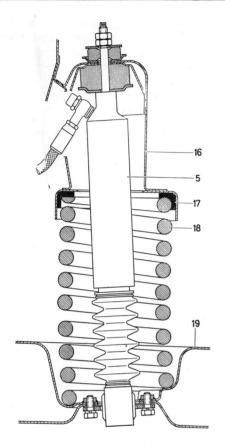

5. Suspension unit
16. Dome on chassis base panel
17. Rubber mounting
18. Rear spring
19. Oblique control arm

Level control shock absorber.

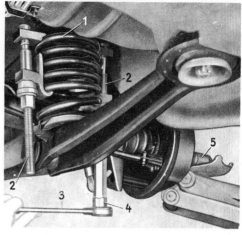

1. Rear spring
2. Spring tensioner (111 589 04 31)
3. Ratchet ½" square
4. Hexagon special socket (24 mm.)
5. Flange

Rear coil spring removal.

1. Compensating spring
2. Cuff
3. Hose clamp or snap-ring
5. Bearing ring
10. Eye on rear axle housing

Steel coil compensating spring removal.

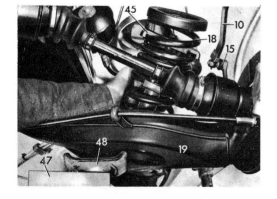

10. Torsion bar
15. Connecting rod
17. Rubber mounting
18. Rear spring
19. Oblique control arm
45. Spring tensioner (115 589 00 31 00)
47. Angled intermediate brace
48. Jack cradle

Removing rear coil spring—phase II models.

Hydropneumatic compensating spring removal.

illustrated until tension on the right axle tube bracket is relieved, then unbolt the bracket and remove the spring. *NOTE: On 230 SL and 250 SL, it may be necessary to detach the lower shock absorber bolts to allow the axle tubes to swing downward far enough for spring removal.*

### HYDROPNEUMATIC-TYPE

Jack up the car from the rear and support on jack stands. Unscrew the Allen bolts that hold the ball joint bracket, then unscrew nut (7) and remove spring and washer. The left shock absorber lower mounting must be removed and the control arm supported with a jack to allow the axle tube to drop low enough for installation.

## Rear Wheel Camber

Rear wheel camber is adjusted by turning the lower spring plate (5) or by installing upper rubber mounting pads (2) of different thicknesses. On phase II models, rear wheel camber is adjusted by changing the actual position of the trailing rear control arms, each specific arm position corresponding to a specific camber value.

On early models, remove the rear coil spring, then unbolt the lower spring plate and adjust, or use thicker or thinner upper spring pads.

# Differential

## Differential Removal

### MODELS HAVING ENCLOSED AXLE SHAFTS

Jack up the rear of the car and remove the rear wheels. If equipped with drum brakes, remove the drums; if equipped with air suspension, remove the sway bar. Remove the rear exhaust pipe and the two mufflers, then loosen the parking brake adjuster wingnut and disconnect the brake cables. Disconnect the rear universal joint and push the driveshaft forward, then remove the compensating spring. Remove the rear coil springs, as described previously, and, on cars with air suspension, disconnect the spring piston from the torque arm. *NOTE: Do not remove from bellows.*

1. Compensating spring
2. Cuff
3. Hose clamp or snap-ring
4. Hose clamp
5. Bearing ring
6. Washer
7. Hexagon nut (polystop)
8. Hexagon socket screw

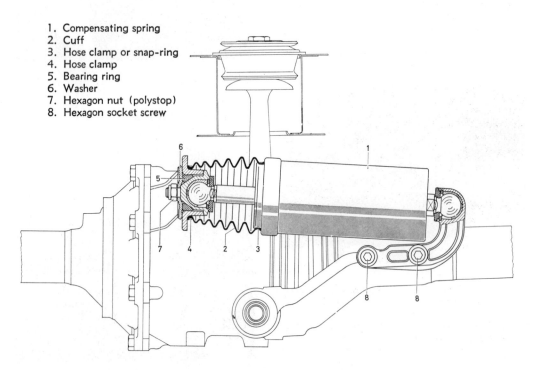

Hydropneumatic compensating spring.

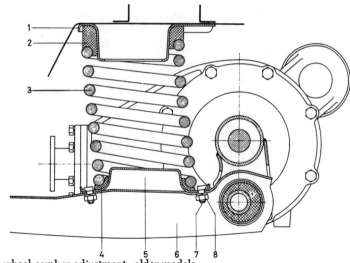

1. Upper spring plate on chassis base panel
2. Upper rubber mounting
3. Rear spring
4. Lower rubber mounting
5. Lower spring plate
6. Torque arm
7. Screw for fastening the spring plate to the torque arm
8. Hexagon nuts with lock-washers

Rear wheel camber adjustment—older models.

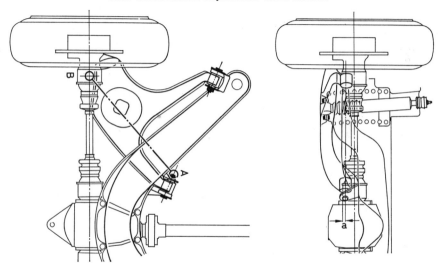

a = oblique control arm position (difference in height between the axis of the rear oblique control arm mounting (A) and the lower edge of the cup for the outer homokinetic joint (B).

Rear wheel camber adjustment—phase II models.

1. Rear shock absorber
2. Rubber buffer for axle tube
3. Rear spring
4. Brake line
5. Brake hose
6. Distributor fitting
7. Rear brake cable
8. Torque arm
9. Brake line (connection to left brake hose)
10. Main muffler
11. Rear exhaust pipe
12. Intermediate muffler
13. Compensating srping

Rear suspension—cars with enclosed axle shafts.

1. Cheese head screws     3. Hexagon nuts
2. Locking plates           4. Oil drain plug

Rear universal joint removal.

1. Hexagon nut and locknut
2. Cup
3. Rubber buffer
4. Retainer on chassis base panel
5. Cross strut
6. Hexagon nut (locknut)
7. Rear link
8. Hexagon screw and spring washer
9. Front link
10. Hexagon screw and spring washer
11. Hexagon screw for connecting pin of the rear axle suspension
12. Support for rear axle suspension
13. Hexagon screws (clamping screws)

Rear torque link removal—190c, 190Dc, 220b, 220Sb, 220SEb, 300SE models.

If car is equipped with drum brakes, disconnect the brake lines from the wheel cylinders and brake hoses, then remove lines and retainers from axle tubes. If equipped with disc brakes, disconnect hoses from lines at the calipers.

Remove the front link (9) from the cross strut by loosening bolts (8) and (10); push the strut out of the way. Remove the trailing arm brackets (2) from the chassis. *NOTE: Tape any shims found beneath the plate to the appropriate trailing arm.*

If equipped with air suspension, disconnect brake support chassis mount by removing rear seat and unscrewing the castle nut thus exposed. Pull the bolt out from beneath the car. Jack up the axle tubes slightly to unload the shock absorbers, then disconnect the lower shock mounts. Raise the axle tubes to a horizontal position.

Place a 24″ section of 2 x 4 (wood) over the top of the differential housing, the long axis lined up with the axle tubes, then, using short sections of chain or rope, fasten the axle tubes to the ends of the 2 x 4 so that the axle tubes remain in a horizontal position and do not sag at their ends. This is to prevent damage to the inner sliding joint of the axle shafts.

From inside the trunk, unbolt the differential housing from the chassis, then gradually lower the entire rear differential housing and axle tube assembly to the floor.

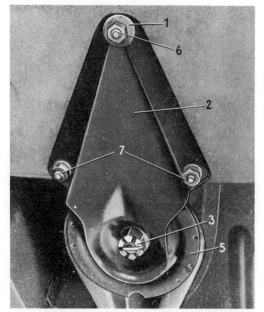

1. Washer
2. Mounting plate
3. Shouldered castle nut
5. Torque arm
6. Welded-in hexagon screw with nut and lock-washer
7. Hexagon screws with nuts, lockwashers and washers

Trailing arm mounting plate.

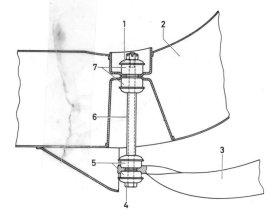

1. Cup
2. Side member
3. Lever for brake support
4. Hexagon screw
5. Lower rubber buffer
6. Spacer tube
7. Upper rubber buffer

Hold-down bolt through chassis base.

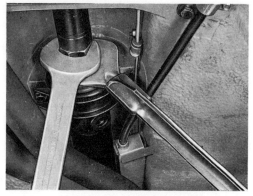

Loosening driveshaft clamp nuts.

Loosening axle bolt.

Lowering differential.

42. Rear rubber mounting
43. Hexagon socket bolt
45. Breather
46. Screw plug for filling
47. Screw plug for draining

Differential mounting bolts.

## MODELS HAVING EXPOSED AXLE SHAFTS

Jack up the rear of the car as high as possible; support rear axle subframe on jack stands (both sides). Drain oil from differential housing, remove hubcaps and the two bolts (one per side) that hold the axle to the axle flange. The rear axle splined shaft then must be pressed from the axle flange. (The illustration shows this being done using the proper tool.) Place a jack under the differential housing and jack up the housing slightly. then unscrew the Allen bolt (43). *NOTE: This bolt is tightened to 87–115 ft.-lbs.*

From inside the trunk, remove the four plugs and unbolt the differential housing from the subframe (17 mm. socket). Now, loosen the driveshaft center bearing support bracket, push back the rubber dust cover and loosen the locknut. Disconnect the rear universal joint from the flange and

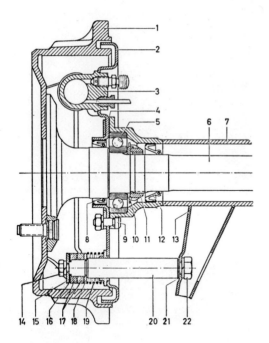

Removing axle shaft.

1. Brake drum
2. Brake anchor plate
3. Wheel cylinder
4. Seal
5. Annular grooved
   bearing
6. Rear axle shaft
7. Axle tube
8. Outer seal
9. Fitted screw
10. Locking plate
11. Grooved nut
12. Inner seal

13. Bracket
14. Hexagon screw
    with lockwasher
15. Washer
16. Brass washer
17. Brake shoe
18. Washer
19. Pressure spring
20. Anchor pin
21. Washer
22. Hexagon screw
    with lockwasher

Axle shaft—drum brakes.

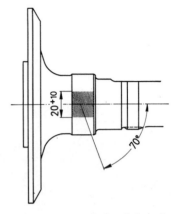

Left rear axle shaft with right-hand thread pattern.

push the driveshaft forward out of the way, then lower the entire rear differential housing assembly and axle shafts to the floor.

## Axle Shaft Removal

MODELS HAVING ENCLOSED AXLE SHAFTS
(190c, 190 Dc, 200, 200 D,
220b, 220 Sb, 220 SEb,
230, 230 S, 230 SL, 300 SE Sedan,
300 SE/c UP TO AUGUST, 1965)

Jack up the rear of the car, remove the wheel and, if equipped with drum brakes, remove the brake drum and shoes. Disconnect brake line from wheel cylinder and remove the backing plate anchor bolt from the rear.

If the car is equipped with disc brakes,

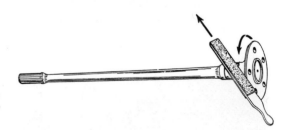

Left rear axle shaft with right-hand thread pattern.
Flange of rear axle shaft pointing to tailstock.

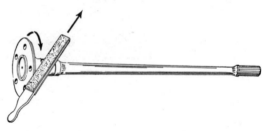

Right rear axle shaft with left-hand thread pattern.
Flange of rear axle shaft pointing to headstock.

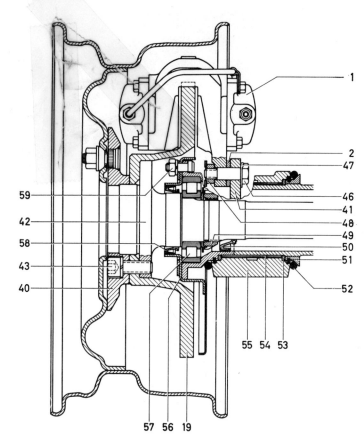

1. Brake caliper
2. Shim
19. Brake disc
40. Wheel fixing disc
41. Fixing eye on the bearing housing
42. Rear axle shaft
43. Hexagon socket screw
46. Hexagon fitting screw
47. Locking plate
48. Bracket
49. Grooved nut with lock
50. Seal
51. Sealing ring
52. Rubber ring
53. Split shim
54. Bearing shell
55. Bearing housing
56. Sealing ring retainer
57. Barrel roller bearing
58. Seal
59. Fitting bolt with hexagon nut and lockwasher

Axle shaft—disc brakes.

remove the brake caliper, the brake disc and the hold-down plate. Remove the backing plate/grease retainer bolts, then, using a puller as illustrated or a slide hammer, pull out the axle shaft. *NOTE: Axle bearings must be removed with a special puller or an arbor press ONLY—never hammer on the bearings.*

If the outer axle seal surface no longer has discernible oil return grooves, recut the grooves using a flat piece of wood (paint stirrer) and 180 grit emery paper. The left axle shaft gets a right-hand pattern; the right axle shaft a left-hand pattern (see illustrations). *NOTE: When inserting axle shaft into sliding joint, anchor joint by removing 10 mm. plug on axle tube and rotating sliding joint so that depression in joint lines up with hole; insert suitable punch.*

MODELS HAVING ENCLOSED AXLE SHAFTS
(250 S, 250 SE, 300 SEb, 300 SE/c
FROM AUGUST, 1965, 300 SEL)

Jack up the rear of the car and remove the wheel, brake caliper and disc, then remove the parking brake shoes (see Chapter 7). Unbolt the backing plate and dust cover and pull the axle from the housing using a puller or slide hammer (see previous section). *NOTE: The grooved nut is threaded to the shaft; bearings must be removed and replaced using an arbor press. Use punch, as previously described, to anchor sliding joint during axle installation.*

MODELS HAVING EXPOSED AXLE SHAFTS
(PHASE II MODELS)

Jack up the rear of the car and remove the wheel and center axle hold-down bolt (in hub). Drain differential oil and place

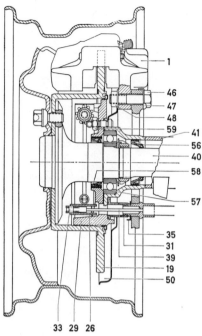

1. Brake caliper
19. Brake disc
26. Expansion lock
29. Back plate
31. Rubber sleeve
33. Pin for brake cable
35. KL lock for brake cable
39. Brake cable
40. Rear axle shaft
41. Axle tube
46. Hexagon fitting bolt
47. Locking plate
48. Bracket with weld-on nut
50. Cover plate
56. Seal
57. Grooved ball bearing
58. Seal
59. Fitting bolt with hexagon nut and lockwasher

Axle shaft arrangement.

Differential mounting bolt (43) and rear mount (42).

9. Rear axle housing
27. Side gear
30. Differential housing
33. Lock ring

Lock ring for axle shaft—phase II models.

a jack under the differential housing. Un-bolt rubber mount (42) from the chassis and the differential housing, then remove the differential housing cover to expose the ring and pinion gears. Press the shaft from the axle flange, as described previously. Using a screwdriver, remove the axle lock ring inside the differential case (see illustration) and pull the axle from the housing. *NOTE: Axle shafts are stamped "R" and "L" for right and left units. Always use new lock rings.*

*CAUTION: Check end-play of lock ring in groove. If necessary, install thicker lock ring to eliminate all end-play, while still allowing lock ring to rotate.*

Removing axle shaft and spacer ring (11).

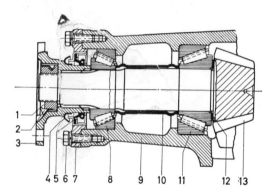

1. Grooved nut
2. Locking plate
3. Joint flange
4. Protective washer
5. Seal
6. Hexagon screw
7. Cover
8. Front annular taper
   roller bearing
9. Rear axle housing
10. Spacer sleeve
11. Rear annular taper
    roller bearing
12. Compensating
    washer
13. Drive pinion

Pinion seal configuration.

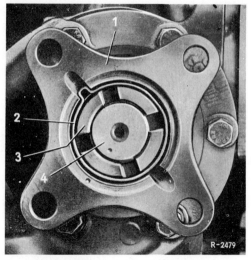

1. Joint flange
2. Locking plate
3. Grooved nut
4. Drive pinion

Grooved pinion nut.

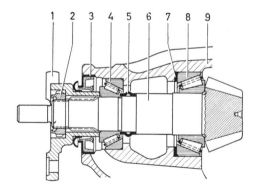

1. Joint flange
2. Self-locking grooved
   nut
3. Sealing ring
4. Front taper roller
   bearing
5. Spacer sleeve
6. Drive pinion
7. Shim
8. Rear taper roller
   bearing
9. Rear axle housing

Pinion seal configuration—phase II models.

Pinion seal removal (3).

## Pinion Seal Replacement

Drain the differential oil, jack up rear of car and remove wheels and brake drums. Support the axle tubes or lower arms on jack stands so that axles are in a horizontal position, then disconnect the driveshaft rear universal joint. Punchmark the flange and housing, then remove the grooved nut.

Using a puller, remove the flange. *NOTE: If flange is scored, it must be replaced.*

Pull or pry the seal from the housing and install new seal (press into place). Reinstall components and carefully tighten the grooved nut until the torque required to turn the differential assembly at the pinion shaft is 26–30 cm.-kg. (22–26 in.-lbs.) for models having enclosed axle shafts and 15–20 cm.-kg. (13–17 in.-lbs.) for models having exposed axle shafts. This corresponds to about 108–144 ft.-lbs. on the grooved pinion nut. If the turning torque is excessive, a new collapsible spacer sleeve must be installed. Never back off on the grooved nut to achieve desirable pinion turning

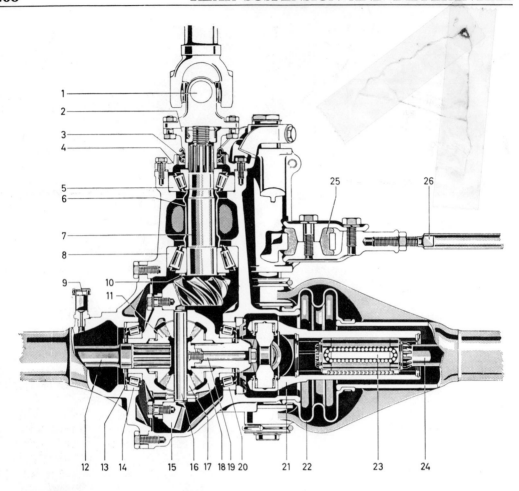

1. Driveshaft
2. Joint flange
3. Seal
4. Cover
5. Front annular taper roller bearing
6. Spacer sleeve
7. Drive pinion
8. Rear annular taper roller bearing
9. Bleed screw
10. Compensating washer
11. Left differential side gear
12. Left rear axle shaft
13. Compensating washer
14. Annular taper roller bearing for differential
15. Ring gear
16. Differential pinion shaft
17. Differential pinion gear
18. Differential housing
19. Clamp screw with lock-washer
20. Annular taper roller bearing for differential
21. Outer yoke with universal joint
22. Rubber sleeve
23. Sliding sleeve with cylindrical rollers
24. Right rear axle shaft
25. Rubber mounting
26. Cross strut for rear axle suspension

Typical differential construction—models having enclosed axle shafts.

torque, as the bearings will be improperly preloaded and eventually destroyed.

**Ring and Pinion Gear Replacement and Adjustment**

(190c, 190 Dc, 200, 200 D, 220b, 220 Sb, 220 SEb. 230, 230 S, 230 SL, 300 SE Sedan, 300 SE/c UP TO AUGUST, 1965)

With the rear differential housing removed, first remove the right-hand axle and tube, then loosen the hold-down bolt and pull out the slip joint. Remove the right- and left-hand axle shafts and unbolt the bearing flange and axle tubes from the housing. The differential now can be removed. Press the outer bearing race from the left axle tube, then remove the lock tabs (2) and unscrew the threaded ring from the housing. Drive the outer bearing race from the right-hand side of the housing, then remove the grooved pinion nut while holding the flange steady in a vise.

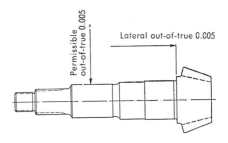

Threaded ring (1) and lock tabs (2).

Left axle tube (1) and breather (2).

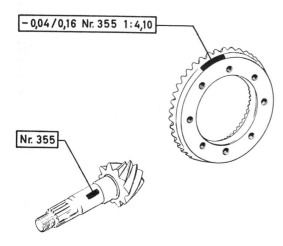

— 0.04  Deviation "a" from basic adjustment
"D nom." in the direction minus 0.04
mm.
0.16  Backlash
No. 355  Gear set (ring gear and pinion) No. 355
1:4.10  Gear ratio drive pinion to ring gear

Ring and pinion markings.

The pinion shaft can now be pressed into the empty differential case and removed. Remove the pinion flange and cover and the inner pinion bearing; the outer bearing race must be pressed from the housing. The inner bearing can now be pressed from the pinion shaft. Check the pinion for runout and the bearing seats for scoring. Don't forget to remove the collapsible spacer sleeve from the pinion shaft.

The ring and pinion gears have several markings etched on their surfaces: the serial number, the pinion depth tolerance deviation (in mm.), the gear ratio and the backlash clearance (in mm.). Backlash is constant, being .0062″ ± .0008″, while the individual gear markings indicate tolerance deviation from the norm for those *particular* gears. For instance, if the ring gear is marked with a minus (—) sign (and a dimension), it indicates the pinion deviation is away from the ring gear; a plus (+) sign indicates the reverse. The proper pinion depth can be computed for any combination of ring and pinion gears, and the thickness of the compensating washer determined, from these markings. Since special tools are required for computation of the proper washer thickness, a "red lead" test will be described later.

The factory procedure involves measuring distance "B", the distance between the front end of a "perfect" dummy pinion shaft of known thickness ("C" nom.) and the center of the ring gear to determine distance "A" (see illustrations). Then the actual distance ("D" act.) is computed by adding to (or subtracting from, as the case may be) the "perfect" distance between the front of the pinion gear as installed, the dimension "a" etched on the gear to be used. (Dimension "a" is the amount of deviation from the "perfect" pinion thickness.) From the illustration, it can be seen that "S", the thickness of the

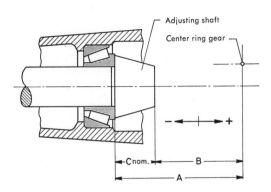

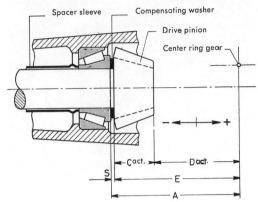

C nom. = Nominal height of adjusting shaft

B = Distance between front end of adjusting shaft and center ring gear

A = Distance between inner race of rear taper roller bearing and center ring gear

C act. = Actual height of drive pinion

D act. = Actual distance between front face of drive pinion and center ring gear (adjusting dimension)

E = Distance between compensating washer and center ring gear

A = Distance between inner race of rear taper roller bearing and center ring gear

S = Thickness of compensating washer

compensating washer needed to bring the pinion and ring gears into perfect mesh, is determined by subtracting distance "E" from the previously determined distance "A". Distance "E" is found by adding the actual thickness of the pinion gear to be used (measured with a micrometer) to the distance "D act.", also previously computed. This enables the washer thickness to be accurately determined before the components are assembled, thus saving much time and trouble over the trial and error "red lead" method.

$$S = (B + 34.50) - [(58.00 \pm a) + C \text{ act.}]$$

  S = thickness of compensating washer
  B = distance between front of dummy "perfect" pinion and center of ring gear
  ± a = manufacturing tolerance deviation etched on gear
  C act. = actual thickness of pinion to be used
NOTE: C nom. = 34.50 (mm.)
      D nom. = 58.00 (mm.)

To assemble, first install the outer bearing races (front and rear) of the pinion shaft into the housing, using a tool similar to the one illustrated. Push the compensating washer "S" onto the pinion shaft and press on the inner bearing race. *NOTE: If "red lead" method of determining washer thickness is to be used, pick a washer on*

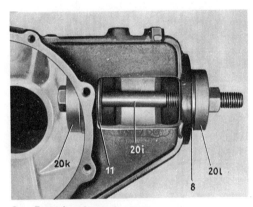

8.   Front bearing outer race
11.  Rear bearing outer race
20.  Fixture (111 589 12 61 00)) or homemade
20i. Hexagon screw
20k. Installing washer
20l. Installing washer

Installing outer pinion bearing races.

*the basis of markings on old gears and old washer thickness. If ring and pinion gears are to be reused, a new washer of the same thickness as the one used before should be installed.*

Install the pinion into the differential housing, slide on a new collapsible spacer sleeve and press on the inner bearing race, after coating it with hypoid lubricant. Press a new pinion seal into place in the housing cover and install the cover. Press

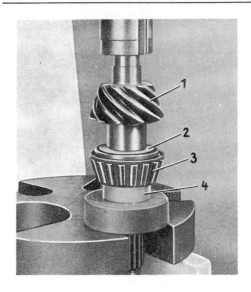

1. Drive pinion
2. Compensating washer
3. Rear annular taper roller bearing
4. Pressure sleeve with support

Pressing on inner bearing race.

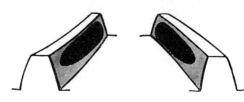

Correct Meshing

Contact at Dedendum (incorrect)

Contact at Addendum (incorrect)

the driveshaft universal joint flange onto the drive pinion splines, after coating splines with Molykote. *NOTE: Observe matchmarks made during disassembly.*

Install the grooved nut and lock plate and tighten the nut until a torque of 16–18 cm.-kg. (14–15 in.-lbs.) for new bearings, or 5–10 cm.-kg. (4–9 in.-lbs) for old bearings, is needed to turn the drive pinion in its bearings. Tap the housing gently with a fiber hammer to seat the bearings. *CAUTION: Remember, as the grooved nut is tightened, the collapsible sleeve is deformed to provide proper bearing preload. As a consequence, the sleeve must be REPLACED if torque on the grooved nut is exceeded. Never loosen the grooved nut to obtain desired pinion rotating torque.*

Insert the compensating washer into the left axle tube flange and press in the outer race of the roller bearing. Screw in the threaded ring about three turns and press the outer bearing race into the differential housing until it rests against the ring. Install the differential into the housing and attach the bearing flange and left axle tube to the housing. Tighten the threaded ring to approximately 25 ft.-lbs. and tap the housing gently with a fiber hammer to seat the bearing. There must be some play be-

tween the ring and pinion gears, otherwise the ring must be removed and a new washer (thinner) inserted.

Set up a dial indicator to measure ring gear backlash at the outer edge of the teeth. Check backlash at four or five points around the gear circumference—it should be .0062″ ± .0008″. *NOTE: Clamp the drive pinion so that only ring gear backlash is measured.*

If backlash is excessive, a thicker compensating washer must be installed between the bearing flange and the outer bearing race (in differential, *not* on pinion) and vice-versa. A .040″ washer results in approximately .003″–.004″ change in backlash.

### Red Lead Tooth Pattern Test

In order to determine whether the ring and pinion gears are in perfect mesh a "red lead" test must be made. This is especially necessary if pinion depth compensating washer "S" was arbitrarily selected without computation. Coat the teeth of the ring and pinion gears with red lead, mechanic's blue dye or lipstick. Rotate the pinion shaft while holding a piece of soft wood against the ring gear (the wood acts as a brake). Compare the tooth pattern obtained with the illustrations. The ideal ring gear "wear" pattern is usually not exactly as shown; it is only necessary that the outer portions of the gear teeth are not touched. If the outer (upper) portions of the teeth are covered, a thicker compensating washer "S" is indicated for the drive pinion. At the same time, a thinner washer is needed in the left axle tube flange to correct backlash. If the inner gear teeth surfaces are covered, a thinner compensating washer "S" and a thicker left axle tube washer are necessary. This will, of course, require complete disassembly of the unit and a new collapsible spacer on the drive pinion. It is for this reason that it is best to have the proper equipment available for computation of compensating washer "S" thickness before assembly, as this trial and error method is most time consuming.

After the proper pinion depth and backlash has been achieved, adjust the initial tension on the differential bearings by tightening or backing out the threaded ring. At the same time, check the torque required to rotate the pinion shaft (and complete gear train). *NOTE: The torque required to turn the pinion shaft before installation of ring gear is known; it should increase by 7–8 cm.-kg. (6–7 in.-lbs.) after installation.*

Continue assembly in reverse order of disassembly.

### Ring and Pinion Gear Replacement and Adjustment (250S, 250SE, 300SEb, 300SE/c from August, 1965, 300SEL

Disassembly is basically the same as in the previous section, although some small design differences are apparent. For instance, the compensating washer "S" on the drive pinion is installed between the outer bearing race of the rear bearing and the front face of the bearing seat (see illustrations).

Computation of washer thickness is the same as in the previous section, with the following exceptions:

C nom. = 67.00 (mm.)
D nom. = 66.00 (mm.)

4. Dished washer
5. Differential pinion
14. Thrust washer
15. Differential side gear
16. Locking pin
17. Differential pinion shaft
21. Bearing ring

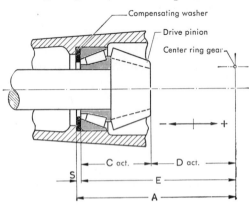

Spider gears and associated parts.

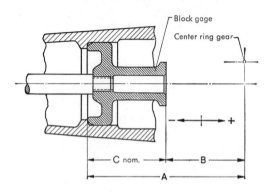

C act. = Actual height of drive pinion plus height of taper roller bearing
D act. = Actual distance between front face of drive pinion and center ring gear (adjusting dimension)
E = Distance between compensating washer and center ring gear
A = Distance between front face of bearing mounting for the rear taper roller bearing and center ring gear
S = Thickness of compensating washer

C nom. = Height of block gage
B = Distance between front face block gage and center ring gear
A = Distance between front face of bearing mounting for the rear taper roller bearing and center ring gear

## Standard Differential

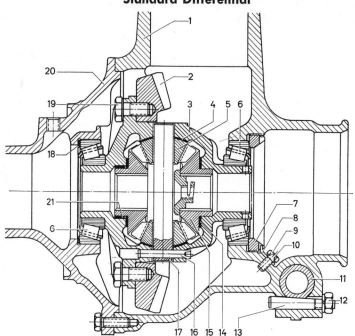

1. Rear axle housing
2. Ring gear
3. Differential gear housing
4. Dished washer
5. Differential pinion
6. Taper roller bearing
7. Threaded ring
8. Lock
9. Hexagon screw
10. Locking plate
11. Connecting pin
12. Hexagon nut with lock-washer
13. Conical screw wedge
14. Thrust washer
15. Differential side gear
16. Locking pin
17. Differential pinion shaft
18. Compensating washer
19. Hexagon screw
20. Bearing flange with left axle tube
21. Bearing ring

1. Ring gear
2. Differential housing
3. Friction clutch
3a. Friction clutch with one-side sinter coating
3b. Friction clutch without coating
3c. Friction clutch with both-side sinter coating
4. Differential side gear
5. Nut for right differential side gear
6. Differential pinion
7. Dished washer
8. Locking pin
9. Differential pinion shaft

Positive traction differential clutch parts.

3a. Friction clutch with one-side sinter coating
3b. Friction clutch without coating
3c. Friction clutch with both-side sinter coating
4. Differential side gear
5. Nut for right differential side gear
6. Differential pinion
7. Dished washer
8. Locking pin
9. Differential pinion shaft

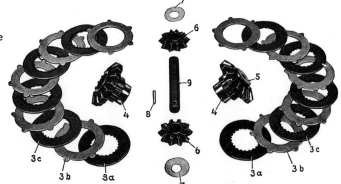

Positive traction differential parts.

## Carburetor Altitude Adjustment

At high altitudes, atmospheric pressure (normally 14.7 psi at sea level) decreases. As a result, carburetors equipped with standard jets supply too rich a mixture to the engine. There are two ways of correcting this—use of special Solex Altitude Correctors with larger air correction jets or use of smaller main jets in the carburetors. Always choose the smallest possible main jet without loss of performance and overheating due to a lean mixture. The chart shows the size of the main jets that give the best results at various altitudes.

| Model | 200, 220/8 | 230 (180.945) | 220 Sb with Zenith Carburetor | | 230 (180.949), 230 S, 230/8 | | 250 S | | 250/8 | |
|---|---|---|---|---|---|---|---|---|---|---|
| | | | | | | Size | | | | |
| Altitude (ft.) | | | Stage | | Stage | | Stage | | Stage | |
| | | | I | II | I | II | I | II | I | II |
| 3,280—4,920 | 90 | 195 | 120 | 170 | 120 | 150 | 130 | 140 | 120 | 140 |
| 4,920—8,200 | 110 | 210 | 140 | 190 | 140 | 170 | 150 | 160 | 140 | 160 |
| 8,200—11,500 | 115 | 220 | 160 | 210 | 160 | 190 | 170 | 180 | 160 | 180 |
| 11,500+ | 130 | 240 | 180 | 230 | 180 | 190 | 190 | 180 | 180 | 180 |

## Distributor Advance Curves

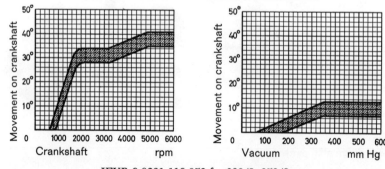

JFUR 6 0231 116 052 for 230/8, 250/8.

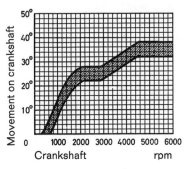 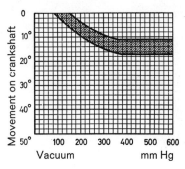

JFUR 4 0231 115 060 for 220/8.

Automatic governor control movement

Automatic vacuum control movement

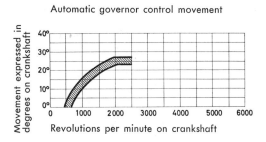 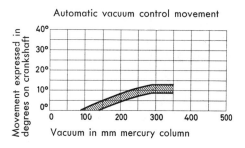

ZVI/PBUR 6 R1 for 300SE.

Automatic governor control movement

Automatic vacuum control movement

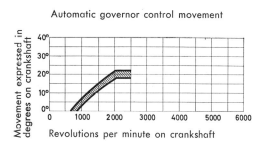 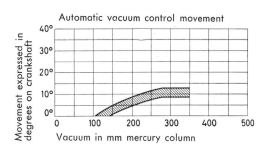

VJUR BR 61 T for 220SEb (third version).

Automatic governor control movement

Automatic vacuum control movement

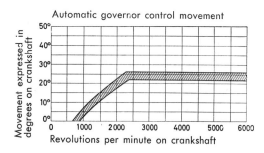 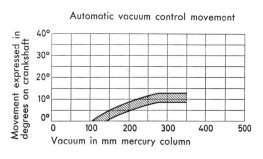

VJUR 6 BR 49 T for 220SEb (second version).

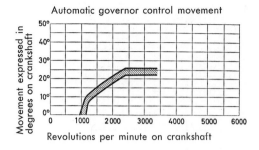
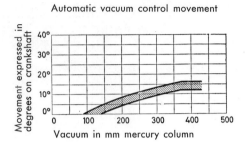

VJUR 6 BR 45 T for 220SEb (first version).

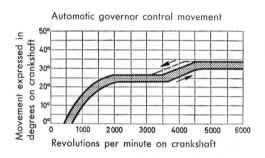
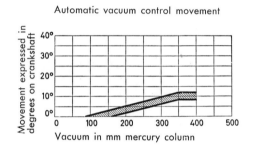

VJUR 6 BR 47 T for 220 b, 220Sb.

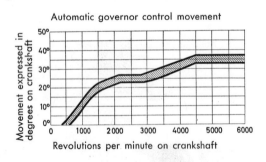
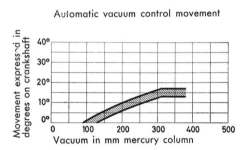

VJUR 4 BR 27 T for 190c.

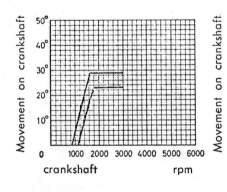
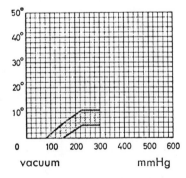

PFUR 6 (R) 0231 141 004 for 300SEb, 300SEL (second version) all manual transmission.

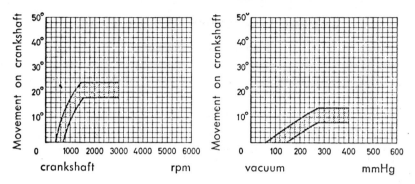

ZV/PBUR 6 R 1 T 0231 141 001 for 300SE (185 H.P.).
PFUR 6 (R) 0231 141 002 for 300SEb, 300SEL (first version), 300 SE (195 H.P.)

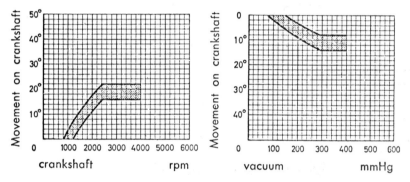

JFUR 6 (R) 0231 116 051 for 230SL (fourth version), 250SE (second version), 250SL.

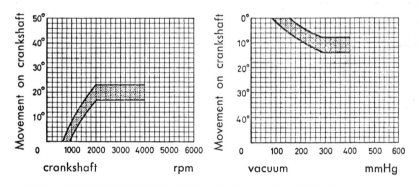

JFUR 6 (R) 0231 116 047 for 230SL (third version), 250SE (first version).

# Exhaust Gas Values (Under Load)

## Fuel Injected Engines

| Model | 230SL, 250SE, 250SL, 300SE, 300SEb, 300SEL (with six-cylinder inj. pump) | | 250SEb, 300SE (with two-cylinder inj. pump) | 280SE/8, 280SL/8, 300SEL/8 | |
|---|---|---|---|---|---|
| Adjustment | Vacuum (mm.Hg./in.Hg.) | Exhaust gas values (% CO/ % SUN) | Exhaust gas values (% SUN) | Vacuum (mm.Hg./in.Hg.) | Exhaust gas values (%CO/ % SUN) |
| Full load @ 3,000 rpm (third gear) ① | | 2.0—3.0/81—83 | 78—80 | | 1.5—2.5/ 82—84 |
| Partial load @ 1,500 rpm (third gear) ② | 300/11.8 | 1.0—2.0/81—85 (230SL— 83—86 SUN) | 83—86 | 300/11.8 | 0.1—0.5/ not readable |
| Partial load @ 2,500 rpm (third gear) ③ | 300/11.8 | 0.5—1.0/84—87 | 84—87 | 300/11.8 | 0.1—0.5/ not readable |
| Idle speed (neutral) ④ | 300—400/11.8—15.7 (six-cyl. pump) 420—480/16.4—18.8 (two-cyl. pump) | 2.5—3.5/80—82 | 79—81 | 300—400/ 11.8—15.7 | 3.0—4.5/ 79—81 |

①    Adjusted at control rod end.
②    Adjusted at black screws.
③    Both vacuum and exhaust gas values must be obtained. On two-cylinder injection pump, adjust at white screws. On six-cylinder injection pump, white screws cannot be moved with pump installed; remove pump first.
④    Check again in Drive range if equipped with automatic transmission.

# Exhaust Gas Values (No Load)

## Carbureted Engines

| Model | Exhaust gas values (% CO/ % SUN) | | | |
|---|---|---|---|---|
| | Idle speed | 1,500 rpm | 3,000 rpm | 4,500 rpm |
| 190c, 200, 220b, 220Sb, 230, 230S, 250S | 3.5—4.5/79—81 | 1.0—4.0/80—85 | 0.2—0.3/82—87 | .05—1.5/84—89 |

# Spark Plug Recommendations

| Model Code | Type Driving | Beru | Champion | Bosch |
|---|---|---|---|---|
| | | | Type Plug | |
| A | Normal | D 215/14/3<br>D 215/14/3S | N6Y | W 215 T 28<br>WG 215 T 28 |
| B | Normal | D 235/14/3S | N6Y | WG 235 T 28 |
| C | Normal | D 250/14/3S | N6Y | WG 250 T 28 |
| D | Normal | D 215/14/3T<br>D 215/14/3S | UN12Y | WG 215 T 28 |
| A | Winter/Town | D 200/14/3 | N5 | W 200 T 27 |
| B | Winter/Town | D 215/14/3s | N7Y | WG 215 T 28 |
| C | Winter/Town | D 215/14/3S | N7Y | WG 215 T 28 |
| D | Winter/Town | D 215/14/3T | UN12Y | WG 190 T 28 |
| A | Hard/Fast | D 225/14/3<br>D 235/14/3S | N6Y | W 225 T 28<br>WG 235 T 28 |
| E | Hard/Fast | D 235/14/3S | N6Y | WG 235 T 28 |
| A ① | Normal* | D 200/14/3 | N5 | W 200 T 27 |
| E | Normal* | D 200/14/3 | N5 | W 200 T 27 |
| C ② | Normal* | D 215/14/3S | N7Y | WG 215 T 28 |
| D | Normal* | D 215/14/3T | UN12Y | WG 190 T 28 |

*For USA versions with exhaust emission controls

① Except 280S/8    A—200, 230, 230S, 250S, 220/8, 230/8, 250/8 sedan, 250/8 coupe, 280S/8
② Plus 280SE/8    B—280SE/8, 280SL/8 (USA), 300SEL/8 (USA)
                 C—250SE, 300SEL/8, 230SL, 250SL, 280SL/8, 300SE/C, 300SEb, 300SEL
                 D—300SEL/8 6.3
                 E—280S/8

# Tune-up Values for U.S. Versions with Exhaust Emission Controls*

| Model | Point Gap (In.) | Dwell Angle (Deg.) | Dwell Angle (%) | Ignition Timing at Idle Speed | Basic Timing at 4,500 rpm | Ignition Timing at 1,500 rpm | Ignition Timing at 3,000 rpm | Compression Pressure (psi) | Spark Plug Type |
|---|---|---|---|---|---|---|---|---|---|
| 200 | .016—.020 | 50 ±2 | 55 ±3 | TDC ±2° B ④ | 43° B | 24—31° B ⑤ | 31—37° B ⑤ | 142—156 120 min. | Bosch W215T28 Beru D215/14/3 |
| 230, 230S | .012—.016 | 38 +3 −1 | 63 +5 −2 | TDC ⑤ | 37° B | 19—28° B ⑤ | 29—35° B ⑤ | 142—156 120 min. | Bosch W215T28 Beru D215/14/3 |
| 250S | .012—.016 | 38 +3 −2 | 63 +5 −2 | TDC ⑤ | 37° B | 19—28° B ⑤ | 29—35° B ⑤ | 142—156 120 min. | Bosch W215T28 Beru D215/14/3 |
| 250SE, 250SL | .012—.016 | 38 +3 −1 | 63 +5 −2 | 2A ±2° ④ | 30° B | 12—19° B ⑤ | 30° B ⑤ | 156—170 127 min. | Bosch WG235T28 Beru D235/14/3S |
| 220/8 | .016—.020 | 50 ±2 | | 3A +3° ④ −2 | 43° B | | | 142—156 120 min. | Bosch W200T27 Beru ED200/14/3 |
| 230/8 | .012—.016 | 38 +3 −1 | | TDC ④ ⑤ | 37° B | 19—28° B ④ ⑤ | 29—35° B ④ ⑤ | 142—156 120 min. | Bosch W200T27 Beru ED200/14/3 |
| 250/8 | .012—.016 | 38 +3 −1 | | TDC ④ ⑤ | 37° B | 19—28° B ④ ⑤ | 29—35° B ④ ⑤ | 142—156 120 min. | Bosch W200T27 Beru ED200/14/3 |
| 280S/8 | .012—.016 | 38 +3 −2 | | TDC ⑤ | 37° B | 19—28° B ⑤ | 29—35° B ⑤ | 142—156 120 min. | Bosch W200T27 Beru ED200/14/3 |
| 280SE/8 | .012—.016 | 38 +3 −1 | | 2A ±2° ④ | 30° B | 12—19° B ⑤ | 30° B ⑤ | 156—170 127 min. | Bosch WG215T28 Beru D215/14/3S |
| 280SL/8 | .012—.016 | 38 +3 −1 | | 2A ±2° ④ | 30° B | 12—19° B ⑤ | 30° B ⑤ | 156—170 127 min. | Bosch WG215T28 Beru D215/14/3S |
| 300SEL/8 | .012—.016 | 38 +3 −1 | | 2A ±2° ④ | 30° B | 12—19° B ⑤ | 30° B ⑤ | 156—170 127 min. | Bosch WG215T28 Beru D215/14/3S |
| 300SEL/8 6.3 | .012—.016 | 36 ±2 | 60 ±3 | 2A ±2° ⑤ | 26° B | 13—21° B ⑤ | 26° B ⑤ | 156—170 127 min. | W215P21 D215/14/3P |

*This chart covers U.S. versions exclusively. If the car is of European origin, for that market, specifications may differ slightly.

① P or N unless otherwise noted.
② Manual or automatic — no accessories operating other than alternator.
③ Adjusted if a 1.0 mm. (.039") ring placed under float needle.
④ With vacuum.
⑤ Without vacuum.

⑥ In 2, 3, 4 or R range only.
A. After top dead center.
B. Before top dead center.
F. Front.
R. Rear

| | | | CARBURETION | | | | | | | EXHAUST GAS VALUES (% CO/% SUN) | |
|---|---|---|---|---|---|---|---|---|---|---|---|
| Model | Carburetor Type | Main Jet (No.) | Air Correction Jet (No.) | Idle Fuel Jet (No.) | Idle Air Jet (mm.) | Injection Tube (mm.) | Injection Rate (cc./stroke) | Fuel Level (mm.) | Idle Speed ② in N (rpm) | Idle Manual Trans. | Idle Auto Trans. ① |
| 200 | Solex 38 PDSI | 137.5 | 80 | 62.5 | 1.6 | 0.5 | 0.7—1.0 | ③ | 850—900 | 2.0—2.5/82—83 | 2.0—2.5/82—83 |
| 230, 230S | 35/40 INAT Zenith | 115F 120R | 100F 130R | 45 | 1.3 | | 0.7—1.0 | 21—23 | 800—850 | 0.5—1.0/85—86 | 0.5—1.0/85—86 |
| 250S | 35/40 INAT Zenith | 115F 125R | 100F 120R | 45 | 1.3 | | 0.7—1.0 | 21—23 | 800—850 | 0.5—1.0/85—86 | 0.5—1.0/85—86 |
| 250SE, 250SL | Fuel Inj. | | | | | | | | 700—750 | 2.5—3.5/80—82 | 2.5—3.5/80—82 |
| 220/8 | Solex PDSI 36—40 | 137.5 | 80 | 62.5 | 1.6 | 0.5 | 0.7—1.0 | ③ | 850—950 | 2.0—2.5/82—83 | 2.0—2.5/82—83 ⑥ |
| 230/8 | 35/40 INAT Zenith | 115F 120R | 100F 130R | 45 | 1.3 | | 0.7—1.0 | 21—23 | 800—900 | 1.5—3.0/81—84 | 1.5—3.0/81—84 |
| 250/8 | 35/40 INAT Zenith | 115F 125R | 100F 120R | 45 | 1.3 | | 0.7—1.0 | 21—23 | 800—900 | 0.5—1.0/85—86 | 0.5—1.0/85—86 |
| 280S/8 | 35/40 INAT Zenith | 115F 125R | 90F 110R | 45 | 1.3 | | 0.7—1.0 | 21—23 | 800—900 | 0.5—1.0/85—86 | 0.5—1.0/85—86 |
| 280SE/8 | Fuel Inj. | | | | | | | | 700—800 | 3.0—4.5/79—81 | 3.0—4.5/79—81 |
| 280SL/8 | Fuel Inj. | | | | | | | | 700—800 | 3.0—4.5/79—81 | 3.0—4.5/79—81 |
| 300SEL/8 | Fuel Inj. | | | | | | | | 700—800 | 3.0—4.5/79—81 | 3.0—4.5/79—81 |
| 300SEL/8 6.3 | Fuel Inj. | | | | | | | | 550—600 | | 2.0—3.0/81—83 ⑥ |

# Conversion Tables

## Linear Measure—Millimeters into Inches—1 mm. = 0.0394 in.

| MM. | 0.00 | 0.01 | 0.02 | 0.03 | 0.04 | 0.05 | 0.06 | 0.07 | 0.08 | 0.09 |
|------|------|------|------|------|------|------|------|------|------|------|
| | | | | | Inches | | | | | |
| 0 | 0 | .000394 | .000787 | .001181 | .001575 | .001969 | .002362 | .002756 | .003150 | .003543 |
| 0.1 | .003937 | .004331 | .004724 | .005118 | .005512 | .005906 | .006296 | .006693 | .007087 | .007480 |
| 0.2 | .007874 | .008268 | .008661 | .009055 | .009449 | .009843 | .010236 | .010630 | .011024 | .011417 |
| 0.3 | .011811 | .012205 | .012598 | .012992 | .013386 | .013780 | .014173 | .014567 | .014961 | .015354 |
| 0.4 | .015748 | .016142 | .016535 | .016929 | .017323 | .017717 | .018110 | .018504 | .018898 | .019291 |
| 0.5 | .019685 | .020079 | .020472 | .020866 | .021260 | .021654 | .022047 | .022441 | .022835 | .023228 |
| 0.6 | .023622 | .024026 | .024409 | .024803 | .025197 | .025591 | .025984 | .026378 | .026772 | .027165 |
| 0.7 | .027559 | .027953 | .028346 | .028740 | .029134 | .029528 | .029921 | .030315 | .030709 | .031102 |
| 0.8 | .031496 | .031890 | .032283 | .032677 | .033071 | .033465 | .033858 | .034252 | .034646 | .035039 |
| 0.9 | .035433 | .035827 | .036220 | .036614 | .037008 | .037402 | .037795 | .038189 | .038583 | .038976 |

| MM. | 0 | 1 | 2 | 3 | 4 | 5 | 6 | 7 | 8 | 9 |
|------|------|------|------|------|------|------|------|------|------|------|
| | | | | | Inches | | | | | |
| 0 | 0 | 0.039370 | 0.078740 | 0.118110 | 0.157480 | 0.196850 | 0.236220 | 0.275591 | 0.314961 | 0.354331 |
| 10 | 0.393701 | 0.433071 | 0.472441 | 0.511811 | 0.515181 | 0.590551 | 0.629291 | 0.669291 | 0.708661 | 0.748031 |
| 20 | 0.787402 | 0.826772 | 0.866142 | 0.905512 | 0.944882 | 0.984252 | 1.023622 | 1.062992 | 1.102362 | 1.141732 |

## Cubic Measure—Cubic Centimeters into Cubic Inches—1 cm³ = 0.0610 cu. in.

| CM³ | 0 | 0.1 | 0.2 | 0.3 | 0.4 | 0.5 | 0.6 | 0.7 | 0.8 | 0.9 |
|------|------|------|------|------|------|------|------|------|------|------|
| | | | | | Cubic Inches | | | | | |
| 0 | 0 | .0061 | .0122 | .0183 | .0244 | .0305 | .0366 | .0427 | .0488 | .0549 |
| 1 | .0610 | .0671 | .0732 | .0793 | .0854 | .0915 | .0976 | .1037 | .1098 | .1159 |

## Liquid Measure—Liters into Pints—1 L. = 2.113 U.S. pints

| L. | 0 | 0.1 | 0.2 | 0.3 | 0.4 | 0.5 | 0.6 | 0.7 | 0.8 | 0.9 |
|------|------|------|------|------|------|------|------|------|------|------|
| | | | | | Pints | | | | | |
| 0 | 0 | .2113 | .4226 | .6339 | .8452 | 1.0565 | 1.2678 | 1.4791 | 1.6904 | 1.9017 |
| 1 | 2.1130 | 2.3243 | 2.5356 | 2.7469 | 2.9582 | 3.1695 | 3.3808 | 3.5921 | 3.8034 | 4.0147 |
| 2 | 4.2260 | 4.4373 | 4.6486 | 4.8599 | 5.0712 | 5.2825 | 5.4938 | 5.7051 | 5.9164 | 6.1277 |
| 3 | 6.3390 | 6.5503 | 6.7616 | 6.9729 | 7.1842 | 7.3955 | 7.6068 | 7.8181 | 8.0294 | 8.2407 |

## Weight Measure—Grams into Ounces—1 g. = 0.0353 oz.

| G. | 0 | 1 | 2 | 3 | 4 | 5 | 6 | 7 | 8 | 9 |
|------|------|------|------|------|------|------|------|------|------|------|
| | | | | | Ounces | | | | | |
| 0 | 0 | 0.0353 | 0.0705 | 0.1058 | 0.1411 | 0.1764 | 0.2116 | 0.2469 | 0.2822 | 0.3175 |
| 10 | 0.3527 | 0.3880 | 0.4232 | 0.4585 | 0.4938 | 0.5295 | 0.5643 | 0.5996 | 0.6349 | 0.6702 |
| 20 | 0.7055 | 0.7408 | 0.7760 | 0.8113 | 0.8466 | 0.8823 | 0.9171 | 0.9524 | 0.9877 | 1.0230 |

## *Pressure—Kiloponds per Square Centimeter into Pounds per Square Inch—1 kp/cm² (at) = 14.22 p.s.i.

| kp/cm² (at) | 0 | .01 | .02 | .03 | .04 | .05 | .06 | .07 | .08 | .09 |
|------|------|------|------|------|------|------|------|------|------|------|
| | | | | | Pounds per Square Inch | | | | | |
| 0 | 0 | .1422 | .2844 | .4266 | .5688 | .7110 | .8532 | .9954 | 1.1376 | 1.2798 |
| 0.1 | 1.4220 | 1.5642 | 1.7064 | 1.8486 | 1.9908 | 2.1330 | 2.2752 | 2.4174 | 2.5596 | 2.7018 |
| 0.2 | 2.8440 | 2.9862 | 3.1284 | 3.2706 | 3.4128 | 3.5550 | 3.6972 | 3.8394 | 3.9816 | 4.1238 |

| kp/cm² (at) | 0 | 1 | 2 | 3 | 4 | 5 | 6 | 7 | 8 | 9 |
|------|------|------|------|------|------|------|------|------|------|------|
| | | | | | Pounds per Square Inch | | | | | |
| 0 | 0 | 14.22 | 28.45 | 42.67 | 56.89 | 71.12 | 85.34 | 99.56 | 113.78 | 128.01 |
| 10 | 142.23 | 156.45 | 170.68 | 184.90 | 199.12 | 213.35 | 227.57 | 241.79 | 256.02 | 270.24 |
| 20 | 284.46 | 298.69 | 312.91 | 327.13 | 341.36 | 355.58 | 369.80 | 384.03 | 398.25 | 412.47 |

\* *Kiloponds* per square centimeter is the same as *kilograms* per square centimeter

# Where to Write
# for Diesel Station List

American Oil Company
    Standard Travel Center
    918 South Michigan Avenue
    Chicago, Illinois 60680

Atlantic Richfield Company
    Atlantic Division
    260 South Broad Street
    Philadelphia, Pennsylvania 19101

    Richfield Division
    555 South Flower Street
    Los Angeles, California 90017

Chevron Oil Company
    225 Bush Street
    San Francisco, California 94120

Cities Service Oil Company
    Attention: Merchandising Manager
    P. O. Box 300
    Tulsa, Oklahoma 74102

Continental Oil Company (Conoco)
    Attention: Asst. Director
    of Merchandising - Wholesale
    P. O. Box 2197
    Houston, Texas 77001

Douglas Oil Company
    Douglas Oil Building
    816 West 5th Street
    Los Angeles, California 90017

Gulf Oil Corporation
    1350 South Boulder
    P. O. Box 661
    Tulsa, Oklahoma 74102

    City Ave. at Schuylkill Expressway
    P. O. Box 8056
    Philadelphia, Pennsylvania, 19101

    1375 Peachtree Street, N. E.
    Atlanta, Georgia 30309

    222 South Prospect Avenue
    P. O. Box 427
    Park Ridge, Illinois 60068

    Avenue of the Stars
    P. O. Box 54064, Terminal Annex
    Los Angeles, California 90054

Humble Oil & Refining Company
    Hutchinson River Parkway
    Pelham, New York 10803

    P. O. Box 1288
    Baltimore, Maryland 21203

P. O. Box 367
Memphis, Tennessee 38101

P. O. Box 420
Charlotte, North Carolina 28201

1105 West 22nd Street
Oakbrook, Illinois 60523

34th Floor
Southland Center
Dallas, Texas 75201

1800 Avenue of the Stars
Gateway East
Century City, California 90067

Mobil Oil Corporation
    150 East 42nd Street
    New York, New York 10017

Phillips Petroleum Company
    Sales Department
    National Accounts
    Bartlesville, Oklahoma 74003

Pure Oil Company
    Attention: W. D. Johnson
    Division of Union Oil Company
    of California
    200 E. Golf Road
    Palatine, Illinois 60067

Shell Oil Company
    Attention: J. H. Harahan
    50 West 50th Street
    New York, New York 10020

Signal Oil Company
    1010 Wilshire Boulevard
    Los Angeles, California 90017

Sinclair Refining Company
    Fleet Sales Division
    600 Fifth Avenue
    New York, New York 10020

Standard Oil Company
    225 Bush Street
    San Francisco, California 94120

    P. O. Box 1446
    Louisville, Kentucky 40201

Sun Oil Company (Sunoco)
    1608 Walnut Street
    Philadelphia, Pennsylvania 19103

Texaco, Inc.
    Manager
    Truck Service Center Development
    P. O. Box 52332
    Houston, Texas 77052

Union Oil Company of California
    Union Oil Center
    Los Angeles, California 90017

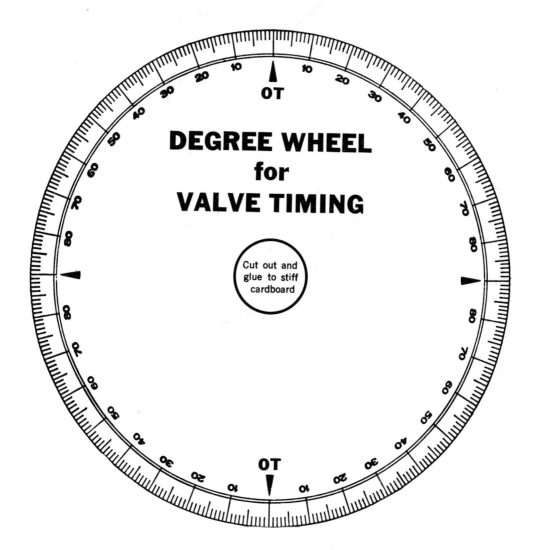

DEGREE WHEEL
for
VALVE TIMING

Cut out and
glue to stiff
cardboard